THEOLOGICAL DIVERSITY AND THE AUTHORITY OF THE OLD TESTAMENT

by John Goldingay

WILLIAM B. EERDMANS PUBLISHING COMPANY
GRAND RAPIDS, MICHIGAN

Library of Congress Cataloging-in-Publication Data

Goldingay, John.
    Theological diversity and the authority of the Old Testament.

    Bibliography: p. 240
    Includes index.
    1. Bible. O.T.—Theology. I. Title.
BS1192.5.G65   1986   221.6   86-19638

ISBN 0-8028-0229-X

Contents

CONTENTS

Preface

I am concerned in this volume with how we handle the theological diversity in the OT: with how we can recognize it rather than sidestep it, with how we can interrelate the diverse viewpoints represented in the OT rather than (consciously or unconsciously) disregard some of them, and with how we can thus allow all these varied viewpoints to function theologically. I have sought to analyze three approaches to the question. One suggests that different viewpoints are appropriate to different contexts, another that they reflect different levels of insight, and a third that they are all expressions of one underlying theology. The first approach, I believe, needs to recognize that some contexts allow particular themes to be developed more profoundly than others do. The second needs to evaluate levels of insight on the basis of criteria internal to the material rather than ones brought to it from outside (so that we may come to some positive evaluation of even the material that speaks to people's "hardness of hearts"). The third needs to acknowledge that the one coherent OT theology which the interpreter seeks cannot be discovered beneath the surface of the OT but must be built up from the raw materials that the OT provides.

The analyses of these approaches in chapters 2, 4, and 6 below include brief examples of how they might be applied to specific themes in OT theology, and each is followed by a chapter which works out an example more systematically. Some themes appear in the context of more than one approach, and although it may be that for each theme one approach will be especially illuminating, all three will generate insights. Norbert Lohfink's study of "Man face to face with death,"[1] for instance, illustrates how the differences between the various OT perspectives on this theme reflect their differences in context (see chap. 2 below), the variations in what people can accept

---

[1]*Christian Meaning of the OT,* 138-69; cf. pp. 55-56 below.

(chap. 4), and the complexity in the range of attitudes which the subject itself justifies (chap. 6).

Doing OT theology is more important than discussing its methodology. In theology, as in other arts and sciences, correct method does not in itself guarantee worthwhile results, but consideration of method can help to sharpen insights, test hypotheses, and point the creative mind in the right direction. I am excited at the way creative minds are at work on the theological significance of OT faith, and look forward to seeing more insight emerge from the Hebrew Bible on what it means to be human and to be Christian in our day.

I am glad to acknowledge here the wisdom and criticism of my supervisor and examiners, the Rev. Dr. Henry McKeating, the Rev. Professor John Heywood Thomas, and the Rev. Professor John Rogerson, when the material in this volume started off life as a doctoral thesis examined in the University of Nottingham in 1983; as well as those of my colleagues at St. John's College, Nottingham, especially Edward Ball. I am also grateful to the college for granting me periods of research leave during which some of the work was done; to the college library, the university library, and the college bookshop for obtaining material for me; to the libraries of Cambridge University, of Tyndale House, Cambridge, and of King's College, London, for their facilities; to Sue Elkins, Barbara Walters, and especially Karin Thut (who processed words until square brackets danced before her eyes) for their secretarial skills; and last, of course, to Ann, Steven, and Mark, who don't let the Old Testament interfere with psychiatry, computers, or electric guitars (indeed, Steven has given me much help with the indexes to this book), and who thereby free me from (often) feeling guilty about the possibility that it might.

Some of the work in the volume takes up material I have published elsewhere; I have not generally referred to this in the text or notes, but include the items in the bibliography. I am grateful to Inter-Varsity Press for their goodwill in connection with my taking up matters already treated in my *Approaches to Old Testament Interpretation*.

In the text and footnotes, books and articles are referred to by the author's name and a brief title or periodical reference. Unless otherwise noted all references are to the latest edition of a work. Full information concerning these works appears in the bibliography. Abbreviations are those used in the *Journal of Biblical Literature* (see volume 95 [1976] 335-46, reprinted in *Society of Biblical Literature Member's Handbook* [1980]). Emphasis in quotations is that of the original author unless otherwise stated. Where alternative forms of biblical references are given (e.g., "Hos 2:1 [1:10]"), the first denotes the versification which appears in printed Hebrew Bibles, the second that in English Bibles.

INTRODUCTION

Chapter 1
THEOLOGICAL DIVERSITY IN THE OLD TESTAMENT

Over its two-hundred year life as a scholarly discipline independent of dogmatics, biblical theology has had difficulty in doing justice both to the conviction that there is a coherence about the teaching of the one book "the Bible," and to the awareness that the actual statements of the various "scriptures" are rather diverse in content. Precritical biblical study read the scriptures in a static way, assuming that the same truths were taught in both Testaments and that Christian beliefs could be read out of the OT in ways that now seem to pay insufficient attention to the meaning that statements had for their writers and their original readers. The nineteenth century set its mind to tracing the history of biblical religion, and perceived vast differences not only between OT and NT, but also between earlier and later forms of OT faith, and between Jesus and Paul. Neo-orthodoxy and the biblical theology movement, seeking not to ignore biblical criticism but to build on it, nevertheless reemphasized the one biblical faith's content, truth, and relevance. Now during the past three decades the theological pendulum has swung once again to an affirmation of "the multiplex nature of the Old Testament tradition" which includes representatives of "completely divergent 'theologies'" and "struggling contradictions."[1] The concern of this present study is to reconsider how the theologian is to handle the diversity of viewpoints within the OT.

For a Christian, that theological question cannot ultimately be considered without reference to the NT. Yet questions about diversity and unity in the NT and about the relationship between the Testaments are major topics in themselves which require study in their own right. Reference to the NT cannot be

---

[1]So, respectively, Barr, *Old and New,* 15; von Rad, *Theology,* 2:412; Eichrodt, *Theology,* 1:490 (Eichrodt's German original comes from the 1930s, of course.) Käsemann (e.g., *NTS* 19:242-43) speaks similarly of the NT.

omitted, then, but it can be attempted here only in a marginal way.

FORMS OF DIVERSITY IN OLD TESTAMENT FAITH

The diversity of viewpoint in the OT with which we are concerned takes various forms. These may be instanced as follows.

Diversity in the Meaning of Concepts, Themes, and Institutions

Themes, concepts, and institutions often have widely varying meanings in different books. If we ask what the OT means by God,[2] we discover that it is ambivalent over whether Yahweh is the sole divine being or whether in some sense divinity attaches to other supernatural beings. Yahweh sometimes belongs to a particular place, at other times he can be encountered anywhere. While his power and involvement in his worshipers' lives is generally emphasized, and one psalmist denies that he ever sleeps, another psalmist challenges him to awake from the sleep of inactivity (Ps 44:24 [23]; 121:4). He can be described as changing his mind, and can be seen withdrawing a commitment he has made to a particular people or individual or city, even though his consistency and faithfulness are emphasized and it is specifically denied that he changes his mind (e.g., 1 Sam 15:11, 29, 35). Further, while the OT as a whole sees Yahweh as supremely the just God, the NT places more emphasis on his love. It is thus possible to speak of "the transformations of God":[3] he is known in changing ways as times change.

The theme of the people of God is a main focus of OT thinking correlative to that of the person and activity of God himself, and there is also considerable diversity over the meaning of this theme. The people of God can be a pastoral clan, constituted by kinship but separated from the world and called to live by faith in God's promise. It can be a theocratic nation, directly governed by God and challenged to live in the world by his standards. It can be an institutional state, ruled by human kings

---

[2]Cf. Schmidt, *Das erste Gebot,* 7-11.
[3]Bultmann, *ZTK* 60:344-48; the phrase *die Wandlungen Gottes* comes from the work of Ernst Barlach, the dramatist and sculptor. Cf. Landau, *Werden und Wirken des AT,* 335-38.

like the nations and open to the nations' influence on its faith, its administration, and its culture. It can be an afflicted remnant, revealing God's standards by experiencing his judgment on its sin, and called to accept affliction as a strange form of real service to Yahweh. It can be a religious community, in various ways living with a tension between its self-understanding before God and its position in the world. It can be, in the NT, both the Israel that rejects its Messiah and the Israel that recognizes and proclaims him.

The contexts or forms by which God and his people relate show further diversity. History can be Yahweh's means of fulfilling his purpose for Israel and for the world, or it can be Israel's means of fulfilling its own purpose until Yahweh intervenes to bring history to its end; or history can simply be ignored. The covenant can be a relationship of promise between God and the ancestral clan leader. It can be a relationship of commitment between Yahweh as the one who brought Israel from Egypt, and this redeemed people who at Sinai pledge themselves to live by his demands. It can be a relationship modeled on that of secular treaties and law codes between Yahweh, the emperor and lawgiver, and Israel in the plains of Moab, the underling and subject, whose disobedience would lead to the annulling of the relationship. It can be a special relationship between Yahweh and the Israelite king. It can be a relationship not yet actual and dependent on new acts of Yahweh which will be needed to bring all Israelites into personal commitment to Yahweh. It can be, in the NT, a relationship between the God and Father of Jesus Christ and those who believe in him.

The monarchy as an institution can be radically rejected (in one strand of Judges, 1 Samuel, and Hosea), accepted with qualification (Deuteronomy), accepted wholeheartedly (another strand of Judges, Samuel-Kings, and Psalms), accepted as a right hope for the future even though it is one not yet realized (the "messianic hope" of some prophets), or, in the NT, can be reinterpreted as essentially not of this world (cf. John 18:36). The law, as the God-given means of Israel's expressing its commitment to Yahweh, can be the seal of its relationship with him, constitute a threat of judgment for those who ignore it, be the means of making clear how those who heed its warnings can avoid judgment, or explain judgment for those who have been judged; it can thrill the believer's heart with joy and delight, or, in the NT, it can be so much rubbish compared with the joy of knowing Jesus Christ. Israel's future with Yahweh can be seen as his involvement with them in their own this-worldly political decision-making and acts, or as his own bestowing of a marvelous redemption from exile which nevertheless still presupposes a this-worldly experience, or as an even more supranaturalist transformation of people, land, and temple, or as a thoroughly otherworldly creating of a quite new order; such hopes may center on an earthly leader, a new David, or may reinterpret the traditional Davidic idea, or may ignore it altogether; or national and cosmic hopes may themselves be ignored and the focus of hope may be on personal release of some kind, personal renewal, or personal resurrection. The Day of Yahweh which is the object of such hope may be seen as far off, or near, or at hand, or actually present, or past.

Different Israelites had different understandings of the nature of the response to God which he sought. In the patriarchal stories, it is a trustful following of his promise. In Exodus-Deuteronomy it is a wide-ranging and detailed subordination of the whole of life to Yahweh: but the laws in Exodus place more stress on the demands of life in the world, while Leviticus is more concerned with the offering of worship according to right forms, and Deuteronomy emphasizes both the general attitudes of trust, fear, and commitment, and (in its regulations regarding actual behavior) recourse solely to the shrine which Yahweh chooses. The Psalms are much more concerned with the life of praise and prayer lived by the believer and the believing community. The preexilic prophets, however, so stress justice and faithfulness rather than temple worship of any kind that they can be plausibly portrayed as rejecting the latter altogether; yet their postexilic successors take a quite different attitude to the temple. Meanwhile the wisdom writers, while not ignoring morals or even worship, show more interest in the living of everyday life in a successful and satisfying way, an interest markedly different from that of prophets who urge their hearers to trust in Yahweh rather than in worldly wisdom.

God's commitment to Israel can be seen as unqualified and permanent, made for the people's blessing as an end in itself; or it can be seen as inherently conditional and always open to being terminated, and as intended not to exclude other peoples but to be a means of drawing them to Yahweh. Further, that commitment can be seen as working itself out with manifest fairness and justice for each generation, community, and individual, or as a rather more complex affair in which the individual sometimes suffers because of the sin of the community as a whole or of other individuals within it (esp. its leaders), or as one in which the community as a whole suffers because of the sins of others within it, or as one in which one generation's sin has consequences for another generation, or as only working itself out with fairness if there is judgment and reward after death, or as an inherently mysterious process which we can hardly pretend to understand at all.

The total thrust of Israelite faith may thus be seen in quite varied ways. How is one to understand and approach one's life in an ever-changing world?[4] By clinging to the forms of the past (as the Nazirites and Rechabites did)? By seeking God's blessing through the outward rites of cultic worship or by a detailed obedience to laws governing the conduct of everyday life? By trusting in a special commitment of Yahweh's to the Israelite people? By investigating the order embodied in the world itself and the laws by which life may be successfully led? By hoping for a future act of God which will be the key to life in the present? By accepting a challenge which is itself present, a challenge to repentance before God, trust in God, and commitment to God, which will issue in living for him in his world and transforming it? All these diverse overall approaches to life are represented in the OT.

Diversity in the Messages Brought by Different Old Testament Books and Traditions

Discussion of OT theological themes or concepts has to proceed largely by abstraction from actual OT material. Writers, teachers, prophets, and traditionists must work with some understanding of the world and life and of God and humanity, even if it is only half-conscious, and we may validly seek to articulate and explicate their work's implicit theology. But generally the OT material itself does not take the form of a series of discussions or presentations of such a worldview or theology; this is not the expressed message of the writer's work. The latter is something more specific, pointed, concrete, conscious, and addressed to a particular situation. One may thus investigate the overt messages of OT books as well as their underlying theolo-

---

[4]For what follows, see Fohrer, *Theologische Grundstrukturen*, 51-94; also Crenshaw's study of the difference between prophet, priest, and sage, and between Yahwism and wisdom, in *Tradition and Theology*, 237-39, 245-49.

gies, and one will find as considerable a diversity among the former as among the latter.

This diversity has been particularly illumined by Gerhard von Rad. His *OT Theology* makes clear, first, a basic distinction between the approach of Israel's historical traditions and that of its prophetic traditions. The former utilize stories about the great events of Israel's *past* to suggest how God's people are currently to see their position in the world; von Rad sees this approach as characteristic of the books from Genesis to Kings. Then, when he comes to the prophets, von Rad sets on the title page of Part One of his treatment the words "Remember not the former things nor consider the things of old. For behold, I purpose to do a new thing" (Isa 43:18-19). There is "a definite break between the message of the prophets and the ideas held by earlier Jahwism." The prophets turn their backs on finding the meaning of Israel's existence in events of the past, and testify to "the approach of entirely new and terrifying divine acts of salvation."[5]

Nor is the break between narrative and prophetic traditions the only major disjunction within the OT. Although von Rad divides his *Theology* into these two major parts, each includes other strands of thinking which do not entirely fit under either heading. Wisdom is a particularly significant such strand. In *Wisdom in Israel*, von Rad develops his treatment of this subject, and in effect adds a third volume to his *Theology*.[6] Prophecy, with its forward look, was not Yahwism's only alternative to history, with its backward look. Wisdom's empirical, existential approach stands alongside these as a third way.

The diversity of the OT's messages is illustrated further by the divergences that appear within such overall strands, divergences (for instance) between different pentateuchal sources or between Kings and Chronicles, between prophets such as Isaiah and Jeremiah, and between different wisdom books (notably Job or Ecclesiastes over against Proverbs). It is also illustrated by contrasts between works from different strands. The hierocratic or theocratic view of P or the Chronicler is the one contested by a prophet such as Amos.[7] Both Deuteronomy and Isa 40–55 speak

---

5*Theology*, 2:3, 299.
6Cf. Bryce's comments in *TToday* 30:436-42.
7Cf. von Rad, *Problem of the Hexateuch*, 253; Smend, *EvT* 23:404-23; Geyer, *EvT* 25:222-23; Schmitt, *Textgemäss*, 149.

of Yahweh's sole power and deity, Israel's blessing, victory, and fame, the covenant theme, and the servant theme; but the meaning, role, and importance of these motifs in the two books differ. The same theological statements function in different ways, and "one must not ask simply what was said, but rather which way what was said cut, what happened when the language was used."[8] Deuteronomy and Isa 40–55 have individual themes in common, yet the thrust of their messages is quite different. In the NT, Deuteronomy finds its affinity more with James or nomism, Isa 40–55 with Paul or antinomianism.

Diversity among the messages contained within the OT also appears in the varied responses offered by contemporary documents to the same historical situation. For instance, the considerable body of material connected with the exile sets forward a number of possible understandings of this experience.[9] For Lamentations, the exile is especially the result of placing false trust in the security of Jerusalem; for the Deuteronomistic History, of ignoring the fundamental Deuteronomic requirement that Yahweh be worshiped exclusively at the shrine he would choose; for Ezekiel, of the unfaithfulness of the temple worship itself; for Jeremiah, of the people's political, social, and moral waywardness, as well as the unfaithfulness of their worship.

The practical responses to the exile expressed or urged by these books also varies. Lamentations bewails it, the Deuteronomistic History by implication simply accepts it, Jeremiah urges people to submit to the Babylonian yoke and settle down under Babylonian authority, the Jeremiah prose tradition urges the taking up of a life of obedience to God's word.

The books vary, too, in the way they look to the future. Lamentations casts itself on God's mercy without indicating explicitly what its hope is. The Deuteronomistic History merely hints that the God who promised to restore those who return to obey his law, to listen to prayer directed toward the temple even from exile, and to be faithful to David's line for ever, may not have finished with Israel. In the Jeremiah prose tradition and in

---

[8]J. M. Robinson, *Trajectories*, 69.

[9]On what follows, see R. W. Klein, *Israel in Exile*; Janssen, *Juda in der Exilszeit*; Ackroyd, *Exile and Restoration*; Nicholson, *Preaching to the Exiles*; Albrektson, *Studies in Lamentations*, 214-39; Westermann, *Isaiah 40–66*. If P is exilic, it adds a further distinctive strand to those mentioned here.

Ezekiel there appears explicit hope for a new David, a fresh branch to grow from the Davidic tree. But Isa 40–55 turns its back on such ideas, reallocating the Davidic role to the servant, to Cyrus, and to the people as a whole. Isa 40–55 promises a revelation of Yahweh in a new exodus and restoration of Jerusalem, but Ezekiel (at least in the book's final form) gives most prominence to the new temple to which Yahweh will return to dwell.

An even more striking diversity of approximately contemporary and apparently rival views can be documented for the postexilic period (see pp. 21-23 below).

Diversity in the Significance Found in Particular Events or Motifs

One of the ways in which OT writers formulate and express their message for their particular hearers is by considering the significance for their day of archetypal events or motifs such as the exodus or God's covenant with David, which belong to their people's history and are continually reinterpreted and reappropriated in the context of Israel's tradition. The kinds of significance that an event can come to have for later generations can be quite diverse.

The OT's first "event" is the creation of the world.[10] In Gen 1:1–2:3 the significance of creation includes the fact that it is the act of the God of Israel in his freedom and sovereignty; he has no conflicts to resolve in his work. The sun, moon, and stars are not gods to be acknowledged (as the Babylonians believed), but mere lamps in the sky; nor does the establishment of the state go back to creation. The sabbath, however, is part of the pattern of God's activity, revealed to Israel so that they might follow it, yet not (as the exiles might be tempted to believe) a merely Israelite peculiarity. In Gen 2:4–11:9, however, creation suggests God's loving provision of life and all else that humanity needed, which contrasts with the manifold alienation of humanity (from each other, from work, from the world, from God, from life itself) which the chapters also portray; so that the story claims that these issue not from the imperfection of the creation or from the problems, the bloodiness, and the bloody-mindedness of

---

[10]For what follows, see von Rad, *Problem of the Hexateuch*, 131-43; B. W. Anderson, *Creation versus Chaos*; Westermann, *Creation*, 17-31; Lindeskog, *Root of the Vine*, 1-22; Mowinckel, *Psalms*, 1:106-92.

the supernatural powers, but from the acts of humanity itself.

The creation event has further meanings for the book of Exodus. One way of linking the creation event with the event of redemption which Exodus celebrates is to see the former as preceding the latter in time; Israel's redemption has its background (via the patriarchal promise) in the creator's concern for his world. But another way is to describe the redemption event itself in terms of creation: the exodus is an occasion of creation (see the creation imagery of Exod 15) and the gifts of creation are the gifts of redemption (see the significance attached to Israel's harvest festivals in Exod 34:22-23; Deut 26:5-10). Yahweh's grace and power shown in creation appear again in Israel's hymnody, and encourage a hope that they will also be experienced in his people's own history (Pss 74; 89); but his creative power can also be applied to the punishing of Israel for their failure to respond to him (the creation hymn in Amos 4:13; 5:8-9; 9:5-6). Elsewhere in the Psalms, creation is simply the basis for worship of God. Thus in Ps 104 the sky speaks of his splendor (vv 1-4), the act of creation itself reflects his power (vv 5-9), and its living things experience his continuing creative provision (vv 10-30) (see also, e.g., Pss 8; 29; 33). When Israel celebrates Yahweh's kingship (perhaps in the context of a special festival designed to mark his taking up his kingship for a new year), it affirms his kingship as the creator (Pss 93; 95-99), the one who once again guarantees the rebirth of nature, the renewing of creation which each new year brings (Pss 65; 67).

The events of history as well as the annual cycle of nature bring their experiences of creation seeming to collapse; God's judgment is an act of uncreation (cf. Jer 4:23-26). One way of coping with such an experience is to recall that things were not always this way: the world came into being through an act of purposeful creation, so that emptiness and formlessness are not history's intrinsic characteristics. This is part of the significance of Gen 1-2 as introductions to the narrative from Genesis to Kings. This narrative closes with the exile; in that same context, however, the exilic Isaiah again appeals to the creation theme as one familiar from Israel's worship ("Have you not known? Have you not heard?"), to remind his hearers of the present significance of creation faith (Isa 40:12-31). The exiles are naturally impressed by the nations' power (Israel is a humiliated remnant), by their idols (the Jerusalem temple lies desolate), by their rulers (Judah's King Jehoiachin is in prison), and by their cosmic deities (Yahweh has disappeared). But they are encouraged to recall that this Yahweh is the creator of the whole world, their experience of abandonment is therefore not their final destiny. Yet another response to the experience of uncreation is to look to the future, not to the past, in a different way, by projecting onto the future the vision of a created order which is the antitype of present experience, a new heaven and a new earth (Isa 65:17-25). Thus creation comes to be a way of thinking about the End.

The wisdom books see the significance of the creation event in further directions. Prov 1–9 as a whole is concerned to inculcate wisdom in the sense of insight, prudence, sense, and shrewdness about life. Chapter 8 commends wisdom for its value in connection with doing right (vv 1-11) and with the exercise of leadership (vv 12-21), and then points to God's own use of his wisdom in creation (vv 22-31). When you look at creation, it suggests, you can see what God achieved by using his mind, therefore creation encourages you to use your own. Job suggests links between an appreciation of creation and an understanding of human suffering. At the climax of the book Yahweh directs Job's attention to the creation, which challenges him to acknowledge both Yahweh's power and also the purposefulness of his government of the world: he is the one who put Behemoth and Leviathan in their places (Job 40–41). The world of God's creation is not one in which chaos rules (cf. Isa 45:18), and this should provide the context for interpreting the chaos which apparently prevails at present in Job's life. Creation provides reason for trusting God even when one cannot understand him.

In each of these examples, the writers allude to creation because of an interest in other themes which are their real concerns; they are thus able to attribute to creation quite diverse significances. The process continues in the NT, where the question now is "How are we to understand Jesus of Nazareth?" Here, one way of expressing his significance is to associate him with creation, as the means of God's self-expression through whom all things were made (John 1:2-5; cf. Prov 8:22-31), or as the image of God, his firstborn heir of his creation, in whom all things were created and now hold together (Col 1:15-17).

Succeeding archetypal events in the OT story such as Yahweh's special dealings with Abraham[11] and his rescue of Isra-

---

[11]See Martin-Achard, *Actualité d'Abraham*; Clements, *Abraham and David*.

el from Egypt[12] are the subject of parallel sequences of reapplications. In Genesis, for instance, Abraham is the bearer of a promise of blessing which is ultimately designed to benefit all the nations (J), he is the committed believer who submits to God's will
even when God's demand seems to imperil God's own promise
(E), and he is also the recipient (on behalf of his heirs) of an irrevocable covenant between God and his chosen people (P). Elsewhere in the Hexateuch, God's word to him is the basis for confidence that Yahweh will complete the purpose of redemption
which he has begun, for the conviction that the land of the
Canaanites does belong to the Israelites, and for a challenge to
commit oneself to the God who had kept his word to Abraham.
Abraham influences the portrayal of David; his testing on a
mount in Moriah is now part of the justification for building a
temple there, and his acknowledging of Melchizedek is part of
the justification for acknowledging David, who has inherited
Melchizedek's position. In the prophetic books, God's commitment to Abraham is the basis for confidence that God will once
again grant blessing, land, and increase to Abraham's descendants; but this argument from the story of Abraham can be denied (Ezek 33:24) as well as affirmed (Isa 41:8-10; 43:5; 51:1-3).
In the NT, too, the argument from God's commitment to
Abraham can be both affirmed (Acts 3:25-6; Gal 3–4) and denied
(Matt 3:9; John 8:31-40).

The exodus is, in the book of Exodus, the magnificent and
unique act of Yahweh's power, faithfulness, and justice, whereby
the descendants of Abraham are freed to serve and acknowledge
Yahweh as his own people. In Hosea, too, the exodus is the paradigmatic act of Yahweh's love and the act that made him their
God. But Yahweh now declares that it is not a once-for-all event;
for failing to maintain its commitment to the God of the exodus
Israel will return to Egypt (where for political reasons they are
inclined to resort anyway)—even though Yahweh then promises
that his love will have its way in a new exodus from there in the
end. Amos, too, sees Israel's apostasy as having dissolved the
commitment that the exodus signified; he declares that it was
merely one of the many ancient Near Eastern migrations of
which Yahweh has been Lord. In Jeremiah, the exodus period is
the time of Israel's first love (Jer 2:1-3), but in Ezekiel it is merely

---

[12]See Sahlin, Root of the Vine, 81-95; Nixon, Exodus in the NT;
von Rad, Theology, 2:413.

the time of Israel's initial faithlessness (Ezek 20). Isa 40–55 takes up Hosea's vision of a new exodus, but its own vision of the servant role reinterprets the significance of the exodus in a radical way. Then, in the NT, the exodus motif is reapplied as a metaphor for another kind of deliverance that Jesus' dying will achieve (see esp. Luke 9:31).

More generally, von Rad notes that the "foundations" or "bases of salvation" or "initial appointments" upon which OT traditions build (the patriarchal covenant, the Sinai covenant, the Davidic covenant, and the foundation of Zion) are highly heterogeneous in content. Further, "as a result, each promise gave its own characteristic theological stamp to the progression of historical events which led to its fulfilment," and to the prophetic preaching which takes these same initial appointments as its model for looking to the future.[13] So diversity is an essential characteristic of OT tradition.

REASONS FOR THE DIVERSITY IN OLD TESTAMENT FAITH

One normally expects a book to manifest a unity of perspective, theme, conceptuality, and aim; one might expect the same of the text acknowledged by a religious community. Indeed, the Bible's failure to fulfill this expectation marks it out in the history of the world's religions.[14] Why does it do so?

Some of the reasons are historical. The Bible is a compilation of *biblia*, of scriptures; the words are plural. A collection of shorter works published as one volume is not necessarily expected to have the same unity as a single work, even where all are by the same author. In the Bible's case, the works are not all by the same author: it is more a symposium than someone's collected works. Prophets such as Jeremiah and Ezekiel speak different messages, even where they address the same people, because they are different men with different backgrounds, experiences, and attitudes to life. Similar results follow from the variety in the tradition circles that influenced the OT. Multiplicity of authorship is bound to imply some diversity of viewpoint.

The books of the Bible were written to a variety of audiences, living in varying periods and situations. Jeremiah and

---

[13]*Theology*, 2:411-12.
[14]So Vawter, *Biblical Inspiration*, 1-2.

Ezekiel differ, though they are contemporaries; Isaiah and
Jeremiah or Jeremiah and Zechariah differ in other ways because
they are not contemporaries, and their message is related to the
circumstances and attitudes of their hearers. The book of
Jeremiah specifically enunciates the principle that God's dealings with people varies with the response he meets from them
(Jer 18:7-10) and the story of Jonah's self-falsifying ministry illustrates this principle at work (Jonah 3–4). Both Chronicles'
emphasis on the importance of Israel's worship and Amos's dismissal of it reflect the kind of attitude toward God and the kind
of spiritual need which the writers find among the people of
their day. Different "appointments" (e.g., the call of Abraham,
the exodus, the covenant with David) disclose different contents
as they find different "actualizations" when set in different perspectives by different contexts.[15] On one side and the other of
the fall of Jerusalem in 587 a different message is brought not
only by different prophets (e.g., Jeremiah and the second Isaiah)
but also within the ministry of a single prophet (esp. Ezekiel).
Different social contexts may need to be addressed in different
ways: the same message may not seem appropriate for
Abraham's pastoral clan and for David's urbanized state; patriarchal religion reflects the former while J and the wisdom writings
reflect the latter. Like any religion, Israelite faith changes with
the changing world; theology is a historical affair.[16]

The variety in the external contexts of Israel's world also
contributed to the variety within the OT itself. These contexts
affect Israel's faith partly by direct influence, partly by constituting an aspect of the situation which has to be addressed. The
occupation of Canaan, for instance, leads to Israelite faith being
expressed in terms derived from the Canaanites (e.g., in the
"Zion theology" represented particularly clearly in the Psalms),
and also in terms which show that it is different from that of the
Canaanites (e.g., in the stress on avoiding Canaanite practices
which appears in many laws). The exile leads to renewed influence of Near Eastern myth but also to polemic against it; both
may be evidenced in Isa 40–55 and in the P creation story.

A theological account of this diversity may sometimes be

---

[15]See again von Rad, *Theology*, 2:413.
[16]Cf. Hempel, *Das Ethos des AT*, 1-19, on the variety of backgrounds,
political and economic situations, and ideologies to which OT teaching on behavior has to relate.

appropriate, to the extent that the OT pictures God himself as
having different things to say at different periods. In part this is
because he is responding to varying situations in the way described above. It is also because the ongoing historical process
requires something different to be said at a later period from
what was said earlier, partly as a consequence of what was said
earlier and on the basis of what has followed from it. Whereas
Yahweh once spoke much about the exodus from Egypt, later he
wants his people to look forward to a new event in history. Indeed, where he once seemed to work within history, a time
comes when he seems to have abandoned history.

The changes in God's speaking and acting are not merely
responses to particular human situations or to the point reached
by the ongoing historical process. In part these changes emerge
directly from his own initiative, independent of external stimulus such as the biblical writer can observe. There is an unpredictability about how God will choose to act or speak. Why should
the "new thing" of prophecy have happened when it did? Perhaps
the factors which decide such changes arise in part from God
himself, and one cannot necessarily explain why God should at
this particular moment have something different to say from
what he has said before; such changes are involved in living as a
person, for God as much as for human beings.[17]

The complexity of the realities of which the OT speaks accounts for some of the diversity within the OT. While there are
many matters of which one can give straightforward explanations on which competent authorities can be expected to agree
(characteristically, subjects studied by disciplines such as mathematics, geography, and the natural sciences), there are other realities (and questions about what lies behind the concerns of these
disciplines), belonging more to the realm of the humanities,
where straightforward explanations are rarer and disagreement
among competent authorities is more common. What is a
human being? What is right? What is the nature of Being? What
is ultimate reality? Where is history going? Such questions are
complex because the realities that they are seeking to grasp are

---

[17]See further Bultmann, *ZTK* 60:344-48 (cf. n. 3 above); also Ogden, *Reality of God,* 144-63. Cf. also the NT's picture of God knowing throughout
OT times that he would cause his gospel to be proclaimed throughout the
world through the "gentile mission," yet keeping this μυστήριον secret until he
decided it was time to reveal it (Eph 1:9-10; 3:1-13).

complex, and it is not surprising if within a document such as
the OT a variety of aspects of these complex wholes appears. If
there were no tensions in the Bible, one might infer that it was
too simple in its understanding of such questions.[18] The variety
of "actualizations" of "appointments" such as the call of Abraham similarly reflects the depth of these symbols, which are inherently capable of a wide range of application.

Imagine, then, "Gibbon's *Decline and Fall of the Roman
Empire*, the collected poems of T. S. Eliot, the *Textus Roffensis*,
Hamlet, Robinson's *Honest to God*, *The Canterbury Tales*,
Holinshed's *Chronicle*, the *Cathedral Statutes of Rochester*,
Hymns Ancient and Modern (Revised), Bonhoeffer's *Letters and
Papers from Prison*, Hammersjkold's *Markings*, *The Thoughts
of Chairman Mao*, *Pilgrim's Progress*, the *Sixteen Satires* of
Juvenal and the *Book of Kells*" deprived of indications of date
and authorship, all printed in the same format and bound together as a single volume;[19] the analogy suggests that it is natural
that the library comprising the Jewish and Christian scriptures
manifests such diversity of viewpoint.

DEGREES OF DIVERSITY AND FORMS OF
CONTRADICTION

"The Bible is full of contradictions."[20] If this is so, then it will be
a tour de force to interrelate its various viewpoints. But the
statement is an exaggeration, arising partly out of a rather loose
use of the word "contradiction." Such a looseness of usage is instanced by Bultmann's describing as contradictory features of
the NT that "the death of Christ is sometimes a sacrifice and
sometimes a cosmic event. Sometimes his person is interpreted
as the Messiah and sometimes as the Second Adam."[21] Such variations, like the OT's various reapplications of the creation event
or of the Abraham story (see pp. 10-11 above), indicate that the
Bible is highly diverse, and they invite the interpreter to take up
the challenge of relating them to each other as part of the task of
their theological explication, but they do not involve mutual op-

---

[18]Cf. Rahner, *Theological Investigations*, 5:35-36.
[19]Blanch, *The World Our Orphanage*, 16.
[20]Dahl, *Studies in Paul*, 159; the essay deals with the approach to this
issue in the Hebrew Bible as it appears in Jewish exegesis and in Paul.
[21]*Kerygma and Myth*, 11.

position. It is quite possible for one person to be both the Messiah and the Second Adam; the descriptions are very different, but both can be accepted without inconsistency. Such variations do not raise a problem of contradiction versus harmony.

On the other hand, some diversity does entail opposition and not mere difference. At least four forms of contradiction may then be distinguished.[22]

Formal Contradiction

Formal contradiction involves a difference at the level of words which is not a difference at the level of substance. P. D. Hanson opens his study of *The Diversity of Scripture* (pp. 1-4) by noting that such inconsistency is natural to "the language of confession" as it expresses depth of personal response. Material in which symbolic language has a prominent place particularly raises this problem. As we noted above (p. 2), the OT both states and denies that God changes his mind, even in the same chapter (1 Sam 15:11, 29, 35; each time נחם). There is a clear formal contradiction, but the presence of both assertions in one text invites us to seek to relate them as well as to contrast them. To speak of God changing his mind about an act or regretting it suggests the reality of his interacting with people in the world. People make real decisions which do not necessarily correspond to the will of God, and which thus introduce an element of novelty into history; they are not the result of God's direct determination. God thus reacts to them as a person reacting to the deeds of other persons, with pleasure or surprise or sadness or regret, and as a person reacting to the deeds of other persons he relates his own subsequent decision-making to these acts. On the other hand, to speak of God not changing his mind, as a human being does, safeguards his faithfulness and consistency (לא ישקר). His reactions to the deeds of others reflect a coherent pattern rather than randomness. Further, whereas human beings make their decisions unaware of all their consequences, so that those consequences can catch them out, God (so the OT assumes) can fore-

---

[22]Cf. Martin's discussion in *SR* 8:143-52, which also takes up Lonergan's work in *Method in Theology*, esp. 128-29, 235-37. Of the nature of the case, opinions may vary as to which category different examples may belong to, though in itself this hardly makes attempts at categorization questionable.

see not only the consequences of his own actions but also the nature of the responses they will meet with and the nature of other human acts, so that he can in turn formulate his response to these in advance. So the interaction between divine and human decision-making is real (there are genuine human acts to foresee), yet God is not caught out by the latter, and in this sense he does not have to change his mind. Thus both the affirmation and the denial are part of a coherent analogical description of God's involvement in the world, and each would be misleading without the other. There is a formal contradiction between them, but the statements can be seen as complementary.[23]

There is a formal contradiction involved in "the prophetic 'no' to Israel's traditions."[24] Amos, for instance (5:18-20), denies that Israel will experience a coming Day of light and salvation, as contemporary tradition apparently believed[25] and subsequent canonical material certainly declares. But in doing so he was "restoring the theology of the tradition that had got lost," pointing to that tradition's actual witness to Yahweh as opposed to its mere outward form,[26] a witness to "the nearness of the One who is free, the One who shows himself as the Lord."[27] Elsewhere, Amos utters the "heresy" that the exodus is no more significant than the migrations of other nations (9:7); yet we must not interpret literalistically a challenge designed to startle Israel out of their complacency regarding Yahweh's commitment to them.[28] Isaiah and Micah contradict each other over the destiny of Jerusalem; but in Micah "Jerusalem" stands for the leadership of an oppressive state, in Isaiah it stands for

---

[23]On the relationship between God's consistency and his mutability, see Barth, *Dogmatics*, 2/1:496-99. The affirmation of an element of contingency in God's acts as developed in process theology is applied to the OT by L. S. Ford in *Lure of God*, 15-44 (cf. *Int* 26:198-209); by Janzen in *Magnalia Dei*, 480-509, and in *Encounter* 36:379-406; also by Cooper in *USQR* 32:25-35; but this approach questions whether divine foreknowledge (probably implied by the denial that God changes his mind) can be reconciled with this contingency and with real human freedom (cf. Ford, *Int* 26:208).

[24]Zimmerli, *Tradition and Theology*, 69; cf. Smend's study of Amos's no to Israel's understanding of history (*EvT* 23:409-13). See also chap. 2, n. 102 below.

[25]The question of the origin of the idea of the Day of Yahweh remains controverted; cf. Zimmerli, 75.

[26]Laurin, *Tradition and Theology*, 269.

[27]Zimmerli, 76.

[28]Cf. Schmidt, *Zukunftsgewissenheit und Gegenswartskritik*, 79-80, with Gese's response, *Textgemäss*, 33-38.

the presence of Yahweh in judgment as well as in grace.[29]

In the study of the NT, Bultmann himself suggests instances of merely formal contradiction: for example, Paul says that the earthly Jesus was emptied of his glory, while John declares that glory shines out from the earthly Jesus. Both would agree that there was no "heavenly luminosity" about the earthly Jesus, but that the cross does reveal a paradoxical glory visible to the eyes of faith.[30] More generally, if we are given the impression both that human life is determined by cosmic forces and that we are challenged to decision, then the former is a metaphorical equivalent of the latter.[31] A comparable approach might be taken to the differences between ways of conceiving the End in the OT. All are metaphorical projections (whether or not they require demythologizing in order to interpret them existentially), and the divergence between them may be formal rather than substantial. Widely divergent conceptualizations can reflect the same preconceptual vision of reality.[32]

OT attitudes to nations other than Israel also vary in ways which are in part formally rather than substantially contradictory. A number of OT passages envisage the nations as sharing with Israel in the worship of Yahweh and in the blessing of Yahweh. Isa 2:2-4 (= Mic 4:1-3) pictures the nations converging on Jerusalem to receive Yahweh's teaching and his judgment which go forth from there; Isa 19:18-25 portrays Egypt (and Assyria) praying for deliverance and healing from Yahweh and receiving his blessing through Israel; Ps 117 exhorts all nations to praise Yahweh. But elsewhere (e.g., Joel 4 [3]; Nahum) the nations' destiny is only punishment.

The difference between these two descriptions of the nations' destiny is in part formal rather than substantial, first in that both descriptions are essentially Israel-centered. It is for Israel's sake, as a measure of his blessing of them, that Yahweh will make them an indispensable means of blessing to the world. The function of such a statement as a reassurance of Yahweh's attitude toward them is similar to the function of an assertion that the nations who have oppressed Israel will be judged. Sec-

---

[29]So Hermisson, *KD* 27:98.
[30]*Faith and Understanding*, 281.
[31]*Kerygma and Myth*, 11-12.
[32]So Griffin, *TToday* 28:281-83. As Voegelin puts it, diversity of symbolization disguises "equivalences of experience" (*Eternità e storia*, 215-34).

ond, to the extent that such prophecies declare Yahweh's actual purpose for the nations, they implicitly place two possible destinies before them as comparable passages place two possible destinies before the people of God themselves. Either they respond to Yahweh and receive his healing and blessing, or they resist him and expose themselves to his punishment. The function of the two types of passage is to open up alternative scenarios rather than to offer contradictory predictions.

A formal contradiction, then, is one which is more a matter of words than of substance. Beneath the words at the level of substance are statements which are complementary or at least reconcilable.

Contextual Contradiction

Contextual contradiction denotes a difference reflecting the variety in circumstances which different statements address; if the two speakers were confronting similar circumstances, one might find them speaking in similar terms. Isaiah urges Judah to trust in God's commitment to Jerusalem and to David, in the assurance that he will not leave them; Jeremiah denies that Judah can trust in such a commitment and warns that God will leave them. But the two prophets address different audiences (a people who are over-fearful and a people who are over-confident). Hananiah may be seen as proclaiming the same message as Isaiah, but he is a false prophet because that message is inappropriate to his particular audience. It is at least possible that, addressing Jeremiah's age, Isaiah might speak like Jeremiah rather than like Hananiah.

Similarly Ezek 33 denies, but Isa 51 affirms, the possibility of taking God's dealings with Abraham as a paradigm for the way he may be expected to deal with his people in the exile. Ezekiel addresses people at the beginning of the exile, when they have not yet learned how searching must be God's chastisement of his people, while Isa 40–55 addresses people near the end of the exile, who have become demoralized by their experience of it.[33] Again, the preexilic prophets indict Israel for their preoccupation with worship at the expense of morals, and imply that the temple means nothing, while postexilic prophets and the Chronicler emphasize worship as much as morals, and imply that the

---

[33]See Sanders, *Canon and Authority*, 29-41.

temple means everything. The former confront misapprehensions of one day and the latter misapprehensions of another. Similarly, the Chronicler's "corrections" of Samuel-Kings (e.g., 1 Chr 21:1) in part reflect the fact that a different religious context from the one in which Samuel-Kings was written may demand the clarifying or safeguarding of different theological points (e.g., the emphasis on God's fairness which especially characterizes Chronicles). Different national and personal contexts may require different explanations of the problem of suffering: some experiences may be the direct result of wrongdoing (Ezek 18), some may result from wrongdoing which goes back to earlier generations (Kings), some may reflect a presence of evil in the world that goes back to humanity's earliest days (Gen 2–3), some may be a means of dealing with evil and restoring right relationships (Isa 40–55), some are not explicable in moral terms at all (Job, Ecclesiastes, many laments in the Psalter).

1 Kings 19 may be taken as an instance of contextual contradiction. J. Gray sees the theophany here as implying an abandonment of eschatological hopes of supernatural judgment, once fostered in the cult, and an outgrowing of belief in a revelation of God in phenomena such as storm, earthquake, and fire (expressed in Judg 5; Pss 18; 68; Hab 3). These are replaced by human political initiatives arising out of revelation in the form of intelligible communication, "an advance in man's conception of God as personally accessible and intelligible to man within the framework of human experience, anticipating the prophetic conception of the expression of the divine will in contemporary history and the divine revelation in Jesus Christ."[34] The developmental understanding embodied here is questionable. The story's view of God, as Gray describes it, is as old as any material in the OT, and the eschatological hope of supernatural judgment, with the attendant picture of storm, earthquake, and fire, continues to appear through subsequent OT material and in the NT. Further, it is dubious whether this story is to be seen as denying that God once appeared at Horeb to such accompaniment; the main thrust of Elijah's concern is that people are not affirming the commitment made there.[35] If the story is concerned to

---

[34]Gray, *Kings*, 410-11; cf. Fohrer, *Theologische Grundstrukturen*, 36-37, referring to Eichrodt, *Theology*, 2:20-21.

[35]Note the parallel references to the covenant and to destroying altars, and the correspondences between Yahweh's appearance to Moses and to Elijah, which emerge from a comparison of 1 Kgs 18–19 with Exod 19–24; 32–

deny anything, it may be a denial that Yahweh is like Baal,[36] or a denial that this particular moment is one when God is acting in judgment by means of tempest, earthquake, and fire;[37] but it does not thereby deny that he can be so portrayed, or that he so acts, in other contexts.

Substantial Contradiction

Substantial contradiction involves a true divergence in viewpoint on the part of speakers whose disagreement is neither merely verbal nor merely contextual. It arises rather out of differences in their own background, overall perspective, or personality which cause them to see a situation differently or to perceive different aspects of it or to assess it differently and thus to respond to it in different ways. They have divergent views on what Yahweh is concerned about at a particular point and thus on what his word is. B. Vawter suggests that Jeremiah and Ezra, for instance, have quite divergent religious attitudes; they would have been "completely at loggerheads over the first principles of man's relation to God."[38] Their differences cannot be explained on a merely contextual basis.

In some instances, speakers were contemporary and may have been consciously confronting each other. Particularly marked tensions appear in postexilic OT material.[39] A major fea-

---

34; Deut 4–5. See further Carlson, VT 19:416-39. Lust (VT 25:110-15) thinks that the קול דממה דקה is itself "a roaring thundering voice" like the one at Sinai. This view removes any suggestion of contradiction from the passage.

[36]So Cross (Canaanite Myth, 190-94) and Macholz (Werden und Wirken des AT, 325-33).

[37]Perhaps these phenomena are to be understood as a means of judgment, rather than as accompaniments of revelation; they are directly analogous less to the phenomena of Horeb or those of Ps 29 (Macholz) than to the tempest, earthquake, and fire of judgment (cf. Isa 29:6). קול דממה דקה is then the sound of gentle stillness (RV mg) which replaces catastrophe and turmoil (cf. Ps 107:29), rather than a revelation in a still small voice. Cf. Coote, Traditions in Transformation, 115-20, for the view that the event reveals that Yahweh is not coming in judgment.

[38]Biblical Inspiration, 2, 3.

[39]These have been analyzed by Plöger, Theocracy and Eschatology; Steck, Israel, also his articles in EvT 28:445-58 and in Tradition and Theology; Hanson, Dawn of Apocalyptic. In Post-exilic Theological Streams, a critique of such analyses, Hall warns against too sharp a dividing of these "streams," which are capable of intertwining and mingling; cf. Peterson, Late Israelite Prophecy, and Williamson, Israel in the Books of Chronicles. Indeed, Steck (EvT 28:453) begins his contrast over against the Chronicler's position with

ture of the period is that the experience of the Jewish community fell considerably short of that described and implicitly promised in earlier narratives of Israel's history,[40] and of that explicitly promised by Israel's prophets. Many postexilic documents
embody responses to that situation. The differences between
them may be portrayed by characterizing the nature of the beliefs and message of Chronicles and contrasting the emphases of
other postexilic writings with these. Chronicles suggests the response, "You *have* returned and rebuilt the temple as the prophets said you would, you *do* enjoy the privilege of knowing Yahweh as his people and of worshiping Yahweh in his temple as
David arranged, you *can* experience his blessing as you respond
to him with simple trust and obedience in the concrete present
in which you have to live; so do not undervalue what Yahweh
gives to you and what it means to have him among you." But each
of these statements was a controversial one, contradicted by
other strands of postexilic material.

First, postexilic prophecy (e.g., Isa 56–66) is inclined to respond to this situation by pointing to what Yahweh is going to do
rather than to what he has done. "Yes, it is true that Yahweh's
promises have not been fulfilled, but one day they will be—even
more spectacularly than earlier prophets said. So keep your eyes
watching keenly for that future day when Yahweh acts." Two
quite divergent contemporary viewpoints are expressed in
Chronicles and Isa 56–66.[41]

Second, the questioning of Job and Ecclesiastes may plausibly (though more inferentially) be seen as a protest at another aspect of the thinking represented by the Chronicler, his emphasis
on the manifest fairness of Yahweh's dealings with each king and
each generation, which he pictures at work in Israel's history
much more systematically than do the books of Kings with
which this "Deuteronomic" principle of "retribution" is often

---

the penitential prayers in the Chronistic work itself. Brueggemann (*JBL*
98:180) sees Steck's analysis as too diffuse, though when he traces these
streams into the preexilic period Brueggemann has to acknowledge the
diffuseness of the picture there (see 173-74). Kellermann (*Nehemia*) and
Ackroyd (e.g., *TD* 27:323-46) show the diversity even within a work such as
Ezra-Nehemiah.

[40]On the essential, though implicit, forward-looking orientation of OT
narrative, see p. 198 below.

[41]But Peterson (chap. 3), taking up Welch's investigations in *The Work
of the Chronicler*, 42-54, notes that prophecy is an important feature in
Chronicles.

especially associated.[42] Job and Ecclesiastes fundamentally dispute the claim that Yahweh's fairness can be perceived at work in human life, whether in the experience of the individual (Job) or in the events of history (Ecclesiastes).

A third central feature of the Chronicler's theology mentioned above, his stress on the privilege of worshiping Yahweh in the company of Yahweh's people in the temple, may be implicitly contested by the spirituality of Pss 1, 19, and 119, which places paramount stress on the individual's response to God expressed in his keeping the law.[43] Such an attitude may be more characteristic of Diaspora Judaism, for which Jerusalem could not be an everyday physical focus of spiritual life as it could be in Judah. For the writer and readers of Esther, too, Diaspora Judaism, not Jerusalem Judaism, is the locus of God's activity. Esther also emphasizes the significance of human initiatives and decision-making in a way that Chronicles with its stress on a passive trust in Yahweh does not.[44]

A fourth feature of the Chronicler's work is his emphasis on Israel and his concern with the definition of the community. Even if Chronicles and Ezra-Nehemiah take different attitudes to Judeans who had not gone into exile or to the inhabitants of Samaria,[45] both assume that "Israel," however defined, must maintain a distinctive identity over against other peoples; it is doubtful if the author of Chronicles would be any more sympathetic to intermarriage than Ezra and Nehemiah were. There is thus a contrast between the attitudes of Chronicles-Ezra-Nehemiah and those of Ruth, Jonah, and Isa 19:18-25, which are commonly connected with this period. Here an ancestor of David marries a Moabitess, an Israelite prophet is rebuked for resenting God's forgiving the Ninevites, and another prophet promises that Egypt will enjoy deliverance and (with Assyria) blessing like Israel's.

---

[42]On this protest in wisdom's "literature of dissent," see Crenshaw, *Tradition and Theology*, 249-58. More directly, of course, Job and Ecclesiastes are disputing the general tone of Proverbs: see further chap. 7 below.

[43]Cf. Mantel, *HUCA* 44:55-87; also Noth's discussion of the absolutizing of the Law (*Laws*, 85-103); see further pp. 44-48 below.

[44]Cf. Berg, *The Divine Helmsman*, 107-27. See further pp. 48-55 below.

[45]So Williamson, *Israel*; cf. R. L. Braun, VTSup 30:52-64. Braun's understanding of the origin of Ezra-Nehemiah as a continuation of Chronicles within the same tradition but with some differences in views now seems to me the right one.

There are direct contradictions between these various viewpoints. Historically those who held them do sometimes seem to have been opposed to each other. On the other hand, for all the differences between them, they all arise from faith in the one Yahweh; in this sense they are "on the same side."[46] This distinguishes such contrasts from a fourth form of contradiction.

Fundamental Contradiction

Fundamental contradiction denotes a disagreement which is a matter of substance and which indicates a basic disharmony at the level of "ethical stance" or "religious outlook."[47] The ultimate form of this disharmony related by the OT is the conflict reported in Elijah's day, for instance, over whether Baal is God or Yahweh is God. In Jeremiah's day it is the question of allegiance to Yahweh or to the Queen of Heaven. In analyzing the theological tensions of the postexilic period, referred to above (pp. 21-23), Morton Smith sees the fundamental conflict which has "shaped the Old Testament" as that between the "Yahweh-alone party" and the "syncretistic cult of Yahweh."[48]

Even some conflicts within "mono-Yahwism" may be seen as instances of fundamental contradiction. Jeremiah might have seen his conflict with Hananiah in these terms, for the two prophets ultimately differ quite radically over the meaning of the name Yahweh and over the actual content of Yahwism. G. Fohrer implies that the approaches to life of the wisdom material, the cultic material, the classical prophetic material, and other strands in the OT are so distinctive and mutually exclusive that they deserve to be seen as basic disagreements of this kind.[49] That possible view raises most sharply the question whether or

---

[46]Barrett's comment on the NT writers (*Horizons in Biblical Theology*, 3:4); Barrett goes on, "even though, like the armies in *King John*, in attacking the same city from opposite points they sometimes succeed in shooting each other."

[47]Lonergan, 235.

[48]*Palestinian Parties and Politics That Shaped the OT*, e.g., 81, 82. Smith's work is also discussed by Hall (see n. 39 above).

[49]*Theologische Grundstrukturen*, 51-94; cf. Vawter's remarks on Jeremiah and Ezra quoted in n. 38 above. Clavier sees these divergent outlooks as merely different "currents" (the more traditional term "means of revelation" has similar meaning) carrying similar content (see *Les variétés de la pensée biblique*); but this understates the difference.

how far one may expect to find a theological coherence in
the OT.

IS IT APPROPRIATE TO LOOK FOR THEOLOGICAL
COHERENCE IN THE OLD TESTAMENT?

Given the fact that the OT documents are of such diverse viewpoints, for the reasons we have outlined, it may seem questionable whether we should look for any form of theological unity in
them. It has been objected that this quest mistakenly posits some
metahistorical entity standing behind the various historical expressions of OT faith, risks betraying the historical significance
and distinctiveness of witnesses who were sometimes opposing
each other, ignores the OT's own reticence over any quest for a
systematic view, takes no account of the primitive mind's toler-
ance of what the western analytic mind calls contradiction, and
disregards the deliberate concern of those who collected the
scriptures with accepting representatives of divergent views.[50]

Objections to this quest are thus both theological and historical; equally the possibility, the likelihood, and even the inevitability that some form of theological unity can be expected of
the OT can be argued on both theological and historical grounds.

P. D. Hanson suggests that it is dishonest to attempt to account for contradictory perspectives within a document in theological terms if the document itself does not point to a theological explanation for the contradiction.[51] Perhaps it is correct that
such an activity is extrinsic to the exegesis of the actual document (though no more so than the attempt to uncover the factual
historical events referred to by a narrative and to investigate
similar questions which have been the classic concerns of
exegetes). This does not make the task illegitimate, however, except on the assumption that historical exegesis of individual
documents is the sole valid interpretative activity. An alternative assumption is that while this is one valid enterprise, an
equally valid one takes account of the fact that these documents
became part of the scriptures of particular religious communities. Τά βιβλία became τό βιβλίον.[52] To look for theological expla-

---

[50]Cf. Otto, *Kairos* 19:60; Smend, *EvT* 23:423; Gottwald, *Contemporary OT Theologians*, 52-53; Koester, *Trajectories*, 115; von Rad, *Theology*,
1:116; 2:427.

[51]*Canon and Authority*, 118.

[52]Clavier, xi-xii.

nations for contradictions in such documents seems, on theological grounds, a possible task. It is important to acknowledge that we are engaged in a quest which may not have concerned the individual OT writers; but it is also important to acknowledge that this may be a valid quest from other perspectives.[53] Indeed, the theological perspective which sees the various OT writings as part of that defined collection of scriptures which express the self-understanding which the Israelite tradition developed over a long period and portray the character of the one Yahweh[54] compels the expectation that the OT scriptures as a whole can be brought into some coherence. Even if it rejects the traditional view that God was the real author of scripture and that its historical features were incidental to its true nature, a community which believes that in some sense it receives the scriptures from God and not merely from human beings will find it quite natural to look for such a coherence. It will then be only by presupposing that such a coherence exists that we shall be able to discover what that coherence is (or to confirm whether or not it exists).[55]

The expectation that the OT will be theologically coherent has historical as well as theological grounds. First, the suggestion that historical priorities rule out even the *possibility* of looking for such theological coherence should surely be rejected. A historical approach to interpretation indeed presupposes that we seek to understand documents in terms of their meaning in their historical context as exercises in communication between an author and his readers. But this approach does not exclude the possibility that the diversity of views in a particular collection of documents (such as "the Old Testament") can be embraced within some larger coherence, whether or not the conviction that they do so cohere had its origin in historical considerations.

Indeed, this is more than merely a possibility, even on historical grounds. It is a reasonable working assumption that a religious community will believe that documents which it accepts as its scriptures mutually cohere. Certainly this assumption is appropriate to the Jewish community in the period during which the Hebrew canon was coming into its final form. Jewish exege-

---

[53]Cf. Spriggs, *Two OT Theologies*, 90-91; also Wood, *Formation of Christian Understanding*, 19-22, 67-75.

[54]Cf. Zimmerli, *EvT* 35:99-100; *Theology*, 13-14.

[55]Cf. C. A. Baxter's comment on Barth, *Movement from Exegesis to Dogmatics in Barth*, 221.

sis of the period between 200 B.C. and A.D. 200 is particularly interested in the coherence of the biblical text, whose apparent inconsistencies it works hard to resolve: "the first and foremost of all exegetical imperatives was harmonisation and reconciliation."[56] If the formal reason for the forming of a collection of Hebrew scriptures was to make them available as a resource for worship and teaching,[57] it was natural that such activity followed.

It is not by accident or oversight that a collection of scriptures made by people of this period embraces diverse or conflicting material. Such people are aware of a need to unify divergent material that they cannot disregard.[58] So "through canonization various separate strands of tradition, which were originally self-sufficient and were not orientated towards mutual supplementation, were accommodated to one another," to the huge enrichment of the tradition.[59] And while it is true that "no one redacted the Bible as a whole,"[60] so that no one author's work can be the focus of an attempt to interpret the Bible as one document, the process of collecting and defining the scriptures is nevertheless one with implications for the interpretation of the resultant collection as a unified whole. Indeed, the midrashic instinct features within the individual books that eventually came to be regarded as scriptures. It appears at a late stage in the process of reediting, rereading, and supplementing whereby earlier works are accepted but also modified in order to speak to different situations and to solve problems felt by later readers. A unifying concern also underlies the earlier, broader development of the OT tradition, which worked in such a way as to portray the one God of the one community, and allowed that tradition to embrace only works in which he could be recognized.[61]

It is historically certain, then, that the Jewish community believed that its scriptures were theologically coherent and that the divergent material they included was capable of coalescing

---

[56]Vermes, *Cambridge History of the Bible*, 1:209.

[57]Cf. Barr's definition of "canon," *JTS* 25:274, though I have here avoided the word *canon* both because it is a "hurrah" word for some and a "boo" word for others, and because it is difficult to define the distinctive connotations that cause it to provoke these reactions.

[58]Cf. Vawter, *Inspiration*, 6.

[59]Ebeling, *Study of Theology*, 15.

[60]Barr, 274.

[61]So Patrick, *Rendering of God*, 56.

into a form of unity, and the first Christians naturally shared such a belief.[62]

Further, although the conviction that the OT documents belong together did not arise from historical considerations, it is in part capable of being tested historically. It need not be (and ought not to be) in conflict with historical considerations. The exegetical methods by which Jews and Christians two millennia ago sought to vindicate this conviction do not find acceptance in the world of twentieth-century scholarship. Our attempt to see how diverse viewpoints within the OT may be acknowledged, interrelated, and allowed to function theologically is in part, then, an exercise in discovering whether this conviction can be vindicated by the methods now used by scholarship. But more broadly, it is concerned to see how we can speak of theological unity in such a way as to release rather than to lose the value of the OT's diversity, in the context of Christian theology and biblical interpretation.

In the investigation which follows, we shall examine three chief approaches to the diversity of viewpoint in the OT, each of which may offer some insight on how OT texts in their diversity can function theologically in the church and in the world.

---

[62]See, e.g., Dahl, *Studies in Paul*, 159-77; Laurin, *Tradition and Theology*, 271 (with disapproval).

Part I

A CONTEXTUAL OR HISTORICAL APPROACH

Chapter 2

CAN WE EXPLAIN DIVERSE THEOLOGIES BY THEIR CONTEXTS?

DIVERSITY WITHIN THE BOUNDARIES OF MEMBERSHIP OF ONE "FAMILY"

One approach to theological diversity in the OT is simply to acknowledge the variety of viewpoints and to accept all of them as potentially instructive. The OT writings may then be likened to a collection of paintings of a landscape, portrayed from various angles during different seasons and in various periods, some in the manner of van Gogh, some in that of Cezanne, some in that of Picasso, some portraying a whole vista, others concentrating on a stream here or a ruin there. Our response to such a collection is not to try to unify them in some way, but to enjoy each of them individually. In turn, it is precisely the range of insights incorporated within the OT which opens up the possibility that among them I may find some insight that relates to my own situation. S. Mowinckel speaks of "God's word— concrete and relevant";[1] its concreteness, far from threatening its relevance, enables it to be relevant.

In what sense, then, do these viewpoints cohere? To refuse to harmonize conflicting viewpoints by reducing their individual distinctiveness is not to deny the existence of any form of unity in their theological perspective.[2] That unity can be envisaged in formal or in material terms.

---

[1] *OT as Word of God*, 119.

[2] Barth, for whom the unity of scripture is of great importance, himself warns against a failure to do justice to historical particularity (*Dogmatics*, 1/1:179-81).

29

Formally, all these writings belong to one history; they are the deposit of the historical experience of Israel in its pre-Christian period. Together they are thus also the deposit of one unified religious tradition,[3] whose development is one aspect of that history. Further, and more specifically again, they all belong to the form of that tradition which came to have the status of a canon of normative writings in Judaism. While the OT is not "a consciously formulated propositional confession," neither is it merely a collection of *disiecta membra*; it is "a *corpus*, or, if you prefer, a collection of *corpora*, which both issued from and moulded the life of a religious community," embodying that community's many-colored confession of faith, and manifesting not the structured unity of a carefully articulated statement, but "the organic unity which is given to it by a worshipping community."[4]

Certain books within this canon themselves model the formal unifying of highly diverse viewpoints within one document. Job, for instance, offers a range of responses to the questions about the nature of the relationship between God and humanity which are raised by the fact of human suffering: the beliefs expressed by the prologue, by each of the three friends, by Job himself at different points, by the wisdom poem, by Elihu, by the Yahweh speeches, and by the epilogue, all contribute insights on these questions.[5] In Proverbs, "individual fragments of knowledge are listed one after the other, and contradictory experiences are not reconciled, but consciously opposed to one another, in order to attain a comprehension of reality as full and extensive as possible";[6] the juxtaposed antinomies of Prov 17:27-28; 26:4-5 illustrate particularly vividly the book's willingness to hold together diverse facets of experience.[7] Ecclesiastes, too, though working out the balance of various types of sayings very

---

[3]Gese's emphasis: e.g., *Tradition and Theology*, 307-17; idem, *ZTK* 67:424-26; idem, *Essays*, 9-33.

[4]G. W. Anderson, *SJT* 16:280, 284. Anderson is here referring both to the Psalter and to the OT as a whole, which he believes the Psalter exemplifies (see the next paragraph).

[5]Jacob (*Grundfragen alttestamentlicher Theologie*, 23-24) sees Job as the OT's deepest statement on the nature of God, made in the course of insisting on the complexity of his one person (over against the limits set by systems and dogmas).

[6]Lohfink, *Christian Meaning of the OT*, 138-39.

[7]Cf. von Rad's comments, *Wisdom*, 311.

differently, embraces material of different viewpoints, while OT apocalyptic (specifically Daniel) holds together law, prophecy, and wisdom with their different dynamics.[8] The Pentateuch combines material of highly diverse viewpoints into a formal narrative unity;[9] thus in their final form the story of the crossing of the Red Sea in Exod 13-14 and the story of the spies in Num 13-14 interweave at least two different understandings of the relationship of divine and human acts and of how Yahweh can be both judging and merciful.[10] The book of Isaiah holds together materials which both confront and reassure the people of God; they challenge its readers to responsible action themselves, envisage God's action in their own experience, and promise God's action at the last great Day; they both look forward to new growth from the tree of Jesse and see Cyrus as Yahweh's anointed. The Psalter embraces a wide variety of responses to God, of adoration, wonder, gratitude, commitment, testimony, trust, repentance, grief, doubt, complaint, anger, perplexity, resentment, longing. It rejoices in (or misses) his activity in nature and in history, in the story of Israel and in the experience of the individual. It acknowledges Yahweh in all the multiplex aspects of his character. Thus in its "comprehensive variety" it "supplies the data for an epitome of Old Testament theology,"[11] so that H.-J. Kraus can describe his *Theologie der Psalmen* as "a kind of OT theology *in nuce*."[12] Each of these OT books thus models a formal unifying of diverse perspectives.[13]

Scholars who urge that OT theology must take seriously the contextual variety of theological viewpoints expressed in the

---

[8]See Beauchamp, *L'un et l'autre Testament*, 200-228.

[9]Cf. Clavier, *Les variétés de la pensée biblique*, 2; also von Rad's observations on the interweaving of J, E, and P (*Genesis*, 28).

[10]See Schmitt, *Textgemäss*, 139-55; Sakenfeld, *CBQ* 37:317-30. See further pp. 193-97 below.

[11]H. W. Robinson, *Inspiration and Revelation*, 269; cf. Anderson, 277-85; also Kapelrud, *Tradition and Theology*, 113-23.

[12]ET from p. 5; he notes that Luther in his "Preface to the Psalter" suggests that the Psalter "might well be called a little Bible," comprehending as it does everything in the entire Bible (*Luther's Works*, 35:254). Kraus himself later (p. 11) calls the theology of the Psalms a *biblical* theology *in nuce*.

[13]In *The Varieties of NT Religion*, 285-96, E. F. Scott suggests that later NT books such as Matthew, Acts, and John seek a more comprehensive perspective than earlier books or traditions which strongly asserted one view; e.g., Matthew both affirms and denies the significance of the Law, maintaining both views but not indicating how they may be related. Cf. J. M. Robinson's comments on "early catholicism" in the NT, *JES* 3:46-51.

OT do not assume that they constitute merely a formal unity. They believe that these viewpoints also have a degree of material unity about them. First, they not only derive from and belong to one people: they concern one people. What it means to be the people of God varies over the centuries (see pp. 2-3 above). But a concern with Israel as the people of God runs through the OT.[14] Second, since the OT's concern is Israel as the people of *God*, a further unifying strand in its thinking is the person of that God himself. He is the keystone that holds the OT's diverse materials into one building.[15] He may change his mind or change his name or change his way of acting in relation to Israel and to the nations, but the OT assumes that he remains the one Yahweh. The fathers were addressed in many differing ways, but by the same God (cf. Heb 1:1). Third, as Israel's history provides a fundamental aspect of the OT's formal unity, so its history constitutes one aspect of its material unity. The OT constitutes not a collection of mutually contemporary descriptions of the relationship between Yahweh and Israel, but the story of a people living in history and changing with history. This history can be seen as the story of a struggle with some basic issue or question, to which a variety of approaches is possible: the nature of God's purpose,[16] or the establishing of "order" and meaning,[17] or the tension between unpredictable divine initiative (symbolized by Abraham) and regular historical institution (symbolized by Moses),[18] or an experience such as God ever turning to humanity to speak what needed to be said in different situations.[19] Throughout it is one story, "a single drama of divine and human action" which embraces the diversity of different times, personalities, and viewpoints as the plot develops, but locates all within the outworking of one purpose.[20] Even the development of

---

[14]Cf. von Rad, *Theology,* 1:118; see chap. 3 below.

[15]See Jacob, *Grundfragen,* 41; cf. Schmidt, *Erste Gebot,* 7-11; McKenzie, *Theology,* 26; Zimmerli, *EvT* 35:102-17 (illustrating how this includes the wisdom literature); idem, *TLZ* 98:81-85; Kraus, *Biblische Theologie,* 384; Laurin, *Tradition and Theology,* 266-67; Ebeling, *Study of Theology,* 36; Patrick, *Rendering of God,* 56-60 (emphasizing the coherence of the OT's portrayal of God).

[16]So von Rad, e.g., *Theology,* 2:357-58.

[17]Voegelin, *Israel and Revelation,* ix.

[18]So Leenhardt, *Two Biblical Faiths.*

[19]Cf. Wagner, *TLZ* 103:794-95.

[20]H. R. Niebuhr, *Meaning of Revelation,* 135-36; cf. B. W. Anderson, *TToday* 28:326-27; Laurin, 267.

forms of faith that rather turn their backs on history as the locus of God's activity with Israel is part of that history.[21]

The World Council of Churches *Study on Biblical Hermeneutics*[22] speaks of an acceptance of the manifold richness of the Bible and a satisfaction with identifying "family resemblances" among its varied witnesses. The notion of family resemblances was developed by L. Wittgenstein[23] in the course of seeking to define a "language-game," to penetrate the essence of language. He compares the proceedings we call games: nothing is common to all games, yet games manifest a complicated network of similarities overlapping and crisscrossing, which are like the various resemblances within a family, such as build, features, color of eyes, and temperament. Thus "games" form a family. The varied messages of the OT might also be seen as sharing a family resemblance. None may manifest all aspects of the family profile, but all share common features visible when they are compared with each other or with those who are outside the family. All may therefore be treated as members of the OT family, and all should be taken seriously.

DIVERSITY OF VIEWPOINT AND DIVERSITY OF CONTEXT

If these viewpoints are so diverse, however, it will be easy for some to be ignored or dismissed. How can they be understood and acknowledged? One response to this question is to emphasize that the OT material is related to different historical contexts and needs to be viewed in the light of this variety of contexts. Isaiah and Jeremiah, or Ezekiel and the second Isaiah, can speak opposite messages because they address very different situations (see pp. 19-21 above). The differences between them are not to be toned down; they arise from the directness with which each is responding to a particular context, and their oneness lies in the way they are doing this in Yahweh's name, not in a unity at the level of the content of their messages.[24]

L. R. Bailey offers a contextual explanation of different biblical perspectives on death: "It is precarious to speak of *the*

---

[21]Cf. Barr, *RTP* 3/18:210-12.
[22]New England Group Report 14; cf. Bright, *Authority of the OT,* 124.
[23]*Philosophical Investigations,* §§ 65-67.
[24]Cf. Diem, *Dogmatics,* 234-38.

biblical response to death. Rather, there is a variety of responses, depending upon the time and circumstances. . . . Since all of the responses are (at least to some extent) historically conditioned, and since all of them have been preserved (canonized) by communal decisions, any one of them need not *automatically* be considered superior to the others. Since more than one stance was 'normative' for its time and proved to be an effective coping mechanism, all of them may have a contribution to make to the attitudes of members of the believing communities (synagogue and church) in the present. Rather than *a priori* hierarchical values (such as early is authentic; latest is fullest revelation; the NT alone is binding on the church; Jesus' perspective is ultimate), it may be that the communities' situation in the present will ultimately determine which biblical response is the most meaningful, after dialogue with the entirety of the canon."[25]

The diversity of OT attitudes to suffering[26] may also be understood as reflecting the possibility that God is involved in suffering in different ways in different contexts. Sometimes he is punishing sin, sometimes fulfilling some purpose of edification, sometimes acting (apparently) arbitrarily, sometimes taking people through an unpleasant experience which has a positive purpose for others, sometimes caring for people whose suffering comes through some other agency, sometimes promising future relief from suffering which comes through some other agency. Corresponding to this range of contextual possibilities is a range of possible human attitudes to God in the contexts of suffering: repentance, submission, trust or uncertainty, anger or protest, acceptance, relief, hope.

Contextual differences also underlie instances of diversity that amount more to difference than to contradiction. If the story of Abraham issues a challenge both to a realization of Yahweh's interest in other nations (J), to fear of God (E), and to confidence in his irrevocable commitment to his people (P), this perhaps reflects the circumstances of the united monarchy, the northern kingdom, and the exile, respectively.[27] Differences between the ethical stances implied by different parts of the OT may also be explained contextually, for the Israelite attitude to life is concrete and temporal, not timeless and theoretical; it is a

---

[25]*Biblical Perspectives on Death*, 97.

[26]See recently Gerstenberger and Schrage, *Suffering*; Simundson, *Faith under Fire*.

[27]Cf. Brueggemann and Wolff, *Vitality of OT Traditions*.

matter of specific response to God in a particular situation.[28] OT commands are not so much universal absolutes, designed to be applicable in any circumstances, as specific enactments made in particular historical, social, and cultural situations, and designed to function in those particular situations.[29]

THE USEFULNESS AND LIMITATIONS OF THIS CONTEXTUAL APPROACH

Simple acceptance of the diverse viewpoints expressed in the OT has several considerations in its favor. First, it can take seriously the breadth of the OT canon. Theology can easily be selective in its approach to the sources which in theory it acknowledges as normative. By its variety, the Psalter, for instance, sets before OT theologians an example which can help safeguard them against selectivity by not allowing them to forget the perplexingly comprehensive and divergent subject matter which must be incorporated in an OT theology.[30] Second, it can take the actual text of the OT seriously, allowing passages and books to speak for themselves rather than to be assimilated to the perspective of other books or replaced by an alleged underlying theology. It can thus avoid exaggerating either their intrinsic disharmony or their intrinsic harmony. On one side, it recognizes that the difference between the message of Isaiah ("Relax; Yahweh is with you; he is not going to let the city fall") and that of Jeremiah ("Wake up; Yahweh has abandoned you; he is going to let the city be destroyed") does not necessarily imply that the two prophets are contradicting each other; they spoke to different contexts. On the other side, it recognizes that there are real differences between such attitudes as the confident generalizations of Proverbs and the skeptical empiricism of Ecclesiastes, and does not read the latter as if it were the former in disguise.

The insight that the varying messages in scripture address varying situations is also of significance for the task of seeking to identify what aspects of scripture especially confront us today. On the one hand, where the questions raised in some OT contexts are similar to those raised in our context, we can learn

---

[28]Cf. Hempel, *Ethos des AT,* 89-90.
[29]Cf. Barth, *Dogmatics,* 3/4:12; cf. 2/2:673-74 with reference to many of the commands in Exodus.
[30]So G. W. Anderson, *SJT* 16:283, 284.

directly from the message addressed to that context. The believing community seeking inspiration for its worship, or unsure of the security of the world, or uncertain of the power of its God when its own fortunes seem to be at a low ebb, or having difficulty trusting in his goodness, can learn directly from the way the creation theme is brought into relationship to these questions.[31] Thus we give formal recognition to all the scriptural material, yet we find that certain elements within it especially grasp us, because the message addressed to their context is also that which especially speaks in the context in which we live.[32] On the other hand, the path the "creation trajectory" takes as it reacts to OT questions may also enable us to extrapolate the path it might be expected to take in relationship to questions which are not raised in the OT, such as ecology, world development and world food needs, and the search for meaning in life. Thus the contextual nature of the OT also functions as a model for our attempt to see what new thing God may have to say in contexts that were unknown in ancient Israel.

An acceptance of the diverse viewpoints expressed in the OT thus makes a good starting point for an attempt to allow the OT to function theologically. Yet it is only a starting point for this task. First, the OT material often has more the character of raw material for a portrayal of some aspect of belief (e.g., God's nature) than that of the coherent and finished portrayal itself. Simply accepting the OT's statements about God falls short of the properly theological task of analyzing these statements reflectively and building with them. Without this, even if the themes of God, his people, and the story of the relationship between them hold together so much of the OT, what these themes mean varies so extensively that the unity they give to the OT remains rather formal.[33] H. Gese argues that acknowledgment of the variety of OT theologies is saved from relativism by recognition that all these theologies belong to one tradition-process; but it is not clear *why* this fact saves us from relativism[34]

---

[31]See pp. 8-10 above.

[32]Cf. Laurin's comments, *Tradition and Theology*, 272.

[33]Cf. Clavier, 319-23; Zimmerli's treatment of the presence of God or of forms of leadership such as kingship illustrate this point (see *Theology*, 70-108). Schlier (*Relevance of the NT*, 20) makes a parallel observation regarding the thesis that the unity of the various NT witnesses lies in the Christ to which they refer.

[34]ZTK 67:425-26.

Recent study of the land as an OT theme illustrates the point. W. Brueggemann, notably, studies this theme diachronically as it appears in various periods in biblical times.[35] But this means that he does not consider the theological questions which the material as a whole raises, such as "Is ownership of real property necessary for either individual or group fulfilment? Is the life of the *fellah* intrinsically better than that of the *bedouin* (many romantics have thought quite the contrary)? What basic principles governed land-ownership in ancient Israel? Do these have any relevance to the possession of land by the nation (surely they do)? By what moral standard can one justify the divine gift of land once occupied by the Canaanites to people who were historically not even their enemies? Why did the historical greatness of Israel emerge only in the age when she was becoming detached from the land?"[36]

Questions such as these also point us to a further aspect of the stress on context as a key to seeing how scripture applies today. This stress means putting considerable weight on a historical understanding of both scriptural text and modern situation. Misunderstanding of either may then easily generate misconceived paralleling of biblical message and modern situation and misappropriation of biblical text. Sometimes we do not know what circumstances saw the emergence of a particular text. Sometimes the same context (e.g., the exile, or the postexilic situation in Judah) generates several types of response, and the differences between them cannot be explained contextually. Sometimes scripture offers several possible paradigmatic responses to a recurrent set of circumstances: for instance, for a landless or insecure people, is the matching scriptural message that of Joshua (attack), that of the exile (wait for Yahweh to act), or that of some postexilic thinking (accept the situation)?

Decisions between alternatives are involved here. Even if we accept a theoretical commitment to all these varied perspectives, we do not expect to maintain such an undifferentiated commitment in practice. All the OT's perspectives on the people of God or on the land may contain insights, but all those insights cannot be normative in the same way at the same time. The in-

---

[35]*The Land.* See also Diepold, *Israels Land;* Eckert, ed., *Jüdisches Volk—gelobtes Land* (esp. Rendtorff, 153-68); H.-R. Weber, *Promise of the Land* (*Study Encounter* 7:4); von Waldow, *A Light unto My Path*, 493-508.
[36]Dentan, *JBL* 97:578.

terpreter has to move from a theoretical commitment regarding the whole OT to a practical commitment regarding some aspect of it rather than others. On what basis is one to do so? If we make our choice on the basis of our own preferences and person, or our own understanding of the world and the church to which we wish to relate the OT's insights, or on some similar basis, from the perspective of the OT tradition as a whole, this approach will be arbitrary,[37] and ignores the possibility that some perspectives are appropriate to some situations but not to others, or that some perspectives are theologically preferable to others.

Similar consequences follow in practice from the fact that it is not actually the case that even the most fundamental OT theological themes appear throughout the OT. The people of God and the history of the relationship between God and his people are missing from the wisdom books, while some of the prophets attack the idea that Yahweh is tied to Israel and assert Yahweh's concern with all peoples.[38] Indeed, even God receives no overt mention in Esther or the Song of Songs.[39]

For some years OT study emphasized the distinctiveness of the Israelite emphasis on God's activity in history, and rather neglected the wisdom books because of their relative independence of this perspective. Over the past two decades, however, the wisdom literature has become a focus of interest. While this is partly the correcting of an earlier imbalance, it also reflects the fact that theology generally has taken a more philosophical turn. Wisdom's concern with secular life, its empiricism, its internationalism, and its concern with the individual all currently make wisdom's perspective attractive; it might even seem to be the gospel for our time, as W. Brueggemann suggests in another work with a strikingly twentieth-century title, *In Man We Trust.*

---

[37]Cf. Schmitt, *Textgemäss,* 141.

[38]Schmidt, *Erste Gebot,* 51; cf. the passages noted by Schmidt, p. 9. Wisdom's creation- and experience-based theology is also rather in tension with it (see further chap. 7 below).

[39]Admittedly Yahweh's involvement in history on his people's behalf may be a covert theme of Esther (so, e.g., Berg, *Esther,* 178-79); but it no longer seems plausible that the relationship between God/the Messiah and Israel is the covert theme of the Song of Songs. There may be indirect allusions to the name of God in the Song (see Gordis, *Song of Songs,* 26-28; idem, *JBL* 100:360-64, 375-78); while Cant 8:6 may include the divine name as an expression of the superlative (cf. JB; but Tromp, *La sagesse de l'AT,* 88-95, takes the expression to refer to love as a creative divine power). But these exceptions prove the rule.

It is inevitable that different aspects of the biblical material speak particularly clearly in different periods, and it is advantageous in a pluralistic culture that people of different backgrounds can find different traditions with which to identify.[40] But it is consequently easy for the Bible to become merely a means of confirming what we are already inclined to believe or hope for other reasons; we look down the well and see our own faces at the bottom. The parts of the Bible that seem more alien are the ones that provide needed correctives to the partial insights which we have already grasped and thus find mirrored in parts of the Bible with which we feel more at home. An acceptance of the variety of OT messages must therefore be followed up by a consideration of how they are to be interrelated and allowed to function in practice, so that we hear all of them and not only those to which we are already attuned.

Similar considerations emerge from Bailey's approach to the variety of *Biblical Perspectives on Death*. We noted above (pp. 33-34) his suggestion that different situations may make different perspectives more meaningful than others. He instances "the modern Christian's increasing inability to accept the idea of an afterlife" and suggests that "at a time when ability to believe in that doctrine is on the wane . . . it might be helpful to remember other perspectives within the tradition," such as the general OT acceptance of mortality as natural and its rejoicing in the ongoing life of one's own people, in the survival of one's own memory, and in the eternity of God himself.[41]

Bailey does not raise the question whether the idea of an afterlife might be a truth rather than merely something helpful if we find it congenial. If the former is the case, then it cannot simply be abandoned because those other perspectives seem more congenial. Bailey speaks of "dialogue with the entirety of the canon,"[42] but he does not make it clear how his approach lets the whole canon be canonical. Nor does the contextual emphasis explain the fact that sometimes the same context in Israel's life meets widely different theological responses, or that sometimes different contexts utilize the same elements within the tradition (which then "cut" in varying ways).[43]

---

[40]So B. W. Anderson, *TToday* 28:327.
[41]Pp. 102-3, 105-6; cf. 47-61.
[42]P. 97.
[43]Cf. J. M. Robinson, *Trajectories*, 69.

Although the unity of OT faith has often been overestimated in the context of monolithic theology, it would be as mistaken to settle too simply for mere acceptance of diversity in OT faith. An emphasis on the contextual variety of theologies in the OT may be just as much an unhistorical mirroring of our pluralistic culture and theology (or of existentialist concerns) as was the emphasis on one system of biblical doctrine an unhistorical mirroring of a monolithic culture and faith.[44]

ARE SOME CONTEXTS MORE ILLUMINATING THAN OTHERS?

The work of James M. Robinson, who makes the observation just noted that an emphasis on contextual diversity may in part mirror our own pluralistic attitudes, suggests one way of safeguarding against this danger (though he does not himself develop the point). With Helmut Koester, Robinson has applied the model of trajectories to the development of movements of thought such as the Christian faith. His suggestion is that such movements of thought need to be seen not as fixed collections of specific beliefs or attitudes, but as processes on the move. He contrasts this view with one in which "the fixed point was taken for the historical fact, whose degree of reality was hardly equaled by the penumbral areas of influences that led up to it and consequences that grew out of it," so that "the movement itself would tend to be a deficient mode of reality, the space between discrete atoms of factual reality."[45] On the contrary, Robinson suggests, the historic reality is the movement itself. This is true both for the Christian faith and for the other movements which have been viewed as the "background" against which it has to be understood (Rabbinic Judaism, Gnosticism, Hellenism). These are not static, fixed contexts but moving trajectories, jostling each other and modifying each other as they move, and also affected by the gravitational pulls of the plurality of spinning worlds between which they move. The Christian trajectory inevitably shared many features of the trajectory (trajectories) of its overall culture(s). Thus what is distinctive about it is not what distinguishes it from our own way of thinking ("We

---

[44]Adapted from an observation on NT theology by Robinson, loc. cit.; for its application to the OT, see B. W. Anderson, loc. cit.
[45]*Trajectories*, 11.

talk a lot about the uniqueness of Christianity; but on further study much of its uniqueness, at least on the surface level, turns out to be the unusualness of Hellenistic thought patterns in the American culture").[46] It is how it related to the trajectories among which it was inevitably caught up.[47]

So a statement about Jesus—or about Yahweh's activity in Israel—gains its meaning from its place and function in a trajectory. This both facilitates and hinders (even both enables and prevents) the grasping of what the event means. As well as making it clear, it obscures it, because the terms used bring the overtones and nuances that history has given them, and these contribute negatively as well as positively to apprehending and expressing the point that needs making. There is a potential tension between point and language.[48] Further, the cultural conditions that facilitate an apprehension of certain aspects of an event's significance also prevent the apprehension of other aspects where that same context lacks the symbols or questions or framework which make a response to them possible.[49] There may be quite a sharp conflict between the historical particularity, the "facts," to which the faith feels compelled to witness, and the cultural and religious expectations and ideologies available in a certain culture to express the meaning of those "facts."[50] In a context in which testimony to these facts has become written scripture, a new aspect of this reality emerges: there are certain aspects of this written witness which one generation can "hear" in the way that another cannot, so that interpreters who want to appropriate the text's significance as fully as possible are willing

[46]Robinson, *JES* 3:53-54.

[47]Cf. Robinson, *Trajectories*, 15-16. As well as the other essays in that volume see also Koester, *Future of Our Religious Past*, 65-83; Brueggemann, *JBL* 98:161-85.

[48]Cf. Robinson, *JES* 3:42-43; also Hart, *Unfinished Man*, 27, 87: apprehension has to create a new "house of meaning" using the available "linguistic debris" (Merleau-Ponty, *Signs*, 87) if it is to execute its "raid on the inarticulate" (T. S. Eliot, "East Coker," *Complete Poems and Plays*, 182).

[49]Cf. Koester, *Trajectories*, 208-9. Saggs's contrast of the patriarchal and the Mosaic God (*Encounter with the Divine*, 37-38), though overstated, perhaps provides an OT instance: the exodus context allows certain features of God's character to emerge more clearly (his dynamism and the real interweaving of his decisions and human decisions) but also brings overtones and nuances that obscure other features (his concern for the whole world and his prosecuting a coherently thought-out purpose).

[50]Cf. Koester, 279.

to look at it through the eyes of other generations' exegesis as well as those of their own, which are inevitably blinkered in certain respects.

Some conceptualities, questions, symbol-systems, or frameworks, then, will provide a better match than others do to some realities, and one particular context may allow the fullest and most challenging understanding of some reality to emerge.

Now it is possible to see a work such as G. von Rad's *OT Theology* as following the trajectory of the OT kerygma through the OT period. It is also possible to see historical treatments of OT themes such as M. Noth's study of Law,[51] W. Zimmerli's study of *Man and His Hope in the OT*, W. Brueggemann's study of *The Land*, or various individual chapters of W. Eichrodt's *Theology of the OT*, as seeking to follow the trajectory of a particular symbol or concept, freezing that trajectory at various points in order to see what aspects of its possible meaning are allowed to emerge in various contexts.

A strictly contextual approach to diversity in the OT simply notes that different statements are then appropriate in different contexts. But Robinson's observation that a particular cultural context both facilitates and hinders the interpretation of an event or a concept suggests the possibility that more of the event's or the concept's intrinsic meaning or depth will be allowed to emerge in some contexts than in others. All may be illuminating, and all are of theological significance. But some may be more illuminating and of more theological significance than others.

Now this is not to imply that because more of this depth emerges in specific contexts, material which emerged from other contexts is of no significance or value. The whole trajectory is potentially illuminating; the way that insights emerge at varying points contributes to our understanding as a whole. It is not the high point of the trajectory which alone counts. Nevertheless, some contexts may be relatively more illuminating and of greater theological significance than others.

This can be illustrated from the NT by E. Käsemann's analysis of the way the NT deals with the tension between Spirit and order. There the church starts off manifesting the dynamism of the Spirit, but is threatened by enthusiasm and Gnosticism and, beginning to appeal to the authority of tradition and ministry,

---

[51]*Laws*, 1-107; see further pp. 44-48 below.

comes to manifest even within the canonical period the characteristics that were to come to full flower in catholicism— order without Spirit. Käsemann has no doubt that it is the church manifesting the dynamic of the Spirit that is the real church, nevertheless, "the historical necessity of this transformation should not be overlooked. The Pauline understanding of office, worship, Christian freedom and responsibility was apparently unable to curb the ferment of enthusiasm in the churches. . . . The revolution can be called legitimate" in that "the Holy Spirit manifests itself in the Church most clearly when, in the midst of pressing need and perplexity of men, it awakens the courage and spiritual gifts for new ways which are appropriate to the situation." Nevertheless, we have to ask about "the price which early catholicism had to pay for the preservation of the Christian Church in the defence against enthusiasm," namely, that "the Church was compelled to bind the Spirit to the office" and thus rejoice in the uncomfortable fact that occasionally "the real Paul . . . is rediscovered" through the fact that "the Church continues to preserve his letters in her canon and thereby latently preserves her own permanent crisis."[52]

Clearly the fullest understanding of any reality is in theory available at the end of the trajectory, when it can be surveyed as a whole. In this sense the end of the trajectory contains or reveals the significance of the whole. And yet, this instance makes clear that the most *penetrating* grasp of some reality may emerge at a much earlier point. Further, while the fullest understanding only becomes theoretically *available* when the trajectory is complete, it may not be actually accessible to people at that point. As seems to have been the case with early catholicism, they may be able to perceive the trajectory only from their perspective.

INSTANCES OF THEMES EMERGING AT THEIR MOST ILLUMINATING IN PARTICULAR CONTEXTS

In the OT, too, there is a tension between ideal and history. Particular contexts allow some themes to be stated with particular degrees of truth or depth. The trajectory traced by a motif may allow that motif to be seen with special clarity at certain points.

---

[52]*NT Questions*, 247, 248, 249, 250.

Covenant and Law

What is the place of a stress on human obedience to God's commands, in the context of a relationship between God and people? In his influential essay on "The Laws in the Pentateuch," Martin Noth emphasized that the starting point for understanding the OT's theology of the law is that the law belongs to the covenant relationship between Yahweh and Israel (essentially Israel as the people of God; the law is not state law). Further, the order of these two concepts is significant. The covenant relationship existed first, established on the initiative of Yahweh. The giving of the law followed Yahweh's establishing of his relationship with Israel; it was designed to demonstrate and safeguard the distinctiveness of Israel as Yahweh's covenant people. To put it theologically, grace is prior to law in the OT.[53] It can further be noted that the Pentateuch itself (or, better, the Hexateuch, since the story finds its conclusion in Joshua) is, after all, really a narrative in which laws are set, rather than a lawbook.[54]

Noth goes on to observe that the exile signified the terminating of this covenant relationship, upon which the law's own validity depended. Some of the prophets spoke of the establishment of a new covenant, but the reorganization of the community under Persian patronage, recorded in Ezra and Nehemiah, hardly constituted the fulfillment of such a hope. The covenant had been the basis of Israel's community life in relation to God, and thus of the validity of Israel's laws. Now it was in abeyance, and, in contrast, the acknowledgment of the law by Israel constituted the basis of the covenant relationship between God and people. Eventually, the law comes to have a status of its own, independent of the covenant, and emphasis swings completely from divine activity to individual human behavior. Instead of God taking the initiative and human beings responding, now human conduct is decisive and God only reacts to this behavior according to the standard laid down by the law. Noth draws attention to the stress on the individual's attitude to the law in Pss

---

[53]Noth, *Laws*, 1-60; cf. G. A. F. Knight, *Law and Grace*, 25; von Rad, *Theology*, 1:192-95, 2:390-95. Von Rad relates the giving of the law more integrally to Israel's election by describing the proclamation of the law (embodying Yahweh's will) over Israel as a means of putting Israel's election into effect. Cf. Barth, *Dogmatics*, 2/2:509: the law is "the form of the Gospel," that is "the sanctification which comes to man through the electing God" (562-64 apply this to Deuteronomy in particular).

[54]J. A. Sanders, *Torah and Canon*, 4.

1, 19, and 119, and sees this development bearing fruit in the legalism which Paul attacks.[55] By implication, Christians are ill-advised to try to let OT law shape their obedience to God, lest they repeat Israel's mistakes and end up in legalism.[56]

Noth's scheme embraces understandings of the history, social structure, cultic practice, religious faith, and theological significance of OT Israel, and many specific features of it have been questioned. Since the early creative work of Eichrodt and Noth, emphasis on the covenant's importance has swung right into fashion, but then, partly through its being used uncritically, right out of fashion.[57] Similarly, Noth's belief that the original covenant community to which the laws belonged was the "sacral confederacy of the twelve tribes of Israel" or "amphictyony" first earned widespread acceptance, then became widely questioned[58] —though even if the amphictyony has to be abandoned, something rather like it may nevertheless have to replace it.[59] Among the questions of immediate theological significance which have been raised are the following.

One aspect of the overstress on covenant was the emphasis on the covenantal context of OT ethics. In its pentateuchal setting, most OT law is indeed linked with covenant(s). But much of this law—in particular, central features of its fundamental moral ethos—has an earlier background outside the covenant, reflected also in the appearance of a similar ethos in the prophets and wisdom books without explicit reference to the covenant. The content of the laws can thus be seen as reflecting ordinary human experience, as embodying a conformity to natural order, and as applying as much outside as inside Israel; it constitutes a means of response to the creator as well as to the redeemer, and can be connected with the doctrine of creation as well as with the covenant.[60]

---

[55]So Noth, *Laws*, 60-107.

[56]The classic Lutheran position: see, e.g., Luther's own sermon, "How Christians Should Regard Moses" (*Luther's Works*, 35:155-74); also his prefaces to the OT (see *Luther's Works*, 35:235-333).

[57]Some criticisms are noted on pp. 178-80 below.

[58]For varying views see, e.g., Mayes, *Israel*; idem, *VT* 23:151-70; de Geus, *Tribes*; Smend, *EvT* 31:623-30; Fohrer, *TLZ* 91:801-16, 893-94; G. W. Anderson, *Translating and Understanding the OT*, 135-51; Gottwald, *Tribes*, 343-86, 748-84.

[59]So Gunneweg, *Understanding the OT*, 100-104.

[60]Cf. Barton, *JSOT* 9:44-64; idem, *JTS* 30:1-14; 32: 1-18; Levenson, *HTR* 73:17-33; Gerstenberger, *Wesen und Herkunft des "apodiktischen*

Walther Zimmerli has pointed out that in the prophets God's commands are recalled not merely in connection with exhorting his people to keep their side of the covenant, but also as a means of warning them of the danger they risk in ignoring Yahweh's stipulations.[61] Not that the prophetic corpus is finally negative about Israel's future; on the other side of judgment there will be renewal. But God's commands and God's judgment are connected, and thus Paul's connection of law and condemnation is by no means foreign to the OT.

R. E. Clements has noted that the law-centered approach to the OT was not imposed on it, as something alien, by postbiblical Judaism.[62] The Pentateuch itself is dominated by law, despite its narrative framework, and the Pentateuch as the law provides the concept which coordinates the whole canon. Indeed, the very concept of canon (normative rule) presupposes a quasi-legal approach to the role of the scriptures. Thus even narrative is appealed to as halakah in the NT as elsewhere in Judaism.

H.-J. Kraus has pointed out that Pss 1, 19, and 119 do not have to be read in a "legalistic" way. At most they are ambivalent.[63] On a broader front, E. P. Sanders has demonstrated that the picture of Judaism's law-centered piety as legalistic and guilt-ridden is neither that given by Judaism nor that implied by Paul. Paul and Judaism agree on the relationship between grace and works. What distinguishes them is the embodiment of grace to which they respond, and the character of the works responsive to it which they emphasize. For Judaism generally it is the making of the Sinai covenant, and the response of keeping its

---

Rechts"; idem, *JBL* 84:38-51; Gehman, *Biblical Studies*, 109-22; (Stamm and) Andrew, *Ten Commandments*, 75; Audet, *Twenty-Fifth International Congress of Orientalists*, 1:352-57.

[61]*TLZ* 85:481-98; idem, *Law and the Prophets*, 46-92 (esp. 60); cf. Ebeling, *Word and Faith*, 265-66; Gunneweg, 134-40; von Rad, *Theology*, 2:395-402.

[62]*OT Theology*, 104-20; idem, *Creation, Christ and Culture*, 1-12; cf. Gunneweg, 96-105.

[63]*EvT* 10:337-51; *Psalmen*, in loc.; cf. von Rad's observations in *EvT* 13:408-9 on Baumgärtel's interpretation of Ps 1 in the latter's *Verheissung* (and subsequently in *EvT* 14:312); Wolff's stance on von Rad's side in *Essays on OT Hermeneutics*, 195-96, taking up his own study of Ps 1 in *EvT* 9:385-94; also von Rad's comments on Pss 1 and 119 in his *Theology*, 1:381-82; cf. Gunneweg, 130-31. Conversely, Pss 44; 74; 79 might express a legalistic attitude to the covenant itself: so Eichrodt, *Theology*, 1:64.

laws. For the Christian Jew it is God's power manifested in Jesus as Lord, and the response of faith in him. Thus for Paul, "what is wrong with it [the law] is not that it implies petty obedience and minimization of important matters, nor that it results in the tabulation of merit points before God, but *that it is not worth anything in comparison with being in Christ* (Phil. 3.4-11)."[64] It is not the Torah which is to be identified with the eternal Wisdom or Word, as happens in Ben Sira and the rabbis; it is Christ.

Although Noth's work is thus subject to modification, his essay and these other studies show clearly that the law fulfills many theological functions within scripture.[65] It provides a basis for the declaration of judgment, the key to avoiding judgment, and the explanation for the experience of judgment. As such it prepares the way for a proclamation of God's forgiveness which can only come from beyond the boundaries of its own perspective. But it functions in connection with judgment in these ways because it first expresses the will of God the creator, which he expects his creatures to obey because they are his creatures, and the will of God the redeemer, which he expects his people to obey because they are his people. Israel's hope of salvation is of a day when the law will be obeyed (cf. Jer 31:31- 34), perhaps of a day when a new law will be given,[66] but not of a day without law.

A contextual approach to the place of law in scripture notes that the law functions in these varying ways in different situations, acknowledges in principle the validity of all of these, and asks whether one of them is particularly instructive in a specific contemporary context. This seems entirely appropriate. But one needs to go on to ask whether any particular biblical context allows the essential significance of law to emerge more clearly than others. Does the trajectory traced by the law have a high point?

Noth's thesis, granted the refinements referred to above, implies that it does. Specific instructions on the content of human behavior before God are most at home in the context of a declaration of the Lordship of God over the lives of the beings on whose behalf he has acted in love and power, both in creation and

---

[64]*Paul and Palestinian Judaism*, 550.

[65]Cf. Hübner, *KD* 22:250-76; Stuhlmacher, *ZTK* 75:251-80. Many of these features can be noted in Deuteronomy (see P. D. Miller, *Int* 23:459).

[66]So W. D. Davies, *Setting of the Sermon on the Mount*, 109-315. But the evidence is thin (cf. Banks, *Reconciliation and Hope*, 173-85).

in redemption. His instructions concern the life to be lived by those to whom he has given life and freedom. That understanding of the relationship between covenant and law which Noth especially emphasizes brings out the most fundamental theological significance of instruction material in the OT, an understanding present in contexts where ברית does not have its developed Deuteronomic significance (e.g., some occurrences in Exod 24 and 34) or is not used at all (e.g., Gen 1-3).[67]

One justification for this view is that the other significances of the law noted above depend on or derive from this fundamental "covenantal" significance. A theology of law which begins here is able to give a satisfactory account of the other significances of law; without questioning their value, it sets them in an interpretative context. A theology of law which starts at some other point (e.g., law as judgment, antithetical to gospel; or law as the object of delight by the person who approaches God)[68] cannot do so; its base is too narrow.

The Relationship between Divine and Human Activity

For some years it was a truism of OT study that the OT is the story of Yahweh's acts in history.[69] What, then, is the relationship of God's activity to human activity in history? Emphasiz-

---

[67]I assume here that, even if the developed use of ברית in the OT is Deuteronomic (so Perlitt, *Bundestheologie*, also Fohrer, BZAW 115:84-119, following Wellhausen, *Prolegomena*, 417-19—though see, e.g., McCarthy's response, *Bib* 53:110-21), elsewhere its use is pre-Deuteronomic, less obviously comparable to treaty-forms, but still suggesting fundamentally the same relationship of covenant and law. I also assume that while ברית itself may mean "commitment" (offered or demanded) without any inherent implication of mutuality (so Kutsch, *Verheissung und Gesetz*), the implication of mutuality, with the law taking the role referred to here, is present in the way the relationship between Yahweh and Israel is described in contexts where ברית and law appear. The problem over the actual translation of ברית is probably greater in relation to German *Bund*, which rather suggests a mutual contract, than it is in relation to English "covenant," which is a more open expression (so Barr, *Beiträge*, 23-38; see also Eichrodt's responses to Kutsch [*Int* 20:302-21; idem, *TZ* 30:193-206]; the contributions of Weinfeld [*Bib* 56:120-28] and McCarthy [VTSup 23:65-85]; and the discussion in Brekelmans, *Questions disputées d'AT*).

[68]So Wallis, *TLZ* 105:321-32—the postexilic period represents the highpoint of insight on תורה as Yahweh's means of making his world order available to the person who seeks it.

[69]See, e.g., Wright, *God Who Acts*, 38.

ing the acts of God suggests a distinctly interventionist, supranaturalist understanding of God's involvement with the world, one which underplays the significance of the human role in making history. This view appears most clearly in apocalyptic's portrayal of events which are future from the perspective of its visions, though mostly already past from the perspective of the visionaries' own experience. Thus in P. D. Hanson's words, apocalyptic eschatology focuses on the disclosure to the elect of a vision of Yahweh's sovereignty which "the visionaries have largely ceased to translate into the terms of plain history, real politics, and human instrumentality. . . . The visionaries, disillusioned with the historical realm, disclosed their vision in a manner of growing indifference to and independence from the contingencies of the politico-historical realm, thereby leaving the language increasingly in the idiom of the cosmic realm of the divine warrior and his council."[70] The grand-scale portrayals of aeons of history in apocalyptic also reflect the view that what matters in history is the divine act which brings it to a climax rather than the human initiative embodied in it, which it exposes to be mere pretension.[71] The phrase "by no human hand" (Dan 8:25) epitomizes apocalyptic's loss of connections with politico-historical realities.[72]

A near-exclusive emphasis on *God's* acts is not confined to apocalyptic. Another postexilic work, Chronicles, contrasts with apocalyptic in portraying the decisive events of Israel's history with Yahweh as lying in the past, yet agrees with apocalyptic in seeing Yahweh's as the decisive hand in those events. It is the might of God that decides battles. One person with God is a majority (cf. 2 Chr 13; 25:5-12); indeed, the one does not necessarily even have to fight (20:20-4). Conversely, a majority without God will fail (24:24). The Psalms also view history as the sphere of God's activity. When they speak of Israel's history it is of the wonders that Yahweh has done (e.g., Pss 68; 105). When an individual (admittedly perhaps the king) speaks of affliction and his release from it, it is in terms of what Yahweh could do or has done (e.g., 18; 22). Again, Genesis emphasizes the distinctive-

---

[70]Hanson, *Dawn of Apocalyptic*, 11, 12.

[71]For a modern reassertion of the apocalyptic view that God is not active in history (except in exceptional events such as the Christ event) see Sontag, *RelS* 15:379-90.

[72]Hanson, *Int* 25:476.

ness and finished-ness of God's creative work; human beings make no contribution to it.[73]

These books do assume that there are righteous deeds in history, but they are mainly in the private realm of personal acts of faith, love, and loyalty such as are illustrated by the story of Daniel and professed by the psalmist. Human acts affect political history itself primarily in a negative way, constituting the sinful deeds that God's own acts have to counter. It is this stress on God's acts and a consequent underplaying of the role of human beings as creative participants in the making of history that characterize salvation history as a theological theme of recent years.[74]

It is at the beginning and end of the OT, especially, that we find the nearest thing to a pure expression of an interventionist, supranaturalist view of history. Even here, the picture is not a wholly supranaturalist one. Daniel is deeply involved in the politics of Babylon and Persia. In the Psalms, the king himself shatters the nations like a man shattering pottery (2:9) and exercises authority and bloody power among his enemies (11:2, 6).[75] In Genesis, humanity's original task is to subdue the earth; while human achievements east of Eden are deeply affected by sin, they are not wholly evil (see esp. Gen 4). A visionary such as Habakkuk envisages having to wait patiently for the moment of God's action (2:3), yet assumes that precisely the expectation of God's moment arriving encourages us to "run" actively (2:2) in an involvement with the necessities of the present. The vision encourages engagement, not escapism.[76]

Exodus, a book which gives more classic expression to the theology of "God who acts," also asserts the contribution played by human activity. If there is an ambiguity about Moses' original initiative in Egypt, there is no ambiguity about his subsequent initiative in Midian (Exod 2:11-20). If Moses is the speaker and

---

[73]Cf. Landes, USQR 33:84-86. Landes notes the difference between Genesis's own emphasis and its interpretation by writers such as Gutiérrez (see pp. 238-39 and n. 133 below).

[74]See, e.g., Cullmann's comments on the sense in which salvation history is history, Salvation in History, 78, 150-66; also Tupper's comments on Pannenberg, Theology of Wolfhart Pannenberg, 301.

[75]I am not clear that this "royal theology" has as markedly a "static (mythic) view of reality" as Hanson suggests, Dawn of Apocalyptic, 18, also RB 78:43-44. A worship text should in any case perhaps not be expected to translate the vision of divine activity into the terms of real history.

[76]See Janzen, CBQ 44:404-14.

Yahweh is the real actor in the Exodus story, as is characteristic of Yahweh war narrative,[77] nevertheless there are aspects of the heroic about Moses' role in Exod 17 in the battle with Amalek, about his intercession in Exod 32 where his act shapes the future, and about the accounts of his end in Num 27 and Deut 34 where he dies as the model (though tragic) leader.[78] The Exodus story, then, combines a belief in the active power of God with a belief in creative human initiative.[79] In a similar way, the victory over Sisera comes about because Yahweh routs him, because God subdues Jabin, because of Yahweh's צדקות, because the stars fought from heaven (Judg 4:15, 23; 5:11, 13), but also because Barak actually musters his army, because people came to the help of Yahweh (!), and because a woman saw to the bloody end of an enemy general (4:10; 5:23, 24-27).

Isaiah 40–55 reaffirms the "exodus gospel" that Yahweh has once again raised his arm to liberate his people from bondage in an alien land, but although much of the language used to describe this act of liberation is full of symbol and metaphor, the prophet is referring to a historical people (Judean exiles in the sixth century) under a concrete overlord (Babylon) who will be put down by a specific "anointed" king (Cyrus) so that the people can return to an actual city (Jerusalem)—"this world was still viewed optimistically as the context within which the fulfillment of the divine promises could occur."[80]

Nevertheless, here Israel is the passive benefactor from Yahweh's acts. Elsewhere Israel is itself the actor. The book of Esther places special emphasis on this, avoiding all reference to God's activity. It is an especially striking feature if the book is to

---

[77]There may be hints in 14:20 of a military encounter at the Red Sea (see Hay, *JBL* 83:397-403); but if so this highlights the absence of explicit reference to such on the surface of the text (cf. Coats, *ST* 29:57; also more generally von Rad, *Theology*, 1:356-57; idem, *Der Heilige Krieg*; Lind, *BR* 16:16-31; idem, *Yahweh Is a Warrior*).

[78]See Coats, VTSup 28:29-41; idem, *Canon and Authority*, 107; idem, *CBQ* 39:34-44. Schmitt (see n. 10 above) sees a stress on Moses' activity in the "prophetic" as opposed to the "priestly" account of the Red Sea event (see pp. 150-52). This feature is taken up by process theology; see pp. 16-17 and n. 23 above.

[79]Cf. P. D. Miller's description of holy war as a "synergism," "a fusion of divine and human activity" (*Divine Warrior in Early Israel*, 156; cf. Hanson, *Dawn of Apocalyptic*, 17). Miller grants that the OT text stresses the divine side, as Lind emphasizes especially with regard to the exodus (see n. 77 above).

[80]Hanson, *Dawn of Apocalyptic*, 25.

be seen as a novel diaspora version of the new exodus.[81] "The survival of the Jews . . . results from their own actions. The responsibility for saving the Jewish people rests with the queen who must decide whether to risk her own life. The Book of Esther suggests that each individual Jew who is in a position to do so must use his/her power and authority to assist the people of Israel." Even if God's providential hand is to be seen behind the events in the story, its explicit emphasis lies on the human initiative related by it; it "points to the hiddenness of Yahweh's presence in the world."[82]

Esther's stress on human responsibility for history is particularly marked, but is only relatively greater than that in the stories of the judges, Ruth, Saul, David, Solomon, and Nehemiah,[83] and also in that of Joseph (which counterbalances the subsequent exodus traditions at this point).[84] In differing ways these give overt expression to the conviction that God is at work in history, yet they also strongly emphasize the initiative of human actors. Here, at least, decision history *(Entscheidungsgeschichte)* seems as appropriate a description of the OT as *Heilsgeschichte*,[85] and the narratives seem not far from the understanding of history as a continuous chronological sequence of human acts, linked as cause and effect, which we generally take for granted.

The prophets share the conviction that God is at work in history, but that history also reflects human acts and initiatives. Hanson contrasts them with the apocalyptic visionaries by noting that the prophet announcing his vision of Yahweh's plan for Israel and for the world "translates [it] into the terms of plain history, real politics, and human instrumentality . . . the level of the politico-historical realm of everyday life" forwhich king and

---

[81]So Gerlemann, *Esther,* 11-23.

[82]Berg, *Esther,* 176, 178; cf. Loader, *ZAW* 90:417-21; C. H. Miller, *ZAW* 92:145-48.

[83]Cf. Seeligmann, *TZ* 19:385-411; Kegler, *Zum Verständnis politischen Geschehens im Israel* (cf. *TLZ* 102:315-18); Brueggemann, *In Man We Trust* (!); idem, *Int* 24:18-19. Brueggemann examines this as a wisdom emphasis; cf. McKane, *Prophets and Wise Men,* 128-30.

[84]Berg, 176-77, and elsewhere; cf. Coats, *From Canaan to Egypt,* 86-90.

[85]Fohrer, *Studien zur alttestamentlichen Prophetie,* 289-91; idem, *Biblical Essays,* 31-39 (though Fohrer has in mind human acts in response to God, good or bad). The term fits these narrative works better than the prophets. Cf. also Zimmerli, *VTSup* 29:19; Baumgärtel, *KD* 9:229; Blank, *JBL* 72:1-13 (on "the Promethean element in biblical prayer").

people bore responsibility.[86] The prophets were "the ones responsible for historicizing Israel's religion . . . the ones who forged the visionary and realistic aspects of the religious experience into one tension-filled whole."[87] For Isaiah, then, history is both the sphere in which God fulfills his promise and the locus in which human beings fulfill their answerability to God; the two are essentially linked because for both the object of history is the exaltation of Yahweh as the holy one in צדק ומשפט (5:16; cf. 2:10-21; 11:4-5).[88]

The integration of divine and human activity in history features also in the Deuteronomistic History. J. Ellul observes that 2 Kings "displays concretely the play of what Karl Barth has called the free determination of man in the free decision of God. We are constantly in the presence of the relation between man's action and God's."[89] But the relationship between these acts is different from the prophetic one. There the emphasis is on people being invited and challenged to act in history in fulfillment of God's will. Here in 2 Kings God's will is fulfilled whether they are interested in it or not. "Deliberate acts which men do for their own reasons and according to their own calculations are the very ones which accomplish just what God had decided and was expecting (even though the men often do not know this or are not aware of it at first). These acts enter into God's design and bring about exactly the new situation which God planned."[90] Thus, "whereas Isaiah began with the vision of the cosmic Yahweh and translated that vision into reality, thus balancing vision and reality, the Deuteronomic historian found the historical realm transparent to Yahweh's will. . . . A one-to-one ratio was seen between events of this world and divine action."[91]

The OT, then, allows for seeing God as virtually the sole

---

[86]Hanson, *Dawn of Apocalyptic*, 11, 12. Hanson (p. 19) instances Isa 6-7, which he contrasts with Dan 8:26; 12:4; cf. Hanson, *RB* 78:44-46; idem, *Int* 25:459-60.

[87]Hanson, *Dawn of Apocalyptic*, 17.

[88]Wildberger, VTSup 9:108-9.

[89]*Politics of God*, 15; cf. Deuteronomy's understanding of the land as both God's gift and Israel's achievement (so Miller, *Int* 23:453-56).

[90]Ellul, 16-17.

[91]Hanson, *RB* 78:47. Hanson is deeply critical of the Deuteronomistic approach; in my view he underestimates its strengths, and makes insufficient allowance for the differences between prophecy and history which arise from the fact that the former is prospective (events are open), the latter retrospective. Cf. Zimmerli's contrast between them (VTSup 29:13-15).

actor in history (Daniel, Psalms) or at least as the dominant actor (Exodus, Isa 40–55), for seeing his acts interweaving with human acts without the relation between them being quite clarified (Judges, Saul, David, Solomon, Nehemiah) or immanent in the decisions of human actors (Exod 17, 2 Kings) or interacting with the decisions of human actors (preexilic prophecy), or for seeing God's acts as hidden behind or yielding importance to human acts (Esther). It is likely that different documents take their individual perspectives because of contextual factors; for instance, Hanson suggests it was the special features of the postexilic period that generated apocalyptic eschatology, "a pessimistic view of reality growing out of the bleak post-exilic conditions within which those associated with the visionaries found themselves."[92] Those who had no power to influence the policies of their people could only look for what they saw as the right policies to be implemented immediately by God himself. "In certain 'bottleneck' phases of historical epochs, the requirements of causal efficacy are massive, and the alternatives for negotiation are extremely narrow"; there is little room to maneuver.[93]

At different points on its trajectory, then, the theme of divine and human activity appears in different forms. Hanson's thesis is that the ministry of the eighth-century prophets embodies this theme in its most profound form. In particular, the account of Isaiah's dealings with Ahaz illustrates "the delicate balance achieved by prophetic Yahwism between the visionary element and the pragmatic integration of the cosmic vision into the events of that time. Isaiah, the visionary who received his call by being drawn into Yahweh's divine council (Isaiah 6), was at the same time the statesman standing at the side of the king and relating every major event of his nation to divine will." "In his prophecy vision was integrated into politics without thereby losing its normative character"; he was "a man of faith living out his career within the field of tension between the vision of Yahweh's Kingdom and a sense of responsibility for an earthly community."[94]

It is not that the problem is "solved" in Isaiah. Indeed, per-

---

[92]*Dawn of Apocalyptic*, 11-12.

[93]Janzen, *Encounter* 36:399. It is not merely a question of date, of course; the apocalyptic and the theocratic view are contemporary, as are Esther and Chronicles (cf. Berg, *Divine Helmsman*, 107-27). Sociological factors are involved.

[94]Hanson, *Dawn of Apocalyptic*, 19, 410.

haps it is the high point because it looks most steadfastly in the face the fact that the challenge is to believe and act as if this will work, despite the fact that it often does not, as the experience of Hezekiah and Josiah perhaps showed.[95] In the light of the cross the assumption that suffering and salvation are invariably opposites will be put in question by the reality of the one leading to the other.[96] Yet Isaiah's ministry remains the high point of insight on the two realities we have been considering because it holds them together in the sharpest way, neither letting one overcome the other, nor simply interweaving them, nor assimilating them. Circumstances may make it difficult for this perspective to be maintained in many contexts, but this is the perspective which the OT at its most profound encourages.

Life, Death, and the Possibility of Afterlife

N. Lohfink illuminates this theme by contrasting the attitudes of Israelite wisdom at various stages in its history.[97] Proverbs affirms that life is Yahweh's gift and is good and meaningful. A full life and a long life is to be enjoyed, even though (or because) it ends in death, which must be accepted realistically as something not inherently fearful, though the new form of existence it brings lacks the positive joy and fulfillment of life with Yahweh. For Ecclesiastes, however, human life is "solitary, poor, nasty, brutish and short."[98] The entire landscape of human life is dominated and spoiled by the death which ends it and thereby establishes the limitations of human wisdom and the relativity of human joy in this life. Others respond to the same awareness about present life by looking for a full life to continue in some way despite death (Ps 73:23-26), or for an end to death (Isa 25:6-8) or for resurrection to a new life for some (Dan 12:2-3).[99] The

---

[95]The presentation of Hezekiah in Isaiah itself reflects the need to cope with this.

[96]Cf. Gunneweg, KD 27:170-73.

[97]Christian Meaning of the OT, 138-69. On this subject see also Bailey, Biblical Perspectives on Death; Brichto, HUCA 44:1-54; Brueggemann, IDBSup 219-22; Burns, SJT 26:327-40; Eichrodt, Theology, chaps. 16, 19, 24; Gese, Essays, 34-59, 239-46; Gibson, SJT 32:151-69; Tromp, Primitive Conceptions of Death; Wolff, Anthropology, 99-118; Martin-Achard, From Death to Life.

[98]Hobbes, Leviathan, chap. 13; though this was not in its original context a description of the universal condition of human life.

[99]Lohfink, keeping within a strictly wisdom tradition, confines attention to the book of Wisdom. But the point can also be made by reference to books in the Hebrew canon.

sequence of views which appears here is in part chronological: Ecclesiastes' emphasis is a reaction against an existent confidence about the meaningfulness of this life; belief in an overcoming of death often has as its background the kind of questioning of meaning which appears in Ecclesiastes, even if one cannot say whether, for example, Ps 73 antedates or postdates Ecclesiastes itself.

Confidence about this life, uncertainty about this life, and confidence about an overcoming of death may all be valid in their context. Nevertheless, each follows from the other and seeks to set it in a broader framework. Ecclesiastes would be impossible without Proverbs, Ps 73 without the perplexity expressed in Ecclesiastes. Furthermore, Proverbs must not finally be read in isolation from Ecclesiastes, nor Ecclesiastes in isolation from Ps 73. The variety of views in the OT accumulates, and the earlier have to be read in the context of the later. One cannot simply revert to an earlier view as if the later ones had not emerged.[100]

H. Gese generalizes this point in discussing the theological significance of the traditio-historical process. This process does not imply that what is older is rejected and replaced by what is newer, even where the new clashes with the old. The old is not abandoned but preserved and set in a new light. The history of revelation is not a journey toward truth, but a journey which starts from truth—though not a static doctrinal truth. Gen 2–3, for instance, is not rendered untrue or half-true by having Gen 1 placed in front of it. When we appropriate Pss 49 and 73, we do not abandon psalms that plead for rescue from death in the conviction that this life is all we have. Prayers arising out of such convictions express in the only way possible an attitude which treats life itself with absolute seriousness, and which is therefore in a position to value the notion of resurrection and of a new world.[101] Nor do we abandon old wisdom when we have Job. Indeed, we can only have the latter by way of having the former. As Gese puts it, "In order to become Job, it is necessary first to be his friends"; and the views of Job's friends are to be treated as potentially illuminating, not as inherently erroneous.[102]

---

[100]See the comments on Bailey on p. 39 above.

[101]Cf. Rahner, *Theological Investigations*, 16:186- 87; Bonhoeffer, Letter of Advent ii, 1943, *Letters and Papers*, Fontana ed., 50; enlarged ed., 157.

[102]Gese, *Essays*, 19. Cf. Zimmerli's observations on the way that proph-

In this instance, then, the trajectory keeps rising and reaches its highest point at its furthest distance; this is the vantage point from which the OT's varied statements about life and death have to be appreciated as a whole.

The "trajectory" model might, indeed, suggest that the ultimate destiny of the journey traveled by a particular theme gives the natural perspective from which to understand its path. Thus the history of Israel as the OT tells it (patriarchal promise and exodus/conquest, judges and monarchy, exile and return, submission to Persia and oppression by Antiochus) has a shape or plot that may suggest ways of interpreting individual episodes in the story. The whole is a pedagogic process, a series of responses to the unfolding of a story, forming altogether a total theological statement.[103] But this does not imply that each theme reaches greatest clarity only at the end of the OT period.[104] We have suggested that the OT offers clearest insight on the position of law near the beginning of its story (whereas the position at the end is rather ambiguous), and profoundest wrestling with the tension between divine and human activity in preexilic prophecy. Its understanding of the people of God becomes clearest in the exile.[105]

It is for special reasons that this particular trajectory needs to be appreciated from its end. The point it has then reached (the notion of eternal life) radically affects the significance of the whole, whereas later perspectives on law or on the relationship between divine and human activity do not as fundamentally affect the significance of earlier insights. Indeed, whereas the other trajectories reach their high point before the end of the OT period, this trajectory is still rising as it leaves the OT.[106]

---

ets sometimes have to say no to the way traditions are being appropriated and the tradition process is thereby developing (he instances Amos 9:7; Isa 43:18-19) (TLZ 98:90-92; see also pp. 17-18 and n. 24 above). Despite that no, one may affirm that these traditions were God-given in the context to which they belong, and that they are still fulfilling a paradoxical positive function even in this later context: in order to become a second Isaiah, it is necessary first to have been an exile looking back wistfully to the good old days (see Westermann's comments on Isa 40:6-8, Isaiah 40–66, 40-43.

[103]See further chap. 6 below.

[104]See further pp. 101-4 below.

[105]See chap. 3 below. Zimmerli sees exilic prophecy as also the climax in the OT understanding of God (VTSup 23:48-64) (cf. p. 106 below).

[106]And "disappears behind a wall" (Lys, Meaning of the OT, 106), so that from an OT perspective it could end up in Judaism or in Christianity.

It seems, then, that the world and the people of God are nearer to or further away from fullest insight regarding different aspects of the faith at different periods. Some situations lead to perception in one area but blind spots in another. Thus part of studying the OT's approach to different themes will be to identify the interrelationships between perspectives that emerge from different contexts, and to look for the high points of insight or the points of most creative tension reached by the various trajectories that themes follow. As in other forms of theological study, the insight of interpreters themselves will contribute to their identifying these high points. Their analysis nevertheless aims at an objective understanding of the dynamic of the themes, so that their work is part of OT theology's descriptive task. They can say of their analyses, "Here is a way of interrelating the various OT viewpoints on this particular theme, a way of seeing them in a pattern which is natural to them rather than imposed on them," and they can argue meaningfully with each other as to whether one understanding of a trajectory or another does better justice to its inherent dynamic.

Chapter 3

A CONTEXTUALIZING STUDY OF "THE PEOPLE OF GOD" IN THE OLD TESTAMENT

The question "What does it mean to be the people of God?" received different answers in different historical contexts in OT times, and consideration of this theme thus illustrates the approach to diversity and unity in the OT described in chapter 2. This chapter examines the theme in its various contexts, notes the insights particularly associated with each context and the issues that recur in different periods, but suggests that the period of the afflicted remnant (the exile) allows the deepest insights on the question to emerge, those associated with the idea of theocracy as it is then juxtaposed with the image of the servant.

The people of God is one of the most prominent themes in the Bible. This need not have been so: a religion could give theological significance only to people in general, or to the relationship between God and individuals. It has not always been acknowledged to be so: while Jewish theology has naturally recognized and wrestled with the theme,[1] Christianity has found it easier to be predominantly individualistic, and biblical theology has not always given appropriate centrality to the theme of the community.[2]

As far as the OT is concerned, what it means to be God's people is bound up with history, and that in two senses. First, it is worked out in concrete and changing human situations, with all the diversity we have already noted. We thus find ourselves examining the changing face of the people of God. Second, what it means to be God's people is bound up with "history" in the

---

[1] In his survey *Understanding Jewish Theology*, Neusner sees the three central issues of Jewish theology as God, Torah, and Israel.

[2] Contrast the revised edition of Vriezen's *Outline*, which is largely structured by this theme, with the original edition, where it is virtually absent. On the vital place of the theme see von Rad, *Gottesvolk im Deuteronomium*, 20-21.

sense of "socially significant, public events." God's people is a clearly identifiable social entity, for a significant period an actual nation. It has a culture of its own and is involved in changing mutual relationships with other cultures. Its life has to be lived in this context; its changing social structure affects its faith,[3] and its social and historical experience affects what it means to be God's people.

Its story, as Israel tells it, divides itself by major events that herald new developments. The most significant are Abraham's leaving Haran, the Israelites' departure from Egypt and occupation of Palestine, the institution of the monarchy, the exile, and the partial return of exiles to Palestine. These epochs of salvation history may be seen as a history of their covenant with Yahweh: the Abrahamic covenant, the Sinai covenant, the Davidic covenant, the covenant broken (with the exile) and renewed (with the return). Each epoch brings a change in the mode of being of God's people. It begins as a family (משפחה), one of the families of the sons of Shem (Gen 10:31-32). The fulfillment of God's promise makes it more than a family, a people (עַם; e.g., Exod 1:9; 3:7), and indeed a nation (גוי) alongside other nations, a political entity (e.g., Gen 12:2; Judg 2:20). The monarchy turns it into a state, a kingdom (ממלכה and related words; e.g., 1 Sam 24:20; 1 Chr 28:5). The exile reduces it to a mere remnant (שארית and other expressions; e.g., Jer 42:2; Ezek 5:10). It is restored, to its land and to its relationship with Yahweh, as a religious community (קהל; e.g., Ezra 2:64; Neh 13:1).

THE WANDERING CLAN

Israel's history strictly begins only in Egypt or in Palestine; as the Torah sees it, however, the story of God's people goes back to the family of Abraham (cf., e.g., Neh 9:7; Matt 1:1-18) if not that of Seth (Gen 4:25-26). God's people is thus portrayed as a genetic unit, and in a sense it always remains that.[4] The name Israel

---

[3]Instances in Fohrer, *Grundstrukturen*, 126-32.

[4]Mendenhall believes that these kinship terms are only expressions for social links produced by some other cause, ethnic feeling being a postexilic phenomenon (*Tenth Generation*, 5, 27, 155, 171, 174, 220; cf. Gottwald, *Tribes of Yahweh*, 235-341). But the expressions are too pervasive and their implications are worked out too systematically for this to be plausible. See further pp. 79 and 92-93 below (esp. at nn. 76 and 116). Mendenhall's attack on understanding the patriarchs as nomads or seminomads is more compelling.

marks it as the seed of one man. It is a family (e.g., Amos 3:2; Mic 2:3), a brotherhood (e.g., Deut 15), a tribe (e.g., Jer 10:16), a household (e.g., Exod 16:31; 2 Sam 1:12),[5] a people (עם, too, suggests a kinship relationship; unlike the English word "people," it is rarely used to mean merely "persons in general").

Nothing outward distinguishes Abraham from many other second-millennium figures. It is God's call that marks out from other emigrations his departure from "the ancient and renowned city of Ur."[6] Genesis calls it "Ur of the Chaldeans"; the designation probably belongs to the Neo-Babylonian period and suggests the might and pomp, as well as the arrogance and superstition, associated with the Chaldeans from the seventh century.[7] Abraham leaves such a background in "the first Exodus by which the imperial civilizations of the Near East in general receive their stigma as environments of lesser meaning."[8] It is a calling out of the world.

Yet Abraham is called out of the world for the world's sake. God's purpose is that he should experience such blessing that the world will pray to be blessed as he is blessed (Gen 12:3 NEB). Out of its context, such a promise might seem good news only for Abraham—it does not say that this prayer will be answered. In the context of Gen 1–11, however, it more likely affirms that seeking blessing from Abraham's God is the way that a world under the curse can experience the fulfillment of God's original purpose of blessing. Specific stories (e.g., Abraham and Sodom) offer particular illustrations of the international and open stance of the traditions in Gen 12–50.[9]

The stress on genetic relationship implies that individuals have no choice whether or not they belong to God's people. They have to be born into it; if they are born into it, that settles the matter. Yet if no prior confession of faith or acceptance of obligation is a necessary, or even a possible, condition of belonging to this people, this reflects the fact that it is God's sovereignty, not human initiative, which brings it into existence. It is not a

---

[5]Pedersen suggests that this term, indicating people actually living together, "represents kinship in its most intimate sense" (*Israel*, 1:51).

[6]Speiser, *Genesis*, 80.

[7]Sarna, *Understanding Genesis*, 98.

[8]Voegelin, *Israel and Revelation*, 140.

[9]So Reventlow, *Beiträge*, 354-70; cf. von Rad, *Genesis*, 154-55; Wolff, *Int* 20:131-58; Lind, *Yahweh Is a Warrior*, 40-41; Ellis, *Yahwist*, 204-11; Macquarrie, *Faith of the People of God*, 19-22.

merely natural entity. A special act of God creates it. The notion of election is a key to understanding the notion of Israel. It is not even that God makes an already existent people his own; he brings a people into being. They only exist as a people because of an act of God.[10] More specifically, a special act of a specific God creates it. What is distinctive about Israel is not that they see themselves as God's people (most peoples would make that claim) but that they see themselves as Yahweh's people, and it is this latter phrase that the OT nearly always uses.[11]

In Genesis itself, the divine initiative takes the characteristic form of Yahweh's summons to the particular family of Abraham and his promise to them of blessing, a special relationship to him, and concretely of land and increase. Thus Israel is constituted the people of the promise, a people brought into existence by God's word.[12] The populousness that is intrinsic to being a people will come about not by natural growth but by divine gift which ignores ordinary human expectation, let alone the particular inability of Abraham and Sarah. The land which is also intrinsic to being a people will come to be theirs not by natural inheritance or by natural right, nor by human achievement, but by divine gift which is also of a magnitude to belie both ordinary human expectation and the particular obstacles to its fulfillment which confront Abraham in the land. Thus faith *is* required of God's people: trust in the promise of their God. Obedience is also required of them: yet not a life of obedience to a system of ethical, cultic, and social regulations such as Israel later received, but a commitment to Yahweh's calling which follows where he directs on an individual pilgrimage toward a goal known only to him.[13]

Abraham's call out of the world also involves an exodus from politics; Abraham's family stand outside the power struc-

---

[10]Cf. Macholz, *Jüdisches Volk—gelobtes Land,* 172-77.

[11]Cf. Lohfink, *Probleme,* 275-305; Macholz, 171-72. There has been much recent interest in the theme of the people of God, especially since Vatican II (see "De ecclesia," *Documents of Vatican II,* 24-37; articles in the first issue of *Concilium* [esp. by Congar, Schnackenburg, and Dupont]; Rücker, *Dienst der Vermittlung,* 39; Sloyan, *Standing before God,* 103), but it tends to ignore the particularity of the usual OT phrase (cf. Leonard's warnings, *Communio Viatorum* 19:35-60; also Lohfink, 275-305, on the specificity of the OT usage). Like the term "covenant," "people of God" has come to be a theological technical term of broader meaning than it has in the OT.

[12]Von Rad, *Gottesvolk,* 22; Kraus, *People of God,* 14.

[13]Cf. Watts, *Basic Patterns in OT Religion,* 45.

tures of the land they come to live in. Perhaps the description of them as עברים places them among the many *'apiru* people outside the social structure of second-millennium Canaan. Yet they are not the freebooting mercenaries of the Amarna letters. Military and political involvement comes to Abraham exceptionally and accidentally, and even then Abraham undertakes only a limited rescue operation, by which he refuses to be personally profited (Gen 14).[14] Such an attitude puts Abraham in an exposed position in a ruthless world. But Yahweh will see that he and his descendants are enriched (the term רכש appears in 14:21 and 15:14). Yahweh will be his protector (the term מגן appears as a verb in 14:20 and as a noun in 15:1). Yahweh, not a human ally, will be his covenant Lord (the term ברית appears in 14:13 and 15:18).[15]

Political involvement with the cities of the Arabah brought also religious involvement. The priest-king of Salem attributes Abraham's victory over the Mesopotamian kings to "El Elyon, maker of heaven and earth" (14:18-19). Abraham neither rejects Melchizedek's blessing nor accepts it without qualification: "Yahweh El Elyon" is his Lord. He can accept that the Canaanite high god is God and express his faith in Canaanite terms, as the patriarchs elsewhere happily worship at Canaanite shrines, accept Canaanite observances such as the sacred tree, and acknowledge the Canaanite high god by names such as El Roi and El Olam (though they do not seem to identify with Canaanite Baal worship).[16]

Yet this is not the whole of patriarchal faith, nor its distinctive characteristic. The personal name of the patriarchal God, according to passages such as Gen 14:22, was Yahweh, though if the name was actually known before Moses' time, its significance was only to be revealed then. The distinctive designation of the patriarchal God is as the God of the fathers, the God of

---

[14]Cf. the negative judgment passed on the violent revenge of Simeon and Levi on Shechem in Gen 34 (Lind, 42-45). Mendenhall (*Tenth Generation*, 136-38) and Gottwald (*Tribes of Yahweh*, 391-425, 493-97) exaggerate the significance of Abraham's *'apiru* link. Weippert thinks עברי in Gen 14 has an ethnic sense (*Settlement*, 100-101; cf. more generally Herrmann, *History*, 54, 60, and his references). This undercuts that emphasis.

[15]On this movement from Gen 14 to 15 see Sarna, 121-22; Voegelin, 192-95. Voegelin (p. 194) comments on ברית in 14:13 and 15:18, "the symbol of bondage has become the symbol of freedom."

[16]For the religio-historical considerations here see, e.g., Alt, *Essays*, 1-77; Cross, *Canaanite Myth*, 13- 75; Vriezen, *Religion*, 103-23; Eissfeldt, *JSS* 1:25-37; de Vaux, *Early History*, 267-87.

Abraham, the God of Isaac, and the God of Jacob. Such phrases identify God by linking him with a human individual and with the clan that he leads, wherever they may be. The distinctive faith of the people of God in patriarchal times was thus one suited to their way of life. As they moved about, they needed God to guide them, provide for them, and be accessible to them as they traveled, not to be limited to particular places. As a small landless group their concerns were with progeny and land, and these were their God's promise. It was such needs that the God of the fathers met; he could be identified with El or with Yahweh, but this way of conceiving of God would not match their needs in the same way.

THE THEOCRATIC NATION

Moses is both the last representative of patriarchal religion and the first adherent of the new faith of Israel which he mediates. God appears to him as the God of his father (Exod 3:6, following MT) and he keeps the clan leader's close relationship with the guiding and providing God. Sinai itself is a patriarchal manifestation writ large,[17] and Yahweh relates to Israel as one who chooses to attach himself to a group and then sets before them his expectations of them, his promise to bless them, and his undertaking to accompany them in the vicissitudes of life in the everyday world.

Yahweh, Israel, and the relationship between them are thus one with what we have seen before. Yet the people of God is now in a new situation. The clan has become a people, and one to be reckoned with (Exod 1:7, 9, 20). Expressions such as "Yahweh's people," "your people," "my people," occur for the first time (Exod 3:7; 15:16; Num 11:29).

This increase is an evidence of Yahweh's blessing. On the other hand, Israel is a people in bondage. They have lost the freedom of the patriarchal clan and become an oppressed minority enslaved in a foreign country. By Yahweh's rescue of them from this bondage he makes them not only an עַם but an independent nation in their own right, a גּוֹי. The people of God becomes something not merely different in size, but different in nature. Israel is now a political entity with a place in the history books.[18] A further aspect of God's promise becomes reality (Gen 12:2; Exod

---

[17]So Fohrer, *History,* 81.
[18]Cf. the mention on Pharaoh Mer-ne-ptah's victory stela (*ANET,* 378).

19:6; 33:13) and a further stage in the fulfillment of his purpose is reached.[19]

Yahweh himself thus enters a new sphere of activity. The God of the clan becomes the God of history and the God of politics, battling with the Egyptian pharaoh and defeating him. He meets his people's needs in a new mode of life, though this involves him in taking one nation's side against another in a way he has not done before. He gains new stature as the lord of nature at whose bidding seas part and come together again, as the warrior whose fury brings a shiver even to the hearts of those he aids, as the master of the elements whose coming makes Sinai tremble (Exod 14; 15; 19–20). Although he is Israel's God, "he is not a national god *simpliciter*. . . . Yahweh is too much himself, too free of Israel, for that."[20]

While the OT excludes war from its ideal picture of Beginning and End, and implies that Yahweh is not essentially warlike, it accepts wholeheartedly the warring activity of Yahweh in Israel's history (on their behalf and against them) which is a corollary of his being involved with them as a nation at all. If he is to be the God of all of life, he must be a God of war. Even this area is embraced by Israel's calling "to have the entirety of its life constructed out of its relation to the divine" so that "the separation of religion and politics which stretches through history is here overcome."[21]

This notion is summed up by the picture of Israel as Yahweh's kingdom (Exod 19:6); Israel's song of praise after the exodus comes to a climax with the assertion that Yahweh will reign as king over them for ever (Exod 15:18; cf. Num 23:21). Israel is a theocracy (Josephus *CAp* 2.16-17 [171-75]), Yahweh's personal property (חלק, סגלה, נחלה: Exod 19:5; Deut 4:20), Yahweh's priesthood (Exod 19:6). Their human leaders do not reign by right as kings; they serve under Yahweh by his appointment and only for as long as he wills, and he is capable of directing Israel without using a human intermediary at all (Exod 13:21-22;

---

[19]Cf. Speiser, *JBL* 79:163; also Cody, *VT* 14:1- 6. Rost sees a גוי as a group which understands itself as united in origin, speech, country, religion, law, and leadership, while an עם is a body of citizens living on their own land and possessing the right to take part in war, justice, and cult (*Das kleine Credo*, 89, 92; cf. Gottwald, 510; Bächli, *Israel*, 114-16).

[20]Vriezen, *Religion*, 132. But contrast Saggs, *Encounter with the Divine*, 35-37, emphasizing the more nationalist side to the Mosaic Yahweh.

[21]Buber, *Kingship*, 118, 119; cf. 145; cf. also Fohrer, *History*, 118); Eichrodt, *Theology*, 1:74-75. See further pp. 162-64 below.

23:20-21).[22] Their own priestly tribe cannot claim a position that goes back to the Beginning (the patriarchal clan had no priest except the head of the household himself) or one that will last at the End (see Isa 61:6). They are a peculiar kind of nation with a peculiar kind of religion.

Israel has to be available to Yahweh to treat as his personal possession. Their status is their calling.[23] This calling is itemized at Sinai: the obligation of the people of God now includes a detailed obedience in the ethical, social, and cultic spheres. The covenant shape of Deuteronomy makes the point especially clear. Like a human overlord laying down the law in a treaty, Yahweh the divine overlord details his stipulations to his covenant people.[24] Mesopotamian (and perhaps Canaanite) law is the point of departure for Israel's, indeed, so that the most important distinctive feature of Israelite law may not be so much its origin or actual content but its context in the covenant, in "the framework of relationship which breaks through that which is merely moral."[25]

This context, however, decisively influences the content of Israel's ethic, to the extent that it establishes the notion of the people of God as an ethical principle. In their behavior the people of God are bound to one another.[26] Yahweh being their overlord, they have no human overlords. Theocracy and sociopolitical equality (radical theology and radical sociology) go together.[27]

By stressing the declaring and accepting of Yahweh's will, the covenant motif emphasizes that it is not mere natural kin-

---

[22]Judges 1–12 with its anti-monarchic attitude shows how the will towards actualizing Yahweh's kingship over Israel still lived in the judges period (cf. Buber, 59-84, 164-69).

[23]Cf. Dahl, Volk Gottes, 4, 12.

[24]I assume that even if the Deuteronomic notion of covenant (and the idea of Yahweh's kingship) is retrojected from later times, the belief that Israel is committed to this detailed obedience to Yahweh as their Lord is nevertheless at home in the period before the monarchy. (Perhaps we are compelled to regard nothing as historically certain for this period; if so, then all we can say is that this is the uniform picture of Israel's theological tradition!) Cf. pp. 44-48 and n. 67 above.

[25](Stamm and) Andrew, Ten Commandments, 74-75.

[26]This is applied to the old clan ethos and the covenant by Macholz (Jüdisches Volk, 176-77), to Deuteronomy with its stress on brotherhood by Rücker (Dienst der Vermittlung, 39-47) (see pp. 136-37 below), and to Micah with his sense of scandal at oppression among "my people" by Willis (BZ 14:72-87).

[27]Cf. Mendenhall, Tenth Generation, 16, 19-31; Brueggemann, JBL

ship that makes Israel a people. It is Yahweh's act and his an-
nouncing his will, and their submission to him as their covenant
Lord, that make Israel his people and make them one people.[28]
Indeed, being born into the right clan is not only insufficient but
apparently unnecessary to give someone a place among
Yahweh's people. A rather mixed company leaves Egypt with the
Israelites (Exod 12:38; Num 11:4), Moses marries a Cushite
(Num 12:1), only a Kenizzite matches the faith of Joshua (Num
13–14), and Yahweh's greatness is acknowledged by a Midianite
priest, by a Jericho prostitute, and by the frightened inhabitants
of Gibeon (Exod 18:11-12; Josh 2:1-11; 6:25; 9:9-10).[29]

Most important may be the scene at Shechem where Joshua
challenges his audience to be Yahweh's people rather than worshipers of Mesopotamian, Egyptian, or Canaanite gods
(Josh 24). At this town whose conquest has not been recorded
and which apparently accepted Joshua and his God without resistance, perhaps a very mixed multitude, including many who
had not taken part in the exodus, the covenant-making, or the
victories under Joshua, now accepts the united worship of Yahweh.[30] Even if this theory reads too much into Josh 24,[31] the general point nevertheless holds that the covenant's stress on
human response makes possible a greater openness to admitting
foreigners into Yahweh's people. Israel is still understood in kinship terms and perhaps new members are effectively seen as
adopted into the Israelite family (and receive a genealogy in

---

98:165-67. Gottwald, building on Swanson's *The Birth of the Gods: The Origin of Primitive Beliefs*, sees theocracy or mono-Yahwism as "the function of
sociopolitical equality" (*Tribes of Yahweh*, 611; cf. 622- 49). Gottwald thus
"demythologizes" the OT into sociology (p. 692) as Bultmann demythologizes
the NT into anthropology in the sense of an understanding of the real possibilities of the individual's human existence (see, e.g., *Jesus Christ and Mythology*, 52-54; also H. Braun, *Das NT als Kanon*, 228-29). As Gottwald sees it, we
are therefore not required to appropriate the OT's symbol system by believing
what ancient Israelites believed, but to follow them into freedom and the mas-
tery of our social circumstances, developing such transcendent images as will
help us fulfill that task (pp. 703-9). Social factors no doubt influence people's
theology, but it seems unwarranted to deny that the reverse movement also
takes place (cf. Bowker's critique of Swanson, *Sense of God*, 24-31, 37; also
L. L. Thompson, *JBL* 100:353-58).

[28]See Eichrodt, *Theology*, 1:39; also Rast, *Joshua*, 42-45, on the theme
of one people.

[29]If Rahab was a cult-prostitute (so Fohrer, *History*, 106), this is the
more significant.

[30]So Bright, *History*, 135-37, 143.

[31]So Gray, *Joshua*, 55, 175-76.

keeping with their adoption); there is thus no one who does not belong to one of the tribes. But the qualification for membership is not birth but willingness to commit oneself.

The biblical text itself suggests another reason for seeing Josh 24 as marking an important point in the story of the people of God. It marks the end of the major stage in Israel's occupation of the promised land, the land itself having now been distributed among the tribes. The final aspect of the patriarchal promise is fulfilled. The land becomes ארץ ישראל, the holy land, Yahweh becomes the God of this particular country, Israel becomes the people of the land. Land, people, and faith are henceforth bound together.[32]

This line of thinking is a dangerous one. It threatens to reduce Yahweh's stature; it also obscures the fact that Israel had become Yahweh's people before the settlement, so that actually possessing land was not intrinsic to the meaning of "Israel." Nor can they presume assured possession of the land, for this depends on continuing obedience to Yahweh. Their historians show how incomplete, precarious, and temporary was their lordship over it, while the fact that the land which before them had been named after the Canaanites was after them named after the Philistines is a parable of the uncertain, ambiguous nature of the relationship between ארץ ישראל and עם ישראל.[33]

The choice which Joshua presses on the people gathered at Shechem contrasts with the patriarchs' easy acceptance of Canaanite El religion. The difference in attitude reflects perhaps the inherently degrading nature of the Baal fertility cult; perhaps the more exclusivist claims of the God of Moses, the jealous God; perhaps Israel's vulnerability to the religion of the more sophisticated Canaanites, a danger whether Israel absorbs them or they absorb Israel; perhaps the specific attractiveness of a religion geared to agricultural life, a realm in which Yahweh had not yet proved his competence. Allowing Baal practices to enter Yahwism will lead to disaster; "saying 'No' to the Canaanite cult" becomes *"articulus stantis et cadentis ecclesiae."*[34]

---

[32]Cf. Dahl, *Volk Gottes,* 17; W. D. Davies, *The Gospel and the Land;* Borowitz, *HUCA* 40-41:391-408; Brueggemann, *Land;* Wirth, *Jüdisches Volk,* 312.

[33]Cf. Dahl, 19; also M. Weber's understanding of Israel as the model pariah people or guest people, sitting loose to their social surroundings (*Ancient Judaism,* 3; see also Rodd in *SJT* 32:457-69).

[34]Von Rad, *Theology,* 1:25; cf. Vriezen, *Religion,* 154-78; G. W. Anderson, *Peake,* 132.

The danger that Israel and its distinctive faith would disappear after the occupation of Canaan was the more real as it entered a period when the clans were divided from each other by Canaanites and Philistines and when relations between them were rather loose.[35] Yet their inclination to turn their back on Yahweh goes back into the wilderness period. Indeed, their complaints and their attempts to go back on their election calling begin when they are hardly out of Egypt (Exod 14– 17).[36] At Sinai Moses only delays a while on the mountain and Israel has hastened into a well-meaning but guilty assimilation to heathen religion, while in the tabernacle story no sooner is the priesthood consecrated than alien fire is offered on Yahweh's altar (Exod 32; Lev 10). "Embedded at the heart of the sacred tradition lies Israel's disobedience and rebellion";[37] the OT acknowledges the original sin of the people of God, a rebelliousness that goes back to their beginnings (cf. Ezek 16).

Yet Israel cannot get away from Yahweh. Formally they have opportunities to refuse the covenant relationship (Exod 24:3; Josh 24), but in reality it is too late for that, and these are only occasions for public plighting of troth. Israel cannot go back to Egypt. They can attempt to ignore Yahweh, but they will find that he will not let them alone.

THE INSTITUTIONAL STATE

The judges period establishes that Israel cannot exist in Canaan as a Yahwistic nation. Social, moral, religious, and political pressures threaten to demolish both their inner and outer life. Although God's promises have been fulfilled and Israel lives in Yahweh's land as Yahweh's people, their subsequent experience is an unhappy one. They return to a life not so very different from the one they had once known in Egypt.

Although the rule of the individual leaders of this period was occasional and limited, it showed that with strong leader-

---

[35]I take it that Noth's amphictyony model overestimates the extent to which the tribes of this period could gather for cultic, judicial, or military purposes, and that it is more likely that by the judges period an earlier unity had been fragmented than it is that no unity has yet been reached (see references at chap. 2, n. 58 above).

[36]On this theme see Coats, *Rebellion in the Wilderness;* Tunyogi, *Rebellions of Israel.*

[37]Childs, *Exodus,* 579.

ship, crises can be overcome, and the latter part of the book of Judges adds to its lament "everyone did what was right in his own eyes" the explanation "there was no king in Israel" (e.g., 21:35). There was thus a historical inevitability about the transition from (nominally) theocratic nation to monarchic state.[38] The alternative to such a development was to cease to exist. Thus this transition takes Israel from fragmentation to the peak of its historical achievement in the time of David and Solomon. Both the writing of connected history and the development of wisdom may reflect the monarchy's opening people's eyes to the regularities and interconnections of human life.[39]

The monarchy also brings developments in Israel's worship as Canaanite forms are allowed to influence the worship of the Jerusalem temple, and the worship of El is once more appropriated by the worshipers of Yahweh.[40] Like the development in their thinking just noted, this is a matter of inner beliefs, not merely of outward form. Yahweh becomes more explicitly the universal creator, who rules the world through his Davidic viceroy in his chosen city (see Pss 2; 46–48; 93; 96–99; Isa 2:2-4). The story of the acts of God continues in the covenant with David and the building of the temple, and even the failure of the kings generally leads not to disillusion with kingship but to the hope of a future king who will fulfill the kingship ideal—a hope which provides the most familiar way of understanding the significance of Jesus of Nazareth, the *Christ* coming in his *kingdom*. Human kingship can be a means of Yahweh's kingship receiving more effective concrete expression in the encouraging of justice, peace, and true religion.

Von Rad thus portrays the "Canaanisation of Jahwism" as an enriching of Israelite faith that enables its own inherent dynamic to emerge more clearly.[41] This "paganization" of Israel

---

[38]Cf. Flanagan's study of this process as an instance of an ancient and modern pattern (*JSOT* 20:47-73). A positive theology of the monarchy receives clearest expression in the Judean theology of 2 Sam 7; Ps 89; and later in Chronicles (see, e.g., 1 Chr 28:5, with Zimmerli's comments, *Theology*, 92).

[39]Cf. Eichrodt, *Theology*, 1:452-54; von Rad, *Theology*, 1:48-53.

[40]Cf., e.g., Clements, *God and Temple*, 40-62.

[41]So von Rad, *Theology*, 1:19-30. Cf. Koch's positive assessment of Israelite faith as a syncretism (*KD* 8:112); also L'Hour's suggestion that the contrast between Israel and Canaan lay in the former having the reason for living (in their experience of Yahweh) but not the means or structures for doing so, while the latter have the means but not the content or motivation (*Documenta Missionalia* 5:78-81). But the extent of the Canaanite contribution to "Zion tradition" has been questioned (cf. Roberts, *JBL* 92:329-44).

can, however, be evaluated much more negatively.[42] It includes the narrowing of Yahwism to a matter of piety and worship and a divorcing of Yahwism from politics, justice, and fertility, and of these from each other. The monarchy encourages the replacement of a clan system by a class system, with its inequalities, unfairnesses, and excesses (cf. 1 Sam 8:10-18; 1 Kgs 21). Like the transition from clan to people or nation, becoming an institutional state turned Israel into a different entity, and one with the same structure as other contemporary states: there was no other model to follow. The "liberation theology" of the exodus tradition no longer began where an imperial society found itself, even if in reality the monarchy meant that "Israel had reversed the Exodus and re-entered the Sheol of civilizations."[43] Further, the request for a king implies the rejection of Yahweh as king (1 Sam 8:7). Theocracy is incompatible with any humanly devised form of settled government; earthly leaders must be those he appoints, and they have authority only until he removes them.

Although Yahweh allows the introduction of institutional leadership, henceforth there is always the possibility of a clash between the institution which he once established and the person without strictly institutional authority who nevertheless declares "thus says Yahweh," and may be right. Indeed, the real activity of Yahweh is now more clearly seen confronting the institutions of Israel (not necesarily from outside, since prophets had a place in cult or court) because they have not taken the rule of Yahweh seriously and held together faith, fertility, politics, and social order. The prophets take up the key question of the relationship between the sovereignty of the human king and that of the divine king, the question of "the politics of God and the politics of man."[44]

---

[42]42. So Mendenhall, *Int* 29:155-70. See also *BAR* 3:19-22; Flanagan, *JAAR* 47:223-44; Neufeld, *HUCA* 31:31-53; Boecker, *Law and the Administration of Justice*, 92-93.

[43]Voegelin, 142. The anti-monarchic material in the OT itself has often been dated rather late; but see Eichrodt, *Theology*, 1:441; McCarter, *1 Samuel*, 8; Weiser, *ZTK* 57:141-61 = *Samuel*, 25-45; Mendelsohn, *BASOR* 143:17-22; Crüsemann, *Widerstand gegen Königtum*, 122-27; McKenzie *BR* 7:3-18. This little affects the theological discussion, however.

[44]Cf. Ellul, *Politics of God*; Kraus, *People of God*, 31-33. Renckens comments that what happens here is that the central locus of Yahwism, the real activity of God, is dissociated from the institution—and thus does not fall with it (*Religion*, 237-39). The prophetic hedging of the monarchy (designating kings, judging kings, directing holy war) especially characterizes northern Israel (cf. Cross, *Canaanite Myth*, 219-65; cf. Galling, *TLZ* 76:133-38; Vawter,

The tension between prophecy and kingship is paralleled by tensions between prophecy and priesthood and prophecy and wisdom; the period of the institutional state is also the period of the first temple and of the development of Israelite wisdom. Priesthood can encourage stability in a vital religion by the use of sacred forms, application of that religion to life by means of teaching and counseling, costly self-offering to God in response to his self-giving, safeguarding of the true faith, and personal encounter with God; it can also encourage people to replace divine lordship by human authoritarianism, divine nearness by divine inaccessibility, ethical commitment by outward observances, and openness to God by attempts to manipulate God and human beings. The wise can enable the affairs of state and family life— as these are lived together before Yahweh—to be conducted in accordance with the nature of the world as Yahweh makes it function; or they can enable people to organize their lives in such a way as to eliminate Yahweh from them. The verdict of the prophets is that the ambiguity of kingship, priesthood, and wisdom is generally resolved in the period of the institutional state by the latter sets of tendencies coming to predominate.[45]

The account of the monarchy's origin (1 Sam 8–12) illustrates the OT's ambivalence about kingship, which reflects the ambiguity of this institution itself. "Without the monarchy, the Israel of the confederacy might have disappeared without leaving much of a trace in history; with the monarchy, it survived but betrayed the Mosaic institutions."[46] Apparently Israel could

---

JES 15:267). While Genesis-Numbers is perhaps implicitly negative about the monarchy, as is Isa 40–55, Hosea takes the most unequivocally critical stance (*pace* Ackroyd, *TD* 27:337-38) (see esp. Hos 1:4-5; 9:15; 13:11). Schmidt suggests that a concern to leave room for God's activity in Israel runs through the OT material critical of the monarchy (*Probleme*, 440-61).

[45]Prophecy has its own ambiguity, of course, as kings, priests, and wise men would have emphasized. But the OT traditions regarding the preexilic period generally resolve its ambiguity the positive way.

[46]Voegelin, *Israel and Revelation*, 180; cf. Ackroyd, 338; Brueggemann, *Israelite Wisdom*, 86-87; Eichrodt, *Theology*, 1:441-42, 455-56. Thus alongside the negative view expressed in 1 Sam 8–12, the appointment of a נגיד is the gift of Yahweh's saving initiative (9:16), reference to המלוכה comes in 10:16, and Saul is made מלך before Yahweh (11:15). Judges, too, combines a negative attitude (chaps. 8–9) with a positive one (17:6; 21:25). There is a contrast between these OT accounts and the Mesopotamian picture of kingship descending from heaven (cf. Jacobsen, *Treasures of Darkness*, 78-79, 83, 114; Frankfort, *Kingship and the Gods*, 237-38, 398 [see also his comments on the Egyptian Memphite Theology, p. 33]).

only develop this way. They could not ask whether it was better to be "charismatic" or "institutional"; they could only ask how they were to be what historical forces compelled them to be. They had discovered what it meant to be a Yahwistic theocracy, though they had not succeeded in realizing the ideal. Now they were challenged to discover what it meant to be a Yahwistic institution.[47]

They failed here, too, and ultimately the institutional state is put under the judgment of Yahweh which the prophets declared. Yet this no to Israel as they exist is not a casting off of Yahweh's elect people. It is, indeed, designed to elicit a response from them.[48]

THE AFFLICTED REMNANT

Prophecy thus demands a reversal of the paganization of Israel; the alternative is a judgment that would decimate them.

Although the picture of Israel surviving judgment as a mere remnant begins as a negative idea, the fact that a remnant will survive becomes a basis for hope. The felled tree can produce new growth; the decimated nation can increase again. Beyond judgment there will be salvation, because it is still true that Yahweh has taken hold of Israel and will not let them go.

In some sense the remnant preexists the exile; it goes back at least to Elijah and the seven thousand who refused to acknowledge Baal, and it persists in Jeremiah, Baruch, and those associated with them. When a remnant survives judgment, however, it does not do so because of its righteousness; its salvation is of grace. The call to the remnant to be righteous is made on the basis of the fact that it has been preserved. It is exhorted to give Yahweh the response which should characterize the whole people; after being a warning and a promise, the remnant idea becomes a challenge (Isa 10:20-21; Ezek 18).[49]

Thus, when God abandons the people as a whole, it is not to the individual that he turns.[50] Perhaps one can say that the

---

[47]There is a strand of idealism in the enthusiasm of Gottwald and Mendenhall for the "Mosaic" period, which has not faced up to the failure of the theocratic order (see the comments on p. 107 below).

[48]Cf. Dahl, *Volk Gottes*, 32.

[49]On the remnant, see, e.g., de Vaux, *Bible and the Ancient Near East*, 15-30; Hasel, *Remnant*.

[50]Cf. Vriezen, *Outline*, 358, against Causse, *Du groupe ethnique*.

origin of the idea of the church lies in the idea of the remnant;[51] even if so, the remnant idea does not signify the abandoning of the idea of a people of God. It is rather a means of its continuance.

The end of the northern kingdom comes soon after the emergence of the "writing prophets"; Judah's political, moral, social, and spiritual disorder also portends their judgment. Before the axe actually falls on the tree, Josiah makes a final attempt to preserve it whole by providing the turning back which Torah and prophets demand, seeking to implement Deuteronomy's vision of a holy nation and insisting that the whole (surviving) people commit itself to living in the light of its election as the people of God, in every aspect of its life (inner attitude, cultic practice, social life, religious commitment, moral standard).[52]

If their inadequacy was not apparent in his lifetime, Josiah's reforms died with him at Megiddo. His sons' reigns see religious, social, and ethical degeneration. The Josianic reform comes to a "miscarriage" which reflects the story of the OT as a whole.[53] There is a more profound problem about Israel's human nature than can be solved by a lawbook. A new kind of circumcision, a new kind of relationship to the law, and a new kind of covenant are needed (Deut 30:6; Jer 31:31-34).[54] The idea of Israel being the people of God becomes future prospect, not present reality (Jer 31:1; Ezek 11:20; cf. Hos 1:9–2:3, 25 [1, 23]).

As with the transition from theocratic nation to institutional state, there is a certain logic about the failure of the institution which turns it into a remnant. To the extent that the people of God is where the kingship of God is a reality (a notion given outward form by the theocratic nation), it forms a microcosm of what the whole world is called to be. But in that this kingship is in practice rejected, this people becomes instead a microcosm of what the world itself also is. If the state's importance and sovereignty compete with those of God, it has to be

---

[51]So Eissfeldt, TSK 109/2:10, 13; Hertzberg, Werdende Kirche, 12.

[52]Cf. Eissfeldt, 15; von Rad, Gottesvolk, 9-11, 14-16, 19, 50-51, 60 (noting the difference from the prophetic view, which had ceased to regard Israel as a whole as the chosen people).

[53]Cf. Bultmann, Essays on OT Hermeneutics, 72-75.

[54]See Nicholson, Preaching to the Exiles (esp. 81-84) on these and related passages.

judged.[55] The people of God is not a means of God's revelation, but a threat to it; for the sake of that revelation Israel therefore has to be cast off. The people of God has no security independent of their obedience. They are not indispensable; rather, God will reveal himself through them by judging them, if not by blessing them. They thus represent in microcosm the judgment of all those who go against God.

Although the exile makes real the nightmare that Israel will be turned into a mere remnant, their religion absorbs the experience of exile rather than being absorbed by it. The survivors take up anew the challenge to keep Yahweh's law, meditate anew on the lessons to be learned from their history as a people, and ask anew whether there might be some future for them. It is, however, a demoralized remnant that hears a second Isaiah proclaiming that they *are* God's people, that they are not finished, that they are Yahweh's servant and have not been abandoned by him.

In Isa 40–55, the description of Israel as Yahweh's servant is the key motif to designate Israel as the people of God. Their servanthood is the guarantee of God's concern for them (41:8-10). It also implies their responsibility to him (42:1-4, 5-9). The trouble is that they are too deaf and blind to meet this responsibility, and in need of enlightenment themselves (42:18-20).[56] God first promises that he will restore them to the land, though the anointed king through whom he will do this is not a son of David—Jehoiachin or Zerubbabel—but the Persian Cyrus (45:1). They need to be "on the way," however, in another sense, on the way from sin to new creation,[57] and the prophet himself hears Yahweh calling him to minister to these inner needs, to be the servant to them, and to accept the affliction this will bring him (49:1-6; 50:4-9).[58]

The last major servant passage (52:13–53:12) develops the motif of the servant's affliction, which has been gaining increasing prominence through chapters 40–55. The portrait of Yahweh's arm revealed in his servant's humiliation suggests that it is through his acceptance of affliction and suffering, not

---

[55]Cf. Mendenhall, *Tenth Generation*, 100.

[56]I have argued for the understanding of the servant passages presupposed here in *VT* 29:289-99, though the points made here are not necessarily dependent on this particular understanding.

[57]Congar, *Concilium* 1/1:15.

[58]I take the "obvious" view that in chaps. 49 and 50 when the prophet says "I" he means "I": see further p. 190 below.

through his exercise of triumphant power, that humanity's inner needs find their fulfillment. It would be an oversimplification to say that Israel *is* this servant (earlier chapters have made it clear that Israel needs to receive such a ministry) or that the prophet *is* the servant.[59] Yet to the extent that Israel is God's servant at all, this is their calling; and both the nation's experience of exile (which for some Israelites was undeserved—though Isa 40–55 does not explicitly refer to this point) and the prophet's experience of opposition contribute to the insight expressed in this portrait. The calling of the people of God is the calling of the servant; the calling of the servant is a call to die. That is the exile's deepest insight on what it means to be the people of God.

THE COMMUNITY OF THE PROMISE

In later times, the notion of exile or diaspora deeply influenced both Jewish and Christian thinking about the people of God.[60] The same is true of the servant idea, which both Jews and Christians see as a (if not the) high point of the OT. Yet the idea all but disappears from the OT after the exile, except for enigmatic passages such as Zech 12:10–13:1 and Dan 11:32–12:3.[61] It seems to have exercised little influence on ideas of what it means to be God's people after the return. Not unnaturally, the glorious promises of restoration were what caught people's enthusiasm.

In the event, the restoration fell far short of the glory of these promises, as Haggai, Zechariah, and Ezra 1–6 make clear. It is no triumphant return winning all the nations' acknowledgment of Yahweh. Though free to return to their land, Israel remains a subject people. In a way history does repeat itself; the situation in Ezra 4 resembles that of the judges period. The question now is how such a subject people can live faithfully as the people of Yahweh.[62]

---

[59]The same logic that points to the prophet being the servant in chaps. 49 and 50 (the use of "I") works against it here. Whybray advocates this identification (*Isaiah 40–66*, 169-83; cf. *Thanksgiving for a Liberated Prophet*), but has to ignore the context.

[60]For the latter, see, e.g., 1 Pet 1:1.

[61]Cf. Chary, *Aggée-Zacharie-Malachie*, 200-207; D. R. Jones, *Haggai, Zechariah and Malachi*, 161-62; Plöger, *Theocracy and Eschatology*, 16-17; Ginsberg, *VT* 3:400-404.

[62]62. Cf. Ackroyd, *Age of the Chronicler*, 10.

Israel actually threw off statehood along with monarchy with remarkable ease—"the state as such was somewhat of a borrowed garment for Israel."[63] They had been the people of Yahweh before, and could be after. They had been the Israelite קהל, the assembled community, before, and they could be again.[64] Becoming a community does not mean becoming a church in the sense of a body with no awareness of itself as a people; the קהל bears a people's traditions and hopes.[65] Yet as a people they are in a different position because they have been through nationhood, the experience of Yahweh acting in their political history, and the receiving of his promises that he would do so again. They are now the community of promise. We noted above (pp. 21-23) that the failure of the promise to live up to expectations forces Israel to find ways of living with God's promises; it leads to the emergence of at least four models of what it must mean to be the people of God now.[66]

First, the OT's chief postexilic narrative presentation of Israel's story portrays Israel as a *worshiping* community. This understanding presupposes that God's promises have been fulfilled in the restoration: he is still present and active with his people. The "branch" may have disappeared, but the high priest has not:[67] Yahweh's activity is seen in political events (the Persian authorities serve him), though more significantly in Israel's religious life, which he established in the first place and where the promises of the prophets are fulfilled. He calls the Israelite קהל to be also the עדה, the community gathered for worship. It is this that Ezra established,[68] and this that the Chronicler provides with its ideological base—still, significantly, in the form of narrative history. It was of course true that Israel had been a worshiping community from the beginning, and that Ezekiel's prophecies had this at the center of their vision. Indeed, "we

---

[63]Von Rad, *Theology*, 1:90.

[64]Eichrodt notes that these terms referred originally to the assembly of the Israelite tribes (*Theology*, 1:40); cf. Macholz, *Jüdisches Volk*, 170, 175-76).

[65]Cf. Dahl, *Volk Gottes*, 36.

[66]The analysis which follows may be compared with Baumbach's division of Judaism from the second century into a pietist-nomistic tendency (embracing [2] and [3] here), a particularist hierocratic tendency (corresponding to [1] here), and a universalist tendency, prepared to abandon Jewish distinctives, much of it with a wisdom connection (a descendant of [4] here?) (see *Kairos* 21:30-47).

[67]Cf. Vriezen, *Outline*, 360.

[68]So Koch, *JSS* 19:173-97.

must always ask whether a theology which saw Israel's existence in the eyes of Jahweh as so strongly conditioned by praise could have strayed so very far from the proper road."[69]

In theory, at least, the community welcomes all who are willing to join God's people in Jerusalem to worship with it; yet there is an unresolved tension in its attitude to outsiders. It is still a people, organized by tribe and family—as the Chronicler especially emphasizes. Indeed, community leaders such as Ezra and Nehemiah perceive a need to close the ranks against alien influence if Israel is to survive as a distinct entity in the pressures of their time. They are less tolerant of the "mixed multitude" than Moses had been (Neh 13:1-3). Such a protectionism may have enabled Judaism to survive, even if it could not enable it to triumph.[70]

Second, other Jews approached exilic prophecy in a different way and saw the people of God as called to be a *waiting* community. If God could not be seen as presently active in history, faith's response was not to narrow his sphere of activity to a cultic focus, but to look to God's future. One should not despise the day of small things, but one should not be satisfied with it either. The time will come when he brings to an end this God-forsaken order of history in judgment and salvation.

Some of the tensions between the vision of the worshiping community and that of the waiting community perhaps reflect the respective positions of different groups in the power structure of the postexilic community as a whole.[71] Yet they are also intelligible as alternative responses to a real problem of faith. Nor should the tensions between those who hold these viewpoints be exaggerated. As well as visionaries such as Ezekiel, Haggai, and Zechariah having a distinctively temple-focused faith, worship-focused figures such as Ezra and the Chronicler still look to the future for God to bring about a more satisfactory restoration of his people's fortunes than the one they experience in the present.[72] The cultic and the apocalyptic are both concerned for purity over against outside influence; they stand together over against the views of the Samaritans, of the Jews of El-

---

[69]Von Rad's comment on the Chronicler, *Theology,* 1:354.

[70]Cf. Chamberlayne, *Man in Society,* 176. Williamson in *Israel in the Books of Chronicles* argues that Chronicles takes a less protectionist stance than Ezra and Nehemiah.

[71]So, e.g., Hanson, *Dawn of Apocalyptic.*

[72]Cf. Koch, 197.

ephantine, and of those who were prepared to accept (or to take up arms against) the hellenizing pressures of the Maccabean crisis.[73] A concern for purity over against outside influence thus involves a concern for purity within the people of God, and this, too, apocalyptic and Chronicles share. The division between righteous and wicked is not only one between Israel and the world but one within Israel.[74]

Third, others emphasize *obeying* the pentateuchal law. We noted above (pp. 44-48) that in the context of the covenant the law functioned as an expression of God's grace which provided his people with the framework for a response to his redemptive acts. After the exile, the law seems to function more independently of the covenant, and gains a central place in its own right as a means of people relating to God. The law is the direct object of the believer's meditation, delight, hope, longing, trust, and love (e.g., Ps 19:8-15 [7-14]; 119:14-16, 40-49).

In Mendenhall's view, postexilic Israel becomes for the first time ethnocentric, not least in connection with its observance of the law (see Neh 13).[75] It is implausible in this way either to remove the ethnic base from early Israel, or to remove the confessional base from the postexilic community, for the idea of conversion to Judaism, of becoming a Jew by taking on the demands of the law, begins in postexilic Judaism.[76] It is the postexilic community's focusing on the law which opens up the possibility that any who respond to God's law, whatever their race, can belong to his people—the openness illustrated by Ruth and Jonah, if they belong to this period. Yet this same focusing on the law issues in the exclusivist attitudes of Ezra and Nehemiah, noted earlier in this section.

There are other drawbacks about an emphasis on law. Turning Israel's faith into a religion of a book releases the community from having to listen for the living word and from the

---

[73]There is some *Persian* influence on apocalyptic, but it is of a marginal kind and provides new ways of expressing tendencies inherent in Yahwistic faith rather than introducing quite alien features to it (cf. Ackroyd, *Israel*, 340-44).

[74]Cf. Mowinckel, *Psalms*, 1:207.

[75]*Tenth Generation*, 5.

[76]Cf. Milgrom, *JBL* 101:169-76; Neusner, *Understanding Jewish Theology*, 63. Mendenhall himself later notes (p. 153) that a concern with exogamy in passages such as Deut 7 actually arises from ethical or religious considerations; it is not merely ethnic.

tension of living with God in history.[77] It may imply that the relationship between God and people depends on people rather than on God, and may turn the religion which had been Israel's freedom at the beginning of their story into their bondage at the end of their story.[78] Yet with this faith, Jews can live without national existence, staying on in Babylon and Egypt. They can find a unity based on commitment to the Torah,[79] a commitment which embodies Deuteronomy's demand for a response of love, trust, and fear, and brings a partial fulfillment of the vision of people's hearts being circumcised and of the law being written on them (Deut 30:6; Jer 31:33). Here is the birth of a confessing church.

The fourth model is *questioning;* even more than the third, it appeals as much to the individual as to the community as such. The postexilic community is usually reckoned to be the home of the OT's most serious wrestling with doubt and uncertainty, in Job and Ecclesiastes. Here the exceptions to such confident affirmations as characterize Proverbs are felt more keenly than are the rules themselves. The fact that the rules do not always work must have been apparent before the exile, and doubt and uncertainty about basic affirmations of the faith find periodic expression throughout OT times.[80] The exceptions can be accommodated as long as people retain a living conviction that the world does make sense, a conviction reinforced in Israel by the experience of God's great acts of redemption in their history.[81] The exodus is now ancient history, however, and it is a demanding venture of faith to recognize the restoration as a genuine new exodus. Disappointment with historical experience of this kind seems likely to have contributed to doubt becoming so articulate in Job and Ecclesiastes. In their circles within the postexilic community, it feels impossible to make the ancient faith very meaningful. They recognize that there is nowhere else to look for answers; the situation can be faced only by discovering new bases for believing in Yahweh. But they find it is easier to pose questions than to reach satisfying answers.

---

[77]So Jacob, *Theology,* 133-34; Voegelin, *Israel and Revelation,* 374.

[78]So Mendenhall, *BA* 25:86-87, with Blenkinsopp's comments, *Sketchbook,* 69. Wellhausen saw individual commitment to the Torah as the essence of postexilic religion and evaluated it negatively (*Prolegomena,* e.g., 424-25).

[79]Cf. Koch, *JSS* 19:197.

[80]See further pp. 195-96 below.

[81]Cf. Bowker, *Problems of Suffering,* 9.

THE CONTINUING STORY OF THE PEOPLE OF GOD IN JUDAISM AND CHRISTIANITY

We have reached the end of the story of the people of God as the Hebrew Bible reflects it, yet that story has not come to a proper conclusion. "Colonial dependence" in the Persian and early Greek periods is followed by "wars of independence; controlled independence; and then a last revolt leading to annihilation."[82] From either a rabbinic or a primitive Christian perspective this postcanonical history of the people of God involves a repoliticization which is discredited by its results.[83]

Rabbinic Judaism sees itself as taking up where the OT leaves off. The ghetto comes to stand not only for the Jewish people's continuing calling to a distinctive obedience, but also for their continuing election to the suffering of the servant, in which once again their God seeks to reveal himself.[84] Zionism preserved the vision of being "a model for the redemption of the entire human race."[85] Understandably tired of being treated as the afflicted remnant, however, they have once again repoliticized their life and sought to be a nation like the other nations, guided as much by Joshua, the Maccabees, and Bar Kochba as by Moses, and experiencing the same effectiveness as they once enjoyed under David and Solomon, with the same risks.

A Christian perspective is more impressed by the lines that lead from the OT to Jesus than by those that lead to Rabbinic Judaism; it finds the continuing existence of the Jewish people a theological puzzle. Among the streams of thought represented in the late OT period, Jesus has obvious affinities with the community waiting for the coming of the Day of God, but it is to representatives of the worshiping community that the coming of this Day is first announced (Luke 1:5-25), while the community concerned with obeying the law ought also—so Jesus claims— to find itself drawn to him (John 5:39),[86] and the new revelation

---

[82]Dumas, *Political Theology*, 118.

[83]So Mendenhall, *Tenth Generation*, 101; Schoeps, *Church and the Jewish People*, 65.

[84]Cf. Rengstorf, *Church and the Jewish People*, 34-35.

[85]David Ben Gurion, quoted by Elon and Hassan in *Between Enemies*, 12.

[86]Baumbach too, sees equivalents in subsequent NT theologies to his three types of ecclesiology in Judaism (see *Kairos* 21:46-47).

and new events he brings offer some response to the doubt and questioning of those for whom the traditional faith no longer carries conviction.

Thus Jesus addresses himself to Israel and forms around him the nucleus of a responsive remnant of Israel: not a replacement people of God, but a group through whom Israel as a whole will be reached.[87] In fact, Israel as a whole rejects him. As there were lines that could lead from the OT to Jesus, there were others that could lead to Rabbinic Judaism, to his rejection, and to the OT's own miscarriage. Thus the OT functions both positively and negatively in relation to Jesus, and Christianity's relationship to it is ambivalent.[88] In rejecting Jesus Judaism in general stands self-condemned as the anti-people of God, and the nucleus becomes only a remnant. Not that the church can dispense with Israel; to attempt to do so is "perilously like playing Hamlet without the Prince of Denmark,"[89] and Israel still belongs to the God and Father of our Lord Jesus Christ.

Meanwhile it is this remnant that receives the Holy Spirit, the distinctive foretaste of the End with its blessings, which makes it the community which both lives by and looks for the End of all things. It becomes the church, the gathered community (Christian faith is no less corporate, no more individualistic, than OT faith was). Far from settling down as a remnant, it is expected to take an essentially outward-looking, open stance, expectant of growing into not only the fullness of Israel but—as a means to that—the fullness of the gentiles, who are fellow-heirs with the saints in a body which sees itself as the same old people of God yet at the same time as a new entity in which ethnic distinctions cease to count. All become one in Christ Jesus, for the people of God now focuses on a person, on shared relationships with him, and on a shared acknowledgment of him as Lord; the people of God itself is thus less central than it was in OT times.[90] It is called to preach and to embody his calling as the crucified one, relying on the cross, accepting the cross, and preaching the cross.

---

[87]See, e.g., Flew, *Jesus and his Church*; Küng, *The Church*, 72-74; E. Schweizer, *Church Order*, chap. 2.

[88]Cf. Barr, *Old and New*, 161.

[89]Sloyan, *Standing before God*, 113.

[90]C. W. Williams asks whether the church is central to God's purpose, or whether ecclesiology is but a paragraph from Christology (*The Church*, 17-19). The former is true in the OT, the latter in the NT, as messianism is an aspect of eschatology in the OT, but fundamental to the NT.

On the way to the cross, Jesus had gone through stages in his ministry which in part parallel Israel's experience.[91] He had the power to be the mighty one of Mal 3, exercised the ministry of liberator and savior described in Isa 35 and 61, had the opportunity to become the messianic King of Israel; but found his true calling in the role of the afflicted servant of Isa 40–55.

The church's own story also manifests parallels to Israel's.[92] Perhaps the patterns and recurring developments which can be perceived can be accounted for in sociological terms: the turning of theocracy into state and of church into institution are examples of developments one can perceive in culture and history,[93] while any beleaguered remnant may well cope with and survive its minority situation by turning in on itself.[94] Thus, like Israel, the church begins as a family and spreads through the known world under God's direct leadership. Then it begins to need ordered leadership and to institutionalize the Spirit's lordship. With Constantine, it comes to be accepted by the world and to operate in the world like the world, often on the basis of the world's agenda. With the Enlightenment and the Industrial Revolution, it becomes an exiled remnant, though in some ways thus finds itself. Like postexilic Israel, it now lives with a tension between the way scripture describes the church's significance and the insignificance of its place in the world, often coping with this experience by means of similar devices to Israel's: the agnostic faith of the theological community, or individualistic piety, or a concentration on the church's internal affairs and life of worship, or an escape into hope and striving for a coming Kingdom which contrasts with the present one.

---

[91]For what follows, see J. A. T. Robinson, *Human Face of God*, 80-83.

[92]For what follows, see in part Seebass, *WD* 8:34-35; de Waal, *What Is the Church?* 9-19; Reid, *Elaborate Funeral*, 163-70; Rahner, *Mission and Grace*, 1:31-32; idem, *Shape of the Church to Come*, 29-34.

[93]See, e.g., Melly, *Revolt into Style*, on this phenomenon in music; Reich, *Greening of America*, on its place in the development of the "corporate state" in the USA.

[94]So Berger, *Rumor of Angels*, 31-34. Hanson's work in *Dawn of Apocalyptic* opens up the possibility of a broader sociological analysis of postexilic OT material in particular; see also the general survey by Long, *Int* 36:243-55. The studies of patriarchal religion against the background of parallels among other peoples in a similar social situation by scholars such as Alt and Cross (see n. 16 above) take another incipiently sociological approach to that period. Such approaches need not have reductionist implications, as Berger's work in *Rumor of Angels* and in *Facing up to Modernity* illustrates.

PERMANENT INSIGHTS AND RECURRING QUESTIONS

The contextual approach to the varied theological material we have examined in this chapter begins by noting that these models of what it means to be the people of God are all part of the canonical history; all thus contain material open for our appropriation. The question it then suggests is whether the self-understanding to which Israel gave expression in one or other of these OT contexts is distinctively helpful to us in our context in enabling us to perceive what it means for us to be the people of God.

Permanent Insights

It is not enough that we should simply feel free to choose from the OT tradition those insights which we find immediately helpful. The very way in which the tradition develops reflects the conviction that the insights of earlier periods must be brought to bear on later ones; what it meant to be the people of God in Abraham's time does not cease to be relevant when Israel is no longer a homeless clan. J and P, for instance, speak to the institutional state and the afflicted remnant by retelling the stories of the clan, with their radical implications for each.[95] Arguably the latter traditions become more, not less, important when they offer insights that derive from a quite different social and historical experience.

Conversely, the subsequent history of particular OT traditions or motifs is relevant to our interpretation of the significance of these traditions as they appear earlier. This later history may allow hidden tensions to be revealed or visible tensions to be resolved, intrinsic difficulties to emerge or open questions to be faced, confident affirmations to be qualified or situational overemphases to be set in a broader context. Even if we find it instinctively easy to identify with one model of being the people of God, we must see this model in the context of the others to which it is historically linked. Precisely because the various modes of being the people of God were linked historically and

---

[95]Cf. Lind on J, who "promoted a politics developed in a period of weakness for a time of political strength" (*Yahweh Is a Warrior*, 36).

developed from each other, they may be expected to convey insights of permanent significance.

First, being a wandering family speaks of closeness of relationship, in the present and through the generations. It speaks of mutual love and concern, of the people of God as a brotherhood in which conflict is overcome by reconciliation, and to which all belong as equal partners.[96] Here "the whole of existence is defined by the communal form of the family, a pre- and a-political form of existence."[97] It speaks of being a people on the way, between promise and fulfillment, and dependent on the one who brought it into being by his will (not by the initiative of human beings individually or corporately) to take it to its destiny by whatever route he chooses, willing to sacrifice all securities (even God-given ones) in order to keep receiving the good things of this world anew as the gifts of the God of this world.[98] It must not mean a group turned in on itself, which rests on the mere fact of genetic relationship rather than acknowledging the importance of historical choice, and which may even become settled in an unsettled way of life.

Second, being a theocratic nation speaks of the evident blessing of God demonstrated in the increase he gives; of the experience of him fulfilling his promises; of his direct leading and his people following, of human leadership not allowed to obscure his kingship and of the priesthood of the whole people not annulled by the existence of a priestly tribe. It speaks of living in the world and of learning from it, but of standing over against the world and its religion, though being willing to welcome others to the same commitment to Yahweh as King and Lord which his people themselves must make. It must not mean a confidence in God which produces a false confidence in themselves, in their position and in their response to him; the theocratic nation especially has to recognize that it is the rebellious nation that cannot exist in the world as the theocracy because of its sin.

Third, being an institutional state means that God starts

---

[96]Cf. Dumas, *Political Theology,* 24-42; Lind, 39-42; also the awareness that the theme "people of God" attracted interest in Conciliar Roman Catholicism because it brought out the fact that the church is the total Christian community, not just the clergy (cf. Grillmeier, *Commentary,* 1:138-85; see also n. 11 above).

[97]So Westermann, *What Does the OT Say about God?* 83.

[98]Cf. Gunneweg, *Understanding the OT,* 170; Macquarrie, *Faith of the People of God,* 21-22.

with his people where they are; if they cannot cope with his highest way, he carves out a lower one. When they do not respond to the spirit of Yahweh or when all sorts of spirits lead them into anarchy, he provides them with the institutional safeguard of earthly rulers. It speaks of an openness to learn from the world, to let the world provide the vehicles for expressing the faith, and to attract the world to that faith. It must not mean that the style of the nations becomes the style of the people of God, or that the institution quenches the Spirit and its rulers replace God, or that the gifts of God come to be viewed as inalienable possessions or as rights which God has to defend.[99]

Fourth, being an afflicted remnant means recognizing that the final purpose of God cannot be effected in the regular course of human history, because of the waywardness both of God's people and of other nations. It means that God's people are subject to his judgment, but that all is not lost when God cuts his people down to size. It means reaching one's furthest influence on the world not through the exercise of the world's power or by sharing the world's faith and attitudes but by accepting the affliction that comes from confronting the world, in the awareness that the call of the servant is a call to die. It must not mean trusting in being those who have escaped judgment (by God's grace), or settling down to being the remnant in a ghetto, or morbidly courting martyrdom.

Fifth, being a community of promise suggests a complex set of challenges of its own: of a people that faces up to facts yet recognizes that even when history ceases to be the sphere in which God fulfills his ultimate purpose through them, it does not cease to be the sphere in which they actually have to live; that is honest about what they can believe yet pledged to making sense of the old faith; that is committed to personal discipleship if the corporate seems to lapse; that lives as a people dedicated to the praise of Yahweh for what he has done yet to hope in him for what he is yet to do.[100]

Sixth, being God's people means being especially his, especially responsible to him, and especially likely to reject the Messiah.

Seventh, being God's people means being grasped by the

---

[99]Cf. Gunneweg, 169.

[100]As Congar puts it, the *not yet* must not be allowed to take all the truth from the *is now* (*Concilium* 1/1:16)—or vice versa.

Holy Spirit without being susceptible to the influence of other spirits, being taken out of the world without becoming isolated from the world, accepting the lordship of Christ, the mission of Christ, but also the cross of Christ.[101] It means recognizing that the church remains sinful and that even the NT embraces a concern with law (Matthew), with institutional ministry (the Pastorals), with individualism (John), and with the apocalyptic future (Revelation).

These insights suggested by what it means in different periods to be the people of God may be set up thus as antitheses: they should be this, they should not be that. But the tragic paradox of the people of God is that they are both at once. They are "my people" but "not my people"; a means of God's purpose being effected and also the biggest obstacle to that end; the agent of God's revealing himself and the means of his being obscured; a microcosm of what the world is called to be and a microcosm of what the world already is; set apart and sanctified but also rebellious and indistinguishable from the sinful world; separated from the nations and also a mixed multitude; the event by which God gives expression to his will and the anti-event by which his will is frustrated.

Recurring Questions

Such generalizations lead from a diachronic approach to the material on the people of God—that is, an approach which looks at what it means to be God's people in different ages—to a synchronic approach, which asks what issues recur throughout this material. There are certain constants about the OT's underlying understanding of the people of God, "family resemblances" which generally appear. God's people is that entity which is brought into existence by his historical choice, which lives by his promise and is the heir of his blessing. It is that entity where his kingship is to be made a reality corporately, in a body and not merely in individuals;[102] that entity which accepts Yahweh's

---

[101]See further Käsemann, *NT Questions,* 257-59.

[102]Cf. Hertzberg, *Werdende Kirche,* 5-7, 24, suggesting that the question of the relationship between corporate and individual in the Psalms (who is the "I"?), Isa 40–55 (the servant), and Deuteronomy (which varies over addressing people in the singular or the plural) reflects the fact that both are intrinsically important in the OT; von Rad, *Gottesvolk,* 100, noting that even Jeremiah's vision is of a renewed *people*—it is not individualistic.

lordship and follows his leading. It is a visible body; even where there is a distinction drawn between sò-called Israel and real Israel, that is not a distinction between a visible church and an invisible one, and it lives in the world and in history in order that it may model there the calling of a people of Yahweh, which it is the destiny of all peoples to share.[103]

Such constants which underlie the changing form of the people of God may, however, be less striking and less illuminating than the series of questions which recur throughout the material.

First, what is the relationship between life in the Spirit and life in the world? In Abraham's time, God's people ignore the world and live before God, but eventually find themselves under the world in Egypt. With Moses begins the glorious experiment in which the tension between religion and politics is overcome. But eventually Israel finds itself in a state of religious and moral anarchy—one indeed presaged from the start by the rebellions of Israel—and of political subjection. The monarchy triumphs in the world (at first) but on the whole fails in the realm of the Spirit. The exile again brings earthly humiliation, but new insights to some (though one should not assume a responsiveness on the part of the exiles as a whole). These include the belief that outward affliction may be the means of (others') growth in the Spirit (the servant), though the prophets and preachers of the exile do not abandon the parallel vision of political triumph. The restoration sees only a partial realization of either vision,[104] and the OT thus leaves us with a vision unfulfilled. Israel's story suggests that the relationship between life in the Spirit and life in the world is insoluble. The people of God cannot live as a political theocracy ruling the world in Yahweh's name, but neither can they take the way of separation which evades life in the world.[105] Nor is there any way of living in obedience to God and being organized for existence in history.[106] History, politics, and state-

---

[103]Contrast Baumgärtel's view that Israel mistakenly turned God's promise of a relationship with him into a this-worldly promise involving land (see his *Verheissung*, with Gunneweg's comments, 166-69).

[104]Cf. Eissfeldt's contrast of Deuteronomy with Lev 17- 26, which lacks reference to warmaking and foreign policy and implies acceptance of foreign overlordship (*TSK* 109/2:16).

[105]Cf. Hertzberg, 23, following H. M. Müller, *Das AT: Christlich/ Jüdisch/Weltlich*, 59-61.

[106]Cf. Voegelin, *Israel and Revelation*, 183; also Mendenhall's observation that the biblical tradition has always been most creative when the community lacked political or economic power, while the most corrupt periods are

hood, though inevitable, make it difficult to live as the people of God. The NT has little to add to this OT picture, and church history confirms it.

Second, what is the relationship under God between divine rule and human leadership, and between institutional order and individual freedom and responsibility? The clan leader is taken hold of and guided by God and there is no question of others deciding for themselves where and how they will live their lives, or—as far as one can tell—of their relating directly to God themselves: the clan leader is father, king, and priest. The theocracy emphasizes Yahweh's lordship but the people are slow to follow and both kingship and priesthood fulfill a need for institutional leadership, though not without compromising Yahweh's own position—as the rise of the prophets as an alternative order witnesses. The NT sees the Spirit given to the whole community (or perhaps vice versa), but still the community can be led astray by individuals, and the NT itself develops the features of an institution for similar reasons to the OT's.

Third, what is the relationship between triumph and affliction? The story of the patriarchs is arguably one that takes them from glory to humiliation (in precise contradiction to what had been promised to Abraham), and for no apparent purpose. In the exodus and conquest Israel experiences triumph, but this is followed by humiliation again in the judges period; the pattern repeats itself in the monarchy and exile. Here, however, while political restoration is promised, a new vision appears. It may not be the case that only triumph can win people for God: affliction may do so too. Though the notion of Israel's call to suffering is not further developed in the OT, it has become significant in later Jewish theology. Israel's very election seems to be one to suffering. In the NT, suffering is seen as both preceding glory and as itself a peculiar form of glory, both for Jesus and for the church.

Fourth, what is the relationship between "Yahweh the God of Israel" and "Yahweh the lord of the world"? Israel's story is set on the broadest canvas—the creation of the whole cosmos and the forming of the first human pair by Yahweh Elohim, Yahweh

---

those when it enjoys power (*Tenth Generation*, xi-xii); and Yoder's that the more closely a people is related to God, the less its existence can be tied to the political structures of the institutional state (*Karl Barth and the Problem of War*, 79).

who *is* God, who is worshiped as such from the beginning. The experiences of the patriarchs and of Israel were to be only a paradigm of what God purposed for the whole world. Yet Yahweh's concern with the rest of the world for its own sake is not prominent in the OT. The world is as often seen as the locus of sin before God and enmity toward Israel (and therefore to be punished) as it is seen as living in ignorance and need (and therefore to be saved). Even Jesus' ministry is only concerned with Israel; and—despite the great commission—even the NT's suggestion that the purpose for the delay in the consummation is that this provides an opportunity for the gathering in of the gentiles has the air of an afterthought.[107]

Fifth, what is the relationship between faith in Yahweh and the cultures of other peoples? When the world's concerns are marginal to Israel's and the world's beliefs are less misguided than they might be, God's people are not afraid to identify with it.[108] When they are confronting the world and the world is more degenerate, they resist and attack its beliefs; they thus give expression to their calling to be the people of *Yahweh*. When Israel is itself a power in the world, it allows the nations to influence it, though not without a price being paid. When Israel is being reduced to a remnant and dominated by the world, it again resists the world's beliefs and emphasizes practices that distinguish it. When Israel is lord of its own domain but still under the world's higher overlordship, it is wary still of alien influence and increasingly longing for people to make their individual commitment to Yahweh's way. When Israel ventures confidently with the gospel into the gentile world it is not afraid to reconceptualize that gospel in the terms of Hellenism/Gnosticism. Israel's willingness to be influenced by other cultures is part of its own theologizing; it is also a chief way in which Israel falls into sin and fails to maintain a distinctive faith in Yahweh. The tension between the positive and the negative aspects to this willingness cannot be resolved.

Sixth, what is the relationship between the people of God as a vision and the people of God in reality? The theological statements made about Israel are characteristically larger than

---

[107]On "nationalism" and "universalism," see further pp. 146 and 192-93 below.

[108]Cf. now Dietrich's study in his *Israel und Canaan* of how these two peoples relate (e.g., coexistence, confrontation, integration, secession, infiltration, repression).

life; in that they never correspond to visible reality, they are always open to the explicit eschatological reinterpretation that they eventually receive. The designation of Israel as God's people is not merely a descriptive statement; it is promissory or eschatological, and also prescriptive. There is a danger inherent in the descriptive interpretation (cf. Jer 7:10; Matt 3:9). The image may be absolutized and turned into an idol.[109] If it is not taken prescriptively it is not true at all and becomes only a hope for the future (Hos 1:9–2:1 [1:9-10]; Jer 31:1, 33).[110] The tension between vision and reality is not to be resolved by abandoning the visible people. Throughout the OT the people of God is visibly organized yet based on faith, and has to be viewed in this-worldly terms yet also be viewed theologically.[111] The NT people of God, too, lives with this tension; not least, it both asserts that Christ's community ignores all ethnic boundaries and also believes in the continuing significance of the actual people Israel (see esp. Rom 9–11).[112]

WHAT DOES IT MEAN TO BE THE PEOPLE OF GOD?

Above we noted that the contextual approach to the diverse OT insights on what it means to be the people of God may encourage us to appropriate one perspective or another from within the tradition by pointing to similarities between a specific OT context and our own. For instance, if we locate ourselves as the people of God in a period analogous to that of postexilic times, then it may be natural for us to find the self-understanding of the community of the promise especially helpful; conversely, the church which no longer lives in a period when it exercises political power need not feel guilty at its inability to exercise the power in the world that the institutional state did.

It is a genuine encouragement to find within scripture itself the people of God coping with different modes of being with the ambiguities that we ourselves experience. God has said yes to each of these. The monarchy was part of God's will, even though it had its earthly origin in an act of human rebellion. The community has to find ways of living with the experience of

---

[109]Cf. Marks, *TToday* 29:26.

[110]Cf. Dahl, *Volk Gottes*, 38.

[111]Cf. Hertzberg, 10, 25. Contrast the view that there is a development from people/nation toward church in the OT (e.g., Eissfeldt *TSK* 109/2:9-23).

[112]On this see, e.g., W. D. Davies, *NTS* 24:4-39.

God's promises not being fulfilled, and the OT as a whole includes responses such as the development of apocalyptic
eschatology and of the Chronicler's realized eschatology; even if
cultic observances have a low place on God's theoretical list of
priorities for his people, when they are in danger of disillusion
and loss of identity, the Chronicler's emphasis on God's presence with them in their worship helps to sustain them and keep
them alive. How they understand themselves and live out their
calling has to vary with circumstances; the mode appropriate before may be inappropriate now. The Rechabites' anachronistic
way of life was their calling even in the time of Jeremiah, but it
was not that of the majority.

The danger is that our choice of a perspective from the varied ones the OT offers us may be an arbitrary one. A predetermined understanding of what it means to be God's people may
be bolstered exegetically by appeal to biblical warrants which
support a stance chosen before coming to the Bible.[113] Even the
appeal to context may provide only a rationalization for using
the OT to justify a predetermined stance without examining the
possibility that the OT points in other directions—in other
words, it may function ideologically.

It needs to take account, for instance, of the fact that
some of these modes of being are of more lasting significance
than others. Contrary to common popular assumption, Israel
was not always a nation; still less was Israel always an institutional state. On the other hand, Israel always remained a collection of families, a people, and Israel was from the beginning
a קהל that gathered together for worship, judgment, and war
(e.g., Exod 32:1—the verb; Judg 20:1-2; 1 Sam 17:47). Israel's
history cannot be portrayed as a simple development from
clan to state to religious community,[114] nor in the reverse direction from a community with a distinctive ideology via a

---

[113]E.g., Congar appropriates the model of the institutional state presupposed by Deut 17-18 in justifying the church's possessing a priesthood,
despite accepting that the whole church is God's priesthood—for Israel
possessed kingship and priesthood even though seeing the whole people as
a kingly priesthood (Exod 19:5-6) (*Concilium* 1 / 1:12). Vincent shows how
diversity in the NT view of the church similarly enables different Christian
groups to appeal to different NT images of the church (*Study Encounter*,
SE 55).

[114]So Causse, *Du groupe ethnique à la communauté religieuse*; cf.
Watts, *ExpT* 67:233.

state to a society that now emphasized kinship bonds.[115] Israel was always a community of faith, though always also an ethnic one.[116]

Further, while various contexts enable certain aspects of what it means to be the people of God to find expression, they also impose limits on what can find expression there. Living with the tension between vision and reality is both the strength of the postexilic community and also its limitation. Historical practicalities determine what aspects of "being the people of God" emerge in this context.

Indeed, this is true of any context. Israel finds itself at different points a clan, a nation, an institutional state, a defeated remnant. Each of these experiences has corollaries for what it means to live as the people of God—being unsettled, involving oneself in politics and war-making, taking on the structures of statehood, beginning to be scattered over the known world. It cannot be simply assumed that any of these are intrinsic to being the people of God; they may simply be the chance results of historical particularities, part of the context in which Israel had to discover what it means to be the people of God and not part of the meaning itself.[117] We need to look not only at the historical accidents of the form of the people of God, the ways in which they could not help following the drift of history, but at the way they modified the trajectory.

By implication, then, the people of God cannot take it for granted that each of these models of what it means to be the people of God is equally available for appropriation. Although God says yes to each of them, at each point his activity with and through his people necessarily means he involves himself with them where they are; he does not thereby designate that place as an ideal one. Although he then takes them some way along a

---

[115]So Mendenhall, *Tenth Generation;* idem, *Magnalia Dei,* 132-51; Gottwald, *Tribes of Yahweh,* 235-341; cf. p. 60 and 79 above.

[116]Cf. Vriezen, *Outline,* 346. Thus Bossmann points out that Israelite law and custom always opposed intermarriage, though for changing reasons (*BTB* 9:32-38, following L. M. Epstein, *Marriage Laws);* while the importance of kinship in the Bible is further reflected in its interest in genealogies, which are used for a variety of theological purposes (e.g., in Chronicles-Ezra-Nehemiah and in the Gospels) (see M. D. Johnson, *Purpose of the Biblical Genealogies,* esp. 77-82). An awareness of or a claim to close relationship found its "natural" explanation in kinship terms. Further, it is the family, not the city or the temple, which is traced back to creation (Vriezen, *Outline,* 371-72).

[117]Craigie emphasizes this point in his study of *The Problem of War in the OT* (see also idem, *SJT* 22:183-88).

road, this does not mean that they have thereby arrived. His purpose and his vision for his people has to interact with the intransigent realities of the situation and the flaws in the raw material he has to deal with. His yes to war, kingship, urbanization, cult, apocalyptic, and early catholicism may thus be a qualified one. His grace in the story of his people manifests itself not least in his staying with them out of his willingness to adapt his will to historical and human realities—yet without abandoning his ultimate will and vision.

So "when is Israel really Israel?"[118] Hardly at the very beginning of the story, in the patriarchal period, despite the far-reaching significance of both the emphasis on kinship and that on promise. The OT itself recognizes this period as prehistory, as the time of the ancestors; Israel in the strict sense is not yet even present.

John Macquarrie suggests that the trajectory reaches its high point at the end. On his view, the postexilic community's self-understanding is the noblest and clearest, recognizing as it does that peoplehood is based on faith and is not bound to any natural community, nation, or political institution.[119] But this perspective oversimplifies the postexilic community's self-understanding, under the influence of a churchly perspective which prefers to regard nationhood and land as accidental rather than intrinsic to the being of the people of God. Whether or not this view does justice to the NT, it makes an inadequate starting point for the dynamic of the OT's own perspective on "when is Israel really Israel?"

Nor is Israel really Israel at the center of the story, in the period of the monarchy, for the story makes quite explicit that the trappings of state are at best ambivalent in significance, that the dynamic of God's dealings with Israel during this period resides in the prophets, not in the official institutions of state, and that the exile constitutes an eventual negative judgment on the period of being a state like other states.

The modern State of Israel has found its model and support for its self-understanding and stance in political affairs in the exodus from bondage among the nations and the confident aggressiveness of the conquest of the promised land.[120] For liberation

---

118Gunneweg, Understanding the OT, 172.

119Faith and the People of God, 25. Cf. Saggs's reasons for preferring the patriarchal God to the exodus God (see n. 20 above).

120Cf. Grollenberg, Palestine Comes First, 130-31.

theology, too, the exodus was the paradigm experience of Israel which the church sought to experience for itself.[121] It will hardly do, however, to reassert the triumphalism of the theocracy as if it had not collapsed into the disorder of the judges period and, via the monarchy, into exile. If we will not learn from history, we are condemned to repeating it. A central question for modern Judaism has to be the relationship of the humiliation of the holocaust and the triumphs of the State.

Precisely because being cut down to size by exile was God's act of judgment, Israel is admittedly not really Israel when it is the afflicted remnant. Increase, not decimation, was Israel's destiny (Gen 12:1-3). Yet in certain respects God's people "found themselves" in exile, and the vision of the afflicted servant has often provided Israel with the model that has most meaningfully interpreted their position in the world to themselves, even if (as we noted above) after Auschwitz the Jews have shown signs of declaring that enough is enough.

Similarly, Latin American Christians cannot be expected to accept that humiliation and oppression are their lot for ever. Yet they, too, need a theology of exile.[122] In the light of the experience and the achievement of Jesus, the vision of the afflicted servant has also often seemed to Christians the point of deepest insight and moment in the Hebrew Bible. Thus, whether or not the question of the relationship between humiliation and triumph is raised for the church by its present experience, it is raised by the church's origins: both the experience of Jesus and that of his apostle to the gentiles (see esp. 2 Cor 4) open up the question of the relationship between suffering and death on one hand, resurrection and gift of the Spirit on the other. Either a Jew or a Christian might be in danger of imposing this question on the OT if it were not there; but it is there, in the issue raised by the relationship of Israel's two paradigm experiences, exodus and exile.

So the trajectory traced by the motif of the people of God reaches its first high point with the theocratic nation, but (to allegorize) blows a fuse at this point which ultimately requires a massive mid-course correction with the afflicted servant.

While it will not do to ricochet back from the exile to the

---

[121]The exodus is "the original principle on which the whole biblical concept of God and faith is based" (Assmann, *Practical Theology of Liberation*, 35).

[122]Cf. Yoder, *Missionalia* 2:29-41; Dumas, *Political Theology*, 87-106. See further chap. 6, n. 91 below.

exodus as if intervening history had not taken place, neither can we regard exile as the people of God's ultimate destiny. The midcourse correction does not go back on the fundamental insight of the theocratic nation; this is reasserted in the exile. It does, however, suggest a radical reformulation of what is involved in being the theocratic nation. So we discover what it really means to be Israel when the vision of the theocratic nation and the vision of the afflicted servant come together in the exile.

The two do so, in particular, in Isa 40–55, though not in such a way as to make the relationship between them completely clear. Indeed, as these chapters unfold, both visions come into increasingly sharp focus, but the relationship between them becomes less and less clear. Yahweh makes bare his arm before the nations in the triumphant restoration of the suffering exiles and in the suffering and triumphant restoration of his servant (52:10; 53:1); but these two very different manifestations of his might are juxtaposed without being brought into relationship with each other. It is when the two come together, however, that Israel is really Israel. It is from this vantage point that the OT material on the people of God can most satisfactorily be perceived as a whole. What precedes, leads here; what follows, leads from here without exactly taking us further—until (if we see the continuation of the story of Israel in the NT) Jesus brings glory and humiliation together in his own person and passes on this vision to his followers.

The people of God, then, are called to follow God's lead wherever it takes them, expectant of being led into their inheritance, yet also obliged to accept that their calling takes them via affliction and death. The church is the community led by the Holy Spirit in the way of the crucified one. Neither aspect of this calling comes naturally, and neither has the church found easy to accept; a fortiori, to hold them together is more difficult. Often the church, like Israel, has only been able to fulfill some less demanding calling, but God's way of relating to Israel shows that, even so, he will not abandon them. If the church's situation most resembles that of the postexilic community and the church can only subsist as (for instance) a cult community, the acceptance of the cult community in OT times and the presence of Chronicles in the canon indicate that God will not cast it off. It may not fulfill his highest will, and triumph, but it may at least survive.

Nevertheless, theocracy tempered by the call of the servant remains the calling.

Part II

AN EVALUATIVE OR CRITICAL APPROACH

Chapter 4

CAN WE AFFIRM SOME VIEWPOINTS AND CRITICIZE OTHERS?

In chapters 2 and 3 we have noted how different parts of the OT reflect varying levels of insight as different historical contexts allowed these to emerge. Analyzing these involved a form of critical evaluation of the material, made in the light of the shape of a trajectory as a whole. The critical evaluation we consider in chapters 4 and 5 begins from the variety in attitudes which sometimes appears within the same document, or which in some other way does not seem to reflect primarily historical factors. In chapters 2 and 3 we began from contextual diversity, and the response of formal commitment to all the diverse material in the OT which is apt accidentally to collapse into an actual commitment only to those parts of the OT that seem directly applicable to the interpreter himself, his world, and his church. This phenomenon reflects the fact that certain parts of the OT speak to me in a way that others do not. In itself this carries no implication that these other parts were never God's word; they may simply be parts that are irrelevant to me at present. I inevitably operate in practice with a "canon within the canon,"[1] an effective canon narrower than my formal one.

In this chapter we begin from a different response to the diversity of viewpoints represented in the canon. Since the Reformation and the Enlightenment it has become the common view that Christian theology can and must seek to identify within the formal canon of the OT that element which is truly normative for it. Thus G. Fohrer speaks of the need to decide which of the

---

[1]On this phrase, see pp. 122-27 below.

various human understandings of life embodied in the OT are the true ones, to discern where the OT is right and where wrong; he instances the contrast between the attitudes of Elisha and Isaiah to involvement in political insurrection, and between Ps 137:9 and Ps 46 or Isa 2 in their attitude to other peoples.[2] In what sense can we affirm some viewpoints and criticize others, and what are to be our criteria for doing so?

Interpreters have undertaken this evaluative task in a variety of ways; I have categorized these below (pp. 98-116), though no doubt they overlap at various points. Later (pp. 116-27) I relate the discussion to recent theological study of *Sachkritik* and of the canon within the canon. The view of the chapter as a whole is that an evaluative, critical approach to diversity in the OT has to seek to do justice to the OT as a whole, and not to simplify its diversity by discarding some elements of it.

EVALUATION ON THE BASIS OF THE MATERIAL'S MORAL CONCERN

Many of the early biblical critics and other thinkers of the seventeenth and eighteenth centuries were not consciously or overtly seeking to question the truth or authority of parts of the biblical canon. Thomas Hobbes, for instance, was concerned to apply scripture to life,[3] J. G. Herder to appreciate it as the inspired creation of the human spirit;[4] neither declared a concern to criticize it. Even Benedict de Spinoza claimed to attribute to scripture "as much, if not more, authority" as his correspondent William van Blyenbergh, despite the latter's willingness in the end to subordinate the findings of reason to the findings of scripture if the two conflict.[5] Overtly, Spinoza was concerned with interpreting scripture in the appropriate way—that is, in a less partial and less literalistic way than many of his contemporaries.[6] But his "impartial" study of the Bible led him to the conclusion that the

---

[2]*Theologische Grundstrukturen des AT,* 31-32.

[3]*Leviathan* (1651) (see esp. chaps. 12, 32, 33).

[4]*Spirit of Hebrew Poetry.*

[5]Spinoza, letter 21 (1665) (*Correspondence,* 179), in reply to letter 20 from van Blyenbergh (*Correspondence,* 152).

[6]See his criticism of eisegesis in his Preface to *Treatise* (1670) (*Works,* 1:7-8), and his discussion of the parabolic aspect to scriptural language in letter 21 (*Correspondence,* 180).

authority of the prophets' teaching "has weight only in matters of morality, and that their speculative doctrines affect us little. . . . The Word of God has not been revealed as a certain number of books, but was displayed to the prophets as a simple idea of the Divine mind, namely, obedience to God in singleness of heart, and in the practice of justice and charity. . . . Revelation has obedience for its sole object."[7] Spinoza's concern was the general moral improvement of humanity, and this was also (he believed) the real concern of the Bible. Thus his *Tractatus Theologico-Politicus* has been described as "the first attempt at biblical theology, that is, as the process of winnowing out of Scripture what is of enduring worth from what can be dismissed as irrelevant," by a "philosophically determined" process.[8]

There are links between Spinoza and J. S. Semler, though Semler was more directly concerned with biblical study than was Spinoza. Semler's *Abhandlung von freier Untersuchung des Canon* (1771-75) also insists on the distinction between the canon of holy scripture (a collection of books determined historically by the church), and the actual word of God. The former can (and must) be "freely investigated" so that we can discover the word of God within it. Further, Semler's interest, like Spinoza's, lies in what contributes to the betterment and edification of humanity, so that he does not expect a person to approve of aspects of the scriptures which conflict with his own moral awareness just because they belong to the formal canon.[9]

Immanuel Kant, too, in his *Religion within the Limits of Reason Alone* (1793, 2nd ed. 1794), described by H. R. Niebuhr as "the most profound and illuminating of all attempts to interpret Christianity solely in ethical terms,"[10] affirms that since "the moral improvement of men constitutes the real end of all religion of reason," so "it will comprise the highest principle of all Scriptural exegesis."[11] Scriptural narrative exists only to

---

[7]Preface to *Treatise* (*Works*, 1:8-9); cf. chaps. 12–14.

[8]Sandys-Wunsch, *ZAW* 93:339.

[9]Semler, §§ 5 and 11 (Scheible ed., pp. 26-29, 46-47; partial ET in Kümmel, *The NT*, 63-64). Semler uses the word *moralisch* frequently, but Scheible (pp. 5-6), following Hirsch (*Geschichte der neuern evangelischen Theologie*, 4:48-89) notes that this word refers to the realm of mind and spirit generally (it is opposed to *physisch*), not only to the sphere of the ethical.

[10]See the cover of the Harper Torchbook edition, *Religion within the Limits of Reason Alone.*

[11]3 / 1:vi (*Religion*, Torchbook ed., 102).

encourage moral living and must always be expounded in that interest;[12] if a passage of scripture (Kant cites Ps 59:11-16 [10-15]) seems to contradict morality, Kant asks "whether morality should be expounded according to the Bible [as J. D. Michaelis remarked in connection with the passage cited][13] or whether the Bible should not rather be expounded according to morality."[14]

Kant was able to allude to Jas 2:17 to support his contention that "historical faith 'is dead, being alone'"—that is, mere creed without implications for life is pointless.[15] Such an emphasis on the fact that the Bible is designed to affect the way people live corresponds to an intrinsic concern of the OT and NT themselves, a concern that could easily be underestimated by those who stressed "faith alone" in Luther's sense or "*the* true faith" in the sense of seventeenth-century confessionalism. The Jewish exegetes who always saw haggadah as ultimately subordinate to halakah[16] and the liberation theologians who emphasize praxis and suspect ideology[17] are able to appropriate a major thrust of the OT. The very idea of scripture as canon (rule) or of the Bible as a locus of authority more naturally suggests scripture's relationship to people's behavior than to their beliefs, because behavior can more easily be made subject to rules than belief can.

On the other hand, scripture itself holds together beliefs and life, haggadah and halakah, ideology and praxis, more intrinsically than do the views to which we have just referred. Not that OT stories and creeds can be taken as really only covert statements about behavior; the relationship between the two is more subtle and more dynamic than that.[18] Our commitments do reflect our understanding of God and the world (as well as vice versa). A different set of assumptions about God and people would quite likely issue in a different set of commitments, and

---

[12]3/2 (*Religion*, Torchbook ed., 123).

[13]Kant cites Michaelis's *Moral*, 2:202.

[14]3/1:vi (*Religion*, Torchbook ed., 101).

[15]3/1:vi (*Religion*, Torchbook ed., 102).

[16]Cf. Bowker, *Targums and Rabbinic Literature*, 43, with Loewe's comments in *JTS* 21:462.

[17]See, e.g., Miranda, *Being and the Messiah*, 28: the God of the Bible "has no connection with ontology . . . ; *rather* God is identified with the ethical imperative"; cf. Gottwald, *Tribes of Yahweh*, especially 703-5.

[18]See further n. 27 in chap. 3 above.

commitments often appeal to their framework of belief when they are questioned. Writers such as Spinoza accepted this; they worked out their understanding of the world and life empirically and rationally, and their behavioral priorities related to this understanding. But one cannot accept Spinoza's claim to do justice to the Bible if one neglects the way it emphasizes both how one thinks and how one behaves, and the way one interrelates the two.

EVALUATION ON THE BASIS OF THE MATERIAL'S DEVELOPMENTAL LEVEL

In the biblical study of the past two centuries, an evolutionary approach to the development of ideas and ideals has suggested that the OT, too, should be seen as reflecting an unfolding development, the evolution of Israelite faith; the truly normative material in the OT is then that which expresses this faith at its most mature, while other material which reflects more primitive beliefs may be ignored.

Some classic expressions of this developmental or evolutionary view of the OT belong to the nineteenth and early twentieth centuries. Thus S. R. Driver declared his assumption that "progress, gradual advance from lower to higher, from the less perfect to the more perfect, is the law which is stamped upon the entire range of organic nature, as well as upon the history of the civilization and education of the human race."[19] More recent OT scholars express similar evolutionary beliefs.[20]

There are, indeed, specific aspects of biblical faith (e.g., beliefs about Satan, about messianism and eschatology generally, and about the possibility of resurrection and a positive afterlife) which reach fullest or most mature form toward the end of the OT period. Further, beliefs about God that correspond most closely to monotheism appear in the prophetic period, in Amos

---

[19]*Genesis,* 56; cf. the statements of Simpson (*Psalmists,* vi-vii) and Fosdick (*Modern Use of the Bible,* 11-12; also his *Guide to Understanding the Bible*).

[20]See, e.g., Rowley, *Re-discovery of the OT,* 11, 14; Speiser, *Genesis,* xlix; Otto, *ZAW* 84:187-203, taking up the work of M. Weber (*Ancient Judaism,* 129, 297); Shepherd, *ExpT* 92:171-74, taking up the "social evolutionism" of Kohlberg (*Cognitive Development and Epistemology,* 178), in turn based on Hobhouse's *Morals in Evolution* (1906); Eissfeldt's treatment of Jonah and Ruth, *The OT,* 405, 483 (cf. Orlinsky's comments, *Translating and Understanding the OT,* 230-32).

and Isa 40–55, while earlier material reflects beliefs of a more polytheistic appearance.

Nevertheless, an evolutionary understanding of OT faith as a whole does not satisfactorily match OT data. It has been described as a theory which is now quite passé, a mere "historical curiosity."[21] Yet even if the great "myth" of evolution is dead,[22] it refuses to lie down, as the above references illustrate. The weaknesses of developmental approaches thus still need to be pointed out.

First, the clearest alleged example of doctrinal evolution in the OT is the development from animism via polytheism and henotheism to monotheism. But it is questionable whether any of these appear in the OT. There are only the enigmatic relics of animism, while commitment to Yahweh alone is part of the essence of Israelite faith from its beginning. It is doubtful whether the explicit assertions of Isa 40–55 (themselves the result not of the development of ideas reaching a certain point, but of a particular situation provoking particular new assertions) add very much to what is implicit in statements about Yahweh's lordship in creation and history from the earliest period that we have them; indeed, "express references to monotheism are comparatively rare in the postexilic books of the OT."[23] The tension of "the one and the many in the Israelite conception of God"[24] remained through the OT period, and when monotheism came to be taken for granted, it had to be accompanied by doctrines of angels and hypostases to cope with the awareness that there was both oneness and plurality in heaven. A scheme such as the evolutionary one cannot do justice to the material, which has various ways of coping with this tension throughout Israel's history.

Second, tracing development in OT ideas often involves circular argument. Put crudely, the presence of "developed"

---

[21]Smart, *Interpretation of Scripture*, 250; cf. Westermann, *Essays on OT Hermeneutics*, 123-24; Wright, *OT against Its Environment*, 9-15. They refer to the remarks of Driver, Simpson, and Fosdick cited in n. 19; cf. also Bright, *Authority of the OT*, 120. Rowley (p. 18) rejects the idea of an "evolutionary process" at work in the OT, despite the remarks referred to in the preceding note.

[22]So C. S. Lewis, who delivers its funeral oration in *Christian Reflections*, 82-93. Eichrodt describes Fosdick's *Guide to Understanding the Bible* as the "obituary" of an approach to the Bible based on an "evolutionary historicism" (*JBL* 65:205).

[23]Ringgren, *IDBSup*, 603.

[24]The title of a monograph by A. R. Johnson.

ideas on individual religion in Ps 51 shows that the psalm cannot be earlier than the time of Jeremiah; thus the psalm witnesses to the development of individual religion in the time of Jeremiah. The expectation of an individual messiah develops from the exile; therefore material in Isa 1–39 that refers to an individual messianic-type figure is exilic or postexilic.

Third, Wellhausen assumed that J was early and P late partly because of a concept of development. But "what evolution there was, was really devolution, for it was a backward movement from the life of the green tree to the dead wood of legalism";[25] the development/evolution/progress metaphor is thus more complicated than it looks at first sight. On Wellhausen's own assumptions, not all theological maturity belongs to a later period in Israel's history, for J's achievement signified a peak in Israel's theological thinking on creation, sin, salvation, grace, history, and election at a relatively early period. Conversely, the later period marks decline as much as achievement. Although its notable achievements deserve positive theological assessment and it has generally been excessively downgraded,[26] it can plausibly be portrayed as having a certain epigonic character; it cannot as a whole be regarded as the peak of the OT's development.

Fourth, it is questionable whether the idea of gradual development, comparable to the growth of an organism, does justice to the way ideas, culture, or religion change in history. This change involves the dynamic interaction of particular human needs, challenges, and crises with the personalities of insight who can speak to these moments. There is something radically historical and occasional about the message of J to the united monarchy, that of Amos to eighth-century Israel, and that of Isa 40–55 to the exile. It is not simply that ideas had reached this stage of development.

The evidence suggests that the model of evolution, development, or progress is quite misleading if regarded as a key to discerning what is most profound or most true in the OT. There is, of course, development in the sense of change, but this development "follows a zigzag line,"[27] an up-and-down one in which

---

[25]R. J. Thompson, *Moses and the Law*, 36, paraphrasing W. L. Baxter, *Sanctuary and Sacrifice*, 102. On the romantic preference for the old, primitive, instinctive, see also Gese, *Essays*, 24.

[26]See p. 107 below.

[27]Smart, 250; cf. Ackroyd, *EvQ* 25:69-82; M. Smith, *JBL* 71:146-47.

insights are lost as well as gained. Tracing historical movement means perceiving not "development in God's revelation or manifestation, only what is now called *Lichtungsgeschichte*—a similar pattern at various successive crises in the history of Israel's religion."[28] To the extent that there is advance, it is as likely to be by the refinement or explication of earlier insights as by their transformation or replacement. Where something new emerges, it is likely to be added to the old, rather than supplanting it.[29] The OT must be interpreted historically, but this need not mean developmentally.

EVALUATION ON THE BASIS OF THE MATERIAL'S MOSAIC OR PROPHETIC SPIRIT

As we have just noted, though there were evolutionary aspects to his understanding of the development of Israelite religion, Wellhausen was very attracted by its early period, before it became affected by the restrictions of institution, law, and cult, when a "freshness and naturalness" characterized people's behavior and "the divine right did not attach to the institution but was in the Creator Spirit, in individuals."[30] The "properly creative period in Israel's history" is the time of Moses, even though the prophets "gave . . . greater distinctness to the peculiar character of the nation."[31]

Over the past century, much OT scholarship has followed Wellhausen in emphasizing the supreme significance of the Mosaic and prophetic contribution to the OT, though the tendency has been to reverse their relative significance. Thus in his explic-

---

[28]Schofield, commenting on Procksch's *Theologie* in *Contemporary OT Theologians*, 96. *Lichtungsgeschichte* seems to mean more literally a series of patches of clearing in the jungle; according to J. M. Robinson (*Later Heidegger and Theology*, 25-27; idem, *OT and Christian Faith*, 152- 53), the term comes from Heidegger.

[29]Thus Shepherd's examples (see n. 20 above) show that "earlier" moral "stages" persist throughout the OT (and into the NT), while the attitude expressed by the latest stages is actually already present in very early material; his typology may be valid, but the "stages" seem more concurrent than consecutive. Similarly Weber is aware that more rational, more universalist, more transcendent features of Israel's theology, which Otto notes as more developed (see n. 20 above), were present in Israelite faith from the beginning (see Weber, 133-38).

[30]*Prolegomena*, 412.

[31]"Israel," in *Prolegomena*, 432.

itly evaluative comparison of the diverse approaches to life represented in the OT, Fohrer takes the view that the faith creatively
shaped by the experiences of the Mosaic period reaches its
highpoint in the refined form of the prophetic experience. The
inner history of Israel is the story of the struggle between their
distinctive faith with its approach to life *(Daseinshaltung)* and
those of hostile powers that embody typically human approaches to life, namely, magic and wisdom. These latter are humanity's two great ways of mastering life and finding security, and of protecting themselves from the breaking in of that more
or less known transcendent foreign power which would throw
them into shock and bewilderment. OT faith was formed in interaction with these two approaches to life, and the OT itself is the
deposit (or rather the scene) of this struggle. The magical approach appears in OT taboos and elsewhere, but also and especially in the cult and in national religion (e.g., J), which constitute attempts to control and manipulate God and history. This and the
wisdom approach effect a compromise between the distinctive Israelite vision and the ordinary human approaches to life. Only
prophecy (preexilic prophecy; the epigones begin with Isaiah of
the exile) brings to fulfillment the potential of the Mosaic faith in
the thoroughgoing rejection of these approaches and an acceptance of the paradoxical security of naked uncertainty before and
active submission to the mighty God. It is this which constitutes
the permanently significant feature of OT faith.[32]

Although Fohrer's approach is suggestive, difficulties are
involved in locating the normative feature of OT faith in this
feature of prophetic religion.

First, Fohrer does not offer evidence for the view that the
"prophetic approach to life" is the fundamental insight of OT
faith, and one wonders whether he has simply highlighted the
feature he himself finds most congenial. Nor does he offer evidence that the other approaches to life embodied in the OT are
inherently questionable. The notion of God effecting his worldwide purpose through Israel could easily degenerate into mere
national religion, but it need not do so. The notion of salvation
history needs critical handling, but one cannot dismiss it as easily as Fohrer does.[33]

---

[32]See *Theologische Grundstrukturen*, 51-94. In his discussion of diversity and unity in biblical thought, Clavier also seems to see prophecy as the
high point of OT thinking (*Les variétés de la pensée biblique*, 362-63).
[33]Ibid., 42-46; cf. idem, *History*, 275-76.

Second, the prophets, even those of the preexilic period, are not unequivocal advocates of "the prophetic approach." It is doubtful whether promises of salvation can be eliminated from the preexilic prophets to the extent that Fohrer believes;[34] the manifold positive connections discerned by scholars between the preexilic prophets and the cult on the one hand and wisdom on the other[35] set a question mark by the thesis that the prophetic approach to life is incompatible with the latter two; to describe the prophets as universalist rather than nationalist is at best an oversimplification.

Third, the converse of the fact that the prophets are not unequivocal advocates of the prophetic approach is the fact that this approach is not confined to the prophets. Job, notably, embodies a similar rejection of the idea that a person's destiny is in his control, and calls for humble submission before the power of God.

Fourth, the preexilic prophets cannot be identified as the exclusive high point of OT insight. The OT's approaches to suffering may be instanced. Jeremiah and Habakkuk wrestle with this issue, but not as profoundly as Job and Isa 40–55. The OT's concern with creation is rather marginally represented in the preexilic prophets compared with Genesis, Psalms, Isa 40–55, and Job. W. Zimmerli suggests that the high point of the prophets' significance is not reached until the exile, with the exilic prophets' emphasis in that context that we can only live before God by grace.[36]

Fohrer's method of approach to the prophets and to the OT generally is reminiscent of the one we noted in Spinoza. The aspect of the OT and of the prophetic books of which he takes serious notice (in Fohrer's case, their receiving of a personal revelation which urges them to a personal commitment) is the approach to life which the interpreter himself already valued. Thus N. K. Gottwald accuses Fohrer of reading into the OT his own existentialist, personalistic idealism and finding there only the "sensitivities and value judgments which other cultured bourgeois thinkers reach without any appeal to the Bible."[37]

---

[34]See *History*, 272; cf., e.g., his comments on Isaiah in (Sellin and) Fohrer, *Introduction*, 370-71.

[35]See the critical discussions in, e.g., Rowley, *Worship*, 144-75; Clements, *Prophecy and Tradition*, 73-83; and their references.

[36]See VTSup 23:48-64.

[37]JBL 93:594-96.

Gottwald's own personal commitments lie elsewhere. On the basis of a Marxist approach to the OT material, in *The Tribes of Yahweh* he relocates the authentic revolutionary Israelite faith (or rather praxis) in that of Mosaic Yahwism. His emphasis on this early period corresponds to the stress which much of the OT itself places on it, as is reflected in the emphasis traditionally given in the study of OT religion and theology to Moses, the exodus, and the covenant. But Gottwald himself has more than once noted the danger of emphasizing preexilic religion and theology at the expense of postexilic; "early Judaism" is part of the OT, and it cannot simply be ignored.[38] Further, Gottwald's presentation of Israel's earliest period rather idealizes it, resolving likely ambiguities; it also underestimates the positive significance of the monarchic period.[39] The Mosaic or prophetic contribution to OT faith can no more be seen as *the* high point of it than can any other individual contribution.

EVALUATION ON THE BASIS OF A COMPARISON WITH NEW TESTAMENT CONCERNS

A developmental understanding of the growth of OT faith is often accompanied and aided by the assumption natural to Christian interpreters of the OT that the person and teaching of Christ himself provide the criterion for distinguishing between material which may be affirmed and material which must be abandoned. Thus T. C. Vriezen speaks of submitting scripture to the judgment of the preaching of Jesus Christ, judging the message of the OT in the light of the message of the NT, while F. Baumgärtel sees the Christian as considering the OT's self-understanding, its piety, and its religion in the light of Christ to see where in actual fact (as opposed to where the OT writers thought) God was relating to his people in judgment and salvation.[40]

---

[38] *ExpT* 74:212; idem, *Contemporary OT Theologians,* 48, 56; cf. Barr, *RTP* 3/18:209-17; idem, *Judaism,* 12-13; Ackroyd, *Exile and Restoration,* 1-7; Steck, *EvT* 28:449.

[39] Cf. the reviews by Buss and Lenski in *RelSR* 6:274, 276, and by Mayes in *JTS* 32:476, 482-83; also Brueggemann's analysis of the Davidic and Mosaic "trajectories," especially in *Israelite Wisdom,* 86-87.

[40] See Vriezen, *Outline,* 122, 149; also 88-90, 111-13; cf. Bright, *Authority of the OT,* 200, 211-12. (On pp. 95-109 Bright rejects the view that the OT is to be judged in the light of the NT, but here he seems to reappropriate it.) For Baumgärtel's view see *TLZ* 76:262 and elsewhere, especially his *Verheissung.*

Faith in Jesus of Nazareth as Lord and Christ carries bound up with it the assumption that his teaching provides the supreme key to understanding God and his relationship to the world. Things that were ambivalent or ambiguous in the OT become clear and sharply focused in the light of the Christ event.[41] Things that perhaps seemed quite clear turn out to be only partial insights when they are seen in the light of Christ's incarnation, cross, and resurrection.[42] Thus the NT's own criterion for deciding which aspects of the Hebrew Bible to take up is the person and work of Jesus. It is material which illuminates his significance that the NT finds valuable. Jesus himself sometimes offers explicitly negative assessments of material within the Hebrew Bible, rejecting aspects of OT law, moral, religious, and social (e.g., Matt 5:38-39; 15:1-20; 19:3-12; and parallels).

At the same time, however, Jesus and the NT writers share the assumption common to contemporary Jews of all persuasions that the Hebrew Bible is the word of God. For them to assume that certain parts were more important than others implied a relative judgment on the latter, but not an absolute one that effectively decanonized it. This is even true about the attitude that Jesus took to the Torah. By issuing more rigorous moral demands than those of some laws, Jesus does not abrogate these laws (as if the punishment need now no longer fit the crime, or as if adultery were now permitted); rather he indicates that they do not go far enough. By "declaring all foods clean" (Mark 7:19) he does abrogate many OT laws, though this need not imply denying that they had had their rightful place in the law before, and it was not taken to imply that OT cultic law no longer functioned as scripture (the NT writers utilize such law for theological purposes, even though they see its legal function as over; it is still the word of God, even if it is no longer the com-

---

[41]Cf. Ebeling, *Study of Theology*, 33-35; Vriezen, 87, 100; Mowinckel, *OT as Word of God*, 56-59; Kaufman, *Int* 25:106-7; G. W. Anderson, *Peake*, 167; Wagner, *TLZ* 103:797.

[42]See, e.g., Kraus, *Psalmen*, 1:21-22, 329, 337-38, on the revolution brought by the cross to one's understanding of the glory of the king of Israel (cf. Dietrich, *ZTK* 77:267-68); Gunneweg, *Understanding the OT*, 230-31, on the new approach to the this-worldly saving gifts of the OT necessitated and facilitated by the NT understanding of salvation; Vriezen, 98, on the need to confront OT understandings of theocracy or erotics and marriage with the cross.

mand of God). By connecting the divorce law with people's hardness of hearts (Matt 19:8), Jesus indicates that God does not approve of divorce, but he hardly implies that (given the fact of
marriage breakdown) Moses was wrong to provide Israel with
regulations to give order to divorce when it happens. Nor does
he here indicate that he himself brings a new standard. On the
contrary, his concern is to reassert the ultimate standard taught
by the Torah itself.[43]

It is even less likely that the NT writers assume that they
are in a position to decide which parts of the OT are to be regarded as the word of God and which are not. If anything the
question had to be posed the other way: the issue was not
"whether the Old Testament was Christian" but "whether the
NT was biblical."[44]

So the NT as a whole presupposes the theological and
moral foundation laid by the OT, and concentrates on saying
what now needs to be said in the light of the Christ event,
which it sees as the climax of the OT story. It implies that we
must interpret the OT in the light of the coming of Christ, but
also that we must see the Christ event against the background
of the OT's broader concerns. Differences between OT and
NT which indicate that the latter is emphasizing matters that
it regarded as especially important may have various implications. Sometimes they provide Christians with a way in to understanding the OT, but point them toward broadening that
preunderstanding when they discover the wider range of material contained by the OT (rather than confining themselves
to accepting only what conforms to what they already know).[45]
Sometimes they provide the Christian with a definitive
slant on how to read the OT, resolving ambiguities or setting
statements in a broader context. Sometimes they bring out the

---

[43]On Jesus' discussion of divorce, see Westerholm, *Jesus and Scribal
Authority*, 123-25; von Campenhausen understands the reference to "hardness of hearts" differently, though this does not affect his overall view of
the passage (*Formation of the Christian Bible*, 8-9).

[44]J. A. Sanders, *Magnalia Dei*, 552; cf. idem, *JR* 39:233-35; Freedman, *TToday* 21:227-28; Wildberger, *EvT* 19:80-83; and the reaction of
van Ruler, who speaks of the OT as the real Bible, the NT as its explanatory
glossary (*Christian Church and the OT*, 72, 74).

[45]Thus, while faith in Christ helps us to understand the OT, the OT also
helps us to understand Christ. Cf. the comments of Kraus, *Biblische
Theologie*, 320-21; Wildberger, 73-80; Mays, *Magnalia Dei*, 512-13; Barr,
Old and New, 139-40; Grech, *NTS* 19:318-24; *BTB* 5:127-45.

relatively lower standard of material written in the light of people's sin and stubbornness. But they do not suggest that we serve either the OT or the NT by attempting to use the latter as the criterion for deciding which elements in the former we find acceptable.

In the precritical period the NT often functioned as a covert norm in relation to the OT, by determining how the OT was understood; while possessing the form of canonical authority, the OT thus lost much of the reality. Medieval allegorism provides one example of this process, Protestant confessionalism another; both show how the norm is actually not the NT itself but the NT as interpreted within a later theological scheme. In the modern period (when scholars sought to interpret the OT on its own terms, which are by definition pre-Christian, and thus exposed the differences between OT and NT), the NT became no longer a norm of interpretation, but instead an overt norm of evaluation—so that the OT lost even the form of canonical authority.[46]

Even the NT, however, is usually reckoned to contain material that falls shorts of an absolute standard. J. D. G. Dunn suggests that the norm for evaluating the OT is the NT less "passages which remained within the limitations of the old covenant in the light of the overall NT witness to Christ," such as 1 Cor 11.[47] Thus the line between absolute and more relative material cannot be identified with the division between OT and NT; it lies somewhere within the latter.

Jesus' approach to the divorce question, however, suggests that it also passes through the OT. Indeed, the understanding of man and woman's unity and equality by creation in Gen 1–2 could well function as a critical norm in relation to subordinationist aspects of the NT's perspective on man and woman which Dunn notes. The norm for evaluating OT and NT, then, is the biblical witness as a whole in its most demanding form. Christ may be the key to perceiving that witness in the right way; but it is *its* witness to which he draws attention. He helps us to perceive how to interpret it; he cannot impose on it an interpretation that it resists.

---

[46]Cf. Ebeling, *Study of Theology*, 30.
[47]*Churchman* 96:225.

EVALUATION OF THE MATERIAL ON ITS OWN TERMS

We noted above that precritical biblical study practiced a form of covert theological criticism of the OT by means of allegorizing or by interpreting it in the light of confessional statements; the text's own assertions were thereby avoided. An equivalent postcritical maneuver is to regard parts of scripture which we find theologically questionable as witnesses to human sinfulness which point us to Christ in a negative way.[48] Now such maneuvers at least seek to come to some positive interpretation of the material (they differ on how the positive interpretation is to be offered when the material seems resistant to it). Indeed, strictly any attempt to interpret "the Old Testament" (as opposed to interpreting pre-Christian Jewish religious literature) implies a confessional stance in relation to it.[49]

The problem is that their interpretation of this material contrasts with that intrinsic to the material itself (and that which—as far as we can tell—led to its finding a place in the canon). Indeed, generally the preceding critique of approaches to the OT which evaluate material on the basis of its moral concern, its developmental level, its Mosaic or prophetic spirit, or its Christian connections, presupposes the assumption that the OT itself ought to be allowed to determine what is central to its faith and what is peripheral.[50]

Now admittedly there is a tension here. In chapter 6 we shall argue that the task of writing OT theology is inevitably not merely a reconstructive task but a constructive one. We are not merely reformulating the faith explicitly expressed or implicitly presupposed by a believing community of OT times, in order to understand OT faith for its own sake, but formulating the theological implications of that faith in a way that brings them home to us as members of a believing community in our own time.

---

[48]See Mowinckel's treatment of Esther in *OT as the Word of God*, 109-10; Baumgärtel's approach to the OT's (mis)understanding of God's promise, in *Verheissung*, 27, 64-66 (cf. Hesse, *Essays on OT Hermeneutics*, 299-313); and the common understanding of Ecclesiastes as pointing us to Christ in a negative way, by its doubts (e.g., Lauha, *Kohelet*, v, 24, 37, 60); see also more generally Porteous, *ExpT* 75:72.

[49]Cf. Barstad, *SEA* 45:16-17.

[50]Cf. the "Report of the Dutch-German Group" (Smend, Dinkler, Flesseman-van Leer, and others) in the WCC *Study on the Authority of the Bible*, 1—with a recognition of the difficulty of the enterprise.

Nevertheless, when we seek to understand OT faith, we really are seeking to allow that faith itself to have its impact on us. Our aim is not merely to use it as a mirror or aid to reflection which will enable us to express what we believe already, ignoring the meaning of the material for writers and readers of OT times. Nor is our aim merely to utilize it as a resource from which we choose material that deals with questions we are already asking in ways that immediately strike us as helpful, ignoring other traits of the work and priorities of importance that may be intrinsic to the material itself as a whole. Sometimes our study does involve these two features; they are not in themselves wrong, are probably inevitable features of any process of understanding, and may be our way into a fuller understanding of something or someone. My presupposition here, however, is that this fuller understanding (of the OT or of anything else) ultimately involves the attempt to do justice to the material as a whole, understood and evaluated on the basis of interconnections and priorities suggested by the material itself.

Interpreters themselves often explicitly accept this, and their (generally unconscious) utilization of some principle from outside the OT sits in uneasy juxtaposition with their attempt to identify some focal point within the OT itself, such as the theme of communion between God and humanity (Vriezen), or, alongside that, the concept of the rule of God (Fohrer).[51]

Other scholars offer a wide range of suggestions regarding a focal point which provides us with a principle for interpreting the OT as a whole. Indeed, the location of the center of the OT has been discussed so extensively that R. Smend has been able to fill a small book with opinions on the matter.[52] Nevertheless, these can be categorized fairly clearly. Some locate the OT's theological center in some aspect of God himself: God as the holy one, God as the Lord, God revealing himself, God as the sole deity to be acknowledged, God's involvement in history, God's name, God's presence, God's promise, God's reign.[53] It is sim-

---

[51]See Vriezen, *Outline*; Fohrer, *Grundstrukturen*.

[52]*Die Mitte des AT*; cf. Hasel, *OT Theology: Basic Issues*, (3rd ed.) 77-103; idem, *ZAW* 86:65-82.

[53]So, respectively, Sellin, *Theologie*, 2:19; Köhler, *Theology*, 30-35; Reventlow, *TZ* 17:96-98 (but in *KD* 20:211-17, Reventlow stresses Yahweh's claim to exclusive acknowledgment); Schmidt, *Erste Gebot*, 10-11; von Rad, *Theology*, 1:105-28; Zimmerli, *Outline*, 13; cf. idem, *EvT* 35:102-17; Terrien, *Elusive Presence*; Baumgärtel, e.g., *Verheissung*; Seebass, *WD* 8:30-47.

plest to say straightforwardly that God is the center of the OT,[54] though this may seem a truism which is only the beginning of the real discussion.[55] The major alternative to the view that God is in some way the center of the OT is the suggestion that God's relationship with Israel should be the focus of our examination of OT faith. This view is instanced by those who emphasize God's covenant with Israel, his election of Israel, the speaking and responding of "I am Yahweh," "You are Yahweh," or the mutuality of Yahweh as Israel's God and Israel as Yahweh's people,[56] as well as by the approaches of Vriezen and Fohrer just noted.

An alternative approach to identifying a structure intrinsic to the OT itself is to consider the implications of the way the canon is formally structured. Traditional Jewish thinking analyzes the canon as the Torah, the Prophets, and the Writings. These may be understood as concentric circles, the Torah at the center, the Writings on the periphery: only the Torah and the Prophets feature in the weekly lectionary, and the Prophets are essentially preachers of Torah. Although the Pentateuch has a narrative structure, it is dominated by instruction material; it is thus not inappropriate if the key influence of Deuteronomy as Torah has led to seeing the Pentateuch as a whole in this way. Similarly, although there is a more radical side to prophecy, the "Former Prophets" themselves present the prophets as preachers of repentance who called Israel back to the teaching of Moses.[57]

J. A. Sanders, however, emphasizes how significant was the reshaping of the opening books of the OT in the postexilic period, which sought to give especial emphasis and authority to the Torah as the basis for the life of Judaism.[58] Although this made hermeneutical sense, it involved dividing the continuous story from creation to the exile, and made both the Pentateuch and the so-called Former Prophets into torsos. J. Blenkinsopp offers an-

---

[54]See Hasel, 99-103, with references to other works.

[55]Cf. von Rad, *Theology*, 2:362-63, 415; Wagner, TLZ 103:791-92; also (regarding the NT), Koester, *Future of Our Religious Past*, 72.

[56]So, respectively, Eichrodt, *Theology*, 1; Wildberger, *EvT* 19:77-78; Zimmerli, *Probleme biblischer Theologie*, 638-45; Smend, *Die Mitte des AT*, 48-56, following Wellhausen (and for this view see also Jacob, *Theologie* [2nd ed.], xii; Clements, *OT Theology*, 53-103).

[57]So Clements, *OT Theology*, 104-30; idem, *Creation, Christ and Culture*, 1-12.

[58]*Torah and Canon.*

other understanding of the relationship between Torah and Prophets. Torah stands for normative order, needed to undergird the community's life; prophecy exists to ensure that the normative order is free to change rather than bound to freeze in a form that is appropriate only to circumstances now past, yet is prevented from change which merely assimilates to the pattern of a new set of circumstances. Torah becomes canon only after it has allowed itself to take account of the prophetic perspective; prophecy becomes canon alongside Torah, but the price of this status is its independence. The juxtaposition of law and prophecy in the canon as a whole suggests "an unresolved tension, an unstable equilibrium between rational order and the unpredictable and disruptive, between the claims of the past and those of the present and future."[59]

Other scholars have sought to identify further significance in the threefold structure of the canon as a whole, seeing the three divisions as referring to past, future, and present, or as relating God's deeds, God's words, and humanity's response,[60] but neither of these understandings quite corresponds to the content of these divisions. On either understanding, Chronicles, for instance, belongs with Kings in the first section. In fact, the basis for these divisions more likely lies in historical and/or liturgical considerations (the Writings are the books which became canonical last and/or the ones which were not used in the weekly lectionary) than in questions of content or even of relative authority.

It is easier to see a structure based on form or content in the canonical arrangement which appears in English Bibles, which may be viewed as narrative (or narrative/law)—poetry—prophecy, or as past—present—future. This order, which has come down to us via the Septuagint, has often been assumed to be secondary to the Hebrew one, but P. Katz argues that it is as old as the Hebrew order, which artificially divides Joshua-Kings from Genesis-Deuteronomy, separates Daniel from the prophets, and places Chronicles after Ezra-Nehemiah, while J. C. Lebram believes that the oldest approach to the canon, identified on the basis of hints in Ben Sira, emphasizes its prophetic as-

---

[59]*Prophecy and Canon*, 151.
[60]See, e.g., Wolff, *The OT*; Westermann, *What Does the OT Say about God?* Cf. Jacob's identification of a threefold rhythm of the word of God, as law, prophecy, and wisdom (VTSup 28:120).

pect, as testimony to the work of God's spirit in the history of Israel; Torah is linked to prophecy from the beginning in the canon's history, and the law-centered understanding of the canon is only introduced by Ben Sira himself.[61] Such theories at least indicate that differences in approach to the structure of the canon do not necessarily indicate that the whole enterprise of canonical criticism is a subjective one; the extant canons reflect a variety of historical shapings.

Nevertheless, even if one grants that ideally our interpretation and evaluation of the diversity in the OT should reflect its own intrinsic dynamic, so that data from within the OT itself function as a check on our views regarding what is central to OT faith and what is peripheral, the trouble is that the search for a right principle of organization for writing OT theology has been not so much fruitless as overfruitful; and all the principles that have been proposed are more or less illuminating when applied to the OT material itself. If, however, we have not yet discovered the single correct key to producing a satisfactory final synthesis of OT faith, this suggests that there is no such key. Understanding the OT resembles understanding a battle or a person or a landscape more than understanding the layout of an architect-planned new town.[62] We can appreciate a landscape by starting from its roads, its contours, or its water supplies, or by taking as its center a hill or a church or an inn or a bus stop, and each perspective will lead us to a different aspect of its understanding. Similarly, many starting points, structures, and foci can illuminate the landscape of the OT; a multiplicity of approaches will lead to a multiplicity of insights.[63] The possibility of a variety of approaches to appreciating and expressing the thought of the OT does not render impossibly subjective the task of understanding the OT in a way faithful to

---

[61]See Katz, *ZNW* 47:191-217; Lebram, *VT* 18:173-89.

[62]For these similes, see McKenzie, *Theology of the OT,* 20-27, 324-25; Barr, *JTS* 25:272; idem, *Scope and Authority,* 115; Fohrer, *Grundstrukturen,* 54-55.

[63]Kermode (*Genesis of Secrecy,* 16, 147; also 136-37) observes that interpreters may similarly illuminate a literary work by focusing on several different "impression points" (*Eindruckspunkt:* Kermode refers to Dilthey, apparently to *Gesammelte Schriften,* 5:281-82, where Dilthey speaks of a work developing from a *Mittelpunkt* into a world of its own, and of understanding a person by beginning from an *Eindruckspunkt* or point of contact); cf. Müller-*Towards a Phenomenological Theory of Literature,* 151-55.

its own dynamic. The aim of a critical, evaluative approach to interpreting the OT will then be to sense what norms of critical evaluation are suggested by the OT material itself, as we seek to appreciate it in its own terms.

SACHKRITIK

In modern German study, the kind of theological commentary and evaluation of biblical material we are considering in this chapter is often referred to as *Sachkritik*, a term which came into prominence with the Barth-Bultmann debates of the 1920s.[64] In his Preface to the second edition of his commentary on Romans, Barth declares that "true apprehension can be achieved only by a strict determination to face, as far as possible without rigidity of mind, the tension displayed more or less clearly in the ideas written in the text. Criticism (κρίνειν) applied to historical documents means for me the measuring of words and phrases by the standard of that about which the documents are speaking. . . . Everything in the text ought to be interpreted only in the light of what can be said, and therefore only in the light of what is said. . . . The Word ought to be exposed in the words."[65] Barth here implies that the reality of which the words speak is greater than the words; the latter inevitably fall short of the former, just because they are human words. Here dialectical theology follows a tradition represented by Chrysostom, Augustine, and Calvin. Barth himself later quotes Augustine's homily on John 1:1: "For to speak of the matter as it is, who is able? I venture to say, my brethren, perhaps not John himself spoke of the matter as it is, but even he only as he was able; for it was man that spoke of God, inspired indeed by God, but still man. Because he was inspired he said something; but because a man inspired, he spoke not the whole, but what man could he spoke."[66] The words may be the

---

[64]According to R. Morgan (*Nature of NT Theology*, 175), the term goes back at least to I. A. Dorner's *History of Protestant Theology*, 2:186.

[65]*Romans*, 8.

[66]PL 35:1379-80 (ET, NPNF 1/7:7); cf. Barth, *Dogmatics*, 1/2:508). Chrysostom speaks of "condescension" (συγκατάβασις-συγκάτειμι): see, e.g., his homilies on Tit 1:12-14 and Heb 6:13-16 (*PG*, 62:678; 63:91 [ET, NPNF, 1/13:528-29; 14:419]); cf. Vawter, *Biblical Inspiration*, 40-42. Calvin speaks of God "accommodating" (*accommodare/attemperare*): see *Institutes* 1.14.3; 1.17.13; 2.11.13; 2.16.2; commentaries on Gen 2:8; 1 Cor 2:7; cf. Battles, *Int* 31:19-38. See further Rogers and McKim, *Authority and Interpretation*, passim.

best that could be; the reality to which they refer is nevertheless much bigger than they are. The biblical writers are involved in "saying the unsayable," so that even they cannot escape the problem of "the relativity of the word."[67]

To allow this point is in principle to admit the propriety of *Sachkritik*, critical study of the actual theological contents or message of scripture. Barth and Bultmann agree, however, that Barth does not practice *Sachkritik* in the sense that the term has actually possessed in biblical study. Barth says that one must measure the text by the subject matter; but (so Bultmann complains in his review)[68] he does not actually do this. He writes his commentary as if the biblical writer always gave adequate expression to the subject matter, and Bultmann suspects here a revival of some dogma of inspiration.

Barth has both a theoretical and a practical response to this observation. The theoretical one appears in the *Romans* prefaces: it is that if you are trying to interpret someone, it is appropriate to assume that he is talking sense; this principle applies to books both inside and outside the Bible, and, indeed, may sometimes raise more problems when applied to the former than when applied to the latter.[69] Elsewhere, in keeping with the approach stated here, Barth refuses any a priori doctrine of scriptural inerrancy, though he claims no right to pronounce on where scripture has erred: "from what standpoint can we make any such pronouncement?"[70]

As far as Bultmann is concerned, practicing *Sachkritik* does not imply that "the text is criticized from the standpoint of

---

[67]So Bultmann, reviewing Barth's *Römerbrief* in *Beginnings of Dialectic Theology*, 120.

[68]Bultmann, 119-20. Morgan (*Nature of NT Theology*, 42-43) sees Barth's refusal to practice *Sachkritik* as the fundamental distinction between him and Bultmann; cf. the quotation from Dinkler at n. 81 below. The encounter between Barth and Bultmann has recently been reenacted by Stuhlmacher and Grässer in ZTK 77:200-238.

[69]*Romans*, 11-12; cf. later, in response to Bultmann's review, 16-19. Kermode speaks in similar terms of Austin Farrer's attempts to trace the "narrative coherence" of Mark, contemplating "the apparently flawed surface of Mark's narrative" until seeming "fractures of the surface became parts of an elaborate design" (*Genesis of Secrecy*, 62, referring to Farrer, *Study in St. Mark* and *St. Matthew and St. Mark*). Kermode compares such an approach to biblical narrative with ones to extrabiblical literary works (see his chap. 3 as a whole).

[70]*Dogmatics*, 1/2:510.

modern consciousness,"[71] but that it is criticized in the light of that to which it refers. After all, the way a writer expresses his vision of that reality is affected by various factors apart from the inevitable relativity of all words, which make it likely that his words will need criticism in the light of the nature of the reality itself. One factor is his own fallibility; he will not see everything equally clearly. A second is his historicity; he inevitably formulates his views by means of contemporary forms of thought and language (including ones that belong to a prefaith way of looking at reality) and these forms may only facilitate a rather "primitive or crude" approximation to reality. A third is the contextuality of his audience; he formulates his views in the light of the forms used by those to whom he has to communicate, and this may introduce not only further "primitive or crude" approximations, but also tensions and contradictions with ways he expresses himself elsewhere.[72] Thus, Bultmann suggests, one cannot forgo the use of *Sachkritik*, insofar as it "stems from the text itself."[73]

The actual task of *Sachkritik* may proceed on any of several bases. It may involve criticizing the statements in a document on the basis of other statements in the same document,[74] or on the basis of other statements elsewhere by the same author,[75] or on the basis of statements in other documents within the canon (thus Bultmann interprets the NT documents which embody "the development toward the Ancient Church" in the light of Paul and John,[76] and Paul and John in the light of each other).[77]

But to most readers, criticizing the text from the standpoint of modern consciousness is precisely what *is* involved in Bultmann's approach to the Bible. He is offering us an understanding of the reality to which a biblical author points (in his fallible, historically conditioned way) evaluated in the light of

---

[71]*Beginnings*, 241.

[72]See Bultmann's review of Barth's *Romans* (*Beginnings*, 120); his essay on the problem of a theological exegesis of the NT (*Beginnings*, 241, 254-55); his review of Barth's *Auferstehung der Toten* (*Faith and Understanding*, 71-72, 80-81, 83-84); his essay on NT Christology (*Faith and Understanding*, 263-65, 279-84); also his *Theology*, 2:238. Cf. Barth's own remarks in *Dogmatics*, 1/2:507-12.

[73]*Faith and Understanding*, 72.

[74]Cf. Bultmann, 83-86, on 1 Cor 15:1-11.

[75]Cf. Bultmann, 93-94, criticizing Barth.

[76]*Theology*, 2:95-236. Thus he sees his *Sachkritik* as in line with Luther's approach to James and Revelation (2:238).

[77]Cf. Käsemann, *NT Questions*, 17.

the reality itself *as Bultmann perceives it* (in his fallible, historically conditioned way). As Robert Morgan puts it,[78] Bultmann's *Sachkritik* is really a theological and not merely a historical task. The historical task involves evaluating formulations in the text on the basis of other statements in the text (or even elsewhere in the canon). The interpreter is then claiming to be "true to the author (perhaps understanding him better than he understood himself)."[79] But evaluating formulations in the text on the basis of one's own grasp of the reality to which the text refers is a theological, not a merely historical, task, though one which (as Morgan sees it) is inevitable in the modern age because the alternative—that the interpreter accepts the text's statements even where he cannot see how they can be preferable to his own— is impossible. The interpreter is concerned not merely to be true to the author but also to be true to the subject (perhaps understanding *it* better than the author did). He tells us not merely what the author meant as opposed to what he said, but what he should have meant as opposed to what he actually meant.

It may be that German Protestant theologians find it difficult to allow that their criterion for identifying the *Sache* to which the Bible refers does not come from the Bible itself, and hard to make the distinction between a historical and a theological interpretative task because of their commitment to the principle of *sola scriptura*. Anglo-Saxon theologians, uninhibited by such a commitment, have been readier to suggest that "metaphysics and biblical theology, then, stand in a reciprocally constructive and critical relation to each other" or that the criteria for making crucial theological judgments may not come from the Bible at all.[80]

---

[78]*Nature of NT Theology*, 42-62; cf. Dahl, *Crucified Messiah*, 93-95; also Appel, *Kanon und Kirche*, 296-305, on a modern person's self-understanding functioning as the *criterion* for a right understanding of the NT. For the background (or a parallel) to Bultmann's thinking in Heidegger, see Achtemeier, *Introduction to the New Hermeneutic*, 47, 53-54.

[79]Morgan, 46.

[80]Janzen, *Magnalia Dei*, 485; cf. the "Report of British Working Party on Hermeneutics" (including J. Barr, C. F. Evans, E. Flesseman-van Leer, D. E. Nineham, M. F. Wiles, and others) in the WCC *Study on Biblical Hermeneutics*, 47-49, with Barr's comments, 54-55; also Flesseman-van Leer's observations on *sola scriptura* in the Evans volume *What about the NT?* 235, and Bowden's comments on Bultmann's conservatism at this point in his "Translator's Preface" to Schmithals, *Introduction to the Theology of Rudolf Bultmann*, xiv.

In discussing biblical authority and biblical criticism, Erich Dinkler suggests that Barth and Bultmann resemble each other in that both interpret scripture by utilizing insights from church history and contemporary Christian experience as well as from the ancient world; but that "for Barth the meeting of human subject and divine revelation is a heuristic principle, for Bultmann the dialectic [involved in the theological study of the contents of scripture] is a critical principle."[81] For Barth, our own meeting with God is a means of understanding scripture, for Bultmann it is a means of evaluating scripture. The same distinction can be made in OT study by comparing the work of Walter Brueggemann and that of Georg Fohrer. Brueggemann's studies of wisdom, *In Man We Trust*, and of *The Land* as a key biblical theme, are in part prompted, and certainly facilitated, by his awareness of questions, needs, and instincts in the contemporary world and church; these fulfill a heuristic function for him in approaching the OT. Fohrer's work on OT theology in his *Theologische Grundstrukturen des AT* also profits heuristically from his looking at the OT in the light of his own faith, though in his case the latter also provides the basis for his critical evaluation of the OT.

Although (or because) Barth is inhibited from overtly disagreeing with the Bible (as Bultmann is not—even if he feels less free in this respect than some Anglo-Saxon scholars), he does do so covertly by imposing an interpretation on the Bible when the Bible's surface sense seems to him to be non-sense. "Barth's 'criticism' consists mainly in 're-interpretation.'"[82] His treatment of 1 Cor 15 illustrates this point. According to Barth, in 1 Cor 15 Paul was not appealing to the verifiable historicity of Christ's resurrection, and he was right (as the rest of his argument shows).[83] Here, as Bultmann himself asserts, Barth is practicing a surreptitious form of *Sachkritik* (like that of allegory). Bultmann's own understanding is that Paul *was* appealing to the verifiable historicity of the resurrection, and he was wrong (as the rest of his argument shows).[84] Bultmann's *Sachkritik* is quite overt. More plausible (in my view) is W. Pannenberg's position,

---

81ET from *ZTK* 47:89-90.

82Runia, *Karl Barth's Doctrine of Holy Scripture*, 105.

83*Resurrection*, e.g., 137-39; cf. *Dogmatics*, 4/2:143.

84*Faith and Understanding*, 83-86; so also Fuchs, *Marburger Hermeneutik*, 129; *Glaube und Erfahrung*, 216. Cf. Morgan, 47, 175-76; Achtemeier, 112, 159-62, 176, 183.

which (if applied to this particular question) would seem likely
to be that Paul *was* appealing to the verifiable historicity of the
resurrection, and he was right (and is consistent with his argument elsewhere).[85]

Translated into OT terms, Deut 25:4 was concerned about
oxen, and it was wrong to fret about such topics—so Marcion.[86]
Or, Deuteronomy was concerned about people, not about oxen,
and was right to concern itself along these lines—so Paul.[87] Or,
Deuteronomy *was* concerned about oxen, and was right to be so
concerned—so H. Cunliffe-Jones.[88]

One major aspect of the debate between Barth and
Bultmann, then, is a debate over how far we can affirm some biblical viewpoints and criticize others. Bultmann's approach involves evaluating biblical viewpoints on the basis of one's own
grasp of the reality to which they point; Barth's (overtly) allows
only an evaluation of them based on their own internal dynamic.
The present study presupposes an attitude to the canon which
makes the latter approach more appropriate. To put the point
another way, we are here bracketing the question whether a canonical theology is true (whether it has reference) and concentrating on the question what it would be and whether it could be
coherent (whether it has sense). In the light of Bultmann's work,
we are aware of the need to be self-conscious over allowing extrinsic theological considerations to affect our evaluation and
criticism of the biblical material; but in the light of Barth's work,
we are aware of the need to be self-conscious over allowing extrinsic theological considerations to affect our interpretation of
the biblical material. As in the case of the debate between
Bultmann and Barth, the work of those who are not committed
to a confessional stance in relation to the canon is likely to be of
special help to those who are so committed, in enabling them to
see where they are fudging the interpretative task if at certain
points the material ill fits the "biblical stance" to which they
aspire.

---

[85]See, e.g., *Jesus*, 53-114, especially 89; *Basic Questions*, 15-80, especially 53-57.

[86]Cf. Tertullian's appeal to Deut 25:4 in *Adversus Marcionem*, 4:21
and 24 (*PL* 2:409, 419 [ET, *ANF* 3:380, 387]).

[87]1 Cor 9:9; so also in a different sense Carmichael (e.g., *Women, Law
and the Genesis Traditions*, 71-72), who takes the passage as an exhortation to
fulfill the Levirate requirement of the following verses.

[88]*Deuteronomy*, 140.

THE CANON WITHIN THE CANON

The attempt to identify that element in scripture which should be given positive evaluation may be facilitated by, or may result in, the identification of an inner canon within scripture, a canon within the canon. Although widely used, this phrase is a confusing one, with various senses.[89] Understandings of the nature and function of the inner canon, as well as its form and identity, need to be distinguished clearly.

Form and Identity

The form and identity of the canon within the canon have been understood in at least four ways.

First, it may denote a particular book (or books) within the canon. Romans has often seemed to have this position in the Bible as a whole.[90] For the OT, Exodus has been a central book for theologies which stressed the theme of the acts of God in the OT;[91] it is also the "privileged text" for liberation theology.[92] Partly because it more systematically holds together divine initiative and human response, Deuteronomy may alternatively be

---

[89]For instances of the confusing usage see Wright, OT and Theology, 179-83; Ebeling, Word and Faith, 92-93; WCC Study on the Authority of the Bible, 1-11; O. Weber, Foundations of Dogmatics, 1:264-66; Wood, Formation of Christian Understanding, 106-8. The phrase Kanon im Kanon goes back at least to Alexander Schweizer's Christliche Glaubenslehre, 1:165 (1863) (cf. Lönning, "Kanon im Kanon," 45). But the issues encapsulated in the phrase can be traced further back to Semler's Abhandlung von freier Untersuchung des Canon (1771-75) and via him to Luther (see Lönning; also Strathmann, TBl 20:295-310). Semler claims Luther's spirit on his side in distinguishing within scripture between what is or is not God's word—e.g., on how far Moses should be accepted by Christians (2:126-29, apparently referring to Luther's sermon noted in chap. 2, n. 56 above). The theological issues involved are also surveyed in Käsemann, Essays on NT Themes, 95-107.

[90]Strathmann (p. 295) calls Rom 1:17 Luther's "canon of the canon." In his preface to his translation of the NT, Luther himself describes John, 1 John, Romans, Galatians, Ephesians, and 1 Peter as "the true and noblest books of the NT which tell you all you really need to know" (Luther's Works, 35:361- 62); O. Weber (1:265) thus describes these as Luther's canon within the canon.

[91]E.g., Wright, God Who Acts; thus Wright (pp. 102-5) excludes wisdom. Cf. Murphy's comments on Preuss's exclusion of wisdom from his inner canon, which includes only salvation history (No Famine in the Land, 123-25, referring to Preuss, EvT 30:393-417; idem, VTSup 23:117-45).

[92]So Kirk, Liberation Theology, 95.

said to express all the fundamental questions of OT theology in a concentrated form and thus to constitute the natural center for writing a theology of the OT.[93] For the editors of *Interpretation*, Genesis to Kings as a whole "gives the central exposition of the subject of the Old Testament and furnishes the organizing context for its other books."[94] For other scholars, however, the preexilic prophets[95] or Isa 40–55[96] are given supreme significance. In each of these cases, the true locus of revelation or authority may be reckoned to lie in the experience of the great creative individual, or the stream of tradition which underlies the books, as much as or rather than its eventual literary crystallization.[97]

Second, the canon within the canon may denote a key theme within the canon, a theme such as justification by faith or God acting in Israel's history or the covenant or Yahweh alone being Israel's God or the holy God challenging his people to a life of justice or the suffering servant.[98] It is often a conviction regarding the importance of some such theme that leads to the attaching of central significance to Romans, Exodus, Deuteronomy, eighth-century prophecy, or Isa 40–55; little importance is attached to Rom 16, Exod 26, or Isa 15 where the favored theme is less prominent.

Third, the normative element within the canon may be what Bright calls "the essential structure of the biblical faith, which is visible behind the ancient forms and institutions through which it found expression," the "overarching structure of theology, which in one way or another informs each of its texts," and which constitutes what is characteristic, central, and constant, as opposed to what is peripheral, incidental, and

---

[93]So Herrmann, *Probleme biblischer Theologie*, 156, following von Rad, e.g., *Studies in Deuteronomy*, 37; cf. Wright, 75; Deissler, *Grundbotschaft des AT*, 7; also Spriggs's comments on Eichrodt (*Two OT Theologies*, 24-25, 109).

[94]J. L. Mays and P. D. Miller [?], *Int* 29:115.

[95]See the work of Fohrer referred to above, pp. 104-7.

[96]See Westermann's observation (*OT and Jesus Christ*, 16-19) that in Isa 40–55 prophecy, national history, and the people's response to God in praise and prayer are uniquely held together.

[97]Cf. Harrelson's discussion of core traditions, *Tradition and Theology*, 18-30.

[98]See, e.g., Cullmann's assertion of the key significance of salvation history, in the course of considering the question of the canon within the canon (*Salvation in History*, 297-98); but see further the discussion of where the center of OT faith can be located (pp. 111-16 above).

transient.[99] The canonical element of the OT, then, is its distinctive underlying theology or perspective on human existence (even, then, its underlying anthropology).[100] Or the inner canon may denote a particular characteristic or tendency which runs through the canon, "its own particular variant on the cultural trajectories,"[101] such as the liberating dynamic of community ideals such as equality, compassion, and the integrating of social, cultic, and moral concerns which (P. D. Hanson suggests) tend to characterize laws with a background elsewhere in the ancient Near East once they are taken into the laws of Israel.[102]

Fourth, the canon within the canon may denote something which the canon refers to but which is itself outside the canon. If the revelation itself lies in the events scripture refers to rather than in its actual words,[103] then it is these events that constitute the canon within the canon. Whether we think of the line of events that runs through OT times, or of a particular constitutive event such as the exodus which continually receives new interpretations throughout the biblical period, the event lies behind and is primary in relation to concepts or symbols or imperatives or narratives which are built on it; and the event provides the reference point and criterion for what is built upon it.

The referent which constitutes the canon within the canon of the NT for many scholars is naturally Jesus Christ himself.[104] H. Koester notes that the NT indicates that Christianity has no distinctive language, concepts, or images; the early Christians simply took up contemporary ones to express the significance of Jesus. He himself "did not simply confirm or contest the correctness of certain apocalyptic expectations in his preaching, but rather he announced their fulfilment."[105] The Jesus event had to call forth many different kinds of re-

---

[99]*Authority of the OT,* 144-45. On Bright see further pp. 167-72 below.

[100]So H. Braun, *Das NT als Kanon,* 228-29.

[101]J. M. Robinson, *Trajectories,* 16; see pp. 40-43 above.

[102]Hanson, *Canon and Authority,* 115-31. Cf. Rosemary Radford Ruether's identification of a norm critical of patriarchy within biblical religion itself (*JSOT* 22:55).

[103]See, e.g., Wright, *God Who Acts,* 12-13; Pannenberg, *Revelation as History;* idem, *Basic Questions,* 15-80; cf. Kraus's remarks, *Biblische Theologie,* 345.

[104]E.g., Dunn, *Unity and Diversity,* 375-76; Strathmann, 309; Marxsen, *NT as the Church's Book,* 61.

[105]*Future of Our Religious Past,* 75.

sponses, for it was an event of complex significance; the heart of the canon and the reality which actually constitutes the "historical criteria and canons" (or canon within the canon) for us is the Christ event itself.[106] For many Christian interpreters Christ has a similar status in relation to the OT. "The New Testament witness to Christ serves as the primary norm" or "canon within the canon by which to measure and interpret the rest of the canon—the Old Testament."[107]

Nature and Function

The identity of the canon within the canon has thus been understood in a variety of ways. There is a parallel diversity of approaches to its function.

First, it may constitute the real locus of truth, which provides the key to determining the truth of material within the formal canon and outside it. For W. M. L. de Wette, the NT being the canon by which we must measure the OT meant that what is canonical in the OT is that which corresponds to the canon of the NT.[108] For Mendenhall, in effect "the Mosaic-Sinaitic moment in the history of the religion of Israel" has "the status of a 'canon within the canon,' making it the touchstone which enables us to assess the authenticity of any other complex of ideas in the Hebrew Bible."[109] For Fohrer, the preexilic prophets provide the criterion for a negative assessment of OT material which takes a positive attitude toward the cult.[110] For von Rad, the theme of God's acts in history provides the criterion for a negative assessment of Ecclesiastes.[111] For Hanson, the "liberating dynamic" which has to different extents affected different parts of the OT is to be accepted, rather than material not yet affected by it.[112]

Second, in some instances such as these, however, the inner canon may constitute the locus of the deepest insights within the formal canon, compared with which material elsewhere is of a lower status. As is the case with the first approach, here the inner

---

[106]Koester, *Trajectories*, 205-7.

[107]Dunn, *Churchman* 96:216.

[108]*Das Wesen des christlichen Glaubens*, 366. Cf. Jepsen, *TLZ* 74:65-74: what is canonical is what pointed to Christ; Vriezen, *Outline*, 113.

[109]So Levenson, *CBQ* 41:214.

[110]*Theologische Grundstrukturen*, 51-94.

[111]*Theology*, 1:106; cf. 453.

[112]*Canon and Authority*, 115-31.

canon provides a norm for evaluation, but the evaluation is one of relative value rather than of absolute truth and untruth. Thus for Zimmerli the OT's portrayal of the God of Israel and of humanity's encounter with him "achieves its radical depths" in OT prophecy.[113]

Third, the canon within the canon may constitute those aspects of the canon which are directly binding. When Dunn speaks of the NT being the canon within the canon, he does so in connection with Christ's abrogation of OT laws, either because of their "covenantal relativity" (they belonged to the old covenant), or because of their cultural relativity.[114] Some aspects of the canon, then, are directly binding. Others were once binding on people, but are so no longer. As we noted above (pp. 108-9), it might be that they could still function as norms for belief or behavior in an indirect way: for instance, OT cultic laws provide the NT writers with normative concepts for their working out the significance of Christ's "sacrificial" death. But they are not directly binding.

Fourth, the canon within the canon may constitute the center or focus of the formal canon.[115] It comprises "central statements and concepts which offer a perspective or horizon as comprehensive as possible and which therefore can appropriately be treated as the starting point for derivative statements. Beyond this center are inner circles of statements which bring out its immediate implications, and further circles which bring out remoter ones."[116] As such, it relates closely to the canon as what is *directly* binding; but it suggests central (and therefore of greater significance) over against peripheral (and thus less significant), or primary (and therefore more fundamental) over against derivative (and therefore secondary).[117]

Fifth, the canon within the canon may constitute those parts or aspects of the formal canon which are especially impor-

---

[113]*Theology*, 10.

[114]*Churchman* 96:216-17.

[115]Cf. Lönning, 16; see further the discussion of the center or focus of the OT on pp. 111-16 above.

[116]"Report of the Dutch-German Group," WCC *Study on the Authority of the Bible*, 1, 10-11. The group distinguishes this *Sachmitte* or *Beziehungsmitte* from a canon within the canon consisting of writings in the formal canon; yet the group describes the center as binding in a way that the outer circles are not.

[117]Cf. Küng, *Structures*, 148-49 = *Living Church*, 288-90.

tant to a particular generation or community. For Rabbinic Judaism, for instance, it was halakic material in the OT that especially mattered; for Christian Jews, it was prophecy (or narrative and prophecy).[118] In our own century, Brueggemann has noted how the situation of the Confessing Church in Germany led to a stress on historical/covenantal traditions in the OT at a time when the "German Christians" had appropriated something more like a natural religion. At this point, as after the war in East Germany in another way, "cultural pressures and responses to those pressures contributed to that functional 'canon within the canon.'" Brueggemann urges that we recognize the appropriateness of that kind of commitment to particular strands within scripture in certain contexts, and recognize the possibility that an insistence on balance functions ideologically;[119] so, of course, can commitment to a canon within the canon.

AN EVALUATIVE OR CRITICAL APPROACH TO DIVERSITY IN THE OLD TESTAMENT

In what sense, then, and on what basis, can we affirm some of the diverse viewpoints in the OT, and criticize others?

In the approaches we have considered in this chapter, interpreting scripture in its diversity and evaluating it in its diversity are often interwoven, and this can be confusing. At least three forms of this interpretative task need to be distinguished.

The first is the task of understanding the interrelation of themes or motifs, where questions of priority do not arise. For instance, sometimes the OT hope of salvation gives a prominent place to an individual redeemer figure, sometimes such a figure

---

[118]For illustrations regarding the NT's inner canon, see Dunn, *Unity and Diversity,* 375; O. Weber, *Foundations,* 1:264-66; Cullmann, *Salvation in History,* 297-98. Effectively it is Küng's criticism of much Protestant scholarship in its selective use of the NT (e.g., *Living Church,* 269-79); though Küng, too, is selective: the index to the 572 pages of *Die Kirche* lists only one passage from James (but over 400 references to passages in 1 Corinthians) (cf. Lönning, 229).

[119]*JAAR* 38:367; cf. idem, *JSOT* 18:11-14. Smend similarly observes that, though one can build bridges between Amos and P, as Amos's followers did (Smend refers to Weiser, *Prophetie des Amos,* 324), this is to betray Amos himself because these were the bridges he was seeking to destroy (*EvT* 23:422-23); Smend adds that the cross is both a bridge breaking and a bridge building, both God's no and his yes, though even this gives us no excuse for a cheap avoidance of the thrust of Amos's message.

has no place in this hope. Neither form of expectation seems to be theologically prior to or superior to the other; each gives expression to important insights (see further pp. 188-90 below). The interpretative task involves seeking to interrelate the two forms of hope to see what theological insight emerges from setting them alongside each other. It does not involve evaluating one or other as more or less important or as more or less true.

A second form of the task involves analyzing what is more central to OT faith and what is more peripheral to it. Suggestions regarding the central focus of the OT noted above (pp. 111-16) imply that the OT is concerned more about the nation than about the individual, more about Israel than about the world, more about salvation than about creation, more about God's activity in history than about his activity in nature, more about an election relationship than about a natural relationship (in chapter 7 we shall note reasons to qualify such perspectives, but we may assume them for the purpose of illustration here). Such central themes then provide us with vantage points for surveying the OT landscape; they constitute the OT's more important themes, as the OT itself sees it. Interpreting the OT in this way involves an evaluation of the relative importance of diverse materials, though not an evaluation of their degrees of truth.

A third task involves assessing what is more true or more appropriate and what is less so. As we noted above (p. 110), Jesus makes an assessment of that kind regarding the Torah's diverse teaching on marriage. Interpreting this teaching does not involve merely setting Gen 1-2 and Deut 24 alongside each other on the assumption that they are mutually illuminating, nor merely regarding the former as nearer the center of the OT's concerns (the opposite might be maintained), but evaluating the former as the more profound insight, the latter as a concession to human sinfulness.

We shall consider the first form of this interpretative task at greater length in chapters 6-7. At this point we are more directly concerned with the second and third forms, which do involve evaluating some insights as more or less central or more or less profound than others.

With regard to the second, it is illuminating to identify central themes which can suggest linkages between otherwise rather diffuse material; but these interpretative clues are not, as such, a basis for affirming some aspects of the material and setting other aspects on one side. To the extent that interpretation includes identifying what is more central and what more peripheral, it does involve an evaluative task; yet this is not an evaluation of degrees of truth or profundity, but one of degrees of importance. Even the peripheral is true and demands attention; it is on the periphery, not outside it. Distinctions within the biblical material between what is directly and what is more indirectly normative or between what is central and primary and what is more peripheral or derivative are useful ones, though those who emphasize such distinctions do not make clear how distinguishing what is central from what is peripheral helps in the actual interpretation of the latter; it more evidently tends to lead to its being dismissed as of lower value.[120] Nor is it self-evident that later, less primary testimony is necessarily of lower value than earlier material.[121] Further, we have noted that attempts to identify central themes tend to cancel each other out. If central themes constituted a canon within the canon in the sense of a basis for affirming some aspects of the material and setting other aspects aside, this would raise major difficulties. The central themes would need to be unequivocally identified. But if they are only clues for the interpretation of the material as a whole, there is no absolute necessity for them to be delimited in a defined way. Many clues will be more or less illuminating regarding different aspects of the material.

Acknowledging a canon implies an openness to measuring any critical norm against the richness of the whole canon (which can, indeed, be seen as a *complexio oppositorum*) and a resistance to being more biblical than the Bible.[122] Indeed, part of the point of acknowledging a canon is that it faces me with material that confronts me. Even though a particular generation may find particular parts or aspects of scripture immediately helpful and others less so, it is challenged to face and invited to enjoy the whole. "One ought not to make the canon within the canon into the canon."[123] The notion of "the Old Testament" implies that the canon itself is the canon.

---

[120]Cf. Barr, WCC *Study on Biblical Hermeneutics*, 54.

[121]So Küng, *Living Church*, 288-92 = *Structures*, 148-50, with his quotation from Schelkle, *Petrusbriefe*, 245: the Reformed churches may hold to *sola scriptura*, but not to *tota scriptura*.

[122]Küng, *Living Church*, 268-69 = *Structures*, 145-47, with his further quotation from Schelkle, loc. cit.; cf. Appel, *Kanon und Kirche*, 228-65, especially 235-37.

[123]ET from Lönning, 271; cf. Dunn, 376-78, 419; O. Weber, 1:266; Küng, op. cit.; Wood, *Formation*, 107, 125; Gese, *Essays on Biblical Theology*, 32.

This does not necessarily mean that interpreting the OT is only possible for someone who personally adopts this confessional stance.[124] In relation to any religious document, one valuable form of understanding is open to readers who suspend questions about the status of what they are investigating and cultivate an empathy with it which is willing to learn to breathe its atmosphere and put themselves in the place of those who do acknowledge its authority.[125] But it does mean that in that we are seeking to interpret the OT, it is the OT itself and not some abstract from it that we must interpret. In this sense, we cannot accept some parts or views and reject others.

This fact has to be kept in mind as we take up the third form of the interpretative task referred to above, which does involve explicit evaluative judgments about levels in the material, not least in the light of the difficulties involved in maintaining that all the theological perspectives of the OT are equally valid. Recognizing that some perspectives are more profound or more creative than others, many of the evaluative approaches we have been considering draw attention to the need to go beyond formal commitment to the whole OT (without flattening its diversity) by acknowledging that various levels of insight are expressed within it. We do have to look for ways of distinguishing among them. But if we are to maintain an acknowledgment of "the Old Testament" as scripture, this evaluative task must satisfy two criteria that have often not been applied to it.

First, it must be fulfilled on the basis of the intrinsic dynamic of the OT itself, rather than on some base outside the material. A Christian may also allow the dynamic of the Christian canon as a whole to clarify something which the OT leaves uncertain (that, too, is implicit in the fact that we are studying "the Old Testament"—whose identity presupposes the existence of a "New Testament";[126] we are not studying merely the Torah, the Prophets, and the Writings). But even the NT does not decanonize or emasculate the OT.[127] Still less can modern readers

---

124As Porteous seems to imply (Living the Mystery, 23, 44-45); cf. G. A. F. Knight, Christian Theology of the OT, 20.

125Cf. H. W. Robinson, Inspiration and Revelation, 281-82; Dentan, Preface to OT Theology, 114-16; Watson, ExpT 73:200; Gunneweg, Understanding the OT, 93; Crenshaw, Samson, 21-22.

126Cf. Nielsen, Beiträge, 288; Gunneweg, Textgemäss, 46.

127See pp. 107-10 above.

"interpret" it by concentrating on an inner canon which they themselves determine.[128]

The second criterion an evaluative study of the OT needs to fulfill, if the concept of the canon is to retain its meaning, is that we should seek some positive assessment of material which we regard as less close to reflecting ultimate reality. Even if comparing the messages or theological perspectives expressed in the OT reveals that they vary in their depth of insight into truth, and thus in their validity, raising for us the need to seek a way of distinguishing among them and measuring them against each other, nevertheless we will be obliged to offer some positive theological interpretation of the material that seems to be of less value. In this way we may be able to work out the implications of the fact that the material we are studying is of varied value, yet that the whole is to be acknowledged as "the Old Testament." Here, too, interpreting "the Old Testament" involves seeking to relate diverse approaches to each other, rather than to separate insight from error.[129]

An alternative framework to that of *Sachkritik* for questioning how far biblical material expresses ultimate truth is provided by the "hermeneutic of suspicion" formulated by Paul Ricoeur.[130] In interpreting people's statements, we do not take them at face value or presume them to be true just because they are made in apparent good faith; we often look behind them for the real truth that is masked by their rationalizations. People see things as they do because of their prejudices, commitments, vested interests, and limitations; the interpreter seeks to penetrate behind these. But Ricoeur places in tension with his hermeneutic of suspicion a hermeneutic of recovery, which once again affirms the significance of and seeks to listen openly to what one has been approaching "suspiciously." Critical approaches enable one to move beyond the naïveté of a surface reading of a text, a straightforward taking of it at its face value.

---

[128]Cf. Küng's criticism of the subjective nature of Käsemann's approach to the NT (*Living Church*, 263-69 = *Structures*, 143-46).

[129]Cf. Childs, *Int* 18:438-40. Contrast Stoebe's approach which involves affirming diverse viewpoints as all responses of faith, yet viewing this as an "erring faith" (*Gottes Wort*, 207: the phrase *irrender Glaube* comes from Hempel, *Apoxysmata*, 174-97).

[130]E.g., *Freud and Philosophy*, 32-36. Cf. Segundo's "suspicion of ideological interpretation" in the biblical text itself (*Theology for Artisans of a New Humanity*, 5:125) as well as in the utilization of biblical material in Christian doctrine (*Liberation of Theology*, 40-47).

Then, by means of an interaction between a hermeneutic of suspicion and a hermeneutic of recovery, one aims to proceed past this "first naïveté" to a "second naïveté." This second naïveté is once again able to "hear" the text as a whole in an open way, but it "is postcritical and not precritical; it is an informed naïveté."[131]

To Ricoeur's analysis Bernard Lonergan adds that the dialectic between a hermeneutic of suspicion and a hermeneutic of recovery means that while the former facilitates the removing of obstacles that hinder our apprehending what is authentically true in some statement, the latter also "discovers what is intelligent, true, and good in the obstruction."[132] Postcritical naïveté even brings to light what is of positive significance in material which is of lesser value.

A useful instance is provided by Hartmut Gese in his study of the relationship between faith and conceptions of the world, where he discusses the theological significance of creation stories such as Gen 1, which are often dismissed in the name of a scientific worldview. Gese is concerned to recognize the insight expressed not merely in the theological implications of such a chapter, which are less open to criticism in the name of science than many of its direct statements are (though perhaps less immune to such criticism than is often assumed), but also the insight embodied in statements about the world itself: for instance, the "firmament" expresses the perception that space is not endless; the presence of light before the sun's appearance suggests that physical light is secondary in origin to the light of God's glory which it reflects and symbolizes.[133] To express Gese's point in Ricoeur's terminology, the critical, suspicious hermeneutic that queries the scientific factuality of Gen 1 and facilitates a much deeper perception of its kerygmatic significance needs to be accompanied by a hermeneutic of recovery which manifests enough postcritical naïveté to perceive the depth in what has been subjected to criticism; it is willing to allow it to question in return our dismissal of the ancient way of

---

[131]Ricoeur, 496; cf. 28-32. See also Brueggemann's utilization of Ricoeur's work in *JSOT* 17:3-32; and Stuhlmacher's "hermeneutics of consent" (see, e.g., *Historical Criticism and Theological Interpretation,* 83-90).

[132]*SR* 6:355. Cf. Rahner's observations on the theological truth of the OT in *Theological Investigations,* 16:177-90.

[133]Gese, 231-38; cf. Knierim, *Horizons in Biblical Theology,* 3:74-80; also Ricoeur's allusions to "earth, heaven, water, life, trees and stones," p. 7; cf. 30-31.

perceiving the world, a perception which is always open to a spiritual, second-level reading of material realities, such as is actually invited by any symbolic or poetic statement about realities that are deeper than the material.[134]

Variation in levels of insight in the OT can be perceived in matters of theology (such as understandings of God, humanity, and nation), religious observance (such as attitudes to the temple and to sacrifice), and social life (such as attitudes to violence, the city, and the monarchy). As it happens, a number of these appear in the book of Deuteronomy, and in chapter 5 we shall examine Deuteronomy from this perspective.

---

[134]Cf. Gese, 226-31, 234, 245-46.

Chapter 5

AN EVALUATIVE STUDY OF THE TEACHING OF DEUTERONOMY

Deuteronomy illustrates particularly clearly how the standards of attitude and behavior expected within the OT can vary substantially in level. The book has a notably comprehensive and clearly articulated theology, which as such has deeply influenced modern OT theology. It manifests an attractive emphasis on the love of God and on love for God, and on values such as justice and mercy. Yet its comprehensive theological and ethical perspective may also seem nationalistic, discriminatory, and legalistic,[1] while specific requirements such as the slaughter of entire Canaanite communities, the stoning of a rebellious son, and the banning of the deformed, the illegitimate, and foreigners from Yahweh's assembly may seem to clash with its other features. If we are to perceive how these diverse emphases may be related to each other, we need to investigate the principles or values which underlie Deuteronomy's injunctions (e.g., those revealed by recurring themes or expressions, or stated in motive clauses);[2] sometimes injunctions which are more or less congenial to us, because of our values or presuppositions, all reflect one single aspect of Israelite values. We must also seek to discover the values left implicit in other commands, a more hazardous task which can produce disagreement among interpreters,[3] but a potentially rewarding one which can reveal the aspects of a society's thinking which are taken for granted but are thus particularly significant.[4]

---

[1]Cf. Rosemary Radford Ruether's comments on the Bible's "two religions," *JSOT* 22:55.

[2]On these, see Gemser, VTSup 1:50-66; Gilmer, *If-You Form*.

[3]See, e.g., Mayes's survey of approaches to 23:2 (1) (*Deuteronomy*, 315).

[4]See, e.g., Daube, *Juridical Review* 85:126-34; Douglas, *Implicit Meanings*, ix-x, 3-4; Neusner, *Religion* 5:91-100.

DEUTERONOMY'S BEHAVIORAL VALUES

Deuteronomy affirms many values, norms, or imperatives, such as prohibitions on murder and theft, which are standard features of ethical codes in cultures generally. It lays particular emphasis, however, on the following values.

Justice

Deuteronomy's first major challenge to Israel motivates its commands by asserting the supreme justice of them (4:8), a perhaps polemical parallel to Hammurabi's claim.[5] Specific commands seek to guard against business dishonesty, misappropriation of land, and abuse of the right to sustain oneself by eating grapes or corn on the way through someone's land (25:13-16; 27:17; 19:14; 23:25-26 [24-25]); though there is little property law in Deuteronomy compared with Exod 20–23. A number of laws concern the administration of justice in general (1:16-17; 16:18-20; 17:8-11), the handling of evidence (5:20; 13:15 [14]; 17:4; 19:15-21), and the limiting of legal responsibility (4:41-43; 19:1-13; 24:16).[6] Yahweh is the God of justice, and Deuteronomy's overt motivation for a concern with justice lies in the character, behavior, and expectations of Yahweh, whom Israel is expected to resemble, imitate, and obey.

Concern for the Needy

Israel is to see to the needs of various groups who might have no sure means of livelihood, especially through possessing no land: Levites; widows, orphans, and immigrants (גרים); the poor; and slaves. Where necessary this obligation overrides property rights and the right to family privacy.

As members of the priestly tribe, the Levites' need arose out of their calling, and they are to be supported (esp. by means of tithes) whether they live in their home area or join the staff of the (central) shrine (14:22-29; 18:6-8).

Yahweh concerns himself with the rights and needs of orphan, widow, and immigrant, as he had with those of Israel in

---

[5]So Weinfeld, *Deuteronomy*, 150-51; cf. *ANET,* 177.
[6]On this last, see Greenberg, *Kaufmann Volume,* 20-28; idem, *JBL* 78:125-32.

Egypt. He expects Israel to mirror that concern, guarding them from exploitation and taking practical steps to see that they have enough to eat (10:18-19; 14:28-29; 24:17-22; 26:12-13; 27:19).[7] Thus, while Deuteronomy does not disallow property, it requires public tithing and thus public "accounting," and makes possessing things the means by which one expresses a concern for the needy.[8] Yahweh also hears the cry of the poor, those who own land but are impoverished through circumstances such as poor harvests. He expects Israel to take practical steps to protect them and help them reestablish themselves, in an attitude of brotherhood, generosity, respect, and honor (15:1-11; 24:6, 10-15, 17).

A man who could not escape from impoverishment by means of loans could sell himself into temporary slavery. But the God who acted on behalf of slaves in Egypt also cares about those who are enslaved now, and he expects Israel to treat slaves not as mere chattels but as members of the family, who share in the joy of its worship (as do orphans, widows, immigrants, and Levites) and in the sabbath rest (5:14-15; 12:12, 18; 14:26-27; 16:11-12, 14; 26:11). Escaped slaves are not to be returned to their masters (23:16-17 [15-16]);[9] when slaves are due to be set free they are to be given generously of their masters' sheep, corn, and wine, or allowed to stay on as permanent slaves in the household if they wish (15:12-18).

Brotherhood

Deuteronomy frequently uses the term *brother*, more commonly to refer to fellow-Israelites than to literal siblings; it thus motivates commands concerning relationships within Israel by encouraging the hearer to see Israel as the family writ large. This motif appears in commands concerning suspending debts, mak-

---

[7]Widows were also offered some protection by the levirate law (25:5-10; cf. Neufeld, *Ancient Hebrew Marriage Laws,* 29-31; E. W. Davies, *VT* 31:138-44); immigrants can also be given as food animals that have died a natural death (14:21), and they are to be allowed to enjoy the sabbath rest along with Israelites (5:14). Israelites are to "love" them as Yahweh does (10:18-19); here as elsewhere, "love" denotes practical commitment in action, as well as attitude (see n. 44 below).

[8]On Deut 14, see Boissonnard and Vouga, *Bulletin du Centre Protestant d'Etudes* 32:21-32.

[9]Perhaps the reference is to slaves of foreign masters (cf. Mendelsohn, *Slavery,* 58-64); but see Carmichael, *Laws of Deuteronomy,* 186-87.

ing loans, releasing slaves, dealing with perjury, forgoing interest, kidnapping, slave-trading, and avoiding excessive legal pen-
alties (15:2, 3, 7, 9, 11, 12; 19:18-19; 23:20-21 [19-20]; 24:7;
25:3);[10] also concerning the Transjordanian tribes' commitment
to the rest of the tribes (3:18-20).[11] Even Edomites are to be treated in a special way as brothers (23:8 [7]; cf. 2:4, 8).[12] Not that
Israelites have the right to treat non-Israelites as they wish (see
24:14; also 21:10-14 and the unlimited prohibition on murder,
theft, and coveting, 5:17, 19, 21). But how one treats foreigners
is a less pressing everyday question than how one treats one's
fellow-countrymen; it is among such that one's enemies are
probably located, and it is such that Deuteronomy bids one treat
as brothers (cf. the law on accepting responsibility for the animals or property of others, 22:1-4).[13]

Deuteronomy emphasizes that Israel's leaders or representatives (judges, kings, Levites, prophets) are leaders among
brothers (1:18; 17:14-20; 18:1-5, 15-18).[14] The kings are not to
be foreigners who are not brothers, the Levites' needs are to be
the concern of their brothers, the prophets as brothers bring
Yahweh's word by straightforward, nonfearful means (contrast
18:9-14, 16-17), and none is to elevate himself above his brothers (see specifically 17:20: the king "is simply to be the model Israelite").[15] All Israelites are entitled to a common freedom, as
those Yahweh rescued from Egypt, and to a common enjoyment
of the land, as those to whom Yahweh promised it.

---

[10]Contrast earlier versions of these laws, Exod 21:2, 16; 22:24-26 (25-
27).

[11]Contrast Num 32:20-24.

[12]Contrast Num 20:14, where "brother" appears only as a collective
noun.

[13]The earlier version of this law (Exod 23:4-5) makes explicit that the
"brother" (Deut 22:1) is an enemy. Some other occurrences of "brother" which
appear less freighted (e.g., 1:28; 25:11) are also additions to earlier versions of
the material (cf. Num 14; Exod 21:18-22) and presumably do therefore carry
moral overtones. So also perhaps 25:5-10.

[14]There is no reference to "brothers" in the earlier passages on judges
and Levites, Exod 18; Num 18.

[15]Wolff, *Anthropology*, 196-97. In Deuteronomy the verb "choose" for
the first time has Israel, not merely David, as its object (4:37; 7:6; 10:14; 14:2)
(cf. von Rad, *Gottesvolk*, 27-28; Clements, *VT* 15:306; Nicholson, *Deuteronomy and Tradition*, 103); cf. Deuteronomy's little concern with the Levites'
role and its stress on the whole people's joyful worship and involvement in the
covenant (e.g., 29:10-13 [11-14]) rather than on the role of the clergy.

Womanhood

Another aspect of Deuteronomy's interest in attitudes toward fellow-Israelites is its emphasis on the privileges and responsibilities of women as well as those of men.[16] It is concerned to encourage family stability (see pp. 138-39 below), but it does not seek to strengthen the position of the male head of the family in order to do so. It stresses attitudes toward mothers, wives, and daughters, as well as toward fathers, husbands, and sons.

Thus both mother and father have a right to a son's obedience and an obligation to see to the punishment of his rebelliousness (21:18-21). A wife has a right to marital security or to freedom, even if she is a foreigner (21:10-14), and to her son receiving the extra inheritance if he is the eldest, even if his father prefers the child of another wife (21:15-17). A daughter or a female slave has the same right to share in worship and sabbath rest as a son or a male slave (5:14; 12:12, 18; 16:11, 14), and a female slave has the same right to freedom as a male slave (15:12).[17] Daughters as well as sons are protected from intermarriage and from being offered in sacrifice (7:3; 12:31; 18:10).[18] The needs, and also the responsibilities, of women as well as men are the concerns of laws on sexual conduct and marriage (22:13-29; 24:5; 25:11-12),[19] and on apostasy (17:2-3; cf. 13:7 [6]).

Family Order

There is considerable Deuteronomic material concerning the family, marriage, and other sexual relationships, but this material offers little explanation of the basis of its commands. Suggestions as to its underlying values are therefore hypothetical.

The Decalogue and its context emphasize the responsibility of children to parents and that of parents to children (5:16;

---

[16]Cf. Carmichael, *Women, Law and the Genesis Traditions*, 3-7 and generally; Carmichael sees these laws as taking up incidents in Genesis.

[17]Contrast Exod 21:2-11.

[18]Elsewhere in the OT only the offering of sons is mentioned.

[19]On 22:13-29, see Phillips, *JSOT* 20:6-13; Weinfeld, 284-91; on 25:11-12—a converse of Exod 21:22-25—see Daube, *Orita* 3:36-38; Eslinger, *VT* 31:369-81.

4:9; 6:7, 20-25; 11:19; 21:15-21; 27:16; 32:46). The assumption here is that children need their parents' instruction, and parents need their children's care.[20] A related concern that paternity should always be clear underlies the laws about sex outside marriage. A. Phillips notes especially the description of illicit sexual activity (זנות) as an outrage (נבלה) (22:21). The former term denotes extramarital sex, not as positively directed to a financial or religious end ("prostitution"), or as indiscriminate ("promiscuity"), or as unethical ("immorality"), or as specifically involving either unmarried persons or married persons ("fornication" or "adultery"), but as illicit and socially unacceptable. The second term then designates it as an act of crass disorder, threatening the structured arrangement of marriage and the family.[21] The fulfillment of a person's natural right to have children is part of the concern of laws about levirate marriage and sexual assault (25:5-12)[22] and about a newly married man's exemption from military or other public service (20:7; 24:5).

Two passages impose limitations on whom a man may marry or have intercourse with (23:1 [22:30]; 27:20, 22-23). They seem to proscribe such relationships with one's stepmother, half-sister, or mother-in-law, out of a desire to preserve proper order within the (extended) family.[23] The same aim perhaps underlies the expectation that a bride shall be a virgin (22:13-21, 28-29). The safeguarding of the marriage relationship itself is a concern of the Decalogue and of other laws (5:18; 22:22-27); these probably include banning remarriage to one's former wife (24:1-4),[24] though the latter of course presupposes that divorce will happen.

---

[20]If 5:16 at least includes a concern for aged parents (cf. Albertz, *ZAW* 90:348-74). On the rights and responsibility of primogeniture, see Mendelsohn, *BASOR* 156:38-40; Neufeld, 263; Yaron, *Gifts*, 9-10.

[21]*VT* 25:239. Phillips also sees a concern with paternity in the divorce law of 24:1-4 (*Ancient Israel's Criminal Law*, 117-18).

[22]Cf. Neufeld, 47; Phillips, 94-95. Noonan finds the same aim in 25:4, which he sees as prohibiting the prevention of conception (*JQR* 70:172-75).

[23]See Porter, *Extended Family*; Stendebach, *Kairos* 18:277-79; Evans-Pritchard, *Rules and Meanings*, 44. Wenham sees this principle also behind 24:1-4 (*JJS* 30:36- 40).

[24]Cf. Carmichael, *Laws*, 203-7; idem, *Women, Law and the Genesis Traditions*, 16.

Happiness

Only Psalms and Proverbs use the verb שמח more often than Deuteronomy. It occurs in distinctive Deuteronomic contexts in connection with a joy in Yahweh's provision for his people, which finds expression when people gather for festivals and worship; Deuteronomy emphasizes the sharing of this joy by the whole family and other members of the community (12:7, 12, 18; 14:26; 16:11, 14; 26:11). The verb recurs in the exhortation to give a newly married man time "to make his wife happy" (24:5; Targum "to be happy with his wife"). Further, this book which urges people not to desire other people's possessions encourages them to indulge their desires with regard to what belongs to them (5:21; 12:15, 20, 21; 14:26), and rejoices in the idea of eating and being full (6:11; 8:10, 12; 11:15; 14:29; 26:12), even though it recognizes the danger of this experience (31:20).[25] Its joy is thus a rejoicing in the concrete blessings which come to Israel as Yahweh fulfills his promise to give them a good and fruitful land as a secure possession in a situation of relief from the attacks of enemies (see the collocation of words and ideas in 12:7-21; 14:22-29; 16:9-17; 26:1-15).[26]

D. Daube has drawn attention to a less concrete aspect of human happiness or fulfillment which Deuteronomy stresses, honor or good standing as opposed to shame, embarrassment, or degradation (e.g., 22:13-21; 24:10-11, 25:3, 9; 27:16). The opposite of blessing/the feeling of happiness is curse/the feeling of shame (קללה), and Deuteronomy is concerned to avoid this being the experience of its hearers.[27]

Deuteronomy emphasizes, however, that continued enjoyment of this happiness depends on obedience to the laws it sets forth (e.g., 14:29). One underlying feature of some of these laws, and at the same time an aspect of the life of blessing which Deuteronomy wants Israel to enjoy, is an observing of order in the community by means of keeping distinct those things which are distinct: mother and child, war and peace, life and death (22:1-

---

[25]Again, only Psalms and Proverbs use אוה or שבע more often.

[26]See the emphasis on the land as God's gift in Diepold, *Israels Land*, 76-104; Miller, *Int* 23:451-65; J. Plöger, *Literarkritsche ... Untersuchungen*, 61-91; Wildberger, *EvT* 16:404-22; Brueggemann, *Land*, 45-53.

[27]See *Orita* 3:27-52; *Neotestamentica et Semitica*, 236-39; cf. Carmichael, *Laws*, 45-47.

11).[28] Such external structuring of life is an important expression of order, both supporting the feeling that there is order in the community and thereby encouraging that order. The more overtly social and ethical interests of the law, including its concern for consistent legal practice, also play an important role in supporting social stability.[29] Such order contributes to Israel functioning as a people: for Deuteronomy is concerned with the people as a whole as Yahweh's people. It is a community that is addressed, is reminded of its common history and calling, is challenged to a communal obedience, is invited to its common worship, and is promised its communal blessing.[30]

DEUTERONOMY'S THEOLOGICAL PERSPECTIVE

Deuteronomy's behavioral values probably commend themselves to the modern ethicist. But they have their ambiguities. It is excellent to treat one's fellow-countrymen as brothers, but Deuteronomy's stance is not really humanitarian; it takes a very different attitude toward foreigners (e.g., 15:3; 23:21 [20]). The basis for this different attitude lies in its fundamental theological perspective, which is frequently articulated within the book. It involves two correlative convictions: Israel is Yahweh's people and Yahweh is Israel's God (see, e.g., 26:17-18; 29:12 [13]). It is these foundational convictions which are then explicated in the covenantal structure of Deuteronomy's message.

"You Are Yahweh's Special People"

Yahweh is Lord of the whole cosmos, and no other power rules anywhere on earth (4:39). He made all the nations and thus has a natural relationship with them all; but he has a special relationship with Israel by election. He chose Israel to be his special per-

---

[28]So Carmichael, *JJS* 25:50-63; idem, *HTR* 69:1-7; one might add, man and animals (27:21). Carmichael suggests that Deuteronomy's attitude toward animals, birds, and trees (14:21; 20:19-20; 22:6-7) and its prohibition on eating blood (12:23-25) have the same background (cf. also Carmichael, *Laws,* 150-66; Keel, *Das Böcklein in der Milch;* Wenham, *EvQ* 53:6-15). Some of Carmichael's other examples (e.g., *VT* 29:129-42) I find less convincing. For the broader anthropological background, see, e.g., Bulmer, *Rules and Meanings,* 167-93; see further pp. 151-52 at nn. 62-65 below.

[29]Cf. Hanson's comments, *Canon and Authority,* 124-25.

[30]Cf. von Rad, *Gottesvolk,* 10-19.

sonal possession, and to be thus holy to him (26:18, 19; cf. 7:6; 14:2; 28:9; 32:8, 9); holiness designates not Israel's calling (as in Leviticus), but their status as a result of Yahweh's choice of them.

This special relationship between Yahweh and Israel implies a special practical commitment of the one to the other. He loves them, made promises to their ancestors, rescued them from bondage in Egypt. He is close at hand whenever they call to him for help (4:7). He is committed to their survival and success, and in particular to giving them a land which they can possess and regard as their own (ירשה ,נחלה; e.g., 2:12; 4:38).

Such a commitment to Israel raises the question of the significance of other nations before Yahweh; indeed, O. Bächli makes the question of Israel and the nations the focus of his study of Deuteronomy.[31] What it means to be Israel can emerge from consideration of how Israel differs from the nations, what dangers other nations bring to Israel, and how Israel can avoid these.

Bound up in Yahweh's particular commitment to Israel is his ensuring the defeat of enemies who prevent Israel from leaving their land (4:34; 6:20-23), hinder Israel's journey toward the land Yahweh intends to give them (1:4; 2:16–3:11), currently possess this land (4:38; 6:19; 7:1-2, 17-24; 11:23-25), or inhabit cities which subsequently attack them (28:17) or which they seek to conquer in extending their empire (v 20). Israel is to be greater than any other nation on earth (2:25; 11:24-25; 26:19; 28:1, 10, 12, 13). Yahweh fights for Israel and "delivers them all into her hands," enabling Israel itself to defeat them (2:33; cf. chap. 20); and each experience of victory should then build up confidence in Yahweh for the next battle (1:30; 3:21-22; 20:1-4).

Deuteronomy emphasizes, however, that the first three groups of enemies experience defeat at Yahweh and Israel's hand not because they are mere innocent obstacles to Israel's destiny but because they are willful rebels against Yahweh's moral will. The Egyptians had treated Israel as slaves (6:12, 20-23), so that the Egyptian experience had been like being smelted in a furnace (4:20). Sihon of Heshbon and Og of Bashan had made unprovoked attacks on Israel on their journey toward the land west of the Jordan (2:24–3:17). The Canaanites had forfeited that land by their "wickedness" (רשעה) (9:4-5) or by their "abominations"

---

[31]Israel und die Völker.

(תועבות) (18:9-14)—that is, unacceptable religious practices such as child sacrifice, divination, and magic, which were designed to influence the deity, make things happen, or discover the future.[32]

Thus the Israelites themselves have to learn the appropriate lessons from such warning examples. Possession of the land is not the fruit of their own achievement, but Yahweh's gift (6:10-13). It is not given to them as a reward for their uprightness; it is a fulfillment of a promise that has its basis in Yahweh himself and his decision to commit himself to this particular people (4:37-38; 7:6-8; 9:4-5). The wickedness of the Canaanites makes it possible for him to fulfill this purpose, but it also makes clear that Yahweh has certain standards, which apply to Israel as much as to the Canaanites. His commitment to them is not unconditional. In relation to Israel, too, Yahweh can manifest himself as "a devouring fire, a jealous God" (4:24; cf. 5:9; 6:15). They can lose the land and be annihilated, their few survivors scattered and condemned to worship the empty images to which they were so strangely attracted (4:25-28). Indeed, Israel's own story already illustrates this, for Yahweh has had cause to punish them for rebellion already (1:37-38; 4:21-22; 32:48-52). So it can be that Israel will experience trouble rather than success if they ignore Yahweh's expectations of them (chap. 28); he has enjoyed watching them grow, but he could as readily then watch them die (28:63).

Yet for all the warning of annihilation, death, and destruction, Deuteronomy does not picture such punishment as necessarily final. If it brings the scattered remains of Israel to their senses and they seek Yahweh again, they will find him (4:25-30). Because Yahweh was gracious enough to reveal himself to them, they will pay for rebelling against him; but because he was gracious enough to reveal himself to them, he will not avert his ear from their cry even then (4:31-39). He will restore them not only outwardly but inwardly (30:1-10). Although Moses will not set foot on the other side of the Jordan, he casts his eye over the land as the last act of his life (32:1-4).[33]

---

[32]Cf. Bächli's observation (p. 14) that the two main poles of Deuteronomy's treatment of the nations is their cult (as wicked and dangerous) and their land (as forfeited by them and to be given to Israel). On תועבה see further p. 149 below at n. 48.

[33]Perhaps thus taking possession of it in symbol (so Daube, *Studies*, 24-38).

Neither is punishment Yahweh's only word for other peoples. The fourth group of nations referred to above were ones which have not oppressed Israel, hindered their progress to their land, or (apparently) offended Yahweh by their religion; they are destined to be ruled by Israel because that is Yahweh's will, which they are invited to accept, and only if they resist will they be forcibly subjugated (20:1-18). The OT includes no precise examples of the implementing of this set of instructions, though it describes several partly parallel situations (e.g., 2:26; Josh 9:15; 10:1; Judg 1:27-36). Perhaps the instructions would apply to Edom, Moab, and Ammon, peoples who received their land from Yahweh, as Israel did (Deut 2:4-22). Thus he controls the destiny of these nations around Israel, and concerns himself with their well-being.[34] Admittedly he only asserts this regarding the other Abrahamic peoples, the descendants of Esau (who are thus Israel's brothers) and of Lot (2:4, 9, 19). While Deuteronomy speaks of Yahweh destroying Rephaim and the Horites before Ammon and Edom, it offers no such interpretations of the displacement of the Avvim before the Caphtorim (2:23; contrast Amos 9:7).

Other passages may speak more or less narrowly than this one. Deut 23:4-9 (3-8) permanently bans Ammonites and Moabites from Yahweh's assembly, even after ten generations, and allows Edomites or Egyptians to be admitted only after three generations (cf. Ezra 9-10; Neh 9). The passage's background and interpretation are complex. Perhaps a concern to exclude people of uncertain religious commitment or explicitly of other religions underlies these verses (as it may Deut 23:2-3 [1-2]),[35] though they themselves give the ban an ethical rationale which also underlies the permanent punishment imposed on Ammon and Moab (23:5-7 [4-6]; cf. 25:18-19 on Amalek). In any case, the acceptance of Ruth into the community and the promise of acceptance to the convert (Isa 56:3) need not conflict with this law, if its concern is primarily religious/ethical, not racial.[36]

As in relation to the Ammonites and Moabites, Deuterono-

---

[34]Cf. Gese's observations, *Textgemäss*, 36-37.

[35]Cf. Galling, *Festschrift Bertholet*, 176-91; Bächli, 85-87.

[36]Cf. Bächli, 111, drawing a contrast with Ezra 9. Cf. the combination of rigor and openness in Exod 12:43-49; also in Josh 1-12 (cf. Bächli, *Wort—Gebot—Glaube*, 21-26). Admittedly Deuteronomy itself shows no signs of a concept of individual foreigners being able to be converted to Yahwism (cf. von Rad, 39).

my takes an uncompromising stance in regard to the Canaanites. Their worship is abhorrent to Yahweh and they themselves are to be annihilated, not least lest they lead the Israelites astray (Deut 7:1-5, 25-26). Apparently Canaanite worship is seen as distinctively objectionable and dangerous. The Song of Moses (32:8-9) takes a broader view of other nations' worship:

> When Elyon gave the nations their inheritance [הנחל],
> when he divided up mankind,
> he set the boundaries of the peoples
> in accordance with the numbers of the sons of Israel.[37]
> But Yahweh's share [חלק] is his people.

Yahweh allocated (החלק) the planets and stars to the other nations to worship, but expected Israel to worship him because he had taken them as his own people (עם נחלה) (4:19-20). The statement that Yahweh was involved in the destiny of the Abrahamic tribes is here generalized.

Deuteronomy does not make entirely clear the basis of Yahweh's relationship to Israel. Its origin lies explicitly in Yahweh, not in Israel's own achievements or potential. But Deuteronomy is ambivalent over whether its continuance depends finally on Yahweh himself, as the promise of restoration and renewal in 30:1-10 might imply, or depends on Israel's (repentance and) obedience, as Deuteronomy's many exhortations suggest (cf. even 30:1-2; also 4:29-30). Its hortatory emphasis implies that disobedience could ultimately undo Israel's relationship with Yahweh; but the possibility of being finally cast off is never made explicit.

An unclarity over this point appears throughout both Testaments, and perhaps denotes a tension that one should not try to resolve. The relationship between God and his people begins with his initiative, but it cannot survive without their response; even that response is inspired by him, yet it is still *their* actual response. Which of the poles in this tension needs emphasis will vary. Israel between Sinai and the promised land (or on the verge of the Josianic reform) particularly needs to be reminded that the continuance of their relationship with Yahweh depends on their obedience to him. Israel in exile (presupposed by 30:1-10) also needs to be reminded of the persistence of Yahweh's commitment to them.

---

[37]LXX "sons of God" may be right, though the reasons for such a change in MT are not obvious.

Deuteronomy is also unclear—at best—in its understanding of the relationship between Yahweh, Israel, and other nations. While it sees Yahweh as Lord of the nations, it does not work out the implications of its own hints regarding his positive purpose for them. Its perspective is almost entirely Israel-centered. It concerns itself with the nations only to the extent that they are relevant to Israel.[38]

This characteristic of Deuteronomy no doubt relates to the crises it confronts, overtly or covertly, the threat to Israel's survival as the distinctive people of Yahweh constituted by the occupation of Canaan and the apostasy of seventh-century Judah.[39] In such contexts, Deuteronomy has to emphasize the distinctiveness of Israel's calling by Yahweh and their calling before Yahweh, the privilege of their position and the potential of Yahweh's commitment to them.[40] Yet the assumption that Israel's life and calling have to be seen in the context of Yahweh's worldwide power and concern surfaces in the wider literary work to which Deuteronomy belongs, the narrative which begins in Genesis and extends to Kings before it comes to an unequivocal end. This work focuses on the tragic story of Israel from the twin peaks of the exodus-occupation of Palestine and united monarchy to the disaster of exile, but it sets this story in the context of the creation of humanity and of Yahweh's promises to Israel's ancestors. Deuteronomy notes that it is these promises of Yahweh's blessing (e.g., Gen 12:1-3) which are now being confirmed and fulfilled (e.g., Deut 1:8; 6:10; 9:5; 13:18 [17]; 19:8; 29:12 [13]; 30:20), not least in the nations' acknowledgment of Israel (cf. 4:6-8; 26:19; 28:1, 10-13). This context, however, sees both promise and fulfillment as part of Yahweh's way of dealing with the curse which has come upon all humanity.[41]

"Yahweh Is Your God"

Correlative to Yahweh's commitment to Israel is Israel's com-

---

[38]Thus Altmann describes it as particularist and nationalist (*Erwählungstheologie*, 13-18).

[39]Cf. Bächli, *Israel*, 12; Martin-Achard, *TZ* 16:333-41; Nicholson, *Deuteronomy and Tradition*, 105.

[40]Gese, however, suggests that the denial of Israel's distinctive election in Amos 9:7 is a piece of Deuteronomistic redaction, designed to goad Israel toward obedience (so *Textgemäss*, 33-38). If so, a "non-nationalist" point is being made, though for "nationalist" reasons!

[41]See further p. 61 above, and pp. 192-93 below.

mitment to Yahweh. "You are our God" answers to "You are my people."

Yahweh's expectations of his people begin to be expressed in Deut 4; the general attitudes he looks for are prominent in chapters 4-11 and continue to feature as the background to the remainder of the book. Deuteronomy is not seeking a mere formal, external obedience. It repeatedly affirms that Yahweh's people are to obey him, to fear him, to love him, to follow him, to conform to his ways, to hold fast to him, to trust him, to rejoice before him, to remember him, to serve him, to worship him, and to take their oaths in his name. He alone is to be the object of those verbs: they are to love him wholeheartedly, and thus not to love anyone else (6:4-5);[42] to trust him completely, and not to trust in other resources (17:16-20); not to follow other gods or conform to their ways, not to serve them or worship them. Israel is to be תמים with Yahweh (18:13), wholly committed to him. Their offerings are to be unblemished ones (17:1; 15:21). Their vows are to be kept (23:22-24 [21-23]).[43] They are to avoid misapplying his name (5:11) and are to keep his sabbath (5:12-15).

The OT understands the relationship between Yahweh and his people by analogy with human relationships such as those of husbands and wives, parents and children, brothers, friends, and teachers and pupils, and the commitment of which Deuteronomy speaks has all these in its background. Particularly immediate to it is the relationship of an imperial overlord to a smaller nation, expressed in the Near Eastern political treaties of the second and first millennia. These, too, expect the smaller nation to love its overlord (in the sense of being totally committed in loyalty to him),[44] to serve him alone, to follow his policies, to fear him, to hold fast to him, and to obey him. They emphasize the exclusiveness of this commitment: the smaller nation's loyalty to its overlord excludes any similar relationship with any other power.

It may be significant that the divine overlord is not referred to as Israel's king. Where the term "king" occurs, it refers to the human leader Israel is envisaged as seeking. A human king is al-

---

[42]Bächli sees 6:4-5 as the key to Deuteronomy; the whole of the rest is elaboration on this point (pp. 29-30; cf. Alt, *Kleine Schriften*, 2:253-54).

[43]On this, see Weinfeld, *Deuteronomy*, 270-72.

[44]Cf. Moran, *CBQ* 25:77-87; though this is also a wisdom characteristic (cf. McKay, *VT* 22:426-35; Malfroy, *VT* 15:49-65).

lowed, but human kingship is not to be permitted to compromise Yahweh's sole authority (cf. the discussion on pp. 64-73 above). So the king must be Yahweh's choice, his life must reflect Yahweh's standards, he must rely on Yahweh and not on other resources, and he must pay particular attention to the contents of Yahweh's law, so as to give the exclusive and complete obedience to Yahweh that is expected of the whole people (17:14-20).

Yahweh, then, looks for an exclusive commitment to him; any other commitment (specifically, one to the local deities of Canaan) is impossible.[45] This is where the ten covenant words begin (5:7); it is the content of Israel's basic belief in one Yahweh (6:4-5); it is implied by his being a jealous God, who tolerates no other loyalties (6:10-15); it in turn implies a fierce policy toward rebels (17:2-7; cf. 29:17-27 [18-28]; 30:15-20) and those who encourage rebellion (13:2-19 [1-18]).[46]

Worshiping other gods than Yahweh is only slightly more reprehensible than worshiping Yahweh himself in ways in which other gods are worshiped but which he forbids. Thus the ten words immediately follow the prohibition on worshiping other gods by a ban on images in worship (5:8-10; cf. 8:25-26; 27:15). Although these would be strictly or theologically images to represent Yahweh, they arouse Yahweh's jealousy, for worshiping an image comes to be merely another way of worshiping a god other than Yahweh.

The importance of the ban on images is emphasized by its being the central concern of the opening chapter of Moses' actual instructions to Israel. The chapter begins with reference to obeying Yahweh's commands and holding fast to him (4:1-5), but almost imperceptibly comes a transition to the ban on worship by means of images, based on their inappropriateness to a God whose self-revelation did not have a shape which could then be imitated, but comprised only words which were to be obeyed as expressing the will of one who was personally responsive to his people's call and personally active on his people's behalf (4:6-40). An image suggests another kind of God altogether.[47]

---

[45]Hence von Rad's overstated observation that in Deuteronomy the direct link between religion and farming is broken (*Gottesvolk*, 30).

[46]Note the political terminology; cf. Weinfeld, 91-100; also Bächli's remark (pp. 68-69) that Deuteronomy is concerned with Israel's attitude toward other peoples only because it is concerned with Israel's attitude toward the gods of those peoples.

[47]Cf. Deuteronomy's stress on remembering (cf. Blair, *Int* 15:41-47), which reflects the fact that Yahweh is the kind of God who speaks and acts memorably.

The principle that total loyalty to Yahweh demands not only avoiding the worship of alien gods but also avoiding alien ways of worship underlies many other laws. It is epitomized by the description of various practices as abhorrent to Yahweh (תועבות). The term applies especially to features of Canaanite religion and to attempts to introduce these into Israel (7:25-26; 12:29-31; 13:15 [14]; 17:4; 18:9-14; 20:18; 23:18-19 [17-18]; 27:15; 32:16).[48]

As Deut 23:18-19 (17-18) illustrates, Deuteronomy's concern with sexual behavior arises in part from the latter's link with religion. In ancient Near Eastern religions, this link might involve a girl experiencing sexual initiation in the shrine, as a way of opening herself to the god's power of fertility;[49] or temple personnel engaging in sexual intercourse to represent the marriage between god and goddess which was the key to the land's fertility; or lay devotees of a god or goddess seeking divine life and power by intercourse with such temple personnel. Deuteronomy bans Israelite involvement in such practices and the payment of vows to Yahweh out of the proceeds of participation in them (23:18-19 [17-18]).[50] Its exclusion of the ממזר and his descendants from Yahweh's assembly may presuppose that these are children born as a result of this involvement (23:3 [2]).[51]

Deuteronomy is violently anti-Canaanite, and it is possible to overstate its rejection of Canaanite forms of worship. While it condemns some Canaanite practices that are accepted elsewhere in the OT (see 14:1-2; 16:21-22; 26:14),[52] presumably because it believed

---

[48]See also 17:1 (a practice regarded as just as bad as following Canaanite ways, rather than as actually Canaanite practice?); 23:8 (7) (the denominative verb תעב). On תועבה see L'Hour, *RB* 71:481-503; Humbert, *ZAW* 72:217-37. Deut 24:1-4 more resembles the application of the word to noncultic sexual irregularities in Lev 18:22, 26-30; 20:13; so also Deut 22:5, though this might refer to a Canaanite cultic practice (so Driver, *Deuteronomy*, 250; Römer, *Travels in the World of the OT,* 217-22). Deut 25:13-16 uses the word as a general expression of disgust, resembling that in Proverbs (e.g., 11:1; 20:10, 23).

[49]Cf. Wolff, *Hosea,* 14, 85-88, on Hos 1:2; 4:13-14; Rost, *Festschrift Bertholet,* 451-60; Boström, *Proverbiastudien,* 103-55; though there is some danger of reading too much into the evidence (Rudolph, *ZAW* 75:65-73; Fisher, *BTB* 6:225-36).

[50]On 23:19 (18) see Thomas, *VT* 10:424.

[51]23:2 (1) may similarly refer to intentional mutilation in connection with the service of one's god (on 23:2-3 [1-2], see Galling, *Festschrift Bertholet,* 178-79; Craigie, *Deuteronomy,* 296-97).

[52]On 14:1-2, see Mayes, *Deuteronomy,* 238-39; on 26:14, see Cazelles, *RB* 55:54-71.

they could particularly easily carry Canaanite connotations, many aspects of worship remained common to Canaan and Israel.

As a concern for loyalty to Yahweh leads to the proscription of certain Canaanite forms of worship, so this proscription leads to a further ban on the use of the former Canaanite shrines, and the concentration of worship on the shrine "which Yahweh your God will choose out of all your tribes" (12:5). This requirement is integral to the opening chapter of detailed commands (12:1-31) with its concern for avoiding pagan rites (12:29-31). It means that if it is impracticable for a rite to take place at Yahweh's chosen shrine, it must nevertheless not take place elsewhere; such rites must cease to be sacral occasions. Thus Deuteronomy permits people to kill animals for food at home and to convert tithes and firstlings into monetary offerings (12:15-16, 20-25; 14:22-27), and it removes the cultic aspect to the provision of justice, to the ceremony whereby a slave opted to become a permanent family slave, and to the provision of asylum for someone who has committed homicide (15:16-17; 16:18-20; 19:1-13; contrast Exod 21:5-6; 22:6-7 [7-8]; 21:12-14).[53] Its law of unsolved homicide (Deut 21:1-9) achieves a delicate compromise between the need for the cultic rite to take place at particular locations in the land and the principle that sacrifice itself is confined to Yahweh's chosen shrine. It is difficult to imagine a rite which is nearer to being a sacrifice without actually being one.[54]

The effect of several of these measures is to remove various activities from the sphere of the sacred to that of the secular and/or to change their motivation and effect from a sacral one to a humanitarian one. But it is misleading to describe Deuteronomy's ethos as secularizing or anthropocentric.[55] While Deuter-onomy makes certain events less sacral occasions, at other points it makes people more dependent on Yahweh's shrine. Passover/Unleavened Bread, Pentecost, and Tabernacles

---

[53]Weinfeld (p. 237) comments that the place of asylum, which is a shrine in Exod 21:13-14 (מקום—cf. Deut 12:5!) and Num 35 (a place to stay until the death of the high priest), is solely a place of protection and not a place of atonement in Deut 19:1-13.

[54]I think Weinfeld (p. 210) underestimates the sacral nature of this rite (cf. Roifer, *Tarbiz* 31:119-43; McKeating, *VT* 25:62-64; Zevit, *JBL* 95:377-90). There *is* miasma needing to be removed, and expiation is effected not by confession (there is no confession) but by the rite itself.

[55]So Weinfeld, e.g., *Deuteronomy*, 188-90, 214-17; cf. Milgrom's objections and Weinfeld's clarifications in *IEJ* 23:156-61, 230-33; also von Rad's remarks, *Gottesvolk*, 34.

must be celebrated here (16:1-17);[56] all offerings and sacrifices
are to be brought here, and account is given here of the
worshiper's faithful distribution of tithes at home (12:6; 15:19-
20; 26:1-15). Appeal beyond a local court is made to the priests
and the judge here (17:8-13). Whether Deuteronomy is
desacralizing rites or transferring them to the chosen shrine, it
does so out of the same concern to ensure that Israel's religious
life is focused on Yahweh. The fact that it pays little attention to
how offerings and sacrifices are to be made reflects its central
concern with *to whom* and *where*.[57]

Indeed, it is not only its cultic law which is concerned with
the acknowledgment of Yahweh. Religious life, social life, and
family life are all interwoven in Deuteronomy.[58] Its interest in
the family, the community, and the nation all relates to its concern that Israel should live their whole life before Yahweh;[59] it is
not really so much a book of law as a book of preaching, a book
of Yahwistic moral wisdom.[60] Matters that are of strictly legal
concern elsewhere in the ancient Near East (e.g., adultery or
even murder) and matters of purely private morality are treated
as part of the people's relationship with Yahweh; hence the way
they are approached and the punishments applied to them.[61]

If an anthropological approach to them is right, instructions regarding the external structuring of life also carry a significance in relation to people's religious and ethical commitment
to Yahweh.[62] Preserving distinctions is part of Israel's holiness;
it is for Yahweh's sake that Israel embodies the distinction between life and death (see 14:2, 21 in the context of 14:1-21).[63] It
is also a metaphor for the distinctiveness Israel is to maintain in

---

[56]Exod 12 presupposes that the whole community has easy access to
the/a shrine, so the assumption that people sacrifice there and eat at home is
not impractical.

[57]Cf. Bächli, 94-97. Von Rad questions whether "centralization" is of
focal importance to Deuteronomy (*Studies*, 67). The wide range of passages
related to this concern suggests it is (cf. Nicholson, *Deuteronomy and Tradition*, 54-55).

[58]Note also its concern with the home's religious significance (6:7-9;
11:19-20)—a different matter from its sacral significance (Carmichael seems
not to distinguish the two; see *Laws*, 56-57).

[59]Cf. von Rad, *Gottesvolk*, 55-56; Horst, *EvT* 16:49-75.

[60]Cf. von Rad, *Deuteronomy*, 19-24; idem, *Int* 15:3-13; Carmichael,
Laws, 17-52.

[61]Cf. McKeating, *VT* 25:61-68; L'Hour, *Bib* 44:1-28; Kornfeld, *RB*
57:92-109; Horst, 58-67.

[62]See pp. 140-41 and n. 28 above.

[63]Cf. Soler, *NY Review*, 14 June 1979, 24-30.

relation to the nations (7:1-6), and a means toward it—because these laws *are* part of Israel's distinctiveness.[64] Holiness is embodied in wholeness; this, too, may underlie the categorizing of clean and unclean animals (14:1-21),[65] as well as the concern about bodily emissions (23:11-15 [10-14]) and about completing what you have begun (20:5-7). Thus every aspect of life is capable of reflecting the confession that "Yahweh is our God and we are his people."

Other Nations, Other Gods

The strength and the limitation of Deuteronomy's theology is this systematic focusing on Israel as Yahweh's people and Yahweh as Israel's God. Its strength lies here because it makes possible a sustained exposition of the central message that Deuteronomy sees Israel to need in the period it addresses. Its limitation is that this is not all that needs to be said about Israel or about Yahweh. By focusing on Israel's privileged calling and responsibility and the importance of Israel's distancing itself from the nations, Deuteronomy obscures the fact that it is ultimately for the sake of the nations that Israel is called at all. This, apparently, was what it saw the situation to demand; and "it may well be the case, in any given situation, that that which we *can* say, responsibly and intelligibly, is not that which, were we to abstract from the two poles of concrete speech, we might have wished to say, or felt entitled or obliged to say."[66]

Similarly, in focusing on Yahweh as the exclusive object of Israel's actual commitment, Deuteronomy takes the existence of other gods for granted (they are worshiped, therefore they exist). It satisfies itself with mono-Yahwism; it does not explicitly press toward mono-theism. Yet in an inherently polytheistic context, perhaps a person who commits himself exclusively to Yahweh is nearer the God of Israel and the God of our Lord Jesus Christ, and closer to the truth, than a person who attempts the impossible task of being a theoretical monotheist.[67]

---

[64]Some backing for this approach to such laws is provided by the way that in apocalyptic clean animals symbolize Israel, unclean ones or hybrids the gentile nations or Israel's enemies (cf. J. Massyngberde Ford, *JSJ* 10:203-12).

[65]Cf. Douglas, *Purity and Danger*, 51-56. It is, however, a problem that this approach can suggest several different explanations of the same passage.

[66]Lash, *Theology on Dover Beach*, 39.

[67]So Rahner, *Theological Investigations*, 16:186.

There is a specific tension between Deuteronomy's stress on the rights, privileges, and responsibilities of womanhood, and its masculine understanding of God himself *(sic)*, though it has a little of the "appeal to the maternal side of divinity" which can sometimes be found in the OT:[68] Yahweh does appear as the eagle caring for her young as they learn how to fly, and as the mother who gave birth to Israel (32:11, 18). Nevertheless Deuteronomy distinguishes itself over against Canaanite religion in its reticence over the feminine in theology. In Canaanite religion, however, women were seen so predominantly in sex and fertility terms, to the exclusion of personal ones, that avoiding a feminine portrayal of God may have been the most radically nonsexist response Deuteronomy could have made to its context.[69]

DEUTERONOMY'S PASTORAL STRATEGY

Deuteronomy's behavioral values would be acceptable to most ethicists, and its theological perspective (with the further values this implies) would be acceptable in the context of biblical faith as a whole to anyone who was fundamentally sympathetic to that faith. Other features of Deuteronomy that seem odd, embarrassing, or objectionable need to be considered in connection with the practical object that Deuteronomy shares with other pentateuchal law collections. It wishes to influence people's actual behavior. To do this involves inculcating certain values and encouraging a certain perspective. But these are rather rarified and demanding, whereas instructions regarding behavior also need to start where people are and point out specific steps that lead toward where they should be.

Deuteronomy itself urges obedience to its law on the grounds that it is not נִפְלֵאת, not rarified, incomprehensible, or inaccessible (30:11-14). This is so partly because OT law starts

---

[68]Terrien, *Elusive Presence*, 310; cf. idem, *Horizons in Biblical Theology*, 3:141; also Trible, *God and the Rhetoric of Sexuality*, 31-71; Hamerton-Kelly, *God the Father*, 38-51.

[69]Cf. Rosemary Radford Ruether, *JSOT* 22:59; Segal, *JJS* 30:121-37; Hanson, *Ecumenical Review* 27:317-18; de Boer, *Fatherhood and Motherhood*. To speak of a patriarchal understanding of God is misleading, for the OT rarely describes Yahweh as father, partly for similar reasons to those which may have led to avoiding female terms for deity generally (so Hamerton-Kelly, 13-18).

from the same legal tradition as Israel knew from their environment in Mesopotamia and Canaan, as well as from the ethos of the clan as this had developed over the centuries. Israel's versions of such laws are set in a revolutionary new context, that of a personal relationship with Yahweh, but they are not always markedly different in content.[70] Sometimes Deuteronomy's behavioral values give its law a more exalted spirit that that of Mesopotamian law,[71] but this is not invariably the case.[72] Israelite law (like any law) has to start where its own people are. Its relationship with Mesopotamian and Canaanite law presupposes that it starts where people are as sinners, and starts where they are in their cultural context.

Starting Where People Are as Sinners

A suggestive insight on the nature of Deuteronomic (and other) law emerges from Jesus' discussion with the Pharisees concerning divorce (Mark 10:2-9), noted above (p. 110). The Pharisees, invited to answer their own question concerning the legality of divorce, do so by referring to Moses' acceptance of divorce in Deut 24. Jesus responds by drawing their attention to other passages from the Torah relevant to the topic under discussion, Gen 1:27 and 2:24; these by implication make divorce a much more questionable practice. Jesus explains the difference between them and Deuteronomy's provision by seeing the latter as given because of their stubbornness and unteachability (σκληροκαρδία).

Jesus' suggestion that within OT law we may distinguish between what expresses the absolute will of God and what is given as a result of human sin and to limit sin's consequences is not alien to Deuteronomy itself.[73] Throughout the framework to its laws, it places great emphasis on the sinfulness of those to whom they are given. The historical survey of Israel's journey from Sinai to the plains of Moab which opens Moses' speech begins by recalling the burden that the people's contentiousness (ריב) placed on Moses; this contentiousness against God and

---

[70]Cf. (Stamm and) Andrew, *Ten Commandments*, 75; cf. pp. 45-46 above.

[71]Cf. Eichrodt, *Theology*, 1:74-82.

[72]Hammurabi's code limits slavery for debt to *three* years (*ANET*, 170-71).

[73]Cf. Daube, *JJS* 10:1-13.

against Moses continued in their rebellious unwillingness when challenged to enter the land from the south (1:26-27, 32, 41, 43). Exodus and holy war traditions are turned upside down.[74] After their forty years' chastisement, the land is about to be given to Israel. Now Moses reminds them that they are an inherently sinful people, as their rebellious idol-making at the very moment of the covenant's inauguration had illustrated (9:6-29). The land is to be given them despite their sin rather than because of their righteousness. In describing their stubborn rebelliousness, Moses picks up the expression used to describe them in Exod 32–34, עַם־קְשֵׁה־עֹרֶף (Deut 9:6, 13),[75] the description in turn taken up by Jesus in Mark 10. Moses urges Israel not to continue to be stubborn (Deut 10:16), but he fears that their commitment will not last (5:29), and the Deuteronomic covenant offers more warnings about the consequences of disobedience than it does promises of blessing that will follow on obedience (Deut 27–28). Moses does not believe that Yahweh has yet given Israel a mind to understand what Yahweh has done for them (29:3 [4]), and he foresees the chastisements that their stubborn rebelliousness will bring upon them (29:17-27 [18-28]; 31:27-29). Thus Moses' "Song" is dominated by an awareness of this blindness and rebelliousness (32:4-25).[76] Only when Yahweh "circumcises" Israel's mind and provides them with the ability to commit themselves to him will they begin to live in obedience to his law (30:6-10).

Since the framework to Deuteronomy's laws so forcefully portrays Israel's sinfulness, it is not strange that the laws themselves presuppose acts and events which are less than ideal. The common casuistic form of the laws (e.g., 13:2-3, 7-8, 13-14 [1-2, 6-7, 12-13]) assumes that Israel will sin; the laws' concern is with how that sin is to be dealt with, so as to eliminate the evil from Israel, deter others, and open oneself to Yahweh's mercy and blessing rather than his wrath (13:6, 12, 18 [5, 11, 17]).

The casuistic laws presuppose various realities of a sinful world, such as slavery through impoverishment (15:12-18), the desire to have a king, as other nations do (17:14-20), legal disputes (19:15-21; 25:1-3), war (20:1-20), marital and other family

---

[74]Cf. Lohfink, *Bib* 41:105-34; Moran, *Bib* 44:333-42.

[75]Similar expressions in 9:27; 10:16; 31:27. σκληρός-σκληρότης and compounds are the LXX's equivalents to expressions such as קְשֵׁה־עֹרֶף. σκληροκαρδία itself occurs in 10:16 (elsewhere only Sir 16:10; Jer 4:4).

[76]The blindness and rebelliousness referred to in the rest of the Song is probably that of other nations (cf. Mayes, *Deuteronomy*, 389-92).

problems (21:10-21; 22:13-29; 24:1-4); they do not forbid slavery, monarchy, war, polygamy, or divorce. Each of these is open to the same statement that Jesus actually makes regarding the last of them (Mark 10:6), that they were not part of the way God created the world as the Torah itself describes it; indeed, each of them fits ill with Deuteronomy's ideals considered above (pp. 135-41).

Yet in the light of Israel's sinfulness, simply to ban them would be unrealistic. Deuteronomy's policy is to circumscribe them by, and to harness them to, the values and the theology it propounds. Thus slavery has a time limit set to it, a slave is to be regarded as a brother and allowed to worship as a member of the people of God, and when he is released he is to be given gifts to facilitate his reestablishing himself as a free man. The king is to be chosen by Yahweh, is to remember that he remains only brother among brothers, is not to use his position for his own gain, and is to apply himself to setting an examplary standard of obedience to Yahweh's teaching. The administration of law is to safeguard the innocent, and to be objective but not excessively vindictive with the guilty (for they, too, are brothers). War is Yahweh's means of his people entering into their blessing and of sinful nations being punished, but it does not justify a scorched-earth policy. In marriage a man has much of the power, but he cannot sell a captive wife when he tires of her, he cannot lightly accuse a wife of promiscuity, he cannot play fast and loose with a single girl's honor, and he cannot change his mind when he has divorced his wife.

The instructions concerning how one treats a man who becomes impoverished (15:1-11) illustrate most explicitly the tension between ideal and sinful reality within Deuteronomy itself.[77] Moses promises that there will be no poor in Israel, Yahweh will so bless them in the land (15:4, 6). Yet the instruction concerning giving loans and cancelling debts (15:1-3, 7-11) presupposes that people will become poor and need loans. It does so rightly, because the promise depends on obedience to Yahweh (15:5)—which will not be forthcoming. Thus, despite this promise that there need be no poor people in the land, Deuteronomy can also make the prediction that there will always be poor people in the land (15:11); and just as well, because it can therefore give thought to how their position can be alleviated, including

---

[77]Cf. L. T. Johnson, *Sharing Possessions*, 92-93.

taking into account the sinful nature of those who are more prosperous and will want to look after their own interests (15:9-10; cf. chap. 18).

Starting Where People Are in Their Cultural Context

In a sense any corpus of instruction has to begin where people are in their cultural context. Jesus' expectation that a disciple will volunteer to walk two miles with someone if compelled to walk one presupposes a particular setting in the Roman empire. There, however, the actual command introduces a quite new feature into its context. OT law characteristically works in a different way. It takes up a command or practice which itself belongs to a cultural context and affirms it. An Israelite is thus commanded, for instance, to drain the blood from meat before eating it, to kill and burn animals in worship of God, and to treat his eldest son ("the beginning of his strength," 21:17) more favorably than his other children. These were practices assimilated by OT laws rather than ones devised by them.[78]

Some of the standards that the laws assimilated were ones that are widely evidenced elsewhere. A concern for protecting and providing for people such as widows, orphans, and the poor, and for justice for all, appears throughout the ancient Near East and in other cultures.[79] Sexual requirements such as a ban on adultery and bestiality are also common to ancient Near Eastern and other ancient and modern, "primitive" and "civilized" cultures. Here there is little difference between one cultural context and another.

Practices such as abstaining from eating blood are more culture-bound. While adopting these, Deuteronomy frequently transforms their significance by giving them new meaning. This is a common feature of how cultures develop. Within Christianity, it appears in the NT's utilization of contemporary cleansing rites in baptism and of contemporary leadership structures in

---

[78]On this phenomenon, see Clavier's study of archaic survivals in OT faith (*Les variétés de la pensée biblique*, 62-94); Fohrer's treatment of the relationship between Yahwism and magical views, taboos, and rites (*Theologische Grundstrukturen*, 51-71, 113-20); Horst's similar discussion (*EvT* 16:55-67); and Brichto's examination of the curse, which may have begun as a magical idea but is transformed in contexts such as Deut 29:19-20 (20-21); 30:7 (*Problem of "Curse,"* 31-32).

[79]Cf. Fensham, *JNES* 21:129-39.

the position of elders, and in the later appropriation of the feasts and rites which lie behind festivals such as Christmas and Easter.

Deuteronomy takes over various taboos in this way, including that on working on certain days or in certain years, on eating the whole of each year's produce and of the animals born each year, on eating the flesh of certain creatures,[80] on association with a man who has just built a house, planted a vineyard, or married a wife, on appropriating the property or even the persons of cities given over to the worship of another deity, as well as on eating meat with blood in it. Thus it enjoins rest on the sabbath (5:12-15), release of debts in the sabbath year (15:1-11), draining off blood before eating meat (12:16, 23-25),[81] offering the first of one's crops, the first of the offspring of one's animals, and tithes of one's crops to God, and leaving the final remnants of the harvest uncollected (14:22-29; 26:1-15; 24:19-22), abstaining from the flesh of unclean species (14:3-20), excusing from military service the man who has just built a house, planted a vineyard, or married a wife (20:5-7; cf. 24:5), and destroying the persons and property of alien cities (20:15-17; 13:16-18 [15-17]). It perhaps even devises new taboos, on mixing seed, animals, or fabric (22:9-11).

Similarly, Deuteronomy takes over various rites, including erecting altars and burning animals as a way of offering them to God, hanging a man who has been executed (if this was originally a way of "showing" God that his crime has been dealt with),[82] killing an animal in a community act of contrition following an unsolved murder, and roasting a lamb and daubing its blood on one's doorway on a certain day in spring (27:1-8; 21:1-9, 22-23; 16:1-7).

---

[80]Including the pig? Cf. the evidence for this being a pre-Israelite taboo associated with the pig's role in magical/demonic rites (see de Vaux, *Bible and the Ancient Near East*, 252-69; Stendebach, *BZ* 18:263-71). The religio-anthropological explanation of the taboo on pork could complement rather than rival this interpretation (cf. pp. 140-41 and 151-52 above).

[81]Weinfeld (p. 214) believes Deuteronomy abandons the dogma that blood is sacral. Actually Deuteronomy still treats the blood of sacrificial animals as sacral; it rather changes the definition of sacrificial animals. Blood as such never was sacral (game animals never had to be offered to Yahweh when they were slaughtered), though it was taboo, and remains so in Deuteronomy—with emphasis, indeed (Deut 12:16, 23-25). Deuteronomy's lack of reference to covering the blood may mean it has abandoned one feature of the taboo, or it may be insignificant.

[82]So Phillips, *Ancient Israel's Criminal Law*, 25-26, though bodies could also be exposed as a warning to others (cf. Saggs, *Iraq* 25:149-50).

Deuteronomy also takes over certain property laws. It adapts from Exod 21-22 a law of slavery and a law of seduction (Deut 15:12-18; 22:28-29; cf. Exod 21:2-11; 22:15-16 [16-17]). In Exodus these are aspects of the law of property, because the master bought the slave (21:2, 7; note 21:21), and because seduction threatens to deprive a man of his daughter's dowry (cf. 22:15-16 [16-17]). The law of levirate marriage (25:5-10) is also in a sense a property law, in that it concerns a man's wife and inheritance, as is the requirement that a man shall not deprive his firstborn son of the firstborn's rights (21:15-17).

In adapting such practices, Deuteronomy characteristically transforms their significance by subordinating them to its theological and ethical concerns. Thus it is interested in the laws of slavery and of seduction because they concern the welfare of human beings, and its development of these laws expresses this concern. The other Deuteronomic marriage laws are also primarily concerned "with the violation of family morality rather than with financial liability."[83]

Deuteronomy also transforms the rites it enjoins, by reinterpreting their significance. Passover recalls the exodus; the heifer rite safeguards justice and expresses contrition; the cultic rites on the Jordan bank express joyful worship, mutual fellowship, and the importance of the law (16:1-7; 21:1-9; 27:1- 8).[84]

The process of adapting and transforming is particularly evident in the handling of ancient taboos. The sabbath day enables people to rest, and it recalls being freed from slavery in Egypt (5:14-15). The release of the sabbath year involves not merely letting the land lie fallow but letting debts lie uncollected, for the benefit of one's poor brethren (15:1-11). Surrendering the first of one's crops and of one's flocks, tithes of one's crops, and the final remnants of the harvest enables one to express one's reverence, joy, and gratitude to God and to give to the needy (14:23, 26-29; 24:19-22; 26:3-15). Excusing a newly married man from military service gives him the opportunity to make his wife happy (24:5; cf. 20:7).[85]

---

[83]Weinfeld, 284.

[84]See further pp. 150-51 on the introduction of the principle that sacral rites must take place only at the place Yahweh chooses.

[85]Cf. Seitz's comments regarding 20:5-7 on the turning of a practice with a demonic background into something of humane value (Redaktionsgeschichtliche Studien, 156-57).

The practice of חרם reflects another taboo. Israel is to give to God (and thus to kill or destroy) the nations they displace when they occupy their land (chap. 7; 20:16-20), the inhabitants of any Israelite city that goes back on its commitment to Yahweh (13:13-19 [12-18]) (it is not only חרם but כליל), and the adult inhabitants of any foreign city that refuses to make peace with the Israelite army (20:10-15) (cf. the treatment of Sihon and Og, 2:34-35; 3:6-7, though there the whole population was involved). The Amalekites are also to be destroyed (25:17-19), though here the technical term חרם does not occur, as it does in the story of Saul's actual defeat of the Amalekites (1 Sam 15:6, 15, 20). Although some passages see Israel as free to profit from what they find in a conquered city (2:35; 3:7), elsewhere even inanimate objects are to be destroyed (13:16-18 [15-17]). The nations' objects of worship are particularly contagious; they are to be given over to Yahweh, and their holiness will affect any Israelites who appropriate them (7:26). The taboo reflects the metaphorical contagion of the objects and their owners. If Israel does not destroy the nations, their false worship will infect Israel by leading them astray into the worship of their gods (7:4-6, 16) or into their abhorrent forms of worship (תועבות) (20:18). It is because of such abhorrent practices that these nations are being punished (20:9-13); herein lies their "wickedness" (9:1-5). The custom of חרם is thus made to serve the characteristic Deuteronomic stress on loyalty to Yahweh and is the execution of his judgment on his enemies. In the case of the Amalekites, however, Deuteronomy sees them as guilty of a particularly inhuman attack on Israel which indicated that they had no religio-moral standards at all ("they did not fear God"; 25:18).[86]

There are taboo features about Deuteronomy's concern with the shedding of other human blood. Israel is to see that murderers are to be executed, but that those who commit accidental homicides are protected, both lest "blood be upon you" and so that you "eliminate innocent blood [or the blood of the innocent] from Israel" (19:10, 13; cf. 22:8). The law of unsolved homicide is designed to wipe away this innocent blood (21:8-9).[87] A magical rite designed to deal with an irrational taboo is

---

[86]Cf. Weinfeld, 274-75.

[87]For כפר as having the basic meaning "wipe away," see Levine, *In the Presence of the Lord.* On the concern with blood as pollution in 21:1-9, see also p. 150 and n. 54 above.

thus harnessed to serving an ethical end within a Yahwistic religious context.[88]

It is thus precisely by taking on such legal practices, rites, and taboos that Deuteronomy seeks to make its own ethical values and theological perspective influential on the everyday life of Israel.

Deuteronomy's Compromises

Compared with more radical stances, Deuteronomy's compromises over ritual and over taboos yield considerable concessions. Regarding ritual and worship, it takes a mediating position between attitudes expressed elsewhere in the OT which are more or less critical.[89] It is less enthusiastic than prophets such as Ezekiel and Zechariah, the Priestly and Chronistic narrative works, and many of the Psalms; compared with them, it may seem to be cutting the shrine (and the ark) down to size.[90] On the other hand, it accepts the key place of worship in Israel's life, and offers no equivalent to the dismissive stance of many preexilic prophets to the temple and its worship (see Isa 1:11-17; Jer 7:21-23; Hos 6:6; Amos 5:21-25; Mic 6:6-8; cf. also the awareness expressed in 2 Sam 7:4-7; 1 Kgs 8:12-13, 27; taken further in Isa 66:1).[91]

The setting where Moses delivers Deuteronomy as his final sermon is the setting where Jesus declares that questions about the right "place" are becoming meaningless (John 4:20-24). Nevertheless, the NT does not suggest they were inappropriate in OT times, and the OT is not on the move from a more cultic to a less cultic view;[92] acceptance of cult and attacks on it

---

[88]Seitz (pp. 139-40) draws attention to the addition of the prayer in the Yahwistic/Israelite version of this rite, which transforms it from being simply magical (cf. von Rad, *Deuteronomy*, 135-37).

[89]Cf. H. W. Turner's study of OT attitudes, *From Temple to Meeting Place*, 68-78; also Brueggemann's analysis of the tension between Yahweh's freedom and his accessibility (*IDBSup*, 680-83).

[90]Cf. Clements, *VT* 15:300-312, partly following von Rad, *Studies*, 40.

[91]The stance that Samuel-Kings takes toward the temple is similar to the one it takes toward the monarchy: neither is Yahweh's idea or his ideal, but in the end he accepts each and, indeed, commits himself to each in a far-reaching way. Deuteronomy, too, takes a similar stance to both temple and monarchy: each is accepted, but each is circumscribed. These two perspectives could be interdependent, though they need not be.

[92]*Pace*, e.g., Ringgren, *Sacrifice in the Bible*, 73.

coexist through OT times. Nor does the coming of Christianity abolish cult or sacred space in practice, even though it may do so in theory.[93] The condescension that Deuteronomy shows in relation to people's instincts in Moses' day still seems to be needed. Perhaps it reflects the fact that human beings are physical creatures; as long as they live in this world they may appreciate a house of God they can see.

Deuteronomy's concern with ritual and worship might seem misguided, but fairly harmless. Its concern with slaughtering one's enemies, however, can offer justification for genocide in the name of religion, truth, morals, or even national identity, and it sits in sharp tension with the love and forgiveness of Jesus' teaching.

A theological understanding of Deuteronomy's attitude might begin from its realism. Talk of love and forgiveness in the context of international politics can look like escapist romanticism.[94] War is a fact of international relationships and thus of national life. Nations come into existence through war and maintain their existence through war; even a nation that seeks to remain neutral does not thereby avoid being involved. The question then is, does God involve himself in human life as it actually is, and thus in war as a recurrent feature of it? The assertion that he is a God of war expresses the conviction that he is so involved and can be known. "To describe God as a warrior is thus to say that God participates in human history, through sinful human beings, and through what have become the 'normal' forms of human activity."[95]

In making this affirmation, OT Israel was taking the same perspective as other nations did. Talk of "holy war" in the OT might imply that there is something distinctively holy about war, and something distinctively Israelite about the idea of holy war. Neither of these inferences is correct. In itself, war is no more holy than sheep-shearing;[96] it is simply part of life with

---

[93]On cult, see Mowinckel, *Psalms,* 1:15; on sacred space, see H. W. Turner, 323-45.

[94]Cf. Gottwald's critique of Deuteronomy, *RevExp* 61:307-10. *Tribes of Yahweh* suggests he has now moved to the opposite pole from escapist romanticism.

[95]Craigie, *Problem of War,* 41.

[96]Craigie, 49. "Yahweh war" is nearer to being an OT phrase ("Yahweh is a warrior," Exod 15:3; "Yahweh will have war," 17:16; "the wars of Yahweh," Num 21:14); cf. the comments on "people of God" and "people of Yahweh" on p. 62 above. Writers such as Smend (*Yahweh War*) thus prefer this phrase to

God, because all of life is to be lived before God. In itself, furthermore, there is nothing distinctively Israelite about the belief that the nation's God involves himself in its wars. The attitude of the Moabites or the Assyrians was quite similar to Israel's.[97]

Deuteronomy, then, accepts war as a fact. It then controls, circumscribes, directs, and harnesses it to Yahweh's purpose. Deuteronomy places it under *Yahweh's* control; the one who decides whom to fight and how is not an earthly leader but Israel's heavenly Lord, who wins victories despite his people's feebleness rather than through their strength.[98] It thus harnesses it to a moral purpose; Israel's defeat of the Canaanites is the act of Yahweh's just judgment on a distinctively wicked nation.[99] In case Israel is tempted to treat that as merely a way of providing ideological justification for acts of aggression based on mere self-aggrandizement, Deuteronomy reinforces war's moral significance by warning Israel that Yahweh will make war *against* them if they begin to behave like the nations that are displaced before them (e.g., 8:20; 28:45-68; 32:21-25).

As with the divorce law, Deuteronomy itself does not draw attention to ideals as opposed to sinful realities, though these are again implicit in the wider context of the Torah (in Gen 1–4 with its attitude to peace and violence). Outside Genesis-Kings, the prophets relate their vision of a harmonious world,[100] though that vision also presupposes that violent judgment has to take place before such a world is reached; the prophets are not embarrassed by the חרם idea (cf. Mic 4:13; Isa 34:5).[101] This conviction is maintained in the NT. Part of the unease raised by the חרם law is an unease at the theme of judgment in any form.

The above approach presupposes that the חרם law is to be

"holy war," which was long more usual, especially through the influence of von Rad's *Heilige Krieg*; cf. the discussion in G. H. Jones, *VT* 25:642-58.

[97]For the Moabites, see the Mesha stela (*ANET*, 320-21); for the Assyrians, see Weippert, *ZAW* 84:460-93.

[98]Cf. Weippert, 488; Lind, *Yahweh Is a Warrior*, 50-53, 146-48.

[99]Cf. the comment in Gen 15:16 that Yahweh's promise of the land to Israel could not yet be fulfilled because "the iniquity of the Amorite is not yet full."

[100]Gottwald notes Isa 2:1-4; 19:18-25 (*RevExp* 61:308); cf. the comments on p. 65 above. Craigie (pp. 79-81) wonders whether Israel could develop a vision of peace only on the basis of an experience of war.

[101]Cf. Malamat, *Biblical Essays*, 46.

taken at its face value, as designed to bring about the actual slaughter of peoples such as the Canaanites. Whatever its origin, however, this may be an inappropriate understanding of it, for it does not correspond to what actually happened in OT Israel. The Canaanites were not eliminated. Now there is a gap between law and practice in other areas of law, in Israel and elsewhere, and not one simply attributable to human lawlessness. It seems that laws were not always intended to be enforced; they were promulgated to indicate the moral and social priorities of the lawgiver.[102] The חרם law may, then, be a statement of an attitude to be taken toward Canaanite religion rather than a military policy to be implemented. This view of its significance is the more compelling if the law has its origin in the seventh century, when the question of a military campaign to eliminate the Canaanites was hardly a live one.

Either way, such nations are "no longer . . . simply peoples living in the land which Israel is settling. They are symbolically potent entities whose very existence poses a threat. They are extensions of destructive forces residing in the nature of the gods whom they worship and represent."[103] "All such sanguinary fictions whether in the form of history or prophetic anticipation [or of law] reflect in the contemporary mode of imagination men's acute sense of the struggle against the encroachments of the primeval chaos and for the viability of the human."[104] The חרם law, then, draws attention to the need at certain moments of history to take decisive action in the face of life or death threats from alien ideological forces, and to commit oneself to resist the forces of disorder that threaten destruction. There are moments when compromise is impossible.

Evaluation of Deuteronomy's Compromises

Perhaps it is difficult to see how we could evaluate whether Deuteronomy's compromises yield too much; its decisions were contextual ones, and at this distance we can hardly reenact and criticize them. The question which may underlie unease at some

---

[102]Cf., e.g., McKeating, *JSOT* 11:66.

[103]Rast, *Joshua*, 47.

[104]Wilder, *New Voice*, 59. Contrast Meyers's radically anti-symbolic understanding of the purity and חרם laws as designed to combat the danger of plague and other health problems (*CBQ* 43:108-9).

of its material, however, is whether compromise is acceptable at all, or whether affirming the radical, revolutionary stance more characteristic of the prophets implies rejecting the reformist compromises of the law. Thus Fohrer suggestively sees the OT as making various kinds of compromise between deep-rooted human approaches to life and the revolutionary, distinctive Israelite one with its far-reaching vision and demands; but he regards the compromise as tainted and only approves the revolutionary perspective.[105]

In contrast, Boissonnard and Vouga see Deuteronomy's positive significance as lying in its attempt to *do* something about things that the prophets (merely) lament.[106] This view assumes that half measures are better than no measures, in accordance with Bonhoeffer's observation that "you cannot and must not speak the last word before you have spoken the next to last. We live on the next to last word, and believe on the last, don't we?"[107] Deuteronomy remains a paradigm of a task that ethicist, social worker, social reformer, and legislator have to undertake, as they seek to draw social praxis as near as possible to ideals they may accept, without being unrealistically far away from the ones society actually accepts. They have to be practical. The tension between the praxis they are seeking and the one they start from cannot be too great, or it will simply snap. The necessity of adaptation as a society changes is especially clear with regard to law and praxis regarding marriage, divorce, family, and sexual relations generally.

Like other parts of the OT, Deuteronomy thus both undergirds and subverts the social order it presupposes; it accepts the Davidic institution, with a view to imbuing it with the Mosaic spirit.[108] Formally, it accepts many features of that social order, yet its "creative, egalitarian, and liberating dynamic"[109] explicitly undermines other aspects that it formally leaves untouched. It

---

[105]See his *Theologische Grundstrukturen*, 51-94.

[106]*Bulletin du Centre Protestant d'Etudes* 32:39-40.

[107]Letter of Advent ii, 1943, *Letters*, Fontana ed., 50 (enlarged ed., 157). The Torah (and Jesus), of course, expresses this as a tension between now and the Beginning rather than between now and the End.

[108]Cf. Rosemary Radford Ruether, *JSOT* 22:55; L'Hour, *Bib* 44:26-27.

[109]Hanson, *Canon and Authority*, 129. Hanson is discussing the Book of the Covenant; his argument applies the more clearly to Deuteronomy. Cf. also Russell, *JSOT* 22:68.

works not by stating theoretical theological and ethical principles and working out their implications, but by offering a critique of the theological and ethical praxis of specific sinful
human beings in their concrete social setting.

Rahner suggests that, though we can recognize that this
phenomenon had a right place in OT Israel, it can hardly be appropriate within the church now that "the absolute future" has
arrived in Christ.[110] The church, however, still lives with that
tension between the present age and the age to come (or the age
that is lost) to which Bonhoeffer draws attention. Thus the
church also finds itself driven into compromises over areas such
as divorce that change as society's attitudes change—because
Christians also live in history. This was already the case in NT
times. The issue of divorce illustrates it, if Matthew's μὴ ἐπὶ
πορνείᾳ is not merely an explicating of what is presupposed in
Mark, but a softening of Jesus' stance to meet the pastoral needs
of the church.[111] Less disputably the NT's attitude toward slavery illustrates it. Although slavery in NT times was often a
harsher institution than the one OT laws envisage,[112] and although the fact that all human beings were created free is now
reinforced by the fact that in Christ there is neither slave nor
free, the NT accepts slavery, urges slaves to submit to their masters, and offers no hints that their owners should question their
position.

The NT as well as the OT, then, incorporates a tension between what is and what ought to be, and in both the latter is
often expressed in the stories of the "early days" (creation, the
exodus, the judges period, and the ministry of Jesus and the pre-
Pauline church).[113] Deuteronomy offers us one instance of that
tension, instructive both for its actual content and as a model for
our own theological and ethical thinking.

---

[110]*Theological Investigations*, 16:190.
[111]Cf. also Paul's approach to questions of sexual practice in 1 Cor 7.
[112]Vawter notes that Hebrew has no special word for slave (*JES* 15:268);
and "slavery" was, of course, limited to seven years.
[113]Adela Yarbro Collins, *JSOT* 22:48-49.

Part III

A UNIFYING OR CONSTRUCTIVE APPROACH

Chapter 6

CAN WE FORMULATE ONE OLD TESTAMENT THEOLOGY?

In chapters 2–5 we have discussed and instanced two related approaches to the variety of perspectives in the OT, both of which involved some form of evaluation of the material. In chapters 6–7 we consider approaches to the interrelating of diverse material which do not involve judgments on where a trajectory peaks or where a writer is accommodating himself to his readers. Often diverse material may all seem to be of comparable value. How may it then be interrelated?

THE SEARCH FOR A UNITY UNDERLYING THE OLD TESTAMENT AS A WHOLE

Scholars who have sought to consider directly and systematically what form of theological unity can be attributed to OT faith in its varied manifestations have often posited a uniform structure of faith underlying the outward diversity we surveyed in chapter 1. Like different human beings sharing the same anatomy or a changing landscape built on the same geological features, the OT books in their variety presuppose the same underlying set of beliefs about subjects such as God and his people or humanity and the world. If we wish to discover "the unchanging truth hidden under its [the OT's] bewildering diversity," then, we must take a "cross-section" approach, by which "both the total structure of the system and the basic principles on which it rests can be exposed to view. In other words we have to undertake a *systematic examination* with objective classification and rational arrangement of the varied material."[1]

This cross-section approach can be a considerable aid to the interpretation of individual OT passages. As an awareness of the OT's historical framework aids an interpreter in the attempt to understand the historical significance of a particular passage, so an awareness of the OT's theological framework aids the attempt to understand the theological issues involved in a passage. While such a framework must not be imposed on a text which is not open to it, a provisional understanding of a passage's overall OT theological context may aid detailed understanding of the parts before this latter understanding in turn is allowed to lead to a more refined understanding of the whole. Alternatively, an awareness of the theological framework presupposed by a writer and his culture may help one to make explicit what is actually present in the text, though only implicitly so.

The cross-section approach also effectively translates or converts the kind of statements that appear in the OT into the kind of statements that fit a twentieth-century western Christian scholar's framework of reference. It may thus facilitate the OT's influencing that framework of reference and thus affecting both contemporary Christian theology and contemporary biblical interpretation. In both cases it may then fulfill a positive and a negative function. The positive function is to provide a resource input: systematic theology can be influenced by OT theology, and contemporary preaching can be influenced by the emphases of OT faith. Negatively, it provides a preliminary check on contemporary restatements of the faith and contemporary biblical preaching: if these are inconsistent with the underlying structure of biblical faith, a question mark is thereby placed by them.

DRAWBACKS AND LIMITATIONS ABOUT THE SEARCH FOR A UNITY UNDERLYING OLD TESTAMENT FAITH

Eichrodt's *Theology of the OT* remains, with that of von Rad, one of this century's two classic OT theologies. Nevertheless, it is often illuminating not because of its stated methodology but despite it, because the search for a structured unity of faith

---

[1]Eichrodt, *Theology,* 1:490, 27; the cross-section metaphor appears also in the work of Eichrodt's teacher, Procksch (see *Theologie,* 420). Cf. also Bright, *Authority of the OT,* 124-26; Harvey, *BTB* 1:6-7; Jacob, *Theology,* 11.

underlying the OT text suffers from the following marked drawbacks.

First, the converse of the point made above (p. 168) is that this search does not deal in the kind of statements that the OT actually makes, but only in what hypothetically underlies them. What is reckoned to underlie them is influenced by the interpreter, precisely because he is seeking material that can be related to his own framework of thinking. Von Rad's criticism of it is thus that it makes too far-reaching concessions to systematic theology, risking the imposition on the material of questions and categories that are foreign to it, when it would be wiser to concentrate on "Israel's own explicit assertions about Jahweh."[2]

Second, the underlying structure which this approach seeks to identify is one step removed from a living reality. To examine the frame of a building, the chassis of a car, or the anatomy of a person tells one a little about the reality itself, but by no means all. The examination reveals indispensable features of the reality, but not (necessarily) what is most significant about it. Bright relegates the concrete, living form of the text itself to a secondary place as "transient" and "incidental."[3] Yet the concrete, "incidental" features of the OT portrait of God or Israel are what gives that portrait its identity. What is meant by the confession "Yahweh is God" is only indicated by the specific detail of OT text and story. The abstraction can only live on the basis of it.[4]

Third, it is not clear how moving normative status from the text to the principles of which it is an incidental embodiment (as Bright proposes)[5] helps to allow the text of the OT itself to speak today. Concentrating on the principles that underlie the actual text means bypassing the problem of theological diversity and canonical authority rather than solving it, since it treats the text's diversity as inessential to its significance. It does not help

---

[2]*Theology*, 1:105; von Rad contrasts his approach with Köhler's in his *Theologie* (von Rad, 1:112). He does not deny the existence of an underlying structure of Israelite faith, and examines some features of it (2:99-125, 336-56), but he is more interested in what is "characteristic" or "typical" of it—by which he means the process of reactualization (*Theology*, 2:427, 428). Cf. Clements's warnings about the danger of systematic theology submerging the OT itself, because the latter is more concerned with institutions, rites, and persons than with ideas (*OT Theology*, 2-3, 155).

[3]Bright, 125.

[4]Cf. Wood, *Formation*, 101-5.

[5]Bright, 125, cf. 140-49. See also the discussion on pp. 122-27 above.

us to clarify the relationship between or relative status of Exodus and Ecclesiastes or Amos and Chronicles, even if these are all particular embodiments of the same underlying faith, or to see how specific books should influence doctrine and preaching. Nor does the cross-section approach in itself facilitate the making of strong links between OT and NT. Although it is often assumed that one needs to look beneath the surface of the text to its underlying principles if one wishes to see how the text speaks to today, it is not clear how this procedure helps to this end.[6]

Fourth, what can be said by means of a strictly cross-section approach is rather limited. The range of beliefs explicitly accepted throughout the OT is narrow; it may be virtually nonexistent. Bright summarizes the unique "structure of theology that undergirds the Old Testament"[7] as the belief in one God, to be worshiped aniconically, and to be essentially distinguished from all cosmic and natural phenomena; and the belief that the theater of his activity is the history of Israel, his chosen, covenanted people, whose past, present, and future are the objects of his lordship and the contexts or subjects of their faith, obedience, and hope. Yet even this bare bones of a faith does not actually run through the whole OT: notably, the theme of Israel as God's people is missing from the wisdom books.[8]

Fifth, conversely (as we noted in chapter 3), where a theme such as the position and calling of the people of God features prominently, at least as much theological interest attaches to insights and emphases that occur and then disappear (which would thus not strictly appear in a cross section) and to a series of recurrent questions to which the OT material gives different answers at different points, as attaches to consistent aspects of the way the theme is presented. Thus Gottwald compares Eichrodt's cross section with Max Weber's "ideal type" of culture, and comments that neither can do full justice to the historical data presented in the OT.[9]

A great cross-section OT theology such as Eichrodt's

---

[6]Similar objections (and others) apply to the attaching of special theological sgnificance to the "Hebrew way of thinking" which is said to lie further behind the text and its underlying theology (cf., e.g., Pedersen, *Israel*; Boman, *Hebrew Thought*; G. A. F. Knight, *Biblical Approach to the Doctrine of the Trinity*; with Barr's critique in *Semantics*; also Porter in *ExpT* 90:36-40).

[7]Bright, 126; for what follows, see 126-36.

[8]See the comments on p. 38 above.

[9]*Contemporary OT Theologians*, 31.

achieves much more than this implies, because it does not limit itself to what all the OT books have in common. Thus when Eichrodt studies topics such as covenant, law, the spirit of God, or the relationship between the individual and the community,[10] he does so historically, not merely synchronically. He draws attention to insights which emerge in different books or in different periods, as well as to features that are consistently characteristic of the material. Eichrodt is thus most illuminating when he is not drawing a cross section.[11]

Sixth, contrary to the desires or convictions of many of its advocates, a cross-section approach highlights the similarities between Yahwism and many other religions, ancient and modern, as much as the distinctiveness of Yahwism, for many such religions hold a set of beliefs regarding the deity and his relationship with the world of the kind that Bright lists.[12] Even the conviction of a special relationship between a God and a particular people is a common feature of religions.[13] Theologians of Memphis were proclaiming Ptah as the one God who created by his word two millennia before Israelite theologians made such claims for Yahweh;[14] Mesopotamia knew an equivalent concept to that of the patriarchal "personal God,"[15] and saw divine activity in its history in a way less distinctive of Israel than has often been maintained.[16]

This is not to imply that Israelite faith lacks distinctive features: the Israelite high God occupies the entire sacred domain; he alone is active in the world; as the transcendent God he is even sovereign over (and not immersed in) the natural realms of death and sex; he is mostly pictured in human rather than in animal or

---

[10]See, respectively, *Theology*, 1:36-69, 70-97; 2:46-68, 231-67.

[11]On this ambiguity in Eichrodt's work see further pp. 181-88 below.

[12]Cf. the summaries in Heiler, *History of Religions*, 142-53; Lonergan, *Method in Theology*, 109; M. Smith, *JBL* 71:135-47; Gottwald, *Tribes of Yahweh*, 667-78; and Saggs's treatment in *Encounter with the Divine in Mesopotamia and Israel*.

[13]Cf. Wright, *OT against Its Environment*, 15; Gottwald, 678.

[14]See *ANET*, 4-6 with Koch's comments, *ZTK* 62:253-84; cf. also Koch, *KD* 8:100-123.

[15]See Cross's reference to Jacobsen in *HTR* 55:259 = Cross, *Canaanite Myth and Hebrew Epic*, 75; Jacobsen's own views are now available in his *Treasures of Darkness: A History of Mesopotamian Religion* (see esp. 145-64, 254-56).

[16]See especially Albrektson, *History and the Gods*; but with Lambert's qualifications, *Or* 39:170-77; *OTS* 17:65-72.

inanimate terms, and he cannot be represented plastically in such terms; he is asexual; his people is a body of equals and its leaders are egalitarian rather than authoritarian functionaries.[17] There are differences between the theology of Memphis and the theology of Jerusalem, and we may well prefer the latter.[18] Yet even features central to the total character of Israelite religion, such as the theme of land and of Yahweh's involvement in Israel's history which gave them the land, are what one might expect given Israel's history and geography; and for the same reason some of Israel's peculiarities compared with Mesopotamia and Egypt are points of comparison with Ugarit and even Greece.[19] The distinctive features of Yahwism were functions of its social form.[20]

Finally, the nature of a cross section ought to be a fairly uncontroversial question; yet scholars who agree on the cross-section approach offer significantly different understandings of the cross-section, none of which has won universal acknowledgment in the way one might expect. Eichrodt's own classic attempt to describe a structure inherent in the biblical material rather than one introduced into it from outside has been subject to various criticisms;[21] subsequent OT theologians such as Vriezen, Zimmerli, and Fohrer have analyzed that structure differently, yet each of them illuminatingly. This reinforces suspicion of the view that OT faith is a structured entity with an invariable substructure.[22]

OLD TESTAMENT THEOLOGY AND OLD TESTAMENT SYMBOLS

Von Rad's suggestion that the common systematizing approach

---

[17]Gottwald, 679-91; cf. M. Smith, *JANESCU* 5:395; idem, *JBL* 71:146-47; Gray's emphasis, *Legacy of Canaan*, 162, 203-4, 217; also Saggs's careful treatment, 61-63, 92 (with special stress on Yahweh's negative distinctiveness), 151-52; Spriggs, *Two OT Theologies*, 83 (summarizing material in Eichrodt and von Rad).

[18]Cf. Koch, *ZTK* 62:284-93; in a debate with Koch, Baumgärtel rather emphasizes the differences: see *ZTK* 64:398-416; idem, *KD* 9:223-33 (responding to Koch, *KD* 8:100-123).

[19]So M. Smith, *JANESCU* 5:390-95.

[20]So Gottwald, 679-702; see the comments in chap. 3 at n. 27 above.

[21]See especially Spriggs, *Two OT Theologies*, and Gottwald, *Contemporary OT Theologians*, 23-62.

[22]See further pp. 111-16 above.

to OT *theology* runs the risk of missing the thrust of the OT *message* points us toward a further problem which affects the study of OT theology more broadly. In what sense does the term *theology* apply to the OT?

While the term can be used loosely to refer to any talk of God, more strictly it denotes a particularly analytic, conceptualizing, reflective, systematic way of speaking about God. Eichrodt emphasizes these features of his approach to the OT. Von Rad's point is that these are not characteristic features of the OT's own talking about God: "Israel was always better at glorifying and extolling God than at theological reflexion."[23] Biblical writers tell stories, declare judgment, expound hope, write letters, lay down laws, offer advice, lament affliction, and celebrate blessings, but they do not do theology as such.

If von Rad wished to expound the significance of the OT in its own terms, the logic of his position is that he should have called his work not "the theology of the OT" but "the message of the OT" or "the faith of the OT."[24] In the context of Christians attempting to grapple creatively and rigorously with their faith, however, the term *theology* has value status. Christians concerned for such a grappling with the religious significance of the OT will therefore naturally use the term *OT theology* for this enterprise, and for von Rad not to use that term would have risked his work not being taken seriously *theologically*. Perhaps similar considerations underlie Childs's describing his attempt to forge a new approach to biblical *hermeneutics* as a quest for a "new biblical *theology*."[25] Both von Rad's study of the kerygmatic intentions of Israel's explicit assertions about Yahweh and Childs's study of canonical hermeneutics are open to the comment "magnifique, mais ce n'est pas théologie"; conversely, Eichrodt was right that *theological* study of the OT has grounds for taking a systematic approach, whether or not the OT itself reflects a systematic way of thinking.

The question is, indeed, whether Eichrodt went far enough. In the remainder of this chapter we shall consider ways in which his work might be taken further.

---

[23]*Theology*, 1:122.
[24]Cf. his fondness for the word *kerygma* and his publication of the bulk of vol. II of his *Theology* as *The Message of the Prophets*.
[25]See his *Biblical Theology in Crisis*, 91-122 (my emphasis); cf. P. D. Miller's comments, *JBL* 90:210.

D. G. Spriggs has suggested that despite the consciously different approaches to OT theology taken by Eichrodt and von Rad, underlying their work are certain fundamental similarities.[26] One similarity which Spriggs hints at, without developing, is that both are concerned with the ongoing use and re-use of symbols in the OT. While Eichrodt organizes his work around the topics God and Israel, God and the world, God and man, he shows himself equally concerned with the OT's own symbolism when he superimposes the notion of the covenant on this framework (at least for the first part). He also traces the history of the covenant motif.[27]

Although von Rad, too, from time to time discusses the history of motifs such as the covenant, his approach is more decisively shaped by his related concern with the development of Israelite traditions, since this development (as he sees it) takes the form of a series of reinterpretations of the variety of "foundations" or "bases of salvation" or "initial appointments" of Israelite faith, the patriarchal covenant, the Sinai covenant, the Davidic covenant, and the foundation of Zion.[28] In whatever sense these "appointments" were initially historical events, they soon became symbols by which subsequent experiences were understood and future hopes were articulated—that is, they became types.[29] Thus, although on the surface von Rad's work is structured by tradition-complexes and authors, at a deeper level it is structured by a study of the developing significance of OT symbols.

The view that biblical theology is to be seen as the explication of biblical symbols is more explicit in F. F. Bruce's work on *The New Testament Development of Old Testament Themes*.[30] Bruce suggests that the way to organize an OT theology is to follow the model of the NT's presentation of the OT's theology by studying the ongoing significance and re-use of images such as God's rule, God's salvation, God's people, and God's servant. The study of symbols and the task of theology cannot actually be

---

[26]See Spriggs, *Two OT Theologies*, 60-63.

[27]*Theology*, 1:45-69.

[28]*Theology*, 2:411; cf. p. 12 above. Von Rad outlines the history of the covenant relationship in *Theology*, 1:129-35.

[29]Cf. von Rad's comments on typology in *Essays on OT Hermeneutics*, 17-39; idem, *Theology*, 2:362-74.

[30]The British edition was titled *This Is That: The New Testament Development of Some Old Testament Themes*; see especially p. 20.

equated, however, because symbolism and theology operate on different principles and according to different dynamics.

While theology is characteristically a reflective exercise which involves thinking through the nature, significance, and implications of religious experience and convictions in an essentially cerebral way, symbolism, imagery, and metaphor characteristically work at a more intuitive level and facilitate a more immediate response to and understanding of an experience. They involve the whole person's feelings, memories, experiences, and attitudes, as well as conscious thought-processes. They thus directly and inevitably influence the whole person, by a feedback process. Symbols do things, they do not merely communicate. To identify an event as redemptive or to describe God as a father is not merely to define but to change the event or the relationship. Symbols participate in the power of that to which they point.[31]

As a disciplined, reflective exercise theology depends on clear definition, measured statement, and careful nuancing. But when one uses symbols for relationships with God (such as fatherhood or covenant) or for evil (defilement, sin, guilt),[32] the associations or resonances of these words are as important as their dictionary meaning.

Theology is essentially analytic. It emphasizes the making of clear distinctions, not least between related realities. It probes for the answers to subtle, intricate questions. It will not be satisfied with allusiveness. Its terms are defined so as to be capable of being related to other terms; they are part of a quasi-technical system. Symbolism, however, has a holistic instinct. It is characteristially interested in the links between things. It manages to mean more than it says (and to do more than it says) because it trades on these deep links. It is at home with the paradoxical, living as it does by bringing and holding together things that are not "naturally" compatible. In contrast, theology's analytic instinct nudges paradox into becoming contradiction or dualism or oversimplification.[33]

Symbols such as covenant are thus inherently plurivocal. The language of theology is that of the univocal sign, studied by semantics. It presupposes that we exercise a discipline in using

---

[31]So Tillich, *Systematic Theology,* 1:265.
[32]See especially Ricoeur, *Symbolism of Evil.*
[33]Cf. Bridge, *Images of God,* 135.

religious terms which extends, where possible, to making one
word mean one thing and another mean something else; we do
not encourage them to interchange. Theology uses terms in a
technical way; plurivocity is a vice which produces misunderstanding. Symbols, however, change their meaning and reference. This is not merely incidental to their nature but inherent
in it. If they did not do so, they would cease to function as interpreters of experience; they would then die, and the depth in experiences might no longer be understood or appropriated. Their
plurivocity thus facilitates understanding. Part of the point of
symbols is that there is no one-to-one correspondence between
symbols and defined concepts. So a motif from everyday life
(perhaps one which was already of symbolic significance) such as
ברית is taken up by a biblical writer and turned into a symbol for
the relationship between God and humanity, because it can express familiarly and powerfully certain aspects of that relationship which the writer wishes to emphasize.[34] But because it is a
symbol (and because it has several meanings in everyday life) it is
then capable of various applications. It is "open-ended," like a
parable; it has "the hermeneutical openness of the 'proverb,'
which offers no ready-made interpretation and places no re-
straint on intuition."[35] It can be re-used in new situations with
fresh meanings, and it can survive substantial changes in what it
expresses. If theology relates to semantics, symbols, which mean
more than they say, invite hermeneutics.

Further, theology of course moves between analysis and
synthesis; it does believe in the formal coherence of a systematic
understanding of reality. Perhaps the archetypal symbols belong
to an overall "symbolic and mythic universe" and "unfold a
structure of the World."[36] But if form, coherence, and system belong to symbolism at all, they are of quite a different kind from
those of theology. "Each image will have its own conceptual con-
ventions, proper to the figure it embodies," and the various images will not be open to a single overall conceptual analysis.
Admittedly "they attract one another and tend to fuse, but
they have their own way of doing this, according to their own

---

[34]I here ignore the (nevertheless helpful) classification of symbols into,
e.g., personal, cultural, and archetypal (cf. Wheelwright, *Metaphor and Reality*, 102-11; Perrin, *Jesus and the Language of the Kingdom*, 62, 84-85).

[35]Ricoeur, *Semeia* 4:134, on parable; McKane, *Proverbs*, 23, on משל.

[36]So, respectively, Ricoeur, *Freud and Philosophy*, 40; Eliade, *History of
Religions*, 99.

imagery laws, and not according to the principles of conceptual system."[37]

The Bible characteristically lives in the dynamic, intuitive, holistic, plurivocal, open-ended world of symbolism, not in the disciplined, reflective, conceptual, analytic, measured world of theology. This point can be expressed very radically. Austin Farrer, for instance, approves of the view that "in Scripture there is not a line of theology, and of philosophy not so much as an echo"; not even Paul or John work with a system of theological concepts. Thus what theology since the fathers has done is, however inevitable, alien to the nature of the biblical material itself.[38]

This is, however, too sharp a drawing of the line between biblical symbolism and biblical theology. First, theology itself, for all its concern with definition and analysis, cannot do without symbols. Paul Tillich argues that nothing nonsymbolic can be said about God except that statement and, perhaps, the statement that God is Being itself.[39] If theology concentrates exclusively on being disciplined, conceptual, analytic, measured, etc., it will quite fail to represent its subject even with such adequacy as human language can. In practice, theology inevitably uses the same range of terms as symbolism does, because it needs the kind of facility offered by these symbols if it is to approach its subject at all.[40]

Second, symbolism itself invites, or at least is open to, conceptual explication. Though it is concerned to do more than communicate at the cerebral level, it is not concerned to do less than that. There is a dynamism about symbols which, Paul Ricoeur suggests, "is the primary condition for any move from figurative expression to conceptual expression. The process of interpretation is not something superimposed from the outside on a self-contained expression; it is motivated by the symbolic expression itself which gives rise to thought. It belongs to the essence of a figurative expression to *stand for* something else, to *call for* a new speech-act which would paraphrase the first one

---

[37]Farrer, *Glass of Vision*, 45.

[38]*Glass of Vision*, 44-45; cf. Bridge, 132-38. According to Hart, the actual word *theologia* is not found until the Alexandrians and comes into extensive use only with the high Middle Ages (*Unfinished Man*, 398).

[39]*Systematic Theology*, 1:264-65; 2:10.

[40]Cf. Hart's comments (p. 294) on theology's becoming de-generate when symbols cease to generate life for it.

without exhausting its meaningful resources."[41] Symbols "push toward speculative expression"; they are themselves "the dawn of reflection."[42]

Further, and third, this movement from symbol to system and conceptualization is (despite Farrer and Bridge) already taking place within scripture. If theology is the fruit of an interaction between Palestine and Greece, it is not surprising if Paul and John are par excellence the Bible's two reflective, analytic theologians, whose rethinking of the scriptural message under Greek influence sets the pattern for the work of later theologians.[43] One can, indeed, see the beginnings of dialogue between Palestine and Greece in the later parts of the OT, while there is already evidence of a reflective, systematic way of thinking before the period of Greek influence, notably in Isa 40–55 and in wisdom's philosophical theology.[44]

Symbolism and reflective, analytic theologizing are not alien to each other, but they are different. Part of biblical theology's reflectiveness, then, will be to take account of the distinctiveness of symbolism's dynamic and to seek to do justice to its special characteristics, in the process of seeking to explicate its capacity for articulation in the conceptual terms with which we are at home.[45] It will recognize that translating symbols into theological terms inevitably risks misunderstanding them and loses some of their significance; not all of their significance can be conceptualized.[46] It will also recognize that, because theology uses many of the same symbols as the Bible does, particular care needs to be given to avoiding reading the biblical use of symbols as if it were in fact measured theological use of the same terms.[47]

Covenant provides a convenient and important example.[48]

---

[41]*Semeia* 4:133; cf. idem, *Conflict of Interpretations*, 288. This does not imply that Ricoeur sees the philosophic as more "masterly" (so Vance, *Interpretation of Narrative*, 120-21): contrast Ricoeur's remarks in *Rule of Metaphor*, 22-23, 138 (cf. Crossan, *BR* 24:23-24).

[42]Ricoeur, *Freud and Philosophy*, 39.

[43]Cf. Ricoeur, *Semeia* 4:135-38; Ebeling, *Word and Faith*, 93-94. On other NT "theologians" see Rahner, *Theological Investigations*, 5:28-29.

[44]Ricoeur, 129; cf. Mack, *Int* 24:46-60; idem, *Logos und Sophia*; Beardslee, *Int* 24:62; and Clements's observation that Israelite faith is becoming more amenable to theological treatment the more it becomes a religion of a book (*OT Theology*, 23).

[45]Cf. Ricoeur, 132.

[46]Farrer, 148; Eliade, 98-99; Ricoeur, 36.

[47]Cf. Baker's remarks in *What about the NT?* 167.

[48]On the historical and critical questions, see pp. 44-48 (esp. n. 67) above.

Covenant can have various meanings in the OT, all drawing attention to aspects of the relationship between God and humanity but varying in their emphases. Indeed, the differences in the understanding of the relationship between God and humanity which are expressed in Genesis, Exodus, and Deuteronomy (not to say subsequent books) by the covenant symbol are as notable as the similarities. Conversely, similar emphases concerning this relationship appear (for instance) in Genesis and in Isa 40–55, or in Deuteronomy and Amos, even though in Genesis and in Deuteronomy covenant is an important symbol, while in Isa 40–55 and Amos it is relatively unimportant. Indeed, more significantly, when it does appear in these latter books, it refers to other relationships as well as to the central one between Yahweh and Israel (see Isa 42:6; 49:8; 54:10; 55:3; Amos 1:9).

If covenant were a clearly defined key concept from a systematically thought-out theology, then the unevenness with which it appears in the OT (e.g., its virtual absence from Amos) would be more surprising than is necessarily the case if it is actually, on the contrary, a symbol which a writer may or may not use. As Eichrodt acknowledges, the relationship which he denotes by the term *covenant* is present in the OT both in books such as Genesis and Deuteronomy which use the word rather frequently (though with different emphases in its meaning), and in a book such as Amos where it does not use the word (indeed, the idea is missing where Amos does use the word). It is present in a book such as Hosea on some occasions where Hosea uses the term ברית (6:7; 8:1) and also in other parts of the book where instead and more characteristically Hosea speaks of the relationship between Yahweh and Israel in terms of marriage. He could, perhaps, have used the word of the latter (cf. Mal 2:14; ? Prov 2:17), but does not. When he applies it to human relationships, it is to political ones (10:4; 12:2), so perhaps for Hosea ברית suggested a less personal relationship than the one which he wanted to indicate obtained between Israel and Yahweh in the light of his marriage experience.[49] There is thus a distinction between covenant as a possible technical theological symbol for the relationship between God and Israel (both as pictured by political treaties and as pictured by other relationships) and ברית as an intuitive symbol (which refers in Hosea, and perhaps commonly in the OT, mainly to the former).

---

[49]Cf. Carroll, *When Prophecy Failed*, 14-16.

If theology is to use words such as covenant which are familiar as translations of OT symbols, then at least it needs to be wary of the danger of confusing the two usages. Eichrodt himself explains that he is using covenant not simply as an equivalent to בְּרִית, but as a general term for the relationship between Yahweh and Israel established by God's free act in history which makes Israel his unique people.[50] Nevertheless, it is understandable that critics have misunderstood him at this point.[51] Vriezen preferred to use the word *communion* to describe the relationship between God and humanity suggested by the OT, and to treat covenant as one (central) symbol of this relationship,[52] and this procedure seems preferable to the adoption of one of the OT's terms which is so plurivocal.

Although at one level the unity of the OT lies in the set of symbols which run through it, this unity is not strictly a theological one. Sometimes the language is the same but the meaning or reference changes; sometimes different symbols refer to aspects of the same reality. As diversity of symbolism may obscure theological continuity, so continuity of symbolism may obscure theological diversity. The study of symbolism may give us the impression that there is more theological unity about the OT than is actually the case, or that there is less.[53] Further, it is in princi-

---

[50]*Theology*, 1:18; cf. also his treatment of the history of the covenant idea, which draws attention to the diversity of the OT's own thinking (*Theology*, 1:45-69).

[51]Indeed, Eichrodt himself can sometimes speak of "on the one hand the covenant, on the other the symbols of sonship, marriage . . ." (*Theology*, 1:69). Vogels in his recent study of *God's Eternal Covenant* treats covenant in the Bible as if it were a term of univocal, technical meaning in a systematic, ordered theology. Levenson suggests that scholars have been misled into systematizing (or antithesizing) Moses and David by the mere presence of the word בְּרִית in both contexts—as if this in itself meant that there *must* be a significant theological relationship between them (see *CBQ* 41:215-18).

[52]*Outline*, e.g., 153-62, 166-70. Cf. Gottwald, *ExpT* 74:210; also, again, Eichrodt's own remarks on covenant and other relationship symbols, *Theology*, 1:67-69.

[53]I find many of Tillich's sermons (e.g., in *The Shaking of the Foundations*) illuminating and helpful, partly because I can identify with the symbols he brings to life. But Tillich's more academic works (and indeed, sometimes the sermons themselves) suggest that his underlying view of reality is somewhat different from mine. Eichrodt makes a parallel observation regarding symbolic *practices* such as sacrifice, which can change their meaning even while their form remains the same (*Theology*, 1:167-72).

ple impossible to identify one central OT symbol or to systema-
tize the OT's symbols as a whole.[54]

These considerations suggest that studying OT symbols
cannot itself be the basis for writing OT theology, though it is an
important part of the preparation for this task, in that the scholar can go on from tracing the background, significance, and history of individual OT symbols, moving from one symbol to the
various realities which it may represent, and from a variety of
symbols to the same or related realities, and thus from intuitive
symbols to clearly defined concepts or conceptual symbols. Although the study of OT symbolism is an aspect of OT
hermeneutics, theology itself is not to be reduced to
hermeneutic.

A CONSTRUCTIVE APPROACH

There is a second sense in which Eichrodt's approach to OT theology needs to be taken further. We noted above that there is a
tension in his work between a methodological commitment to a
cross-section approach and an interest in the material's historical diversity which he shows in the course of his actual study of
OT themes. Eichrodt can speak of seeking to identify "the unchanging truth hidden under its bewildering diversity," yet also
acknowledge that "the variety of the OT testimonies" is "the result of observing a complex reality from various angles in ways
which are in principle concordant one with another";[55] the nature of God is such that sometimes only contradictory formulations do justice to it.[56]

Faced with a plurality of approaches to diversity and unity
in OT theology which feature in Eichrodt's work, Spriggs suggests that his fundamental view is the one which allows various
perspectives to contribute to a larger whole.[57] Eichrodt himself,
however, does not work out the implications of this promising
insight, apparently because of his emphasis on underlying unity.
Only rarely does he seek to portray the whole to which the various testimonies refer. He does offer a "synthesis" of the OT picture of God, as holding together the idea of power without limit
(with which holiness and wrath are associated) and the idea of

---

[54]Cf. Porteous, *Living the Mystery,* 25-27.

[55]*Theology,* 1:490, 517. Eichrodt also allows here for contextually derived diversity and for fluctuation between profound insight and relative
impoverishment.

[56]*Theology,* 1:104, 205.

[57]*Two OT Theologies,* 89.

self-limitation in making himself known as a person in love and righteousness through his entering into his special relationship with Israel.[58] He also analyzes the interweaving of "the individual and the community in the Old Testament God-man relationship," acknowledging that the OT is not to be seen as evolving from primitive community thinking toward the developed individualism of the NT, but as holding together an individual and corporate view.[59] But such analyses are the exception rather than the rule.

After tracing the changing "forms of the Old Testament hope of salvation" Eichrodt does consider their implications for "a right understanding of the divine revelation" as a whole: that they portray salvation as something historical, concrete, and earthly (and such therefore is the God who brings it); that nevertheless salvation is of supernatural origin; and that the eschatological hope opens up the possibility of resolving the tensions of Israel's unfulfilled destiny as a nation, of Israel's unfulfilled calling before God, and of the relationship of the individual to the community. He does not go on to reflect on the diverse and contradictory features of Israel's hope of salvation which he notes (whether that hope is for Israel or for all nations, whether it is achieved by political/military means or by nonpolitical/peaceful ones, whether a personal redeemer figure is integral to it). Nor, in consequence, does he seek to identify the truths these tensions witness to or the way the alternatives complement each other. Nor does he make it clear how such theological needs are "fully met in the NT confession of Jesus as the Messiah."[60]

Eichrodt cuts the ground from under much constructive theological work of this kind by appealing to the fact that God is beyond reason and can only be described by means of contradictory formulations; Gottwald perceives the influence of Eichrodt's neo-orthodox background here.[61] Certainly Barth speaks of the impossibility of gaining a systematic conspectus at points where the OT does speak in contradictory ways.[62]

---

[58]*Theology*, 1:286-88. Cf. his observations on God's immanence and his transcendence, represented by the Ark and the Tent (1:109-12), and those on the names of God (1:205).

[59]*Theology*, 2:231-67, though still rather exaggerating the significance of the individual emphasis in Jeremiah and Ezekiel.

[60]*Theology*, 1:472-94; quotation from p. 490.

[61]See 1:205; cf. Gottwald, *Contemporary OT Theologians*, 54-55.

[62]See, e.g., *Dogmatics*, 1/1:179-81, on Exod 19–20 and Jer 31 (and prophecies of judgment and salvation generally). Barth here dismisses harmo-

The warning against a rationalist systematizing is an appropriate one, but it hardly disallows us from thinking systematically about God at all (as Eichrodt and Barth, each systematizers on the grandest scale, must grant). Neither can it determine a priori where the attempt to think constructively about the truth as a whole as the OT witnesses to it reaches its boundary. Eichrodt's own examples point us toward further attempts to explicate the theological significance of the OT material in a way that he did not, partly because he was primarily concerned with his cross section.

The problem is that the cross-section approach does not encourage the interpreter to take up the fact that the OT writers have all perceived some aspect of God and his ways, and thus provide us with a series of complementary portraits of him. As is the nature of a portrait, all these reflect the perspective the artist brings to the subject, yet this perspective also unveils aspects of the real nature of the subject himself. To gain maximum insight into the subject, we look not merely at what they have in common, but also at what they suggest cumulatively; and in studying OT theology, we are concerned not merely with the beliefs actually expressed by individual OT writers and in particular OT books, or with the assumptions which underlie these beliefs, or with the OT faith as "an entity given in finished form at the start and merely unfolding itself in history,"[63] but with the total perspective that these portraits together offer when all have been painted.[64]

OT theology is thus a constructive, not merely a reconstructive, task. The OT itself comprises building blocks (or quarried stone) with which theology can then work. The building materials were finally collected by the Jews who determined the bounds of the OT canon, but they themselves were putting in order materials which had accumulated over centuries; it is not necessarily their vision of the building that is to be implement-

---

nizing, systematizing, measuring one by the other, and balancing one by the other, and allows only a listening to each witness separately. In 2/1:496-99, however, he indulges in such a comparative exercise, in discussing divine constancy and mutability. Cf. C. A. Baxter, *Movement from Exegesis to Dogmatics*, 230-31, 416-17.

[63]Gottwald, *Contemporary OT Theologians*, 52-53, commenting on Eichrodt; also Johnstone's comment that Bright speaks of a theology antecedent to the text, whereas actually a theology is built from it (*SJT* 22:206-7).

[64]Cf. McKenzie, *Theology of the OT*, 20-29, 321-22.

ed, even though in a sense we receive the materials from them. The building must be appropriate to the materials themselves; and (to strain the analogy further) the builder must work on the assumption that even where the stone may seem to have come from several different quarries, it all can be shaped into a satisfying whole. OT theology is more like building than it is like dissecting a body; its new whole is more than the parts it began from, not less than them. But it is even more like the creative activity of a poet or a novelist. They bring something quite new and fresh into existence; yet (if I understand it aright) they feel themselves to be not merely determining something's existence but allowing something to be born.

OT theology's constructive task involves not cutting all the blocks down so that they are the same size, but utilizing them in the potential of their variety. The wisdom books, for instance, contribute to it in their distinctiveness, despite (or rather because of) the fact that their themes are not the more pervasive ones of OT thinking; indeed, especially at those points will they make a key contribution. This is possible precisely through their being set in the context of the rest of the building. Alone they might seem unusable, and consequently they are often left on one side. But in the context of a whole building, they can have a key place (in the foundation, not least, in fact). Working with these materials, we seek to construct a whole which does not correspond to anything that any individual OT writer knew, but which does justice to what he knew. Recognizing the complexity of reality itself, we attempt the task of comprehending as fully as we can that complex reality as a whole, in the light of the witness which the OT has given to various aspects of it in unsystematic ways.

The OT theologian's task can be expressed in terms of a mathematical analogy. The cross-section approach suggests that OT theology seeks the Highest Common Factor in the various versions of OT faith. Preferable is the view that OT theology seeks the Lowest Common Denominator of the various versions of OT faith, that entity into which all the insights that emerge at various points in the OT can find a place because it is large enough to combine them all. It does so taking seriously the historical particularity of OT statements, yet setting these in a broader context shaped by the OT's total range of particular, concrete theological statements.[65]

---

[65]In everyday speech "Lowest Common Denominator" is a pejorative phrase, though not in mathematics and not in the way I use it here.

OT theology's task is a constructive one in a further sense. In analyzing, explicating, articulating, and defining the theological implications of OT faith, interpreters are not merely describing that faith; they are creating new concepts of God and the world through the interaction between what the OT actually says and the tools they bring to it.[66] Not that this work is necessarily alien to the OT's own concerns, even though this task is not one undertaken, to any systematic extent, within the OT itself. The biblical material, Ebeling remarks, "is certainly capable of theological explication" by us, if we need to study it in this way because of who we are, when we live, and how our minds work; indeed, Ebeling goes on to claim (perhaps more disputably for much of the OT), "it does press for theological explication."[67] Such explication, however, by definition goes beyond what the OT actually says.

It is actually unrealistic to maintain that OT theology should be a purely descriptive discipline;[68] it inevitably involves the contemporary explication of the biblical material. Indeed, nothing short of such a task would really deserve the description "theology." "It is in the very nature of theology to concern itself with living faith, rather than with the history of ideas";[69] it is interested in the theological question "What are we to believe the truth to be?", not merely in the phenomenological question "What have various other people believed the truth to be?" OT theology, in particular, then, is naturally concerned to analyze and articulate insight from the OT which remains significant for humanity.

In the 1920s, in the early years of neo-orthodox theology and of the revival of interest in OT theology, Otto Eissfeldt published a famous article in *ZAW* urging that the historical study of scripture should be carried on independent of theological considerations, and that theology's response of faith to purported

---

[66]Cf. Clements, *OT Theology,* 191.

[67]*Word and Faith,* 94. Cf. Kaufman, *Essay on Theological Method,* 33; he instances Mary Douglas's *Purity and Danger,* with its treatment of Levitical law, as an example of explication of what is hardly perceived by the original writer.

[68]So, classically, Stendahl, *IDB* 1:418-32; idem, *Bible in Modern Scholarship,* 205-7. Cf. Gottwald's criticism of Eichrodt's blurring the lines between what ancient Israelites thought of their faith and what he does as a Christian and modern intellectual (*Contemporary OT Theologians,* 54).

[69]Clements, 20, also 10, 155; cf. Porteous, *Living the Mystery,* 22-24, 32, 35-37, 44-46; Reventlow, *JSOT* 11, especially 3-5.

revelation should be made without having to subject itself to this critical study. Eichrodt replied by insisting that historical study of the OT ought to include a concern with identifying the constants in OT faith, which systematic theology can then take into account.[70] Eichrodt is usually reckoned to have had the better of this exchange; but perhaps his solution to the question of how to relate historical and theological study was not as satisfactory as it was neat, while Eissfeldt's presupposition that theology belongs in the realm of faith merits more serious consideration from OT study than it has often received. Eichrodt himself wanted not only "to construct a complete picture of the OT realm of belief" but also "to see that this comprehensive picture does justice to the essential relationship with the NT" which Eichrodt attributes to the OT,[71] and this itself indicates how an interpreter studies the OT out of his own context of faith.

Now admittedly if OT and NT in fact belong together, and the coming of Jesus is the climax of the purpose Yahweh was concerned with in OT times, it will not in itself be unscientific to allow this link between OT and NT to affect the way one presents the OT material. Indeed, this may enable one to see what someone else might miss, or to clarify issues it raises but does not resolve. Ebeling notes that Paul himself seeks to clarify the relationship between the Abrahamic emphasis on faith and the Mosaic emphasis on law which is not made clear by the OT, and adds that the question who Jesus is makes it possible to understand the enigma that the OT exposes but leaves unexplained, the question who Yahweh and Israel are in their mutual relation and contradiction.[72] Nevertheless, a theological judgment interwoven with one's faith in Christ is involved here. Without it, the OT can be read as pointing in one of several directions; written in this faith, OT theology is influenced by judgments which are extrinsic to the OT itself, so that the OT "will appear, considered theologically, not other than it actually is, but with the emphasis laid in a particular way because of the known sequel."[73] Indeed, a

---

[70]See, respectively, ZAW 44:1-12 and 47:83-91; the latter is then Eichrodt's program for his Theology.

[71]Theology, 1:25, 27; cf. Jacob, Theology, 12-13.

[72]Study of Theology, 33-35; cf. pp. 107-10 and 122-27 above.

[73]Porteous, 45; cf. Lys's suggestion that one can determine the general direction of trajectories as they leave the OT, even if it is a conviction of faith that they reach their natural target in Christ (Meaning of the OT, 103-10)— rather as it is a conviction of faith that lines of development in the NT converge in postbiblical orthodoxy (cf. Schlier, Relevance of the NT, 33).

Christian writing OT *theology* cannot avoid writing in the light of the NT, because he cannot make *theological* judgments without reference to the NT. Admittedly the converse is also true: he cannot make theological judgments on the NT in isolation from the OT. Each Testament has to be set in the context of the other, and ultimately *biblical* theology will be the Christian scholar's concern.

This coheres with N. Lohfink's suggestion that we can properly predicate inspiration (and truthfulness) of the Bible only as a whole, and not of its individual authors or of its individual writings, because the latter cannot now be seen as all self-contained and of independent significance. In their diversity they confront and correct each other; but if they all came to be part of one canon, the distinctive assertions and denials of any one part have to be seen in the light of the whole.[74] If the canon comprises a collection of deliberately divergent convictions, this does not mean that the word *canonical* loses its normative reference;[75] it means that all these convictions must be taken into account in attempting to formulate a canonical theology.[76]

Nevertheless, the fact that the emphases of OT and NT are not identical means that the Christian investigation of "biblical" or of OT faith may be in danger of underplaying distinctive and fundamental OT themes such as Israel, the land, law, and worship. There is a case even for Christian scholars to try to write "as if the New Testament did not exist,"[77] in order to do justice to OT faith as a whole. Even scholars who make that their aim are influenced by principles and experience extrinsic to the OT,[78] and are making a statement about beliefs people today ought to take seriously (rather than merely describing beliefs people held in the past), but they are doing so by standing at a particular point in the biblical landscape, which enables aspects of it and links within it to emerge with clarity, whereas they may be

---

[74]*Christian Meaning of the OT,* 33-39.

[75]So Koester, *Trajectories,* 115.

[76]For an example in the realm of ethics, see Childs's treatment of sex ethics in *Biblical Theology in Crisis,* 130-38 (also 184-200).

[77]McKenzie, 319; cf. Fohrer's questioning of the dogmatic assumption that the OT must be understood from Christ and thus from the NT (*Theologische Grundstrukturen,* 29); also Porteous, 45. Works such as Zimmerli's *OT Theology* and Martens's *God's Design* seem to share McKenzie's ideal.

[78]McKenzie, 20-21.

missed if one does not for a while take one's stand at that particular point.

INSTANCES OF THE NEED FOR THEOLOGICAL
CONSTRUCTION WITH OLD TESTAMENT MATERIAL

The Individual Redeemer Figure

Above we noted that Eichrodt does not take as far as he might his
theological consideration of the diverse and contradictory features of Israel's hope of salvation. One aspect of this diversity
concerns the place of an individual redeemer figure in the OT
hope of salvation. What is the significance of the various perspectives on this question?

First, there are certain features of this hope which appear
indiscriminately whether or not it refers to an individual redeemer. These include the expectation of justice for the needy
and upon the wicked, of war and conflict yielding to or leading
to peace and safety, of the renewal of an earthly paradise and of
personal relationships with Yahweh, of recognition for Israel
and through that of blessing for the world. Isa 2:2-4 and Isa 11
instance most of these features without and with reference to an
individual figure through whom these hopes are fulfilled.

When an individual figure has a prominent place in these
hopes, this presumably reflects Israel's understanding of the
way Yahweh has actually acted among his people, particularly in
people such as Moses and Joshua, the judges and the kings, and
also the priests and the prophets. This experience in turn no
doubt reflects the way that human life and history generally
work: a significant role is played by particular individuals. Once
God had begun to work in this way in Israel, particularly
through the monarchy, there is a further reason why an individual figure is integral to Israel's hope. Despite the theological ambivalence that surrounded the origins of Israelite kingship as
these are recorded in 1 Sam 8-12, Yahweh committed himself
unequivocally to the Davidic monarchy (2 Sam 7). The OT assumes that this commitment cannot simply have been abandoned later; hope of an individual redeemer figure is contained
within faith in Yahweh's faithfulness to his commitments. It is a
hope of what Yahweh will do "for David" (Jer 23:5).

The hope of an individual redeemer is qualified, however,
by some of the significance attached to it. As the king was not to
regard himself as more than the leader among brothers (Deut

17:14-20), "the model Israelite,"[79] so the future leader can be pictured less as a redeemer than as one who himself enjoys the blessings of the renewed world, "more a type than a mediator of the Golden Age" (Gen 49:11-12).[80] As the king held authority not for his own enjoyment but for the people's benefit, so the portrait of the future redeemer's activity can yield to that of the world enjoying the fruit of his achievement, so that he disappears from the picture as the prophet enthuses over this prospect (Isa 11:6-9).[81] As the monarchy for a century held the fissiparous tribes in an (admittedly fragile) unity, so the two nations of Israel and Judah will be reunited under one new David (Ezek 37:22-5). As the first man both modeled and reflected the king's calling, with the result that human beings as such are called to a royal role as well as the king being called to fulfill God's purpose for human beings (or Israel) as human beings (Gen 1-3),[82] so the man in Daniel's vision represents Israelites in general when he is given kingly authority (Dan 7). In these various contexts, then, the picture of an individual redeemer figure is tempered by that of the community without which his significance cannot be understood. Further, as the king could never be rightly understood except as Yahweh's servant, Yahweh's anointed, Yahweh's adopted son, and thus as "merely" Yahweh's agent (e.g., Pss 2; 72; 110), since Yahweh is the real King (1 Chr 28:5; 29:23), so the hoped for redeemer is "merely" Yahweh's means of fulfilling his promises to his people.[83]

This second focus, on Yahweh and the beneficiaries of his coming act, dominates a set of passages where the individual redeemer does not appear. Particularly significant is the polemical treatment of this theme in Isa 40-55. Here Israel corporately is a major focus, and the traditional Davidic hope disappears. There is a new exodus, but no new Moses. It is Israel who is Yahweh's servant, whose hand Yahweh grasps, whose fear he reassures,

---

[79]Wolff, *Anthropology,* 196-97; cf. pp. 136-37 above.

[80]Eichrodt, *Theology,* 1:474.

[81]These verses may be of separate origin from 11:1-5 (though see Clements and Wildberger on the passage). Even so, 11:1-9 is a redactional unit with v 9 closing off the whole.

[82]See, e.g., Brueggemann, *CBQ* 30:156-81; B. W. Anderson, *Creation versus Chaos,* 177.

[83]Cf. Gese, *Essays on Biblical Theology,* 114-15, and Gese's subsequent observation that the OT uses priesthood and prophecy, as well as kingship, as models of past and future leadership (pp. 147-51, 155-56).

whose strength he upholds, whose victory he promises (41:8-16):[84] such undertakings would be most familiar as made to the king. It is to Israel that Yahweh's commitment to David now belongs: as Yahweh once worked through David, soon he will work through Israel as a whole (55:3-5).[85] However one is to identify the servant figure in 52:13–53:12,[86] at the heart of his significance is his existing for the sake of the "many" needy and guilty whose testimony the passage includes, and his fulfilling his ministry both in his humiliation and in his triumph by the will of Yahweh.

As the individual element in Israel's hope is tempered by the presence of the corporate, however, so the corporate element is tempered by the presence of the individual, not least in Isa 40–55. While the servant calling and the Davidic commitment belong to Israel, aspects of the Davidic role are nevertheless attributed to King Cyrus. Yahweh's purpose (חפץ) is also fulfilled through him (44:28; cf. 53:10). He is Yahweh's shepherd and Yahweh's anointed; Yahweh also takes his hand, goes before him, names his name (44:28; 45:1-4). Further, a significant individual role is played in these chapters by the second Isaiah himself.[87] He is called to fulfill Israel's own servant role in relation to needy Israel, and thus to be the means of light shining even beyond Israel to the gentile nations (49:1-6). Again, the openness of 52:13–53:12 at least allows for the possibility that an individual should be the unidentified fulfiller of this vision (to which the individual figure of Moses offering himself for Israel contributed). So even these chapters which avoid the traditional individual redeemer figure allow their corporate emphasis to be modified in recognition of the need or possibility of various individual roles being fulfilled in Yahweh's name for the sake of the community.

---

[84]See further 42:1-9, if this describes Israel's calling (see pp. 75-76 above for the assumptions about the servant made here and over the next page). Note the *royal* features of the portrait in 42:1-9, in this connection (see, e.g., Jeremias, *VT* 22:31-42).

[85]For further possible treatments of the nation as the royal son, see Becker, *Messianic Expectation*, 68-78.

[86]In my view, the section describes the calling of the servant (whoever that may be) without identifying him; the passage is a vision or a challenge, not a description of some specific referent, past, present, or future. See especially Clines, *I, He, We, and They*, 59-65.

[87]Against Westermann, who says that the prophet only lets himself be seen in 40:6-7 (*Isaiah 40–66*, 6).

Polarities

In the case of a number of OT themes, a theological approach requires consideration of the relationship between opposed but related polarities.[88] Ebeling has suggested that Luther's thought is constructed around such polarities; he instances letter and Spirit, law and gospel, faith and love, the kingdom of Christ and the kingdom of this world, freedom and bondage, God hidden and God revealed.[89] Elsewhere Ebeling notes that such a polar structure goes back to scripture itself, and that scripture's polar structure reflects "its comprehensive relation to life. If life itself is determined in a polar way—one thinks of birth and death, creating and receiving, subject and object, passivity and activity, the fulfillment and the failure of life, and the like—then when the question involves true life, attention must be directed to the polarities that are determinative and that set it right." In the OT it is the (polar) relationship of Yahweh and Israel, counterparts who belong together and stand in contradiction, which constitutes "the red thread of the Old Testament," and which draws attention to further tensions, between election and universalism, Israel as a political entity and Israel as a religious community, cultic piety and prophetic piety, individual and community in relation to God, openness to the world or to other religions and insistence on distinctiveness or purity, suffering and confidence in God, judgment and grace, law and promise.[90] It is easy to extend this list: creation and redemption (cf. chap. 7 below), exodus and exile,[91] word and event,[92] praise and

---

[88]Cf. Hanson, *Diversity of Scripture*, 4, 148, with his reference to Gebser's *Ursprung und Gegenwart* on the theme of polarities.

[89]*Luther*, 25; cf. idem, "Dogmatik und Exegese," *ZTK* 77:276-77.

[90]*Study of Theology*, 19-20, 34. Cf. Brueggemann, *JSOT* 18:2-18.

[91]It might once have seemed possible to understand the OT (like the NT) as based on an original salvation event, the exodus. But only by an implausible tour de force can the whole OT be seen as a series of outworkings and reinterpretations of the significance of that primal event (as the NT is, in relation to Christ). It would be as feasible to analyze the OT as a series of anticipations of and responses to the exile. Exile, failure, miscarriage (cf. Bultmann, *Essays on OT Hermeneutics*, 72-73), offers a suggestive paradigm for understanding the OT. See also Kitamori, *Theology of the Pain of God*, 69. More appropriately exodus and exile may be seen as two of the poles between which the OT moves; cf. Meeks, *JRT* 33:44.

[92]Belief in revelation in history (see p. 124 and n. 103 above) arose in reaction against belief in revelation as word. But "facts without words are blind; and words without facts are empty" (Braaten, *History and Hermeneutics*, 23, paraphrasing Kant). I have discussed this point further in *Approaches to OT Interpretation*, 74-77, 126-28.

lament,[93] structure and freedom,[94] form and reform.[95] The model of polarity is complemented by that of counterpoint, the interweaving of two independent tunes which combine to form a greater harmony.[96]

We will consider the theological task involved in taking up these polarities by looking at four OT themes; first, universalism and nationalism. As we noted above (p. 146), a book such as Deuteronomy focuses on Yahweh's concern for Israel; his concern for other peoples appears only very marginally. Deuteronomy may then be compared with Nahum, Malachi, Joel, Esther, and the E material in the Tetrateuch (to the extent that this can safely be isolated). The preexilic prophets, Ezekiel, and the Priestly Work also focus on Yahweh's special relationship with Israel, though their direct emphasis lies more on the demand of holiness that this makes on Israel, and they contain more explicit references to Yahweh's lordship over all creation.[97] In contrast, Isa 19:19-25 envisages Assyria and Egypt enjoying the same relationship with God as Israel, Ruth and Jonah take a very positive stance in relation to some Moabites and Ninevites, at least, while the wisdom books make no reference to Yahweh's special concern for Israel and presuppose that he is involved in the life of people as people.

The question of the relationship between the more "nationalist" and the more "universalist" perspectives is raised by their juxtaposition within individual OT books, as well as within the OT as a whole. The OT does not suggest that universalist theology "overcomes" election theology; both viewpoints are present in earlier and later OT books, and in the NT.[98] The theological

---

[93]See Westermann, e.g., *What Does the OT Say about God?* 22.

[94]The OT exemplifies V. Turner's thesis that any enduring social system (including a religion) must hold together structure and anti-structure (cf. institution and community) (see *Dramas, Fields, and Metaphors*, esp. 266-67; cf. Cohn, *Shape of Sacred Space*, 22).

[95]Hanson, 14-36. Hanson sees a fundamental polarity between the visionary and the pragmatic (see pp. 78-79 above and p. 213 below) as the factor which underlies OT diversity in general (Hanson, *Dynamic Transcendence*, 67).

[96]See Lévêque, *Questions disputées*, 183-202, with special reference to salvation history and wisdom.

[97]Von Rad notes P's universal context, though its purpose is to help to understand Israel in the light of creation, rather than vice versa (*Problem*, 155-56, 163).

[98]Against Altmann, *Erwählungstheologie*, 29-30. For their interwovenness, see Danell, *Root of the Vine*, 30-31; Orlinsky, *Translating and*

question concerns the right relationship between them, acknowledging their respective insights but avoiding their respective dangers. The OT's universalist perspective assumes that Yahweh is Lord of the whole world, is creator of that world, cares for the whole world, looks to the worship of the whole world, and makes his ways known to the whole world. Its election theology assumes not that he is ultimately arbitrary or that on its basis Israel can behave as they like, but that he made a special commitment to Israel in connection with his reaching his world through them, and that his purpose and the pattern of his activity can be seen especially clearly through them.[99]

A related polarity is the tension between the picture of Yahweh as the God who is irrevocably committed to his people, ever acting in mercy toward them, and that of him declaring his judgment on his people and threatening to abandon them. This tension appears in the Pentateuch, which speaks both of a permanent covenant commitment to Israel on Yahweh's part and of a covenant which depends on Israel's obedience for its perseverance. The former does justice to Yahweh's sovereign grace but puts his holiness at risk; the latter does the opposite.[100]

The tension between judgment and mercy is particularly overt in the prophecies of Hosea. Hosea emphasizes the inexplicable and paradoxical character of God's love, which is portrayed in terms of the wooing of a wanton, and which is capable of coexisting with anger. "'I will love them no more' (9.15) and 'I will love them freely' (14.4) . . . are allowed to stand side by side with no attempt at reconciliation, signifying that on the

---

Understanding the OT, 206-36; Martin-Achard, *Light to the Nations*. Specifically, the more "universalist" patriarchal God precedes the more "nationalist" Mosaic God (cf. again Saggs, *Encounter with the Divine*, 36-38), while the missionary concern of Judaism suggests that OT faith itself remains open to a concern for the whole world (so I. Epstein, *Judaism*, 144), and the NT mission to the gentiles has its background in the OT (see Jeremias, *Jesus' Promise*; Hempel, ZAW 66:244-72).

[99]Gottwald comments that election is only a problem when the ideology alone is left and the impetus the belief gave to social liberation is gone (*Tribes of Yahweh*, 702-3).

[100]Sakenfeld thus comments on Num 14 that no one model can represent the fullness of God's relationship with his people (*CBQ* 37:330). Cf. also the discussion of Isaiah by Wildberger (VTSup 9:100-108); of second Isaiah by B. W. Anderson (*Magnalia Dei*, 339-60); and the comments on the prophets generally by Fohrer (TLZ 89:481-500), Zimmerli (VTSup 23:48-64), Carroll (*When Prophecy Failed*, 16-27), and Eichrodt (*Theology*, 1:457-511).

basis of the prophetic faith at any rate there is no method of reconciling them. The only answer is to flee from the wrathful to the loving God."[101] Hosea's own concern is not with clarifying theoretical metaphysical questions but with setting before Israel two possible scenarios from which it has to choose. What are the theological implications of Hosea's words, then, and what is the relationship between the two texts and the two "gods"? It is such questions that a *theologian* like Paul cannot help but take up (see Rom 9–11). What has to be said here may be similar to what Paul says in Romans. It is love which is of the essence of deity or of holiness; Yahweh is most clearly the holy God when he is declining to execute his wrath (Hos 11:9). Acts of wrath can be his acts, but they are his "strange" work (Isa 28:21): he is not to the same extent "being himself" when he acts in judgment as when he acts in mercy. Love is his more overarching characteristic and a positive purpose for Israel is one that he is committed to fulfill in the long run. But his love can turn aside from a particular generation, and it is this possibility which faces Hosea's audience.

This resolution of the tension we are considering also appears in the pentateuchal context referred to above. In Exod 32–34 and Num 13–14, Yahweh speaks of utterly destroying Israel because of their sin, but tempers his decision to a punishment of the present generation. In these passages, it is the human response to Yahweh's announcement of judgment (namely, Moses' prayer) which explains the change from destruction of the people as a whole to judgment on the present generation. Such announcements are categorical in form without necessarily being so in reality. They are threats designed to be self-frustrating, by eliciting prayer and repentance.[102] The story of Jonah and the Ninevites well illustrates this point: Jonah knew that his categorical threats were implicitly conditional (Jonah 4:2). The point is explicit in the story of Jeremiah at the potter's house (Jer 18:1-11). It also underlies Hosea's portrait of "two gods." Ultimately, God's positive purpose will be fulfilled, but each individual generation determines by its response to God's message which of

---

[101]So Eichrodt, 1:253.

[102]Sakenfeld (pp. 320-23) suggests that even repentance cannot avert judgment for abandoning Yahweh, but of the passages she refers to, 1 Sam 3:11-14 states only that *offerings* will not avert judgment; Num 13:39-45 is not clearly describing repentance rather than remorse and presumption; 2 Sam 12:10-14 implies that David's repentance averts his death, even though not all other consequences of his wrongdoing.

the gods it meets. How it is that love is more intrinsic than wrath to the personality of Yahweh, or on what basis the former is bound ultimately to prevail over the latter, is further clarified only later, as the cross of Christ becomes both the locus of God's activity in judgment and of his activity in mercy.[103]

A further example of opposed but related polarities which require theological consideration is the relationship between faith and uncertainty. In keeping with Ebeling's thesis that the polar structure of scriptural thinking reflects a polar structure which determines life itself, behind this polarity one may perceive a dialectic between orientation or equilibrium and dislocation or disorientation, a dialectic which characterizes human experience in general.[104] Equilibrium or faith is generally seen (and certainly felt) as preferable to disorientation or uncertainty. But as likely the latter is to be viewed positively, for faith develops not least in the light of experiences which cannot be accommodated by an existent orientation. A new orientation can only develop as the subject accepts and embraces such dislocation, rather than resisting or denying it in holding on to the old orientation. Thus a hermeneutic of suspicion encourages the relinquishing of an old orientation, while in dialectic with that a hermeneutic of recovery encourages the recapture of meaning in a renewed orientation. It is this dialectic that is at work in the alternation between lament and praise in the Psalms. Faith and questioning are essential in relation to each other. Without the context of faith and reorientation in faith, questioning would end up as pessimism. Without the context of doubt and continuing openness to questioning, faith would become sluggish and atrophy; thus in Job "skepticism is the handmaid of religion."[105] It is because faith and questioning belong together that Ecclesiastes manifests both, whether because an originally more unequivocally skeptical book has been tempered by the assurances of the orthodox or because the assurances of the orthodox are Ecclesiastes' own point of departure. It is also for this reason that an uncertainty about basic affirmations of Israel's faith such as God's goodness and accessibility is not confined to Israel's late,

---

[103]Cf. Eichrodt's comments, 1:171-72; Eichrodt also notes that OT sacrifice already holds judgment and mercy together.

[104]Ebeling, *Study of Theology,* 19-20; Brueggemann, *JSOT* 17:5-16, 24-30, building on the work of Ricoeur (cf. the allusions to his work at the end of chap. 4 above).

[105]S. Priest, *JAAR* 36:323; cf. Davidson, *ASTI* 7:41-52.

decaying years or to periods of historical crisis but appears from early times in reaction to over-certainties which seem to ignore contrary evidences.[106] Conversely, the emergence of a "crisis in wisdom" does not mean that people ceased believing that the creation order was intact and secure; "the world of Ps. 104 is not untrue because of Job's situation."[107]

The relationship between oneness and plurality in the OT understanding of God, a fourth example of a polar tension in OT theology, may be connected with the relationship between individual and community at the human level.[108] The OT affirms that Yahweh alone is God: he is the creator, he alone acts in history (see esp. Isa 45:18-23). Such a conviction is not a merely contingent fact (the right answer to the statistical question "How many gods are there?" happens to be "One," though it could have been otherwise); it is a necessary fact (truly understood, the word *God* can only have one referent). Further, this conviction suggests that behind the multiplex nature of reality there is a principle of unity. But the conviction finds expression in specific OT situations not out of abstract metaphysical interests but in connection with some contextual affirmation or denial. It can, for instance, be a response of worship to an experience of Yahweh proving himself Lord over Egypt and its gods and over the natural order (Exod 15). Not that the belief that their God is Lord of all is merely ideological support designed to bolster Israel's self-image as his people (though no doubt it is that); it can be a challenging reminder to them not to overestimate their own significance or underestimate the possibility and the awfulness of being judged by this same God (Amos), or not to infer that their God is to be reckoned powerless or insignificant merely because they have been defeated (Isa 40:12-31).

Once the sole lordship of Yahweh has been asserted, however, it has to be matched by statements which indicate that there is a certain plurality about heavenly reality. The one transcendent God is nevertheless involved in this world in multiplex ways; human experience of the complexity of life and events suggests that these are influenced by a variety of forces, not

---

[106]See Crenshaw, *Divine Helmsman*, 1-19.

[107]Knierim, *Horizons in Biblical Theology*, 3:89, referring to Schmid, *Wesen und Geschichte der Weisheit*.

[108]See Eichrodt, *Theology*, 2:231-67; cf. at n. 59 above. See also A. R. Johnson, *The One and the Many in the Israelite Conception of God*; G. A. F. Knight, *Biblical Approach to the Doctrine of the Trinity*.

merely by one will; Yahweh's own personal nature encourages the assumption that he was involved in interpersonal relationships before there were created beings to relate to. Perhaps considerations such as these underlie the fact that the OT assumes that Yahweh is not alone even though he is unique. There are many sons of God or holy ones or messengers or fighting forces in his heavenly assembly or court or congregation or army. Such talk may sometimes be metaphorical (e.g., Ps 148), but it is hardly always so (e.g., Ps 82). Again, while Yahweh is one, nevertheless the reality of his involvement in the world can be affirmed by speaking of the presence of some part of him (his wisdom, his face, his spirit, his arm) or some expression of him (his name, his word, his glory) or some embodiment of him (his angel).

A tension between oneness and plurality in understanding God can be traced in Israel, in other religions of the ancient and the modern world, and in Christianity. Like other religions, the OT is sometimes willing to acknowledge the continuity among heavenly beings by using its word for deity of them all. But precisely where it calls other beings as well as Yahweh אלהים, in Ps 82, it makes quite clear that all apart from Yahweh lack power and ultimacy (they can die). Here there is an "exclusive exaltation of the one source of all power, authority, and creativity."[109] From a Christian perspective, it is not surprising that further clarifying of the relationship between oneness and plurality in God had to await the Christ event; but this Christian understanding nevertheless still finds itself having to acknowledge the same tension between these two aspects of an understanding of God.[110]

Diachronic Approaches

The instances of theological construction which have been sketched in this section arise out of the cross-section approach to OT theology. Other instances are suggested by more diachronic approaches. Von Rad classically noted the difference between the past orientation of OT narrative and the future orientation of prophecy. To these might be added a more overtly present concern in wisdom and elsewhere.

OT theology, then, has to hold together an involvement

---

[109]Wright, *OT against Its Environment,* 39.
[110]See, e.g., Tillich's analysis of the ways that various types of monotheism handle this tension (*Systematic Theology,* 1:250-54).

with the past, with the present, and with the future, and the attitude toward God the OT looks for thus embraces remembrance,
faith, and hope. The narrative books major on remembrance,
and imply that God's constitutive acts lie in the past; the prophetic books, von Rad suggested, invite Israel to turn from what
God has done to what he is going to do; the psalms and the wisdom books express faith in (and uncertainty about) him in the
present. But the narratives do not speak of the past out of anti-
quarian interest, but because of its relevance to the present and
future of their readers, a relevance which is written into the
story as they tell it; the Bible is a book that "though on a first
level narrating the past, on a deeper level was speaking of the future and for the future."[111] The prophets speak of the future in
the light of the past and in the symbols which have emerged from
past events, and they speak of the future in order to affect life in
the present. The psalms often praise God for his deeds in the
past and/or look to his deeds and their response of praise in the
future; the wisdom books offer advice for the present which is
based on the experience of the past encapsulated in the tradition
of the past, which as such is believed to hold for the future
also.[112] Of course, people may not hold present, past, and future
in right relationship. They may be over-preoccupied with the
past (wallowing in guilt or reminiscence) or with the present (re-
fusing to face up to guilt or to responsibility for the future) or
with the future (escaping into speculation which avoids the implications of the future for the present, or declining to look at
the future in the light of the past). Thus at particular moments
one or other may need emphasis in the light of the corrective
which people's perspectives need. But because all are significant,
in principle all need maximum emphasis at each moment, so
that the tension between them may produce its fruits.

    Another form of diachronic study examines the varied the-
ological approaches that may be perceived in a particular period.
R. W. Klein closes his study of *Israel in Exile* by suggesting how

----

[111]Barr, *Scope and Authority,* 60; cf. 126-27.

[112]This point also emerges from C. F. Evans's study of "The Christian
Past—Tradition," "The Christian Present—Existentialism," "The Christian
Future—Eschatology" (*Explorations in Theology* 2:141-82, 194-95), where
Evans is unable to discuss the gospel narrative, for instance, without noting
that it is written in the light of Jesus' present activity, or to discuss eschatology
without noting that it has implications for protology, or to refer to creation
without noting that it has implications for our future expectations.

the various OT responses to the exile need to be allowed together to offer insight on our "exile." Exile is a time for prayer (Lamentations), for examining ourselves and for turning to God (Deuteronomistic History), for facing facts yet not being overcome by them (Jeremiah), for reappropriating God's old promises (Ezekiel), for reaffirming God's power to save (Isa 40–55), for restoring old institutions in the hope that God may remember his old promises (P).[113]

These various responses also have to be allowed to complement and confront each other. Reappropriation and reaffirmation for the future, for instance, are only legitimate in the context of self-examination and acceptance of responsibility for the past, otherwise they are irresponsible romanticism; restoring old institutions requires the context of turning to God (or it is a reaffirmation of external religion) and of openness to God's power to save (or it is an affirmation of self-salvation).

A parallel approach needs to be taken to the "streams of postexilic tradition" noted above (pp. 21-24). These are responses to a real "theological ambiguity" in the situation of postexilic Israel.[114] One has to affirm both the reality and the incompleteness of what Yahweh has done in fulfillment of his promises. One has to live both in joy and in hope. One has to affirm both Yahweh's fairness and the hard cases which test that affirmation quite severely. One has to affirm a commitment both to the worship of the temple and to the obedience of the individual. One has both to safeguard the identity of the community and to affirm Yahweh's openness to people from outside it.

Analyses of this kind form a proper part of any descriptively understood theology of the OT as a whole. They certainly form part of any attempt to consider the OT's ongoing theological significance. Their findings may be complex and closely nuanced; but that is more likely to mean that they do justice to the OT's own grappling with the complexity of reality itself.

---

[113]*Israel in Exile*, 154; see further, 149-54.
[114]ET from Steck, *EvT* 28:455-56.

Chapter 7

A UNIFYING APPROACH TO "CREATION" AND "SALVATION" IN THE OLD TESTAMENT

This final chapter examines at greater length one aspect of OT theology which is amenable to the approach instanced more briefly above (pp. 181-99). There is a wide divergence between the treatment of God, humanity, and the world which is generally characteristic of the OT's narrative and prophetic traditions and that which characterizes Job, Psalms, Proverbs, Ecclesiastes, and the Song of Songs. The former assume that God made himself and his redemptive purpose known especially to Israel in the course of a particular series of historical events through which that purpose (in which Israel as God's special people had a key place) was put into effect. Motifs such as exodus, covenant, and prophecy are central to this approach. In contrast, the poetic books refer rarely to specific historical events, to an unfolding purpose, or to a particular people; indeed, outside some Psalms they do not do so at all. They concentrate more on the world and on everyday life than on history, more on the regular than on the once-for-all, more on the individual (though not outside his social relationships) than on the nation, more on personal insight and experience than on sacred tradition.

OT study has found it difficult to do justice to both approaches at the same time. Within the OT itself, however, both have a certain importance, and our concern here is to see how they may interrelate theologically.

SALVATION HISTORY EMPHASIZED AND SUBJECTED TO CRITIQUE

The former of the two sets of emphases we have just mentioned has often been described as the salvation history approach. During the middle third of this century it was overemphasized, and the theological significance of the approach which focuses on God's involvement in the regularities of life was somewhat neglected. More recently, interest in the latter has increased, while the emphasis on salvation history has been subject to a wide-ranging critique. Its reference is ambiguous; was it really salvation that Israel found in history, and was it really history that brought Israel salvation? Its importance had been overstated; it could not provide the comprehensive framework for understanding the OT that had been attributed to it, and even the salvation events themselves could not reveal God's purpose without the word of interpretation which explained their meaning. Its basis seemed uncertain; both tradition historians and theologians questioned whether the events of the salvation history had actually happened. Its relevance no longer seemed self-evident: what meaning attaches today to the claim that God is "the God who acts"? Its uniqueness (compared with other religions) was questioned: did not all nations, after all, believe that their gods were active in their history?[1]

Franz Hesse responded to such questions by suggesting that we say "goodbye to *Heilsgeschichte*."[2] This would be an overreaction. While not omnipresent, the salvation history approach outlined above is very prominent in the Bible. The first half of each Testament, for instance, comprises narrative works which, while "precritical" rather than "twentieth-century western" history, offer a series of connected interpretations of events of the past which were regarded as significant for the time of their writers; they assume that certain historical events in the life of one people were of key significance for the unveiling and effecting of the ultimate saving purpose of God. The same assumption is explicit in most of the non-narrative works (the prophets and the epistles) which follow; and it is not absent from some of the other remaining books (e.g., Psalms, Revelation).

The emphasis on salvation history drew attention to the fact that OT and NT faith is not characteristically a system of abstract truths but a message related to certain concrete events. The events only become meaningful as they are understood within a context of interpretation, or are accompanied by words of interpretation, but the "propositional" truth itself is characteristically expressed in the form of comments on historical events.

---

[1]See, e.g., Childs, *Biblical Theology in Crisis*, 13-87, 223-39; Gunneweg, *Understanding the OT*, 173-217, and their references.

[2]See his *Abschied von der Heilsgeschichte*, echoed by McKenzie, *Theology*, 325, and by Bickert, *Textgemäss*, 11.

It is expressed, in fact, as a story. It is not a story like a children's tale or a western, which gives fictional embodiment to what we hope life is like (the good guys win in the end). It is an interpretation, but an interpretation of factual events: these things come to pass so that you will know that Yahweh is God; if Christ is not raised, then our faith is vain. The story is only valid if the events it relates actually took place. Thus, even though talk of "the God who acts" may now raise problems, this way of speaking is too prominent in the Bible for it to be easily sidestepped in biblical study. Indeed, while this way of speaking can be paralleled elsewhere, no other people's literature gives the central place to their gods' involvement in their history that the Bible does. The religions of the ancient Near East, Gnosticism in the Hellenistic period, existentialism and other philosophies in the contemporary world, have all offered worldviews which did not give prominence to once-for-all historical events; they thus contrast with the Bible's perspective.

Nevertheless, the notion of salvation history has long been used uncritically in theological study, and has been allowed to overshadow other biblical themes.

NATURE OVERSHADOWED AND RE-ACKNOWLEDGED

Works such as Eichrodt's and von Rad's Theologies underplay the theme of God's involvement with nature. Various reasons may underlie this neglect. First, "nature" as a self-contained structure with inherent creative power is hardly an OT idea; in OT thinking, the unity and dynamic of "natural" phenomena derive from their dependence on Yahweh. Second, when the OT does refer to Yahweh's lordship over the natural realm which he created, it generally links this lordship with the theme of redemption (so, e.g., Genesis; Amos; Isa 40–55; and such Psalms as 33; 74; 89; 136; 148). Even Hosea and Deuteronomy, where the question of lordship in nature is a point at issue, do not appeal to Yahweh's activity as creator in isolation from his redemptive activity. This appeal develops only under foreign influence, in Pss 19A; 104. It is historically late and theologically secondary. Third, scholars believed that the alien character of such a religious interest in nature was of theological significance. It was the "nature religions" that focused on this interest, and the polemic of Hosea reveals where such an interest leads. Authentically OT faith historicized the farmer's instinctive involvement

with the cycle of nature, subordinating the agricultural significance of the farmer's festivals to a relationship with the salvation events whereby Israel came into possession of the land, and
thus encouraging in them a faith absolutely different from that
of Canaanite religion.[3]

The German-speaking theology of the Eichrodt-von Rad
era was also encouraged to emphasize the negative aspect to a religious interest in nature by seeing the faith of the "German
Christians" as a nature religion from which theologians who
identified with the Confessing Church dissociated themselves
in stressing the particularity of what God did with the *Jews*.[4] Embarrassment with the clash between Gen 1 and Darwinian science perhaps also encouraged the focusing of attention on other
aspects of the OT, though if so the clash between the OT's view
of history (or the role attributed to history by OT theological
study) and the critical historian's view of OT history now pro-
vokes at least equal embarrassment.

Even before the ecological awareness of the 1960s some
scholars who affirmed the primary significance of salvation history wrote as if they partially recognized the imbalance of this
emphasis.[5] After all, Israel had to reflect on Yahweh's relationship to nature, because they came to be involved with land and
agriculture and had to face the question whether Yahweh was the
source of fertility for them, not least in the light of their contemporaries' convictions regarding the link between their gods and
nature, and this is part of the significance of Gen 1-2, as well as
of Hosea, Deuteronomy, and Psalms such as 47; 65; 67; 93; 96–
99.[6] While asserting that Yahweh was lord of the material world
and the source of its life, Israel recognized that this world is a

---

[3]For these reasons, see, e.g., von Rad, *Problem*, 131-43, 152; idem, *Theology*, 1:136-39, 426, 2:103-4; H. W. Robinson, *Inspiration and Revelation*, 1;
Peacocke, *Creation*, 364-66; B. W. Anderson, *Creation versus Chaos*, 52-55;
cf. Knierim's analysis, *Horizons in Biblical Theology*, 3:63-71. Cf. also Barth's
emphasis that God can only be known as creator on the basis of his being our
redeemer (e.g., *Dogmatics*, 3/1:3-41).

[4]Cf. Brueggemann, *JSOT* 18:12; Young, *Creator, Creation and Faith*,
17-20.

[5]Cf. von Rad, *Problem*, 144; Jacob, *Theology*, 136; idem, *Grundfragen*, 36.

[6]Cf., e.g., Harrelson, *From Fertility Cult to Worship*, 12-18; Rogerson,
OTS 20:67-84; Westermann, *Creation*, 118-19; Cross, *HTR* 55:253-54. Contrast von Rad's observation that Deuteronomy dissolves the direct link between religion and farming (*Gottesvolk*, 30).

unity characterized by recurrence and regularity, with a life of its own, and although this is not a view of nature as a system possessing an inherent dynamic, it is a view of nature;[7] it is both interesting to compare with the western metaphysical view of nature which underlies the use of metaphor from nature in poetry, and instructive for our formulating an attitude toward God and natural resources.[8]

Some of the OT's own interest in nature has a practical concern, with learning from it about human life,[9] but elsewhere its joy in the specifics and in the total wonder of nature seems less pragmatic (see, e.g., Pss 139:14; 145; 147). Both in its order and in its wonder it reflects something of its creator, declares his glory (Pss 19; 24; Isa 6:4), and fulfills his will, even when becoming his means of chastisement and not just of blessing for human beings (Gen 3; Deut 28; Joel 3:3-4 [2:30-31]). It thus shares life with humanity; yet it enjoys God's blessing independently of human beings and can be set over against them—so that they sow in tears even though they reap in joy (Ps 126:6).[10]

The fullest OT review of nature in its mysterious detail is given to a man who sows in joy but reaps in tears (Job 38–39). The revelation of its mystery is given neither to explain everything to him nor (ultimately) to confound him, but to reassure him that the mystery of God which lies behind the mystery of nature is one that can be accepted as nature itself can be.[11]

Israel's "reticence about creation in her early traditions"[12] should not be exaggerated.

BLESSING OVERSHADOWED AND RE-ACKNOWLEDGED

To concentrate exclusively on the once-for-all acts of God

---

[7]Cf. H. W. Robinson, 1-48 (with his references esp. to Genesis and Job); Rogerson, 69-73.

[8]Cf. Wicker, Story-Shaped World, 1-8, 50-70; Janzen, Encounter 36:385.

[9]Cf. McKane's comments on Proverbs' interest in nature, and that attributed to Solomon, which is probably practical rather than incipiently "scientific" (La sagesse de l'AT, 167-70, against von Rad, Theology, 1:425); also Song of Songs' appreciation of natural beauty which is fired by and in service to a rejoicing in human love.

[10]H. W. Robinson, 48; cf. Pedersen, Israel, 1:479-80.

[11]H. W. Robinson, 6-8.

[12]B. W. Anderson, Creation versus Chaos, 52.

whereby he effects his purpose in history also involves neglect-
ing God's involvement in the regular and the everyday affairs of
birth and death, marriage and the family, work and society,
which are essential to human life. Salvation is treated as effectively coextensive with acts of deliverance, and the theme of
blessing in everyday life is missed.[13] The overshadowing of this
theme appears also in the longstanding neglect of the Song of
Songs' overt concern with sexual love. It is still illustrated in
Barth's extensive treatment, where the Song is seen as written on
the basis of the nature of God's love for Israel; the covenant between Yahweh and Israel is the original of which the relationship
between men and women is a copy.[14]

As is the case with the theme of nature, even the apologetic
concern that has emphasized the OT's interest in history (because it has seen the cutting edge of the OT's significance for our
own day to lie here) ought to be motivated also to emphasize the
OT's interest in blessing, with its concern for concrete personal
experience and feelings; Yahwism must have a relevance to
everyday human life.[15] Yahweh is involved in the contingencies
of the individual's personal history as well as in those of the history of the nations, involved in the blessings of life itself, of fertility, success, happiness, good health, prosperity, honor, and of
peace in the community; of all the good that comes from having
Yahweh with you. This is illustrated by the stories of people such
as Ruth, Saul, and David, but (again like the theme of nature) it
becomes a focus in the Psalms and Job. In the praise and lament
of the Psalms all the positive and negative experiences of everyday life are treated as part of people's relationship with
Yahweh,[16] while Job focuses on the experience of calamity in
everyday life, of blessing becoming curse. Of the narrative
works, Genesis has most to say about blessing. The concrete
blessings given to all humanity and the struggle between blessing and curse are a key motif in Gen 1-11, while Gen 12-50 is
structured by the theme of blessing promised, sought after, im-

---

[13]See especially Westermann, *Blessing,* 15-17; Westermann's work is of
particular significance throughout this section. ברך and "bless" refer both to
the experience of blessing in fertility, etc., and to the verbal act of blessing.
Here "bless" will refer to the former except where the context makes clear that
the latter is meant.

[14]*Dogmatics,* 3/1:311-29.

[15]Cf. Janzen, 385; Murphy, *No Famine in the Land,* 119-20, 125.

[16]Cf. Westermann, *What Does the OT Say about God?* 69, 71.

periled, sacrificed, bought and sold, fought over, but always vouchsafed and, at least in part, actually experienced. Blessing is also a central theme in Deuteronomy, where it is set before Israel as a prospect to enjoy in the promised land (see, e.g., 7:13-14; 28:3-6; 30:19);[17] it is prominent in the prophets' vision of a future state of salvation;[18] and it is the gift that God gives people in Christ.[19]

WISDOM OVERSHADOWED AND RE-ACKNOWLEDGED

In OT study the term *wisdom* is used in confusingly varied ways;[20] here it chiefly denotes the approach to reality which surfaces especially in the classical "wisdom books." For them, wisdom is both the way to blessing and the embodiment of blessing. The person of insight is the one who can see how to live the blessed life—how to find peace, prosperity, success, and happiness; the blessed person is the one who can give wise counsel and formulate a wise purpose.[21]

As long ago as 1910, Ernst Sellin lamented the overshadowing of wisdom by history and prophecy.[22] One reason for this overshadowing has been the assumption that wisdom is historically and/or theologically dependent on or subordinate to law, prophecy, salvation history, or the covenant.[23]

A disparaging of wisdom can, however, claim a rather contrary justification.[24] It notes the contrast between wisdom and

---

[17]It is *das Heilsgut* κατ᾽ ἐξοχήν (von Rad, *Gottesvolk*, 42).

[18]See Westermann, *Blessing*, 8-11, 33-34, 63-64, 81.

[19]See Westermann, 24-26, 64-101; cf. Bonhoeffer, *Letters*, 126-37; enlarged ed., 374.

[20]On the problem of definition, see, e.g., Crenshaw, *OT Wisdom*, 16-25; also *Studies in Ancient Israelite Wisdom*, 3-5, 481-94.

[21]Cf. Westermann, *Blessing*, 37-40 (noting Job's concern with blessing); Pedersen, 1:183-84, 198-99.

[22]*Introduction*, 207; cf. Priest, *JBR* 31:279.

[23]So, respectively, Wright, *OT against Its Environment*, 44-45; H. W. Robinson, 241; von Rad, *Theology*, 1:355, 452-53; idem, *Problem*, 155-65; Hubbard, *TynBul* 17:3-34.

[24]Bryce notes these two strands to contemporary attitudes (*Legacy of Wisdom*, 189-92, 245-46). They are well illustrated by H. W. Robinson's diagrammatic understanding of wisdom as one of God's means of revelation (p. 238), after he has earlier described it as based on experience rather than revelation (p. 231). Von Rad, too, emphasizes both that wisdom is thoroughly secular and that it is thoroughly Yahwist in presupposition: cf. Towner's discussion of von Rad in *Canon and Authority*, 135-42.

the Yahwism of the rest of the OT, which can make wisdom seem an alien body in the world of the OT. The wisdom writings are the books of the OT most like parallel writings of other peoples, and their understanding of God and humanity reflects the common theology of Mesopotamia, Palestine, and Egypt. Only when they cease to speak in wisdom terms do they begin to speak in distinctively Israelite terms.[25] Indeed, God is really dispensable from wisdom's understanding of reality. Wisdom is an essentially secular, humanity-centered, nonauthoritarian, self-sufficient, pragmatic approach to life, picturing events working out in accordance with cause-effect forces built into them.[26] Israel's wise are committed to taking Yahweh into account (e.g., Prov 16:1, 9; 21:30-31), but the prophets are as rude about them as they are about the wise of other peoples (see Isa 19:11-13; 29:14; 31:1-3). The occupational hazard of the wise is to walk by calculation rather than by faith.

Further grounds for the conviction that the wisdom writings are of rather secondary significance lie in the nature of the development which the wisdom tradition undergoes. J. L. Crenshaw describes it as first secular, then religious, then theological, then nomistic.[27] Old wisdom, that is, had a purely thisworldly concern with finding the successful way to live this life; it was baptized into Yahwism by being set into the context of the fear of Yahweh. Then in Prov 1–9 wisdom is not merely a useful aid to living a successful human life before God, but the very companion of God himself at creation (8:22-31), while in Job the wisdom tradition wrestles with ultimate questions about the nature of God and the relationship between God and humanity. Job 28, however, recognizes how elusive wisdom is, and declares that it is to be found in the fear of Yahweh (28:28); similarly, the apparently *latest* collection in Proverbs is the most explicitly Yahwistic and repeats this motto (1:7; 9:10—a bracket around

---

[25]Cf. Crenshaw, *Studies*, 2 (with his quotation from Gese, *Lehre und Wirklichkeit in der Alten Weisheit* [Tübingen: Mohr, 1958], 2); Preuss, VTSup 23:117-45; Würthwein, *Studies*, 113-33; Schmid, *Wesen und Geschichte der Weisheit*. Mendenhall notes that Solomon received the gift of wisdom at a great pre-Israelite shrine (*A Light unto My Path*, 324).

[26]Cf. Koch, ZTK 52:1-42, on cause-effect thinking in the OT (Koch begins from Proverbs); Zimmerli, *Studies*, 175-207; Priest, *JAAR* 36:312-13; H. W. Robinson, 231; McKane, *Prophets and Wise Men*; Fohrer, *Theologische Grundstrukturen*, 86-93.

[27]*Studies*, 24-26.

Prov 1-9). Even as Job and Prov 1-9 become more "philosophical" and more sophisticated, they come more to appeal to an act of faith in Yahweh, the God of Israel.

The wisdom writings reveal in other ways that their resources do not quite enable them to answer the questions they ask. Proverbs is dominated by confident assertions about the way the world works, but these contrast with the questioning of Job and Ecclesiastes, witnessing to a crisis in wisdom: "Proverbs seems to say, 'These are the rules for life; try them and find that they will work.' Job and Ecclesiastes say, 'We did, and they don't.'"[28]

Of course, Proverbs itself acknowledges that facts must always be preferred to theories; even though it is concerned to wrest order from the chaos of experience, such order cannot be forced to emerge when it is not really present. Job's friends do have to ignore Proverbs' nuances and qualifications in order to generate the dogmatic confidence of the wise men who think they know everything (also derided by Ecclesiastes). Yet the development from generalizaton to dogma to skepticism has a certain inevitability about it. The crisis through which wisdom's way of thinking has to pass is built into its very approach to reality and its quest for understanding.[29]

So how does wisdom handle this threatened skepticism? Job avoids it by working toward an unexpected climax, a theophany, a special revelation, without which the story of Job would come to a stop rather than an end. This event brings no new data for the resolution of the book's theological question, but it brings Job to a trustful submission to Yahweh through the experience of being personally confronted by him. Such a device, however, has no place in a true wisdom book; theophany is a distinctly nonrational, nongeneralizable, noneveryday phenomenon. So the book of Job solves the problem it examines only by looking outside the wisdom tradition, and it does not offer an intellectual solution to the intellectual problem of theodicy, but a nonrational, religious solution to the religious problem of how one relates to God.[30]

---

[28]Hubbard, 6; cf. Gese, Vom Sinai zum Zion, 168-79; Schmid, Wesen und Geschichte.

[29]Cf. Crenshaw, Prophetic Conflict, 123; Preuss, Questions disputées d'AT, 168-71; idem, EvT 30:396-406.

[30]Cf. Rylaarsdam, Revelation, 74-90; Crenshaw, ZAW 82:381.

Ecclesiastes has a more negative final atmosphere than Job, because the author refuses to introduce what he might call a deus ex machina. Ecclesiastes is Job without the theophany. The author is both more rigorous in (and earns more admiration for) his unremitting insistence on a verifiable worldview, and in the end more wrong (if taken as the whole truth). Ecclesiastes takes the wisdom approach to its logical conclusion and proves this to be actually a dead end. He too shows that there is no escape from theological impasse within the wisdom tradition itself.[31] Wisdom records "an unfinished and even unfinishable dialogue about man and world";[32] it can only operate on the basis of an epistemological consensus and with the assumption of an order brought into creation at the beginning, and cannot deal with a recurrent threat to that order or with a questioning of that consensus.[33]

Beyond the OT wisdom books, the wisdom tradition's religious and theological development continues, and escape from the deadlock may be ventured. In the books of Wisdom and Sirach wisdom moves further from being a minority report within Israelite faith toward becoming "the custodian of the centralities of the faith," "the form *par excellence* in which all Israel's later theological thought moved."[34] At this "nomistic" stage חכמה comes to be identified with תורה; God's eternal wisdom is seen as embodied in Israel's law, general revelation in special revelation. From the wisdom tradition's own perspective, this is a step forward; wisdom comes to the center of the stage and the adding of grace to nature points to a way out of Job and Ecclesiastes' impasse.[35] Yet a wider view suggests that it may be a retrograde step either if wisdom is limited to the contents of the Torah, or if salvation history becomes only an instance of a generalization. Wisdom's value lies partly in the independence of its testimony

---

[31]Cf. Crenshaw, 389-90; Würthwein, 123-31; Preuss, *Questions disputées*, 175. Whybray has a less extreme picture of Ecclesiastes' position, reckoning that he keeps faith in a God who is portrayed in a way not totally alien to that of the rest of the OT (*Two Jewish Theologies*, e.g., 15; idem, *Sagesse et religion*, 65-81).

[32]Von Rad, *Wisdom in Israel*, 318.

[33]Cf. Hermisson and Brueggemann, *Israelite Wisdom*, 47-54 and 86.

[34]Von Rad, *Theology*, 1:440-41. See Sheppard, *Wisdom as a Hermeneutical Construct*, for an approach to this development from the perspective of Childs's canonical criticism.

[35]Rylaarsdam (pp. 26-46) notes that mercy, a theme absent from the canonical books, features in Sirach and Wisdom of Solomon.

to God and his truth, in its accessibility to all and its universal appeal. The identification of wisdom and Torah in extracanonical writings solves one problem but exposes a larger one.[36]

The theological limitations of wisdom, brought out by this development, may be seen as underlined by the NT's approach to wisdom. The NT contains no wisdom book. To bring the transcendent creator God near, the NT identifies God's wisdom not with Torah but with the foolishness of the cross.[37] The NT has a certainty about the truth, in the light of the Christ event, which contrasts with the tentativeness and uncertainties of wisdom's insight and advice; it represents a revival of salvation history. It underlines hesitancy over whether wisdom's answers offer an adequate gospel. The NT's failure to quote from Ecclesiastes (and subsequent Christian interpretation of the book as the testimony of humanity outside of Christ) is no coincidence; wisdom has come to a dead end, a miscarriage.[38]

Despite emphasizing salvation history, von Rad offered important insights on both the Israelite view of the natural world and on the theme of blessing. His work on wisdom sits in most systematic tension with his stress on salvation history. Yet its suggestiveness made it an important stimulus to renewed theological interest in wisdom which has been reflected already above.

This interest was encouraged by factors in theology and society generally. One is an appreciation of the radical way in which the question of meaning and the meaningfulness of "revelation" is faced in Job and Ecclesiastes.[39] Both works speak to or for a situation in which the values of society are questioned (as they were in the decade which produced books such as T. Roszak's *The Making of a Counter Culture* [1968-69] and C. A. Reich's *The Greening of America* [1970]), in which there is an ever-pressing awareness of the problem of human evil and suffering (as there was in the Viet Nam decade), and in which traditional ecclesiastical teaching is questioned (as it was in the decade of "the death of God" and of the "crisis" in "biblical theology").

---

[36]Cf. Rylaarsdam, 90-98; Hubbard, 24.

[37]Cf. Hermisson, *Israelite Wisdom*, 55.

[38]Preuss, *EvT* 30:405, 416, alluding to Bultmann's view noted above (e.g., chap. 6, n. 91).

[39]Cf. Crenshaw, *ZAW* 82:395. Cf. Preuss's observation (p. 416) that interest in wisdom merely represented one facet of the decade's reduction of theology to anthropology and ethics.

Wisdom's methodology, moreover, is more akin to the more philosophical style of theology which succeeded "biblical theology" than is the methodology of other biblical traditions. Wisdom is empirical, rational, and experience-centered. It does not appeal to special revelation. Its congeniality to the mind of the 1960s may be seen by comparing its approach with that of an important book from somewhere to the right of the "death of God" movement, Peter Berger's *A Rumor of Angels* (first published in 1969), in which he looks for a way of "starting with man" in doing theology without ending up merely "glorying in man" as secular theology does. Berger suggests that ordinary human behavior and experience manifest certain "signals of transcendence": phenomena within "natural" reality which point beyond that reality. People's attitudes presuppose that there is an underlying "order" in the universe; that the ugly realities are not the final realities, and that to escape from these into creative beauty is not escapism; that a curse of supernatural dimensions—a commitment to hell—is appropriate in response to grossly outrageous behavior; that human finitude can be overcome and can therefore be laughed at. As Berger notes, his examples could be multiplied: for instance, atheists may sometimes feel grateful for life and the world, even though they believe that they have no one to whom they can express their gratitude. People everywhere desire to say thank you.

The point about these experiences is that they presuppose belief in the transcendent. If God is not there, everything is not all right, play is escapism, there is no hope, evil may triumph, there is nothing to laugh at, and no one has given us anything. But people do not believe that and they do not experience life like that.

In starting from these experiences, Berger's methodology is essentially comparable to that of the wisdom books. Both "start from man" and seek to do theology on the basis of how everyday life actually is in the world. It is not surprising if increased attention is paid to the wisdom books at a time when the cultural and theological situation is open to their approach.[40]

---

[40]Cf. B. W. Anderson's observation that most people are more at home in the wisdom literature than in the historical books (*Understanding the OT,* 529) (though McKenzie [*JBL* 86:1] says this has not been his experience!). See also Towner, *Canon and Authority,* 132-47.

A further feature of the theology of the 1960s was its interest in the secular city and in situation ethics. Wisdom's interest in the secular world as *the* aspect of the OT to speak to the modern world was most emphatically asserted by Walter Brueggemann. He expounded his perspective most systematically in his book *In Man We Trust*. The title (with its implicit contrast with the U.S.A.'s more familiar "In God We Trust") expresses his fundamental assertion, that God has committed himself to humanity, "the trusted creature," called to live life itself responsibly and enthusiastically, joyfully, openly, and positively. This attitude to life Brueggemann sees in Proverbs, as well as in the story of David and in other literary productions of the united monarchy (J, the Succession Document). The wisdom tradition is decidedly world-affirming in its attitude to life and learning, and although this characteristic has led to its being neglected by the world-denying church, it may enable it to be God's way in to a world-affirming world.

Features of wisdom that had long seemed its shortcomings now became its assets. Topics such as Jesus as a wisdom teacher, Wisdom as a christological category, and NT documents as wisdom writings gained new interest within NT scholarship.[41] Wisdom has even been called a key to the relationship between the Testaments and to the development of the doctrine of the incarnation, and described as the "pivot of canonical growth"; after a period of neglect, wisdom is queen, at least for a day.[42]

THE POLARITY OF GOD'S INVOLVEMENT IN THE REGULARITIES OF LIFE (CREATION) AND HIS ACTS OF DELIVERANCE (REDEMPTION)

The OT embraces, then, both the theme of God's acts of deliver-

---

[41]In addition to works cited in n. 42 and on pp. 228-29, 233, and 238 below, see, e.g., Robinson and Koester, *Trajectories*; Wilken, ed., *Aspects of Wisdom in Judaism and Early Christianity* (esp. the essays by Robinson, Elisabeth Schussler Fiorenza, and Pearson); Suggs, *Wisdom, Christology and Law in Matthew's Gospel*; Beardslee, *Int* 24:61-73; idem, *JAAR* 35:231-40; idem, *Literary Criticism of the NT*, 30-41; Bonnard, *La sagesse de l'AT*, 117-49; Carlston, *JBL* 99:87-105. An important exception to the earlier relative neglect of wisdom in the NT, and a stimulus to further study, was Bultmann, *History of the Synoptic Tradition*, 69-108, 393-97.

[42]See, respectively, Gese, *Horizons in Biblical Theology*, 3:24-25; Dunn, *Christology in the Making*, 163-212, 324-38; Terrien, *Horizons in Biblical Theology*, 3:139; Crenshaw, *Studies*, 1.

ance in the history of Israel as his special people, and his involvement in the regularities of life which makes it possible for the natural world to be a place of blessing if it is approached in wisdom. How do these two themes relate to each other?

W. Zimmerli has observed that "wisdom thinks resolutely within the framework of a theology of creation."[43] That unequivocal statement can be questioned. Proverbs, at least, specifically appeals to self-interest more often than to creation, while Job's relationship to creation is ambiguous—the theophany appeals essentially to creation, yet Job sees creation's message only when God intervenes to point out what it is; Ecclesiastes is thus the OT's most unequivocally creation-orientated wisdom book.[44] It would be wiser to describe creation as wisdom's premise or domain assumption rather than as its direct teaching.[45] Nevertheless, a theology of creation, which emphasizes God's ongoing involvement in the regularities of the world which he created and maintains in existence, underlies wisdom, as it underlies an emphasis on God's blessing in everyday experience and an emphasis on his involvement in nature. This suggests that we may speak of the two themes we are considering in terms of the theological expressions *creation* and *redemption*.

A polarity between God's more occasional historical acts of deliverance and his ongoing involvement in the regularities of life has been noted on various occasions and analyzed in a number of ways: e.g., as Abrahamic/Mosaic, as Abrahamic/Deuteronomic, as deliverance/blessing, as teleological/cosmic, or as reform/form.[46] Most commonly it is focused in terms of Moses and David.[47] These analyses overlap and contradict each

---

[43]*SJT* 17:148. Cf. von Rad, *Theology*, 1:139, 452-53; idem, *Problem*, 139-43; Procksch, *Theologie*, 400.

[44]Cf. Zimmerli himself on Proverbs in his much earlier article on the structure of OT wisdom, *Studies*, 175-78, 185-88; and on Ecclesiastes, *SJT* 17:155-58 (cf. also H.-P. Müller, *ZAW* 90:238-53).

[45]Cf. Crenshaw, *Studies*, 33-35; Hermisson, *Israelite Wisdom*, 43-44; Barton, *JTS* 32:16-17.

[46]See, respectively, Leenhardt, *Two Biblical Faiths*; P. D. Miller, *Int* 23:462; Westermann (see pp. 204-6 above); Hanson, *Dynamic of Transcendence*, 67-69; idem, *Diversity of Scripture*. For further examples see Brueggemann, *JSOT* 18:3-8; Herion, *JSOT* 21:49-50; Eichrodt, *Theology*, 1:66-67.

[47]See classically Rost, *TLZ* 72:129-34; also Rylaarsdam, *JES* 9:249-70; recently Brueggemann, *JBL* 98:161-85.

other,[48] showing that the models cannot be set up in a sharp-edged way, even though it is heuristically useful to polarize them in one way or another.

A second issue raised by the study of this polarity is that of the relative status of the two models. Generally, one of them is treated as ultimately more significant than the other. To express them as Mosaic-Davidic (or as Abrahamic-Mosaic), for instance, is itself to presuppose terms of reference which emphasize once-for-all acts in history. An interest in nature, blessing, or wisdom is then made to fit a historical scheme, following the OT narratives' own linking of these with the original creation event and with David and Solomon.[49] The assumption that the Torah is normative over the Writings may also make it seem desirable to bring the concerns of the latter under the umbrella of the former. In recent OT study, furthermore, as represented both by the Eichrodt-von Rad axis and the Mendenhall-Gottwald axis, between these two models the Mosaic (standing for a strong interest in history) has the value status.

Such an assumed ordering of priority is to be questioned.[50] Indeed, it is possible to invert the comparative evaluation of the two models and avoid conceiving of the polarity in terms of once-for-all history at all. Thus G. E. Bryce speaks in terms of theocracy/law and kingship/wisdom; H. H. Schmid sees creation with its assertion of order and pattern in the world as the leading feature of OT faith and the true horizon for biblical the-

---

[48]Compare with each other the analyses of Leenhardt, Rylaarsdam, and Brueggemann; see also the critiques of Brueggemann's view of David by Fishbane (*JBL* 93:458) and Myers (*CBQ* 35:368).

[49]Thus Zimmerli links Proverbs with Gen 1-2 (*SJT* 17:151-52), Barth links the Song of Songs with Gen 2:24-25 (*Dogmatics*, 3/1:311-24), Hertzberg links Ecclesiastes with Gen 3-4 (*Prediger*, 230), while Dubarle sees wisdom's theological background as lying in the Noah covenant (*ETL* 44:419). Hendry notes that systematic theology since Origen has generally followed Genesis in seeing creation as God's first act (*TToday* 78:409). Prussner notes that wisdom can be integrated with OT theology via David (*Transitions*, 40-41), while Preuss affirms that linking wisdom to OT history is *the* way to integrate wisdom into biblical faith (*EvT* 30:406-12); cf. von Rad's concern lest wisdom bypass salvation history and legitimate itself directly from creation (*Theology*, 1:451).

[50]Cf. Murphy, *Int* 23:279; Levenson, *CBQ* 41:210-15; and comments on the broader neglect of creation in theology in Hendry, 406; Schmid, *ZTK* 70:1; Landes, *USQR* 33:81-82 (noting esp. Küng's *On Being a Christian*). Brueggemann, however, sees process theology as located on the Davidic trajectory (liberation theology being located on the Mosaic) (*JBL* 98:184).

ology; while R. Knierim, in a wide-ranging study of "Cosmos and history in Israel's theology," turns the whole emphasis on history on its head: the just and righteous order of Yahweh's creation is the fundamental salvation reality to which history belongs, from which it separated, by which it is evaluated, and to which Israel's history of liberation witnesses.[51]

Others vacillate over the question of the two models' relative status.[52] This itself perhaps points toward recognizing the relationship between creation and history, creation and redemption, or cosmos and history as thoroughly dialectical.[53] The OT itself both interconnects them (in the Hexateuch) and sets them side by side (if one considers the broad sweep of the narrative books and that of the poetic books over against each other), without clearly making one subordinate to the other. The OT, then, speaks both of God's everyday involvement in the ongoing life of nature and cosmos, of nation and individual, with the insights that emerge from an empirical study of these realities, and of his once-for-all acts of deliverance on behalf of his particular people Israel, with the specific insights that are given in association with those acts, and raises the question for us here of how we correlate them without subordinating one to the other.

One approach to doing so would involve noting what they

---

[51]See, respectively, *Legacy of Wisdom*, 209-10; ZTK 70:1-19; *Horizons in Biblical Theology*, 3:95, 98. Cf. Priest's stress on creation's fundamental importance in the OT (see *JAAR* 36:315).

[52]See, e.g., H. W. Robinson, *Inspiration and Revelation*, 238 (emphasizing wisdom), 231, 241 (subordinating wisdom); Westermann, *Blessing* (emphasizing the blessing theme), *What Does the OT Say about God?* 11-12, 99-100 (stressing story and events, and excluding wisdom from OT theology); Brueggemann himself, *JBL* 98:161-85 (enthusing esp. over the Mosaic trajectory), *In Man We Trust* and *Israelite Wisdom*, 86-87 (advocating the importance of wisdom and the positive features of the Davidic trajectory) (see also idem, *JAAR* 38:267-80 for this ambivalence).

[53]So Hanson, *Dynamic Transcendence*, 29-30, also now *Diversity of Scripture*. Cf. R. B. Y. Scott, "Priesthood, Prophecy, Wisdom and the Knowledge of God," *JBL* 80:1-15, seeing these as parallel ways whereby God communicates with humanity; also Whedbee, *Isaiah and Wisdom*, 152-53, on the way both visionary experience and empirical observation fed into the insights of Isaiah (cf. Wildberger, VTSup 9:83-117). The three formulations of the dialectic expressed in the text here are those of Westermann (*Gospel and Human Destiny*, 11-38), Lindeskog (*Root of the Vine*, 1-22), and Knierim, 59-123. The last has the advantage of referring clearly to the ongoing state of the world, not merely to an original once-for-all event (which "creation" easily suggests—in line with the OT's own usage of the term).

have in common. Both seek to bring order (continuity, generalization) to the specific and concrete, or to allow such order to emerge from it. Both presuppose a trust in Yahweh as one whose actions are an embodiment of wisdom, ordered, not random, yet free, a trust based on experience of his ways. Both require insight as well as trust; an openness to a secular way of looking at events and their interconnections as well as a sensitivity to God's activity. Both contrast with myth in offering paradigms of the relative, changing, temporal nature of all human experience. Wisdom and other ways of thinking that link with the creation trajectory develop in history and find links with history in the person of Solomon and in the ministry of prophets such as Amos and Isaiah; historical thinking depends on assumptions about God's regular activity and is actually put into writing by "wise men."[54] Redemption might thus be spoken of as an act of creation, and creation as God's first act of salvation.[55]

Creation and redemption are not to be set in too sharp a disjunction. But neither are God's universal involvement in life's regularities and his particular redemptive acts in Israel's history simply to be assimilated to each other. The OT does not systematically integrate statements about creation into the acting of God in history; it does not see creation itself as an act of liberation in the way that other peoples did.[56] The polarity we are concerned with is not to be dissolved by subordinating one pole to the other, or by assimilating the two poles. Our concern is to tease out the various ways in which the two poles relate to each other, preserving the tension between them. Four facets of the relationship between creation and redemption which

---

[54]Cf. Rendtorff, *EvK* 9:216-18; idem, *Beiträge*, 344-51; Schmid, *WD* 13:9-21; idem, *Wesen und Geschichte der Weisheit*; Collins, *CBQ* 41:185-204; Pannenberg, *Gerhard von Rad*, 43-45; Ricoeur's observations on the similarity between history and fiction (*Semeia* 13:177-202); McKenzie, *JBL* 86:1-9; Hermisson, *Probleme biblischer Theologie*, 136-54.

[55]So Gutiérrez, *Theology of Liberation*, 153 (paraphrasing von Rad). Cf. Luther's "in created things lies the forgiveness of sins" (I have not been able to locate the source of this quotation).

[56]Westermann, *Gospel and Human Destiny*, 15; Landes notes that there had been no bondage antecedent to creation from which the world had to be liberated (*USQR* 33:79-81). It is difficult to instance the OT speaking of creation as an act of liberation; it is not clear that the passages quoted by Knierim (p. 98) to make this point (e.g., Pss 74; 77; 89; 136; 148; Isa 51:3-10) refer to creation rather than to the exodus. As Cooper notes (*USQR* 32:25-35), this raises problems for liberation theology's approach to creation (see n. 55).

emerge from the OT material will be considered below.

THE WORLD GOD REDEEMS IS THE WORLD OF GOD'S CREATION

The two ideas, creation and redemption, correspond to two aspects of our understanding of our position in the world. Although the OT sometimes relates these to each other as a chronological sequence (humanity was first created, then redeemed), even Genesis recognizes that the world does not cease to be God's ordered creation when humanity is in a state of rebellion and in need of redemption. The redemptive revelation presupposes an existent relationship of the world and humanity with the creator. Creation is not only the preparation for redemption but its permanent horizon; the total view of created reality expressed in Gen 1-2 continues to take precedence over the narrower concern with a particular redeemed people which follows.[57]

The creation-wide perspective of Gen 1 appears also in many Psalms, especially the hymns, which respond directly to the wonder of God's handiwork still perceptible in his world, and call the whole cosmos to praise him. Like Genesis, the poetic books sometimes refer to creation as a historical event, but characteristically they stress the ongoing activity of God in his creation. To suggest that they think in terms of continuous creation would be anachronistic,[58] but they emphasize that as well as giving life at the beginning, God ever gives life to the world and to humanity; as well as establishing order in the world at the beginning, by his creative power he goes on maintaining the world's order and restrains forces that oppose it.[59] Thus in the poetic books humanity is not just "lost," and the world is not just the sphere of Satan's activity. Humanity in the world is given life by God; he forms each individual as once he formed Adam (e.g., Ps 139:13-16), and humanity is in continuing dependence on God

---

[57]Cf. Knierim, 82-89 and 122 n. 60; Westermann, *Genesis*, 1:175.

[58]Cf. Westermann, *Gospel and Human Destiny*, 23; idem, *Genesis*, 1:175.

[59]Cf. Hermisson (*Israelite Wisdom*, 48-51) on Pss 84; 93; 104; H. W. Robinson (p. 23) on Neh 9:6; Westermann (*Genesis*, 1:2, 46-47) on the different treatments of creation order in Genesis and Psalms; Landes (*USQR* 33:79-80) on Ps 124:8 as holding together present experience of Yahweh's activity and his past creative activity.

for the breath of life, as originally Adam was (Job 34:14-15). Before God as creator, sustainer, and savior, humanity is invited to enjoy life fully, to live it responsibly, to master it actively, to understand it intelligently.[60]

An understanding of God, humanity, and the world which comes from creation, reason, and human experience to human beings as human beings will not be confined to the particular people on whom the salvation history focuses. It is based on principles common to humanity at large. There is therefore a theological rationale for its manifesting parallels to and being overtly open to the thought of other peoples (e.g., Prov 22:17–23:11; 30:1; 31:1; Job). It encourages us to be open to what there is to learn from all of human endeavor and insight, without abandoning the conviction that there is something distinctive about the biblical tradition.

Conversely, God's creation relationship with human beings as human beings implies his concern about all human beings; this concern is not limited to those within the stream of salvation history. "By me kings reign," says the Wisdom inherent in creation (Prov 8:15-16), drawing attention to God's universal revelation of how to live successfully, while Gen 1–11 indicates that "the so-called salvation history can . . . never be seen apart from the universal acting of God."[61] Indeed, his concern is not only with humanity but with the whole cosmos in its own right,with which Genesis begins and to which Yahweh directs Job to warn him against thinking that the universe revolves around him.

Humanity's life as God's creatures has its ethical norms, and creation morality is similar in content to the covenant expectations emphasized by salvation history, and just as authoritative as these.[62] Its basis, framework, and motivation, however, lie elsewere, in the ordered nature of the world, human beings' assumed inherent moral awareness, their experience of life, and their reasoning about it.[63]

---

[60]Cf. Murphy's comments on the stimulus here toward "theological anthropology" (Int 23:292).

[61]Westermann, The Gospel and Human Destiny, 17; cf. idem, Creation, 118; Dubarle, ETL 44:417-19. Landes (pp. 83-84) notes that ultimately this implies God's concern for the liberation of oppressor as well as that of oppressed.

[62]Cf. Gemser, Adhuc Loquitur, 144-49; Crenshaw, Prophetic Conflict, 116-23; Nel, ZAW 93:418-26; against Zimmerli, Studies, 178-84, with which cf. Gese, Horizons in Biblical Theology, 3:27.

[63]See p. 45 above.

Convictions about the ordered nature of the world and life suggest a confidence in the world's trustworthiness which in the OT reflects a confidence in Yahweh himself—or, as the OT itself more often puts it, a fear of Yahweh[64]—and a mutuality between experiences of the world and experiences of God.[65] Among the poetic books the Psalms, of course, take an overtly religious approach to creation. This is inherent in their form; if people were not responding to creation in a theistic way, it would not be psalms that they wrote. The opposite is true about the form of the wisdom books and the Song of Songs, which are intrinsically secular, humanity-centered, experiential, rational. These features are not felt to be in tension with a religious perspective. For Israel secular did not mean secularist, humanity-centered denoted a starting point but not necessarily a total perspective, experiential included experience of God, and rational did not mean rationalist; it included an intuitive aspect. Religious or secular is thus a false antithesis. It is doubtful whether the poetic books—even apart from Psalms—are less religious than the histories.[66]

Indeed, it is the revelation of God that people receive from the created world; created things teach, declare, recount, make known (ידע, ספר, נגד, ירה)(Job 12:7-9).[67] As well as speaking to God in praise, creation speaks to humanity in wisdom. It speaks in grace: not actually using that word, but revealing the creator as the great giver, entrusting life with all its wondrous joys to humanity and not giving up on human beings despite their abusing

---

[64]On " 'Fear of God' and the world view of wisdom," see Barré in *BTB* 11:41-43. Westermann notes that the OT itself does not speak in terms of *faith* in creation or in God as creator; faith applies to the "special" acts of God, to God as deliverer (*Blessing*, 11-12; *Genesis*, 1:42-43). The place occupied by "faith" in the NT as an overall term for human response to God in Christ is taken in the OT by "praise" (so *What Does the OT Say about God?* 69-70). Nevertheless, the OT's attempt to claim Yahweh's sovereignty over nature and its working was in our terms an act of faith, not something inevitable (cf. Rogerson, *OTS* 20:77-79, 84). They could have seen Baal there instead.

[65]Cf. von Rad, *Wisdom*, 62, also 194; cf. 190-93, 307, 317-18. Von Rad actually says experiences of *Yahweh*, not merely of God; the formulation is open to Rogerson's criticism (see n. 64).

[66]Cf. von Rad, 62, 296-98; Priest, *JAAR* 36:314-15; Whybray, *La sagesse de l'AT*, 153-65; Crenshaw, *ZAW* 82:382; also Lys's discussion of the theological significance of the Song of Songs (*Lumière et Vie* 144:35-53).

[67]Von Rad, *EvT* 31:151-52; cf. idem, *Wisdom*, 162-63, 301-3; idem, *Problem*, 159-61.

of that ongoing trust. "Creation is grace."[68] In creation God reaches out in grace to all people, and in living in an ordered, created universe humanity has the prior contact with God and his ways upon which conversation about the possibility of redemption can build.

Not that there is any inevitability about wisdom's revelation reaching humanity (it needs a human teacher to speak for it). Indeed, "revelation" may be a misleading category to apply to creation. First, the concept emphasizes divine initiative and human receptiveness, whereas learning from creation involves human initiative—even if one sees the task as that of opening oneself to the cosmic, moral, and social order, present in the world by God's creation. The discovering of and the living in accordance with the cosmic order are hard work; they are not simply given. They are a "response to God" in the form of a "striving after knowledge."[69]

Second, the concept of revelation suggests an extraordinary activity on God's part, an unveiling of what otherwise conceals itself, whereas the notion of learning from creation presupposes that there is a resource of insight permanently available in creation, not one which manifests itself only occasionally.[70]

Third, "revelation" suggests the manifest, inescapable unveiling of something otherwise hidden, whereas the wisdom books suggest rather that reality is divided between matters of clear meaning (no revelation being required in order to see them) and matters of such deep mystery that they cannot be grasped (no revelation being given in order to grasp them). One may sense their mystery, but not enter into it. For Job, being confronted by this perspective is ultimately reassuring. Ecclesiastes, however, makes a vice out of the necessity that the mystery of meaning is beyond the grasp of human beings.

Part of what creation reveals, or of what creatures discover, is that God is active in the regular, interrelated features of the world, as well as the irregular, the "miraculous," the "acts of God" which "break natural laws." God is the God of the normal chain of cause and effect, who is involved in every historical

---

[68]Barth, *Dogmatics in Outline*, 54 (quoted in Young, p. 90). See also Whybray, *Two Jewish Theologies*, 16; Brueggemann, *Int* 24:12-19; idem, *In Man We Trust*, 119-20.

[69]Von Rad, *Theology*, 1:365; idem, *Wisdom*, 119.

[70]Westermann especially disputes the use of revelation language for creation: e.g., *Genesis*, 1:175; *What Does the OT Say about God?* 21.

event. Indeed, a belief in such a presence of God in the mysterious depths of reality as a whole (an understanding which holds together faith, reason, and experience) is the presupposition of faith in a divine activity in particular historical events. The latter depends on the former. It is because the whole of history can be seen as the act of God that particular events can be seen as his acts of special significance for humanity's salvation.[71] It is because Yahweh is the creator that he can be expected to act in history (cf. 1 Sam 2:8; 2 Kgs 19:15-19), both to judge his people (1 Sam 12:17; the doxologies in Amos) and to save them (Josh 10:12-13; Isa 40:12-31).

In the NT, the creation revelation of God is treated directly by Paul in Rom 1:18-20; the actual language of revelation appears here (ἀποκαλύπτω, φανερόω), though the revelation fails to achieve its goal. The Paul of Acts appeals to what people can know as creatures (and to the limitations of that knowledge) to pave the way for his proclamation of Christ. Jesus' own treatment of this theme is less explicitly theological, but in the end more far-reaching. It is he who appeals to the creator's concern for his world, to the rain falling on the just and the unjust, to nature's embodiment of the ways of God and humanity (see esp. the parables), assuming that those whose eyes are open to the world will also be open to God.[72]

THE WORLD GOD CREATED IS A WORLD THAT NEEDED TO BE REDEEMED

As God's creatures, human beings have to accept certain limits.[73] They are not God, and part of their submission to God is to accept the limits that God places upon them. The OT narrative expresses this in terms of a prohibition of access to the tree

---

[71]Cf. Pannenberg's comments on von Rad, *Gerhard von Rad*, 51; also Hanson, *Dynamic of Transcendence*, 101; Buss notes the affinities with wisdom detectable in Pannenberg (*Theology as History*, 148-49). The link between wisdom and philosophical theology is illustrated by the taking up of the relationship between all events and particular events as acts of God by writers such as Gilkey (*JR* 41:194-205), Ogden (*JR* 43:1-19), and Kaufman (*HTR* 61:175-201).

[72]Cf. Carlston's comments, *JBL* 99:105; also Edwards, *Theology of Q*, 58-79.

[73]On this theme see especially von Rad, *Wisdom*, 97-110.

of the knowledge of good and evil, a prohibition issued at the moment of creation.

Proverbs recognizes its limits by declaring that in principle a grasp of wisdom depends on a prior commitment to Yahweh (1:7), and then by acknowledging that we cannot by thinking, observation, and analysis solve all the questions and problems which our experience of life raises. There remains an element of ambiguity and unpredictability about life, before which the wise person can only acknowledge the hand of God, the "act of God" (see, e.g., Prov 16:1, 9). "The future is largely determined by our present decisions so we should act responsibly," but "in spite of our best planning there is an inscrutable mystery about our experience which we cannot master or manipulate."[74] The wise do seek to bring order to the manifold nature of human experience, but they also recognize the limitations of what they can achieve in this venture.[75] Trust in Yahweh or fear of Yahweh replaces confidence in order; as long as limitations continue to be recognized and trust continues to be the wise person's stance, there is no need for the crisis brought about when dogma devoid of contact with experienced reality causes trust in order to give way to doubt or skepticism. True wisdom involves an unfinished dialogue rather than the construction of a comprehensive system.[76]

The tension between the search for order and the acknowledgment of limits is heightened by Job and Ecclesiastes. Job's friends take their stand on the dogma of order, but they are not rationalists: their world "is surrounded by the insurmountable wall of the inexplicable."[77] Job himself agonizes for an overall perspective that can do justice to his experience, and Eliphaz accuses him of wanting to know too much (15:8). But he early on acknowledges that God the creator can neither be resisted nor comprehended (9:4-14) and returns to this theme near the end of

---

[74]Brueggemann, In Man We Trust, 60; cf. Collins's treatment of the open implications of both a proverb's form (concrete, analogical) and its epistemology (appeal to experience, which is intrinsically historical and unpredictable) (Semeia 17:1-17).

[75]Murphy repeatedly emphasizes this point: see, e.g., Israelite Wisdom, 36; idem, Int 23:294.

[76]Von Rad, 318-19; cf. Crenshaw, RevExp 74:364-65, also noting that חכמה is thus not too easily to be identified with ma'at (cf. von Rad, 106-7; Murphy, CBQ 29:414; Halbe, ZTK 76:381-418; against Schmid, Gerechtigkeit als Weltordnung; Würthwein, Studies in Ancient Israelite Wisdom, 116-23).

[77]Von Rad, 293.

the dialogues (26:7-14); it is expounded in the wisdom poem (chap. 28) and taken further by Yahweh himself in his reply to Job (chaps. 38–39). Ecclesiastes, too, sets the question of a total understanding in the center of his work, and has to acknowledge more grudgingly that he cannot reach the tree; a human being cannot come to any deep comprehension of what God is doing (3:10-11).[78] Ecclesiastes is thus the frontier-guard who leads wisdom back to an awareness of the limitations of her empirical approach—or is himself a danger signal on a dangerous road.[79] Whatever of the ways of God can be perceived in his world, something beyond the witness of nature, reason, or everyday experience is needed if one is to perceive creation's deepest mystery or the creator's identity.[80]

The barring of access to the tree of the knowledge of good and evil suggests limitations which are behavioral as well as cognitive. Human beings are not given total freedom. In Genesis, their power over the created world is given positive direction and is also negatively hedged. There is a certain ambiguity about their position: they are sent into a world which they will have to tame, deprived of access to what looks like a potential key resource, and subject to the blandishment of at least one rather wily fellow-member of God's creation.

The negative aspect of life in God's world is alluded to in material such as the Psalms that focuses on the world as God's good creation. Ps 104 contrasts with J in portraying creation not as a quality of life now diminished or lost but as a present attribute of the natural world.[81] Yet even Ps 104 is aware of the dark side to the created world: the need for the waters to be restrained, hinting at the experienced threat of their bursting their bounds (vv 6-9), the darkness of night itself (v 20), Leviathan albeit reduced to the Loch Ness Monster (v 26), the suffering and death that follow Yahweh's mysterious turning away of his face and taking away of his breath (v 29), the trembling of the earth despite its allegedly secure foundation (v 32), the presence in the world of moral evil yet unpunished (v 35). Ps 93 affirms that Yahweh reigns and that the world stands immovably firm, yet it does so in the context of acknowledging that the floods hurl

---

[78]Cf. Crenshaw, *Studies*, 28-30.
[79]So, respectively, Zimmerli, *SJT* 17:158; von Rad, 235, 315-16.
[80]Cf. Knierim, 91-92.
[81]Steck, *World and Environment*, 79.

themselves against his order. Ps 113 makes similar affirmations in the context of acknowledging the existence of the poor, the downtrodden, and the barren.

The dark side to life also appears in the background of the thanksgiving Psalms, which look back on some experience of it. Proverbs recognizes it when it acknowledges or presupposes the inequalities of life, and when it portrays us wooed not only by Miss Wisdom but by Miss Folly, so that the "organizing voice" of wisdom can be lost if it is not heeded, with catastrophic consequences.[82]

The negative aspect of life becomes more prominent in Genesis with chapter 3. Man's response to hedges is to tear them down (cf. Ezek 28 as well as Gen 3). Human beings' need of redemption now arises not merely from the intrinsic limitations of their creatureliness, but from the added limitations of their sinfulness, climaxing in personal death and cosmic destruction. Their inclination to use power in whatever godless way they like is now not merely possible but actual, in the story of Cain and Abel, in the violence that leads to the flood, and in the instincts expressed in building a tower that will reach heaven. A hedging of human power by God's words is therefore reinforced by his chastisements.[83] That confidence about life in its Gen 1–2 aspect, which also predominates in the Psalms of praise, Proverbs, and the Song of Songs, thus gives way to a more somber perspective in Gen 3–11.

There is, however, an ambiguity about Gen 3–11, the reverse of the ambiguity that appears in Gen 1–2. Life east of Eden is not a reversion to total dis-order. When human beings overstep their limits, they are not thereby deprived of God's effective blessing, nor indeed of his saving acts. Even Cain in his deserved vulnerability is saved by the mark Yahweh puts on him. Even the profoundly violent humanity and the profoundly spoiled world is saved by the preserving of a human and animal remnant and the ebbing of a flood. After that event, furthermore, the permanent preservation and blessing of the world is promised and cov-

---

[82]See Crenshaw, *RevExp* 74:366; von Rad, 161. Von Rad also discusses Proverbs' treatment of some of life's inequalities and unhappinesses, though he notes the substantial absence of value judgments in this material (pp. 115-17).

[83]Coats, *Int* 29:233-34.

enanted (8:15–9:17).[84] There is nothing wrong with the realm of creation in itself. The cosmos was created whole and secure and remains so (Gen 1) even if humanity and history have put themselves out of joint in relation to it, and even if it becomes God's means of chastising man (Gen 3; Deut 28). It still serves God's will; it is not spoiled in itself. The world is established and cannot be moved (Ps 93:1). If the OT comes to promise a new creation it is because humanity's rebellion makes human beings experience the present cosmos as a locus of disorder. It is thus history which is the real locus of disorder.[85]

The Gen 3–11 aspect of life is the focus of the Psalms of lament, Job, and Ecclesiastes. In a lament, sometimes a renewed confidence about life in its Gen 1–2 aspect may appear, so that a lament becomes a psalm of trust or confidence; but alternatively, any residual such confidence may dissolve, so that the afflicted person's eyes focus exclusively on his experience of suffering, isolation, and abandonment, never to be raised again (so Ps 88).[86] The entire books of Job and Ecclesiastes concern how one copes with the experiential and intellectual consequences of life east of Eden, where the creator's revelation seems invisible and his grace obscured. Job (by including the friends' speeches and by ending the way it does) and Ecclesiastes (by including much proverbial material) acknowledge the truth in the more positive teaching of Proverbs—there is an ambiguity here, too—but they insist it is not absolutized, as if we could still live in Gen 1–2. When understanding faces the ultimate questions of reality, it may well feel that it encounters a "merciless darkness."[87]

The poetic books and the histories offer different strategies for coping with humanity's situation thus conceived. The poetic books explore the redemptive potential of the creation order itself. As creation is an ongoing activity of God and a present human experience, so is redemption. Salvation comes to humanity through "factors inherent in creation itself"; "creation theology has a soteriological character."[88]

84Cf. Westermann, *Creation*, 120-21.

85Knierim, 80-81, 94-97, 119-20; Kraus, *Biblisch-theologische Aufsätze*, 157, 168, 172.

86On Ps 88 among the laments, see Brueggemann, *JSOT* 17:8-9.

87Knierim, 91-92, quoting von Rad, *Problem*, 159 (ET there "hopeless gloom").

88ET, from Schmid, *ZTK* 70:8; cf. von Rad, *Wisdom*, 314.

The Psalms of praise, Proverbs, and the Song of Songs still focus more on life in its Gen 1–2 aspect, the Psalms of lament, Job, and Ecclesiastes more on life in its Gen 3–4 aspect; but both seek to overcome the limitations imposed in Gen 3–4, if not those of Gen 1–2. In the Song of Songs "love is represented [in 8:6-7] as a force which is able to overcome the negative forces which threaten the very existence of world and mankind. . . . Love gains the victory over chaos and creates wholesome order and life."[89] In this new paradise-garden with its fruit trees (4:12-13) the tension of Gen 2–3's garden is gone. "No serpent bruises the heel of female or male"; love's lyrics are redeemed and redemptive.[90]

Once more, however, there is an ambiguity in the picture. Ecclesiastes, too, re-creates the outer form of paradise garden with its fruit trees, but he acknowledges that he has not re-created the inner reality (2:5, 11). The Song of Songs is aware of the point: even here death, shame, separation, and domination are still realities of experience, and perhaps the rareness with which the positive note struck in the Song is heard in the OT (and is echoed in the Song's interpretation) reflects the need to see the topic in the light of the limits of life east of Eden.[91]

A comparable recognition that creation theology's resources cannot solve all the problems it can perceive may be implied by the building of bridges with the histories' approach to creation and redemption. Ps 19 and Job 28 suggest that the voice of God cannot be properly heard in creation and that the secret of the universe cannot be found; they go on to express the conviction that one may better understand the cosmos and God's involvement with it, if one understands Israel and God's involvement with them.[92]

Genesis also seeks to relate these two understandings, but from the opposite direction, setting Israel against the background of an understanding of the world. After its gloomy portrayal of the intrinsic limitations of human creatureliness and the added deprivations of human rebelliousness, it reaches a

---

[89]Tromp, *La sagesse de l'AT,* 94.

[90]Trible, *God and the Rhetoric of Sexuality,* chap. 5 and p. 156.

[91]Cf. Landy, *JBL* 98:524; Pope, *Song of Songs,* 668-69; Barth, *Dogmatics,* 3/1:311-29.

[92]Cf. von Rad, *Problem,* 156-63. Von Rad also considers Prov 8 (where, however, it seems to me that a concern to relate creation wisdom and redemption revelation is less marked), and Sir 24.

turning point when God takes hold of Abraham and his family and declares his intention to make him a model of blessing and thus a means of blessing to the world. The ambiguity between the two aspects of human existence, which it portrays as arising in history was—or has begun to be—solved in a particular sequence of events beginning with Abraham and Moses. This sequence of events offers a resolution of the twofold need suggested by Gen 1–11. One need is of a revelation of the mystery of humanity's place in the world and the meaning of reality as a whole. The wisdom books recognize this mystery and do not expect to resolve it; the historians are confident that they can see the heart of its meaning.[93]

The other need is of a release from the bondage into which the human longing for freedom had taken humanity. So alienation from God is replaced by a covenant with him, family disruption (Gen 4; 9:20-27) by a family relationship with him, insecurity by a place to possess, violence and oppression by liberation and a concern for justice. This begins to take place through the once-for-all historical events of the call of Abraham, the exodus, the meeting at Sinai, and the occupation of Canaan. Henceforth the power of creation is enjoyed only through the explicit celebration of the events of God's salvation for his people in their history. They cannot relate to and appropriate the power of creation "directly"; order is not allowed to triumph over liberation.[94]

The difference between the poetic books' approach to redemption and that of the histories should not be drawn too sharply. Ps 19 and Job 28 build bridges between the two from one side. The stories of Saul, David, and Solomon do so from the other side, for they take the wisdom approach and challenge people to follow David's way and avoid Solomon's. Admittedly even they raise the question whether this call can be heeded, whether human beings inevitably fail to live up to the trust placed in them. Even David is, after all, an ideal type; the historical David

---

[93]Cf. von Rad, *Wisdom*, 292-94. Von Rad also suggests that, whereas wisdom teaching was in need of legitimation, for the histories legitimation was superfluous (pp. 291-92). Surely both wisdom and history found their legitimation in the same place, in the factuality of concrete experiences? It is these experiences (historical events) that the histories actually relate; their legitimation is contained within them, in their factuality and meaningfulness.

[94]Cf. Coats, 238; Brueggemann, *JBL* 98:172-74.

betrayed trust and misused power.[95] Nevertheless, the histories assume that it is the God of creation who redeems in history, it is the God who is lord of all history who exercises his lordship in particular in Israel's history; redemption as well as creation is an embodiment of the creator's wisdom, and redemption history serves creation by taking steps toward its restoration.

The creation which history serves also becomes the instrument of history, as Yahweh uses creation (flood and storm, earthquake and plague) as his means of salvation and judgment. The events of Israel's history were of unique significance for the granting of insight into God's ways and for the achieving of humanity's redemption; these events were not merely one manifestation of the creative power that forms the world, but a universally important expression of it.[96] Thus the creation perspective of the poetic books provides the presuppositions for the redemption story, but the poetic books themselves are set in the context of a whole which is shaped by the salvation history approach.

Such conclusions are confirmed by the NT, where wisdom appears in several contexts that are reminiscent of the OT. In the synoptic tradition Jesus proclaims a wisdom designed for life in the last days, its basis modified by the fact that the rule of God is at hand;[97] further, Q's collection of the wise teaching of Jesus is grounded in salvation history by being incorporated in a Gospel. In John 1, the notion of the Logos takes up ideas and terms from the wisdom tradition as well as from Gen 1, but reconnects them with salvation history in declaring that "the word became flesh." Romans asserts that the dis-order of sin and guilt is replaced because of the Christ event by the order of righteousness and forgiveness.[98] 1 Corinthians both utilizes and attacks a concern with *gnosis*, as Isaiah both utilizes and opposes the wisdom approach, while Col 1 reflects the "foundational significance" of wisdom theology outside the area where OT influence was inevitable, and brings together creation and redemption, wisdom

---

[95]Cf. Brueggemann, *In Man We Trust*, 64-77, with Coats's comments, *Int* 29:236.

[96]Cf. Steck, 125-26; Knierim, 97-98.

[97]Cf. Edwards, *Theology of Q*, 78; Gese, *Horizons in Biblical Theology*, 3:40-45.

[98]Cf. Schmid, *ZTK* 70:12-14, trading on his identification *ma'at* = צדק = δικαιοσύνη.

and cross.[99] Blessing becomes a motif expressing what God has done in Christ, fulfilling in him the promise made to Abraham (Gal 3:8-9, 14; cf. also Acts 3:25-26) and bestowing on us in him every spiritual blessing (Eph 1:3).[100] God's involvement in the regularities of life and his acts of deliverance in Israel's history intersect in the life and the achievement of Jesus.

At a moment when the trend of scholarship is to query the notion of salvation history and reaffirm the significance of creation theology, one needs to note how central to the Bible is its stress on particular once-for-all events which are God's means of bringing salvation to the world. It does encourage us to learn from creation, from reason, and from experience, but its understanding of how salvation came goes beyond this, and if this understanding raises difficulties for us, it nevertheless remains part of the *skandalon* of its message which as such requires close attention.[101]

This is not, however, to resolve the creation-redemption polarity in favor of the latter, for this would be to miss the object of redemption itself.

HUMAN BEINGS ARE REDEEMED TO LIVE AGAIN THEIR CREATED LIFE BEFORE GOD

The object of redemption is the restoration of creation. Human beings are redeemed so as to live again their created life before God, the life God still intends for all his creatures.

Most people do not live at a moment when one of the great redemptive events occurs; they have to live their lives before God nevertheless. Even the generation that does live at such a moment has to make the transition from that experience to ongoing life. The climax of the salvation history is thus only the beginning of ours, and salvation history's concern with once-for-all redemptive events achieved by God is its strength, but also its limitation. The salvation-history tradition cannot stand on its own; the events it speaks of have to be grounded and applied, and their consequences for ordinary life worked out. We have to live historically in Pannenberg's sense—to live in the light of those

---

99Cf. Gese, 47-50.

100On blessing in the NT, see Westermann, *Blessing*, 24-26, 64-101.

101Cf. Cullmann's comments on Bultmann, *Salvation in History*, 11-12, 19-28.

once-for-all past historical events which shape the possibilities of life in the present. We have to live historically in Bultmann's sense, too—to make the decisions pressed upon us by our own historicality; and to live historically in Beardslee's sense—to live in time as the "little history" in accordance with the continuities of our existence from day to day and from year to year.[102]

In the OT itself, creation is not a mere subordinate preamble to history; history's purpose is to fulfill the purpose of creation. The OT is as concerned with the mythicizing of history (the bringing out of history's permanent significance for ordered life) as it is with the historicizing of myth; as concerned with the cyclization of history (salvation history's fulfillment in the blessing of the ongoing agrarian life cycle) as it is with a turning away from cyclic to linear history.[103]

This is reflected in the structure of the Pentateuch itself. Exodus (the salvation event) has Genesis (creation and its blessing) behind it; it also has Deuteronomy (renewed blessing in living the created life) after it. The promise to Israel's ancestors is of blessing in the form of increase and of land; the object of the occupation of the land is then life in the land. The promises of God are fulfilled, the Day of Yahweh's blessing is here, Israel has entered into their inheritance and begun to enjoy Yahweh's rest, they have begun the life of love and rejoicing that can be their privilege to the end of the age. The manna, the bread of saving, is now replaced by the produce of Canaan, the bread of blessing (Josh 5:12), as the God of salvation history becomes also the God of fertility.[104]

Deuteronomy holds together Yahweh's special acts of deliverance and his involvement in the regularities of life in a variety of ways. It portrays Israel at the transition point from the one kind of experience to the other, celebrating their arrival in the

---

[102]*JAAR* 35:231; cf. Bultmann's own remarks, *Theology,* 1:25. Rendtorff sees the most significant difference between wisdom and historical thinking as the former's concern with the present life of the individual, the latter's with the future of Israel as a community (*Beiträge,* 352-53). Cf. also Bultmann's understanding of statements about God as creator as confessions of one's dependence on God (*Jesus Christ and Mythology,* 69; cf. idem, *Existence and Faith,* 171-82 and 206-25); with Young's comment that the doctrine of creation thus refers to humanity's historicity, not the origin of the cosmos (*Creator, Creation and Faith,* 130).

[103]Cf. Schmid, 8-10; Knierim, 99.

[104]Cf. Westermann, *Blessing,* 30; *What Does the OT Say about God?* 46; von Rad, *Gottesvolk,* 61-64.

settled, agrarian existence of their "rest" in the land of their secure possession, an existence embedded in "the structure of the
cosmic space and its cyclic time," the life in the presence of the
order of God's creation which was salvation history's goal (cf.
26:1-11).[105] A life of blessing in this land thus becomes part of
the covenant relationship with its focus on the historical relationship between Yahweh and Israel. The covenant relationship
in turn makes blessing in the regularities of life dependent on
obedience to Yahweh; failing that, Israel will experience God's
curse and once again stand in need of his act of deliverance.[106]
The laws which Yahweh gave in history are also an embodiment
of wisdom which the nations will recognize (4:6).[107] Israel's cultic laws introduce them to living in accordance with the orders
of creation in the realm of time (esp. annual festivals, months,
and days), food, and sex; "Israel's arrival in this seasonal-cyclic
life is celebrated as the fulfillment of Yahweh's salvation-history
with Israel," and they now participate in the creation rest of
God.[108]

Creation order is also implemented in the life of Yahweh's
redeemed people in a life of justice and steadfast love in society.
Justice and steadfast love constitute the essence of Yahweh's
moral character as the holy one (see Isa 5:16; Hos 11:9), and
therefore the essential character of the created world as he purposes it to be (see Ps 33:4-5 leading into the treatment of creation and history which follows; also 85:11-14 [10-13]; 89:10-15
[9-14]).[109] Salvation history frees Israel to provide history with a
paradigm of this creation order in Israel's social life. If they do
not (and often they do not), the creation order itself can be called
to witness against them. It is the natural world which is the context of Israel's little history, blessing which is God's ongoing gift
that brings it to its fulfillment, and wisdom which shows them
the way to grasp that gift and to live the life of God's redeemed
creatures in God's created world. The "worldliness" of the OT as
a whole reflects its conviction that humanity's redemption by

---

[105]Knierim, 99; cf. Miller, *Int* 23:461-65.

[106]Cf. Westermann, *Blessing*, 47-49.

[107]See Weinfeld's study of links between Deuteronomy and wisdom,
Deuteronomy, 244-319; also works cited in chap. 2, n. 60 above.

[108]Knierim, 84, 103. Cf. Eichrodt's treatment of time in priestly thinking (*Theology*, 1:424-33).

[109]Cf. Knierim, 87-88, 96, 99-100; also Schmid's thesis that צדק =
ma'at.

God releases us to live life *in* the world which God created, not out of it.[110]

It is perhaps Israel's subsequent experience of "worldwide" empire that leads them to ask questions about the cosmos as a whole and Yahweh's relationship to it. While Israel's significance, and the significance of salvation history, can only be fully appreciated in the light of creation, by a feedback process creation is only fully appreciated in the light of Israel and of salvation history.[111] This involvement with the nature of the whole creation connects also with an awareness that the fulfillment of creation's purpose involves not just Israel but the world. Even if traditio-historically the primeval history is secondary to salvation history, and even if it is added to aid an understanding of Israel's significance, this does not establish that the object of the creation of the world is the existence of Israel rather than that the object of Israel's existence is to stand in service of God's creation of the world.[112] Salvation history finds its context in creation theology and is the context for it.

Thus the creation approach of the poetic books is the presupposition for the histories; yet the poetic books belong within the life of the redeemed people. This is rarely explicit in the way they actually speak, except in some of the Psalms. Elsewhere it appears in the use of the divine name Yahweh—though that is not universal. But a wisdom literature is given a distinctive flavor by its own cultural stream—hence "every wisdom has its own history"; it is only people who know the Yahweh who made himself known in Israel's history who experience and describe life and the world as Proverbs and Psalms do.[113]

Historically, of course, these books belong in the life of the redeemed people in that they were composed (or adopted) here. In the OT itself, they follow the salvation story; they do not precede it.[114] The Psalms, then, are the praises and prayers of the redeemed people of God, whether or not they refer to events such as the exodus; Proverbs teaches people how to live before God

---

[110]Cf. Zimmerli, *OT and the World.*

[111]Steck, *World and Environment,* 125, quoting Link, *Die Welt als Gleichnis,* 103.

[112]Cf. Knierim, 69.

[113]ET, from Schmid, *Wesen und Geschichte der Weisheit,* 198; cf. Steck, 178.

[114]Cf. Murphy, *No Famine in the Land,* 123-24; Zimmerli, *TLZ* 98:92-95.

the everyday life of redeemed creatures; the Song of Songs models for them what it means to love and be loved; Job pictures a human being coping with suffering; and Ecclesiastes reveals the believer wrestling with the doubt that can affect even those who have been on the receiving end of God's saving acts.

Even salvation history itself is only fully grasped in the light of the approach of wisdom. To see Israel's histories as actually deposits of wisdom thinking may be an exaggeration, but these histories do emerge from an interaction between an awareness or conviction about certain once-for-all events and a set of assumptions or questions which are similar to those of wisdom. Wisdom is thus the means of analyzing, understanding, and testing salvation history. It will refuse to let salvation history keep its head in the clouds, and insist on clear thinking even in the area of faith's response to the "acts of God."

The NT is not as "worldly" as the OT, yet it too sees that people have to live their everyday life even when they have been redeemed. It portrays Jesus blessing children, blessing bread, and blessing those he leaves with a peace that will stay with them.[115] It develops the parenesis in Paul's letters (sometimes, as in Romans, manifestly the working out of salvation history's implications for ongoing life). It preserves Q (albeit in its new narrative context), formulates the "new law" of Matthew, and accepts James as a "compendium of wisdom"[116] despite its lack of specific redemption content. It was natural, perhaps, for Luther, at a moment when the Pauline gospel came to life again, to inveigh against James, but life—Christian, redeemed, but created life—has to go on. The cross of Christ is God's wisdom; but Christ's concern with creation theology, as with law, is not to destroy but to fulfill it.[117]

THE REDEEMED HUMANITY STILL LOOKS FOR A FINAL ACT OF REDEMPTION/RE-CREATION

Above we noted that created humanity needed some further act on God's part because of the limits placed on human under-

---

[115]Cf. Westermann, *Blessing*, 83-91. Cf. Bonhoeffer's observations on blessing in the NT in his letter of 28 July 1944 (*Letters*, Fontana ed., 126-27; enlarged ed., 374).

[116]Hubbard, *TynBul* 17:23.

[117]Cf. Hermisson, *Israelite Wisdom*, 55.

standing and because of the bondage imposed on human beings as a result of their rebellion against the creator. God's redemptive acts might be expected to deal with these two needs, but they do so only partially.

We find further reasons why we cannot foreclose discussion of the relationship between creation and redemption by simply declaring that salvation history has solved the problem described by Gen 3–11; the ambiguity of human life remains after Abraham, Moses, Joshua, and David—and after Christ.[118] Gen 12–Revelation is as ambiguous in its way as Gen 1–2 and 3–11 are in theirs. Something of the tension between Gen 1–2 and Gen 3–11, the psalms of praise and the psalms of lament, Proverbs/Song of Songs and Job/Ecclesiastes continues. The inherent limitations and pressures of the created order remain; the added bondages of the rebellious order are not wholly overcome. We live as children of two ages, of this age and of the age to come, or of this age and of the age that is lost.

Still living east of Eden, human beings continue to experience limits; sage (or philosophical theologian) is still unable to formulate satisfying answers to fundamental questions. Indeed, it is God's redeemed people, invited to live full lives in the created world, who most urgently discover the absence of God from their history. It is often in such a situation that an appeal to God's activity in creation becomes particularly forceful—as in Job and in Isa 40–55.[119] God the creator is, of course, central also to Ecclesiastes. "YHWH the Name, has disappeared for Koheleth. Only Elohim remains; but perhaps when one enjoys life and light, the Name, the Presence will reappear."[120] Certainty and doubt, recognition and puzzlement, coexist in the believer's mind.[121]

In some ways Christ is the "answer" to Job and Ecclesiastes.[122] Questions about the relationship between humanity and God, especially as they are raised by the experience of suffering, cannot be the same after the cross, and questions about

---

[118]Westermann, *Beginning and End in the Bible*, 34.

[119]Cf. Brueggemann, *JBL* 98:176-79; Cross, *Canaanite Myth and Hebrew Epic*, 343-46; Steck, 209-13.

[120]J. G. Williams, *Studies*, 191, following Miskotte, *When the Gods Are Silent*, 450-60.

[121]Cf. Lévêque, *Questions disputées*, 200.

[122]Cf. G. C. Morgan, *Answers of Jesus to Job*; Lauha, *Kohelet*, v, 24, 37, 60.

death cannot be the same after the empty tomb. Nevertheless, Christians can and do find themselves in the same position in relation to the tradition of their salvation events as some Jews evidently did in relation to theirs. These events come to seem rather remote (historically they are very remote). Christians can then find that Job and Ecclesiastes speak as powerfully today as they presumably did in postexilic times. The questioning of Job and Ecclesiastes and the reading of earlier parts of the canon through wisdom's eyes may still facilitate a survival of faith which would otherwise be impossible.[123] Israelites experience suffering, defeat, and death, and then a renewed saving activity of God in which his creation power is reasserted (e.g., Ps 18:6-9, 18-19), yet such experiences are never final, and thus they look for a future climactic experience of this same creative-redeeming activity (e.g., Pss 74; 77).[124]

The ambiguity about Israel's position arises not only out of what happens to them but also out of their own life. Rebellion against God is not merely a general human phenomenon which made salvation history necessary. It is also (and more strikingly) a consistent feature of Israel's own relationship with God, from the very moment of the sealing of that relationship (Exod 32–34).[125] Saving acts of God in history were needed because the insights and energy of the created order itself were insufficient to solve the problems caused by humanity within the created order, but even the saving acts of God in history do not solve these problems. The works written for the redeemed people (laws, wisdom teaching, narrative, prophetic books) have that people's continuing sinfulness as a key focus.

In the end, Israel had to give up mythologizing history. It seems to be a good means of bringing judgment, but an ineffective way of implementing creation order. Even Israel's own history does not offer the paradigmatic implementation of Yahweh's creation order on earth that it was meant to be; still less can it take the place of Yahweh's creation and sustaining of the world as a whole. Indeed, Israel's existence and form in history easily becomes an end in itself rather than the means of Yahweh's presence in the world, and when this happens that very history has to be imperiled by Yahweh himself in order to pre-

---

[123]CF. Guthrie, *Wisdom and Canon.*
[124]Young, 66-67.
[125]Cf. Westermann, *What Does the OT Say about God?* 55.

serve an inverted form of witness to the priority of Yahweh's creation purpose. His aim in choosing Israel and involving himself in their history (that he should thereby take steps toward the restoring of creation order in the lives of all nations) remains unfulfilled except in this Pickwickian form.[126] History is then both the locus of Yahweh's activity and of his hiddenness from his people. History itself is not unequivocally revelatory; there is a plan of God being implemented in history (cf. Isa 8:9-10; 14:24-27), but it is a plan that cannot be perceived by human wisdom (cf. Isa 28:21; 29:14).[127]

As well as continuing divine mystery and continuing human sin, a third factor makes for dissatisfaction with the redeemed order: continuing worldly mortality. To compare humanity with grass which springs up in the morning but fades and withers by evening (Ps 90:7 [6]; cf. Isa 40:6) is explicitly gloomy about humanity but also implicitly gloomy about the world around us which mirrors this sad experience. Conversely, to contrast Yahweh's eternity with the perishable, aging, throwaway nature of his creation (Ps 102:27 [26]) explicitly exalts him but implicitly downgrades it.

The story of God's involvement with his people in the OT (and in the NT) is thus one that comes to no final resolution; it continues to drive forward. It cannot merely be seen as a "study in crisis intervention" designed episodically to "re-establish a 'steady-state' universe"[128] (fullness of blessing in the created order). It must have its goal in some fuller realization of his purpose than history has yet seen. Thus some in Israel came to look for a new world, more intelligible, more just, more lasting, more fulfilled than the present one. Von Rad begins his treatment of prophecy in his *Theology* with the exilic Isaiah's exhortation "Remember not the former things nor consider the things of old. For behold I purpose to do a new thing" (Isa 43:18-19). The words are at least open to referring back beyond Israel's history to the event of creation, and forward beyond Israel's history to a new creation (as they do in 65:17).

Such hopes cluster in the book of Isaiah, though they do appear in other prophets and they take up aspects of poetic oracles

---

[126]Cf. Knierim, 61-62, 97, 100-101, 108-9, with his reference to von Rad, *Theology*, 2:374-82, on the hiddenness of God.

[127]Cf. Zimmerli, VTSup 29:7-9.

[128]Patrick, *Rendering of God*, 101.

and other promises of blessing located in the pentateuchal traditions (e.g., Gen 12-13; 49; Exod 3; Num 22-24; Deut 33).[129] No doubt they reflect the diversity of the book's origins, which is matched by their own diversity of portrayal; yet it is striking that they surface in most of the various parts of the book, and give its whole a particular cast. Here Israel's royal ideal is explicitly projected onto the future Davidic ruler they hoped for, and the ideal keeps the notes of wisdom, peace, justice, and harmony in nature; nature will now contain no threat to humanity, and the whole world will be full of the knowledge of Yahweh (9:5-6 [6-7]; 11:1-9; cf. Jer 23:5-6). The "Isaiah apocalypse" portrays final judgment as an act of de-creation affecting both the inhabitants of the world and the powers of the heavens (24:1-23); it also portrays a scene of final blessing and feasting which includes the abolition of death itself (25:6-8), that first undoing of God's creation which Genesis sees as the result of humanity's first rebellion. The further picture of restoration in Isa 35 portrays a blossoming of nature which turns desert into joyful abundance; human disability into joyful strength and wholeness; human danger, sin, and folly into joyful security, holiness, and freedom.

Isaiah 40-55 relates overtly to a specific historical context, unlike most of the other material we are considering here; and these chapters provide evidence for the view that a concern with creation serves a concern with history. Transformation of nature is a means of Yahweh's purpose being effected in history (40:3-4; 43:19-20) or a metaphor for it (41:17-20; 44:3-4) or a sign of it (55:12-13). This last, however, also implies that renewed experience of creation blessing (progeny, land, peace, justice, security) is the object of God's activity in history (cf. 54:1-17).

In several ways, the final chapters of the book of Isaiah go beyond this. They, too, relate specifically to Israel; even the existence of a new cosmic order serves their needs and is part of the transformation of historical experience which they will enjoy (60:19-20). The new creation is embodied in the new Jerusalem (65:17-25). The security of that new heaven and new earth is also the security of Yahweh's people (66:22). At the same time, however, the new life that is here promised is the new life of a new *creation*; the best that can be promised to Yahweh's people is

---

[129]Cf. Westermann, *Blessing*, 32-34; idem, *OT and Christian Faith*, 208-11. Schmid notes that they also correspond to wider ancient Near Eastern beliefs and hopes (*ZTK* 70:10-11).

that they will enjoy long life and security, live in the homes they build, work and eat the fruit of their labor (65:17-25). Paradise is regained. In this sense what the book of Isaiah finally envisages is a restoration of creation order and a reintegration of human history into that order.[130]

In Christ all the promises of God find their yes (2 Cor 1:20). That assertion must include the promise of a new creation. What is true of all those promises is especially clear with this one, that this yes means not that in him they are all (yet) kept, but that in him they are all confirmed.[131] As the one in whom the whole creation holds together and in whom God's wisdom is embodied, and as the resurrected one, he brings new creation now to those who belong to him (2 Cor 5:17); he also guarantees that there *will* be a new heaven and a new earth (cf. esp. Revelation). The Gospel of John begins as the OT begins; the Revelation of John and thus the NT itself ends as the OT (in its Greek/English shaping) ends.

In his study of *Creator, Creation and Faith*, Norman Young considers four theological approaches to his theme: the ontological (Tillich), the transcendentalist (Barth), the existentialist (Bultmann), and the eschatological (Moltmann).[132] The categorization is strikingly similar to the four approaches to creation and redemption that we have been considering, though coincidentally so (I did not discover Young's book until after drafting this chapter). The sharpest contrast, once one considers the content of the theologians' work that Young studies, appears in his chapter on Moltmann, for here the prospect of a new creation becomes centrally a stimulus to Christian action "designed to overcome the gap between what God has promised and what remains to be fulfilled."[133] There are hints of such an understand-

---

[130]See further Knierim, 104-8; Knierim also discusses the alternation between consummation of creation and new creation in Isaiah.

[131]Cf. Vischer, *Witness of the OT to Christ*, 1:24, referring to Barth, "Verheissung, Zeit-Erfüllung," *Münchner Neueste Nachrichten*, 23.12.1930; Dahl, *Studies in Paul*, 13; Vriezen, *Outline*, 123-24.

[132]1Young actually deals with Barth first.

[133]Young, 154; see, e.g., Moltmann's *Theology of Hope*, 19-22, 329-38. Gutiérrez and Alves take a related approach to creation theology more generally: see their discussion of "self-creation" and creation as a "joint enterprise" (Gutiérrez, *Theology of Liberation*, 155-60; Alves, *Theology of Human Hope*, 136-45). Cf. Cooper's analysis of process and liberation theologies' approach to creation (*USQR* 32:25-35).

ing in the NT (notably in 2 Pet 3). Generally, however, the point of creation language is precisely to emphasize the transcendent origin of what God has done, is doing, or will do. The praxis Moltmann desires may be right, but its ideology lies elsewhere.

The biblical material on creation and redemption invites the reader to a highly paradoxical perspective. Each of the four facets of the mutual relationship of these two poles is in tension not only in itself but also with the other facets. The temptation is to opt for one rather than another.[134] The challenge of a constructive approach to OT theology is to hold them together as the varied facets of the dialectic or complementarity or counterpoint suggested by the OT's treatment of God's involvement in the regularities of our lives and his acts of deliverance in history, so that the whole can be fruitful for our own faith and living.

---

[134]Cf. Knierim, 107, on P and Isa 56–66.

Bibliography

The bibliography lists all works referred to in the text and notes of the volume. Where more than one edition of a work is listed here, the reference in text or notes is to the latest edition, except where otherwise stated. As is indicated in the prefatory pages, the form of reference and abbreviation is based on that used in the *Journal of Biblical Literature* (see volume 95 [1976] 335-46; repr. in *Society of Biblical Literature Member's Handbook* [1980]).

Achtemeier, Paul J. *An Introduction to the New Hermeneutic*. Philadelphia: Westminster, 1969.

Ackroyd, Peter R. *The Age of the Chronicler*. Supplement to Colloquium: The Australian and New Zealand Theological Review, 1970.

_____. *Exile and Restoration: A Study of Hebrew Thought of the Sixth Century B.C.* OTL. London: SCM; Philadelphia: Westminster, 1968.

_____. *Israel under Babylon and Persia*. New Clarendon Bible: OT Vol. 4. London: Oxford University, 1970.

_____. "Crisis and Evolution in the Old Testament." *EvQ* 25 (1953) 69-82.

_____. "Faith and Its Reformulation in the Post-Exilic Period." *TD* 27 (1979) 323-46.

Albertz, Rainer. "Hintergrund und Bedeutung des Elterngebots im Dekalog." *ZAW* 90 (1978) 348-74.

Albrektson, Bertil. *History and the Gods*. ConBOT 1. Lund: Gleerup, 1967.

_____. *Studies in the Text and Theology of the Book of Lamentations*. Studia Theologica Lundensia 21. Lund: Gleerup, 1963.

Alt, Albrecht. "The God of the Fathers." In *Essays on Old Testament History and Religion*. Oxford: Blackwell; Garden City, NY: Doubleday, 1966. Pp. 1-77. ET of *Der Gott der Väter: Ein Beitrag zur Vorgeschichte der israelitischen Religion*. BWANT 3/12. Stuttgart: Kohlhammer, 1929. Repr. in *Kleine Schriften zur Geschichte des Volkes Israel*. Munich: Beck, 1953. 1:1-78.

_____. "Die Heimat des Deuteronomiums." *Kleine Schriften zur Geschichte des Volkes Israel* 2:250-75. Munich: Beck, 1953.

Altmann, Peter. *Erwählungstheologie und Universalismus im Alten Testament*. BZAW 92. Berlin: Töpelmann, 1964.

Alves, Rubem A. *A Theology of Human Hope*. New York: Corpus, 1969.

Anderson, Bernhard W. *Creation versus Chaos: The Reinterpretation of Mythical Symbolism in the Bible.* New York: Association, 1967.

_____. *Understanding the Old Testament.* Englewood Cliffs, NJ: Prentice-Hall, 1957; 2nd ed., 1966; 3rd ed., 1975. = *The Living World of the Old Testament.* London: Longmans, 1958; 2nd ed., 1967; 3rd ed., 1978.

_____. "The Crisis of Biblical Theology." *TToday* 28 (1971-72) 321-27.

_____. "Exodus and Covenant in Second Isaiah and Prophetic Tradition." *Magnalia Dei: The Mighty Acts of God: Essays on Bible and Archaeology in Memory of G. Ernest Wright.* Ed. Frank Moore Cross et al. Garden City, NY: Doubleday, 1976. Pp. 339-60.

_____, ed. *Creation in the Old Testament.* Issues in Religion and Theology 6. Philadelphia: Fortress; London: SPCK, 1984.

Anderson, George W. "Israel, Amphictyony: 'AM; ḴĀHĀL; 'ĒDÂII." In *Translating and Understanding the Old Testament: Essays in Honor of Herbert Gordon May.* Ed. Harry Thomas Frank and William L. Reed. Nashville: Abingdon, 1970. Pp. 135-51.

_____. "Israel's Creed: Sung, Not Signed." *SJT* 16 (1963) 277-85.

_____. "The Religion of Israel." *Peake's Commentary on the Bible.* Ed. Matthew Black and H. H. Rowley. London: Nelson, 1962. Pp. 160-67.

Appel, Nikolaus. *Kanon und Kirche: Die Kanonkrise im heutigen Protestantismus als kontroverstheologisches Problem.* Paderborn: Bonifacius, 1964.

Assmann, Hugo. *Practical Theology of Liberation.* London: Search, 1975. = *Theology for a Nomad Church.* Maryknoll, NY: Orbis, 1976. ET of *Teología desde la praxis de la liberación: Ensayo teológico desde la America dependiente.* Vol. 1. Salamanca: Sígueme, 1973.

Audet, Jean-Paul. "Origines comparées de la double tradition de la loi et de la sagesse dans le proche-orient ancien." *Twenty-fifth International Congress of Orientalists* 1:352- 57. Moscow: Oriental Publishing Agency, 1962.

Augustine, S. Aurelius. *Homilies on the Gospel of John.* NPNF 1 / 7. Ed. Philip Schaff. New York: Scribner's, 1887. Repr., Grand Rapids: Eerdmans, 1956. Pp. 7-452. ET of *In Joannis Evangelium Tractatus 124.* 416. Repr. in *PL* 35:1379-1976. Paris: Migne, 1862.

Bächli, Otto. *Israel und die Völker: Eine Studie zum Deuteronomium.* ATANT 41. Zürich: Zwingli, 1962.

_____. "Zur Aufnahme von Fremden in die altisraelitische Kultgemeinde." In *Wort—Gebot—Glaube: Beiträge zur Theologie des Alten Testaments Walther Eichrodt zum 80. Geburtstag.* Ed. Hans Joachim Stoebe et al. ATANT 59. Zürich: Zwingli, 1971. Pp. 21-26.

Bailey, Lloyd R. *Biblical Perspectives on Death.* Overtures to Biblical Theology 5. Philadelphia: Fortress, 1979.

Baker, John Austin. "The Myth of the Church." *What about the New Testament? Essays in Honour of Christopher Evans.* Ed. Morna Hooker and Colin Hickling. London: SCM, 1975. Pp. 165-77.

Banks, Robert. "The Eschatological Role of Law in Pre- and Post-Christian Jewish Thought." In *Reconciliation and Hope: New Testament Essays on*

Atonement and Eschatology presented to L. L. Morris on his 60th Birthday. Ed. Robert Banks. Exeter: Paternoster; Grand Rapids: Eerdmans, 1974. Pp. 173-85.

Barr, James. *Judaism—Its Continuity with the Bible.* Southampton: Southampton University, 1968.

————. *Old and New in Interpretation.* London: SCM; New York: Harper & Row, 1966.

————. *The Scope and Authority of the Bible.* Explorations in Theology 7. London: SCM; Philadelphia: Westminster, 1980.

————. *The Semantics of Biblical Language.* London: Oxford University, 1961.

————. "Le Judaîsme postbiblique et la théologie de l'Ancien Testament." *RTP* 3/18 (1968) 209-17.

————. "Some Semantic Notes on the Covenant." In *Beiträge zur alttestamentlichen Theologie: Festschrift für Walther Zimmerli zum 70. Geburtstag.* Ed. Herbert Donner et al. Göttingen: Vandenhoeck & Ruprecht, 1977. Pp. 23-28.

————. "Trends and Prospects in Biblical Theology." *JTS* 25 (1974) 265-82.

Barré, Michael L. " 'Fear of God' and the World View of Wisdom." *BTB* 11 (1981) 41-43.

Barrett, C. K. "What Is New Testament Theology? Some Reflections." *Horizons in Biblical Theology* 3 (1981) 1-22. = *Intergerini parietis septum: Essays Presented to Markus Barth on His Sixty-Fifth Birthday.* Ed. D. Y. Hadidian. PTMS 33. Pittsburgh: Pickwick, 1981. Pp. 1-22.

Barstad, Hans M. "The Historical-Critical Method and the Problem of Old Testament Theology: A Few Marginal Remarks." *SEA* 45 (1980) 7-18.

Barth, Karl. *The Resurrection of the Dead.* London: Hodder; New York: Revell, 1933. ET of *Die Auferstehung der Toten: Eine akademische Vorlesung über I. Kor.15.* Munich: Kaiser, 1924; 2nd ed., 1926.

————. *Dogmatics in Outline.* London: SCM; New York: Philosophical Library, 1949. ET of *Dogmatik im Grundriss im Anschluss an das Apostolische Glaubensbekenntnis.* Munich: Kaiser, 1947.

————. *Church Dogmatics.* Edinburgh: T. & T. Clark; New York: Scribner's, 1936-69 (Vol. 1/1 rev. 1975). ET of *Die Kirchliche Dogmatik.* Zürich: EVZ, 1932-67 (first volume originally published Munich: Kaiser, 1932 and 1938).

————. *The Epistle to the Romans.* London: Oxford University, 1933. ET of *Der Römerbrief.* Berne: Baschlin, 1919; 2nd ed., Munich: Kaiser, 1922; repr., 3rd ed., 1923; 4th ed., 1924; 5th ed., 1925; 6th ed., 1928.

Barton, John. "Ethics in Isaiah of Jerusalem." *JTS* 32 (1981) 1-18.

————. "Natural Law and Poetic Justice in the Old Testament." *JTS* 30 (1979) 1-14.

————. "Understanding Old Testament Ethics." *JSOT* 9 (1978) 44-64.

Battles, Ford Lewis. "God Was Accommodating Himself to Human Capacity." *Int* 31 (1977) 19-38.

Baumbach, Günther. " 'Volk Gottes' im Frühjudentum: Eine Untersuchung der 'ckklesiologischen' Typen des Frühjudentums." *Kairos* 21 (1979) 30-47.

Baumgärtel, Friedrich. *Verheissung: Zur Frage des evangelischen Verständnisses des Alten Testaments.* Gütersloh: Bertelsmann, 1952.

———. "Der Dissensus im Verständnis des Alten Testaments." *EvT* 14 (1954) 298-313.

———. "Erwägungen zur Darstellung der Theologie des Alten Testaments." *TLZ* 76 (1951) 257-72.

———. "Das Offenbarungszeugnis des Alten Testaments im Lichte der religionsgeschichtlich-vergleichenden Forschung." *ZTK* 64 (1967) 393-422.

———. "Der Tod des Religionsstifters." *KD* 9 (1963) 223-33.

Baxter, Christina Ann. "The Movement from Exegesis to Dogmatics in the Theology of Karl Barth, with Special Reference to Romano, Philippians and the *Church Dogmatics*." Ph.D diss. Durham University, 1981.

Baxter, W. L. *Sanctuary and Sacrifice: A Reply to Wellhausen.* London: Eyre and Spottiswoode, 1896.

Beardslee, William A. *Literary Criticism of the New Testament.* Guides to Biblical Scholarship. Philadelphia: Fortress, 1970.

———. "Uses of the Proverb in the Synoptic Gospels." *Int* 24 (1970) 61-73.

———. "The Wisdom Tradition and the Synoptic Gospels." *JAAR* 35 (1967) 231-40.

Beauchamp, Paul. *L'un et l'autre Testament: Essai de lecture.* Collection "Parole de Dieu." Paris: Seuil, 1976.

Becker, Joachim. *Messianic Expectation in the Old Testament.* Philadelphia: Fortress; Edinburgh: T. & T. Clark, 1980. ET of *Messiaserwartung im Alten Testament.* SBS 83. Stuttgart: Katholisches Bibelwerk, 1977.

Berg, Sandra Beth. *The Book of Esther: Motifs, Themes and Structure.* SBLDS 44. Missoula, MT: Scholars, 1979.

———. "After the Exile: God and History in the Books of Chronicles and Esther." In *The Divine Helmsman: Studies on God's Control of Human Events, Presented to Lou H. Silberman.* Ed. James L. Crenshaw and Samuel Sandmel. New York: Ktav, 1980. Pp. 107-27.

Berger, Peter L. *A Rumor of Angels: Modern Society and the Rediscovery of the Supernatural.* Garden City, NY: Doubleday, 1969; London: Allen Lane, 1970; repr., Harmondsworth: Penguin, 1971.

———. *Facing up to Modernity: Excursions in Society, Politics and Religion.* New York: Basic, 1977; Harmondsworth: Penguin, 1979.

Bickert, Rainer. "Die Geschichte and das Handeln Jahwes: Zur Eigenart einer deuteronomistichen Offenbarungsauffassung in den Samuelbüchern." In *Textgemäss: Aufsätze und Beiträge zur Hermeneutik des Alten Testaments. Festschrift für Ernst Würthwein zum 70. Geburtstag.* Ed. A. H. J. Gunneweg and Otto Kaiser. Göttingen: Vandenhoeck & Ruprecht, 1979. Pp. 9-27.

Blair, Edward P. "An Appeal to Remembrance: The Memory Motif in Deuteronomy." *Int* 15 (1961) 41-47.

Blanch, Stuart Y. *The World Our Orphanage: Studies in the Theology of the Bible.* London: Epworth, 1972.

Blank, Sheldon H. "Men against God: The Promethean Element in Biblical Prayer." *JBL* 72 (1953) 1-13.

Blenkinsopp, Joseph. *Prophecy and Canon: A Contribution to the Study of Jewish Origins.* Notre Dame, IN: University of Notre Dame, 1977.

————. *A Sketchbook of Biblical Theology.* London: Burns & Oates; New York: Herder & Herder, 1968.

Boecker, Hans Jochen. *Law and the Administration of Justice in the Old Testament and Ancient East.* Minneapolis: Augsburg; London: SPCK, 1980. ET of *Recht und Gesetz im Alten Testament and im Alten Orient.* Neukirchener Studienbücher 10. Neukirchen: Neukirchener, 1976.

Boer, P. A. H. de. *Fatherhood and Motherhood in Israelite and Judaean Piety.* Leiden: Brill, 1974.

Boissonnard, Robert, and François Vouga. "Pour une éthique de la propriété: Essais sur le Deutéronome." *Bulletin du Centre Protestant d'Études* 32 (1980) 5-46.

Boman, Thorlief. *Hebrew Thought Compared with Greek.* London: SCM; Philadelphia: Westminster, 1960. ET of *Das Hebräische Denken im Vergleich mit dem Griechischen.* Göttingen: Vandenhoeck & Ruprecht, 1952; 2nd ed., 1954.

Bonhoeffer, Dietrich. *Letters and Papers from Prison.* London: SCM; New York: Macmillan, 1953; rev. ed., 1967; enlarged ed., 1971; London: Collins Fontana, 1959. ET of *Widerstand und Ergebung: Briefe und Aufzeichnungen aus der Haft.* Munich: Kaiser, 1951; rev. ed., 1955; enlarged ed., 1970.

Bonnard, P.-E. "De la Sagesse personnifiée dans l'Ancien Testament à la Sagesse en personne dans le Nouveau." *La sagesse de l'Ancien Testament.* Ed. Maurice Gilbert. BETL 51. Gembloux: Duculot; Louvain: Louvain University, 1979. Pp. 117-49.

Borowitz, Eugene B. "The Problem of the Form of a Jewish Theology." *HUCA* 40-41 (1969-70) 391-408.

Bossmann, David. "Ezra's Marriage Reform: Israel Redefined." *BTB* 9 (1979) 32-38.

Boström, Gustav. *Proverbiastudien: Die Weisheit und das fremde Weib in Spr. 1–9.* LUA, n.s. sect. 1, 30/3. Lund: Gleerup, 1935.

Bowden, John S. "Translator's Preface." In *An Introduction to the Theology of Rudolf Bultmann.* By Walter Schmithals. London: SCM; Minneapolis: Augsburg, 1968. Pp. xi-xv.

Bowker, John. *Problems of Suffering in Religions of the World.* London: Cambridge University, 1970.

————. *The Sense of God: Sociological, Anthropological and Psychological Approaches to the Origin of the Sense of God.* Oxford: Clarendon, 1973.

————. *The Targums and Rabbinic Literature: An Introduction to Jewish Interpretations of Scripture.* Cambridge: Cambridge University, 1969.

Braaten, Carl E. *History and Hermeneutics.* New Directions in Theology Today 2. Philadelphia: Westminster, 1966; London: Lutterworth, 1968.

Braun, Herbert. "Hebt die heutige neutestamentlich-exegetische Forschung den Kanon auf?" *Fuldaer Hefte* 12 (1960) 9-24. Repr. in *Gesammelte Studien* zum Neuen Testament and seiner Umwelt. Tübingen: Mohr, 1962. Pp. 310-24. Repr. in Das Neue Testament als Kanon: Dokumentation und kritische Analyse zur gegenwärtigen Diskussion. Ed. Ernst Käsemann. Göttingen: Vandenhoeck & Ruprecht, 1970. Pp. 219-32.

Braun, Roddy L. "Chronicles, Ezra and Nehemiah: Theology and Literary History." In Studies in the Historical Books of the Old Testament. Ed. J. A. Emerton. VTSup 30. Leiden: Brill, 1979. Pp. 52-64.

Brekelmans, C., ed. Questions disputées d'Ancien Testament: Méthode et Théologie. BETL 33. Gembloux: Duculot; Louvain: Louvain University, 1974.

Brichto, Herbert Chanan. The Problem of "Curse" in the Hebrew Bible. JBL Monograph Series 13. Philadelphia: SBL, 1963.

———. "Kin, Cult, Land and Afterlife—A Biblical Complex." HUCA 44 (1973) 1-54.

Bridge, A. C. Images of God: An Essay on the Life and Death of Symbols. London: Hodder, 1960.

Bright, John. The Authority of the Old Testament. Nashville: Abingdon; London: SCM, 1967; repr., Grand Rapids: Baker, 1975.

———. A History of Israel. Philadelphia: Westminster, 1959; 2nd ed., 1972; 3rd ed., 1981; London: SCM, 1960; 2nd ed., 1972; 3rd ed., 1981.

Bruce, F. F. The New Testament Development of Old Testament Themes. Grand Rapids: Eerdmans, 1968. = This Is That: The New Testament Development of Some Old Testament Themes. Exeter: Paternoster, 1968.

Brueggemann, Walter. The Land: Place as Gift, Promise, and Challenge in Biblical Faith. Overtures to Biblical Theology 1. Philadelphia: Fortress, 1977; London: SPCK, 1978.

———. In Man We Trust: The Neglected Side of Biblical Faith. Richmond: Knox, 1972.

———. "A Convergence in Recent Old Testament Theologies." JSOT 18 (1980) 2-18.

———. "David and His Theologian." CBQ 30 (1968) 156-81.

———. "Death, Theology of." IDBSup. Ed. Keith Crim et al. Nashville: Abingdon, 1976. Pp. 219-22.

———. "The Epistemological Crisis of Israel's Two Histories (Jer. 9:22-23)." In Israelite Wisdom: Theological and Literary Essays in Honor of Samuel Terrien. Ed. John G. Gammie et al. Missoula, MT: Scholars, 1978. Pp. 85-105.

———. "The Kerygma of the Priestly Writers." ZAW 84 (1972) 397-413. Repr. in The Vitality of Old Testament Traditions. By Walter Brueggemann and Hans Walter Wolff. Atlanta: Knox, 1975. Pp. 101-13, 143-51.

———. "Presence of God, Cultic." IDBSup. Ed. Keith Crim et al. Nashville: Abingdon, 1976. Pp. 680-83.

———. "Psalms and the Life of Faith: A Suggested Typology of Function." JSOT 17 (1980) 3-32.

———. "Scripture and an Ecumenical Life-style: A Study in Wisdom Theology." Int 24 (1970) 3-19.

————. "Trajectories in Old Testament Literature and the Sociology of Ancient Israel." *JBL* 98 (1979) 161-85.

————. "The Triumphalist Tendency in Exegetical History." *JAAR* 38 (1970) 367-80.

Brueggeman, Walter, and Hans Walter Wolff. *The Vitality of Old Testament Traditions*. Atlanta: Knox, 1975.

Bryce, Glendon E. *A Legacy of Wisdom: The Egyptian Contribution to the Wisdom of Israel*. Lewisburg: Bucknell University; London: Associated University, 1979.

————. "Wisdom in Israel: By Gerhard von Rad." *TToday* 30 (1973-74) 436-42.

Buber, Martin. *Kingship of God*. New York: Harper & Row; London: George Allen, 1967. ET of *Königtum Gottes*. Berlin: Schocken, 1932; 2nd ed., 1936; 3rd ed., Heidelberg: Schneider, 1956. Repr. in *Werke*, vol. 2, *Schriften zur Bibel*. Pp. 489-723. Munich: Kösel; Heidelberg: Schneider, 1964.

Bulmer, R. "Why Is the Cassowary Not a Bird? A Problem of Zoological Taxonomy among the Karam of the New Guinea Highlands." *Man*, n.s. 2 (1967) 5-25. Repr. in *Rules and Meanings: The Anthropology of Everyday Knowledge—Selected Readings*. Ed. Mary Douglas. Harmondsworth: Penguin, 1973. Pp. 167-93.

Bultmann, Rudolf. *The History of the Synoptic Tradition*. Oxford: Blackwell; New York: Harper & Row, 1963. ET of *Die Geschichte der synoptischen Tradition*. FRLANT 29. Göttingen: Vandenhoeck & Ruprecht, 1929; 2nd ed., 1931; enlarged ed., 1958.

————. *Jesus Christ and Mythology*. New York: Scribner's, 1958; London: SCM, 1960.

————. *Theology of the New Testament*. 2 vols. New York: Scribner's, 1951-55; London: SCM, 1952-55. ET of *Theologie des Neuen Testaments*. Tübingen: Mohr, 1953.

————. "The Christology of the New Testament." In *Faith and Understanding*. London: SCM; New York: Harper & Row, 1969. 1:262-85. ET of "Die Christologie des Neuen Testaments." In *Glauben und Verstehen: Gesammelte Aufsätze*. Tübingen: Mohr, 1933. 1:245-67.

————. "Faith in God the Creator." In *Existence and Faith: Shorter Writings of Rudolf Bultmann*. New York: Meridian, 1960; London: Hodder, 1961. Pp. 171-82. ET of "Der Glaube an Gott den Schöpfer." *EvT* 1 (1934-35) 175-89.

————. "Der Gottesdenke und der moderne Mensch." *ZTK* 60 (1963) 335-48. Repr. in *Glauben und Verstehen: Gesammelte Aufsätze*. Tübingen: Mohr, 1965. 4:107-12.

————. "Karl Barth, *The Resurrection of the Dead*." In *Faith and Understanding*. London: SCM; New York: Harper & Row, 1969. 1:66-94. ET of "Karl Barth, 'Die Auferstehung der Toten.'" *TBl* 5 (1926) 1-14. Repr. in *Glauben und Verstehen: Gesammelte Aufsätze*. Tübingen: Mohr, 1933. 1:38-64.

————. "Karl Barth's *Epistle to the Romans* in Its Second Edition." In *The Beginnings of Dialectic Theology*. Ed. James M. Robinson. Richmond: Knox, 1968. Pp. 100-120. ET of "Karl Barths Römerbrief in zweiter Auflage." *Die christliche Welt* 36 (1922) 320-23, 330-34, 358-61, 369-73. Repr. in *Anfänge dialektischen Theologie.* Ed. Jürgen Moltmann. TBü 17. Munich: Kaiser, 1964. 1:119-41.

_____. *Kerygma and Myth: A Theological Debate.* London: SPCK, 1953. Pp. 1-44. ET of "Neue Testament und Mythologie: Das 'Problem der Entmythologisierung der neutestamentlichen Verkündigung." In *Kerygma und Mythos: Ein theologisches Gespräch.* Ed. Hans-Werner Bartsch. Hamburg: Reich, 1948, 4th ed., 1960. Pp. 15-48.

_____. "The problem of a theological exegesis of the New Testament." In *The Beginnings of Dialectic Theology.* Ed. James M. Robinson. Richmond: Knox, 1968. Pp. 236-56. ET of "Das Problem einer theologischen Exegese des Neuen Testaments." *Zwischen den Zeiten* 3 (1925) 334-57. Repr. in *Anfänge dialektischen Theologie.* Ed. Jürgen Moltmann. TBü 17. Munich: Kaiser, 1964. 2:47-71.

_____. "The Meaning of Christian Faith in Creation." In *Existence and Faith: Shorter Writings of Rudolf Bultmann.* New York: Meridian, 1960; London: Hodder, 1961. Pp. 206-25, 310-11. ET of "Der Sinn des Christlichen Schöpfungsglaubens." *ZMR* 51 (1936) 1-20.

_____. "Prophecy and Fulfilment." In *Essays Philosophical and Theological.* New York: Macmillan; London: SCM, 1955. Pp. 182-208. Repr. in *Essays on Old Testament Hermeneutics.* Ed. Claus Westermann. Richmond: Knox; 1963. = *Essays on Old Testament Interpretation.* London: SCM, 1963. Pp. 50-75. ET of "Weissagung und Erfüllung." *ST* 2 (1949) 21-44. Repr. in *ZTK* 47 (1950) 360-83. Repr. in *Glauben und Verstehen: Gesammelte Aufsätze.* Tübingen: Mohr, 1952. 2:162-86. Repr. in *Probleme alttestamentlicher Hermeneutik: Aufsätze zum Verstehen des Alten Testaments.* Ed. Claus Westermann. TBü 11. Munich: Kaiser, 1960. Pp. 28-53.

Burns, John Barclay. "The Mythology of Death in the Old Testament." *SJT* 26 (1973) 327-40.

Buss, Martin J. "The Meaning of History." In *Theology as History.* Ed. James M. Robinson and John B. Cobb. New Frontiers in Theology 3. New York: Harper & Row, 1967. Pp. 135- 54.

Buss, Martin J., and Gerhard Lenski. "*The Tribes of Yahweh . . .*, by Norman K. Gottwald." *RelSR* 6 (1980) 271-78.

Calvin, Jean. *The First Epistle of Paul the Apostle to the Corinthians.* Edinburgh: Oliver & Boyd, 1960. ET of *Commentarii in epistolam Pauli ad Corinthios I.* 1548. Repr. in *Opera omnia.* Amsterdam: Schipper, 1667. 7:111-216.

_____. *Commentaries on the First Book of Moses, Called Genesis.* Edinburgh: Calvin Translation Society, 1847; repr., Grand Rapids: Eerdmans, 1948. ET of *Commentarii in primum librum Mosis, vulgo Genesin.* 1554. Repr. in *Opera omnia.* Amsterdam: Schipper, 1667. 1:1-245.

_____. *Institutes of the Christian Religion.* Ed. J. T. McNeill. LCC 20. Philadelphia: Westminster; London: SCM, 1961. ET of *Institutio christianae religionis.* 1536; rev. ed., 1559. Repr. in *Opera omnia.* Amsterdam: Schipper, 1667. 9:1-406.

Campenhausen, Hans Freiherr von. *The Formation of the Christian Bible.* London: Black; Philadelphia: Fortress, 1972. ET of *Die Entstehung der christlichen Bibel.* Tübingen: Mohr, 1968.

Carlson, R. A. "Élie à l'Horeb." *VT* 19 (1969) 416-39.

Carlston, Charles E. "Proverbs, Maxims, and the Historical Jesus." *JBL* 99 (1980) 87-105.

Carmichael, Calum M. *The Laws of Deuteronomy.* Ithaca, NY: Cornell University, 1974.

_____. *Women, Law, and the Genesis Traditions.* Edinburgh: Edinburgh University, 1979.

_____. "A Common Element in Five Supposedly Disparate Laws." *VT* 29 (1979) 129-42.

_____. "A Time for War and a Time for Peace: The Influence of the Distinction upon Some Legal and Literary Material." In *Studies in Jewish Legal History in Honour of David Daube.* Ed. B. S. Jackson. *JJS* 25 (1974) 50-63.

_____. "On Separating Life and Death: An Explanation of Some Biblical Laws." *HTR* 69 (1976) 1-7.

Carroll, Robert P. *When Prophecy Failed: Reactions and Responses to Failure in the Old Testament Prophetic Traditions.* London: SCM; New York: Seabury, 1979.

Causse, Antonin. *Du groupe ethnique à la communauté religieuse: Le problème sociologique de la religion d'Israël.* Paris: Alcan, 1937.

Cazelles, Henri. "Sur un rituel du Deutéronome (Deut. xxvi 14)." *RB* 55 (1948) 54-71.

Chamberlayne, John H. *Man in Society: The Old Testament Doctrine.* London: Epworth, 1966.

Chary, T. *Aggée—Zacharie—Malachie.* SB. Paris: Gabalda, 1969.

Childs, Brevard S. *Biblical Theology in Crisis.* Philadelphia: Westminster, 1970.

_____. *The Book of Exodus: A Critical, Theological Commentary.* OTL. Philadelphia: Westminster, 1974. = *Exodus: A Commentary.* OTL. London: SCM, 1974.

_____. *Introduction to the Old Testament as Scripture.* London: SCM; Philadelphia: Fortress, 1979.

_____. "Interpretation in Faith: The Theological Responsibility of an Old Testament Commentary." *Int* 18 (1964) 432-49.

Chrysostom, S. John. *Homilies on the Epistle to the Hebrews.* NPNF, 1/14. Ed. Philip Schaff. New York: Scribner's, 1887; repr., Grand Rapids: Eerdmans, 1956. Pp. 335-522. ET of Εἰς τὴν πρὸς Ἑβραίους Ἐπιστολὴν ca. 390. Repr. in *PG* 63:9-236. Paris: Migne, 1862.

_____. *Homilies on the Epistle of St. Paul the Apostle to Titus.* NPNF, 1/13. Ed. Philip Schaff. New York: Scribner's, 1887; repr., Grand Rapids: Eerdmans, 1956. Pp. 1-269. ET of Εἰς τὴν πρὸς Τίτον Ἐπιστολὴν ca. 390. Repr. in *PG* 62:663-700. Paris: Migne, 1862.

Clavier, Henri. *Les variétés de la pensée biblique et le problème de son unité: Esquisse d'une théologie de la Bible sur les textes originaux et dans leur contexte historique.* NovTSup 43. Leiden: Brill, 1976.

Clements, Ronald E. *Abraham and David: Genesis 15 and Its Meaning for Israelite Tradition.* SBT 2/5. London: SCM; Naperville, IL: Allenson, 1967.

249

_____. *God and Temple: The Idea of the Divine Presence in Ancient Israel.* Oxford: Blackwell, 1964; Philadelphia: Fortress, 1965.

_____. *Isaiah 1–39.* NCBC. London: Marshall; Grand Rapids: Eerdmans, 1980.

_____. *Old Testament Theology.* London: Marshall; Atlanta: Knox, 1978.

_____. *Prophecy and Tradition.* Growing Points in Theology. Oxford: Blackwell; Atlanta: Knox, 1975.

_____. "Covenant and Canon in the Old Testament." In *Creation, Christ and Culture: Studies in Honour of T. F. Torrance.* Ed. Richard W. A. McKinney. Edinburgh: T. & T. Clark, 1976. Pp. 1-12.

_____. "Deuteronomy and the Jerusalem Cult Tradition." *VT* 15 (1965) 300-312.

Clines, David J. A. *I, He, We, and They: A Literary Approach to Isaiah 53.* JSOTSup 1. Sheffield: JSOT, 1976.

Coats, George W. *From Canaan to Egypt: Structural and Theological Context for the Joseph Story.* CBQMS 4. Washington: Catholic Biblical Association, 1976.

_____. *Rebellion in the Wilderness: The Murmuring Motif in the Wilderness Traditions of the Old Testament.* Nashville: Abingdon, 1968.

_____. "The God of Death: Power and Death in the Primeval History." *Int* 29 (1975) 227-39.

_____. "History and Theology in the Sea Tradition." *ST* 29 (1975) 53-62.

_____. "The King's Loyal Opposition: Obedience and Authority in Exodus 32–34." In *Canon and Authority: Essays in Old Testament Religion and Theology.* Ed. George W. Coats and Burke O. Long. Philadelphia: Fortress, 1977. Pp. 91-109.

_____. "Legendary Motifs in the Moses Death Reports." *CBQ* 39 (1977) 34-44.

_____. "Moses versus Amalek: Aetiology and Legend in Exod. xvii 8-16." In *Congress Volume: Edinburgh 1974.* VT Sup 28. Leiden: Brill, 1975. Pp. 29-41.

Cody, A. "When Is the Chosen People Called a Goy?" *VT* 14 (1964) 1-6.

Cohn, Robert L. *The Shape of Sacred Space: Four Biblical Studies.* AARSR 23. Chico, CA: Scholars, 1981.

Collins, Adela Yarbro. "New Testament Perspectives [on the Effects of Women's Studies on Biblical Studies]: The Gospel of John." *JSOT* 22 (1982) 47-53.

Collins, John J. "The 'Historical' Nature of the Old Testament in Recent Biblical Theology." *CBQ* 41 (1979) 185-204.

_____. "Proverbial Wisdom and the Yahwist Vision." In *Gnomic Wisdom.* Ed. John Dominic Crossan. Semeia 17. Chico, CA: Scholars, 1980. Pp. 1-17.

Congar, Yves. "The Church: The People of God." *Concilium* (London) 1/1 (1965) 7-19.

Cooper, Burton. "How Does God Act in Our Time? An Invitation to a Dialogue between Process and Liberation Theologies." *USQR* 32 (1976-77) 25-35.

Coote, Robert B. "Yahweh Recalls Elijah." In *Traditions in Transformation: Turning Points in Biblical Faith.* Fest. F. M. Cross. Ed. B. Halpern and J. D.

Levenson. Winona Lake, IN: Eisenbrauns, 1981. Pp. 115-20.

Craigie, Peter C. *The Problem of War in the Old Testament.* Grand Rapids: Eerdmans, 1978.

————. *The Book of Deuteronomy.* NICOT. Grand Rapids: Eerdmans; London: Hodder, 1976.

————. " 'Yahweh Is a Man of Wars.' " *SJT* 22 (1969) 183-88.

Crenshaw, James L. *Old Testament Wisdom: An Introduction.* Atlanta: Knox, 1981; London: SCM, 1982.

————. *Prophetic Conflict: Its Effect upon Israelite Religion.* BZAW 124. Berlin: de Gruyter, 1971.

————. *Samson: A Secret Betrayed, a Vow Ignored.* Atlanta: Knox, 1978; London: SPCK, 1979.

————, ed. *Studies in Ancient Israelite Wisdom.* New York: Ktav, 1976.

————. "The Birth of Skepticism in Ancient Israel." In *The Divine Helmsman: Studies on God's Control of Human Events Presented to Lou H. Silberman.* Ed. James L. Crenshaw and Samuel Sandmel. New York: Ktav, 1980. Pp. 1-19.

————. "The Human Dilemma and Literature of Dissent." In *Tradition and Theology in the Old Testament.* Ed. Douglas A. Knight. Philadelphia: Fortress; London: SPCK, 1977. Pp. 235-58.

————. "In Search of Divine Presence (Some Remarks Preliminary to a Theology of Wisdom)." *RevExp* 74 (1977) 353-69.

————. "Popular Questioning of the Justice of God in Ancient Israel." *ZAW* 82 (1970) 380-95.

————. "*Wisdom in Israel,* by Gerhard von Rad." *RelSRev* 2 (1976) 6-12.

Cross, Frank Moore. *Canaanite Myth and Hebrew Epic: Essays in the History of the Religion of Israel.* Cambridge: Harvard University, 1973.

————. "Yahweh and the God of the Patriarchs." *HTR* 55 (1962) 225-59.

Crossan, John Dominic. "Paradox Gives Rise to Metaphor: Paul Ricoeur's Hermeneutics and the Parables of Jesus." *BR* 24/25 (1979/80) 20-37.

Crüsemann, Frank. *Der Widerstand gegen das Königtum: Die antiköniglichen Texte des Alten Testamentes und der Kampf um den frühen israelitischen Staat.* WMANT 49. Neukirchen: Neukirchener, 1978.

Cullmann, Oscar. *Salvation in History.* London: SCM; New York: Harper & Row, 1967. ET of *Heil als Geschichte: Heilsgeschichtliche Existenz im Neuen Testament.* Tübingen: Mohr, 1965.

Cunliffe-Jones, Hubert. *Deuteronomy: Introduction and Commentary.* Torch Bible Commentaries. London: SCM, 1951.

Dahl, Nils Alstrup. *Das Volk Gottes: Eine Untersuchung zum Kirchenbewusstsein des Urchristentums.* Oslo: Dybwad, 1941; repr., Darmstadt: Wissenschaftliche Buchgesellschaft, 1963.

————. "Contradictions in Scripture." In *Studies in Paul: Theology for the Early Christian Mission.* Minneapolis: Augsburg, 1977. Pp. 159-77. ET of "Motsigelser i Skriften—et gammelt hermeneutiskt problem." *STK* 45(1969) 22-36.

————. "The Future of Israel." In *Studies in Paul: Theology for the Early*

Christian Mission. Minneapolis: Augsburg, 1977. Pp. 137-58. ET of "Paulus' syn på Israels fremtid." In *Israel, kirken og verden. Nordisk teologkonferanse: Utstein kloster 1971*. Ed. M. Saebø. Oslo: Land og Kirke/Gyldendal, 1972. Pp. 115-36.

————. "Promise and Fulfillment." In *Studies in Paul: Theology for the Early Christian Mission*. Minneapolis: Augsburg, 1977. Pp. 115-36. ET of "Paulus' syn på løftenes oppfyllelse." In *Israel, kirken og verden. Nordisk teologknoferanse: Utstein kloster 1971*. Ed. M. Saebø. Oslo: Land og Kirke/Gyldendal, 1972. Pp. 99-114.

————. "Rudolf Bultmann's *Theology of the New Testament*." In *The Crucified Messiah and Other Essays*. Minneapolis: Augsburg, 1974. Pp. 90-128, 175-77. ET of "Die Theologie des Neuen Testaments." *TR* 22 (1954) 21-49.

Danell, G. A. "The Idea of God's People in the Bible." In *The Root of the Vine: Essays in Biblical Theology*. By Anton Fridrichsen et al. London: Dacre; New York: Philosophical Library, 1953. Pp. 23-36.

Daube, David. *Studies in Biblical Law*. Cambridge: Cambridge University; New York: Macmillan, 1947.

————. "Concessions to Sinfulness in Jewish Law." *JJS* 10 (1959) 1-13.

————. "The Culture of Deuteronomy." *Orita* 3 (1969) 27-52.

————. "*Repudium* in Deuteronomy." In *Neotestamentica et Semitica: Studies in Honour of Matthew Black*. Ed. E. Earle Ellis and Max Wilcox. Edinburgh: T. & T. Clark, 1969. Pp. 236-39.

————. "The Self-Understood in Legal History." *Juridical Review* 85 (1973) 126-34.

Davidson, Robert. "Some Aspects of the Theological Significance of Doubt in the Old Testament." *ASTI* 7 (1970) 41-52.

Davies, Eryl W. "Inheritance Rights and the Hebrew Levirate Marriage." *VT* 31 (1981) 138-44.

Davies, William D. *The Gospel and the Land: Early Christianity and Jewish Territorial Doctrine*. Berkeley and Los Angeles: University of California, 1974.

————. *The Setting of the Sermon on the Mount*. Cambridge: Cambridge University, 1964.

————. "Paul and the People of Israel." *NTS* 24 (1978) 4-39.

Davis, Stephen T. "Divine Omniscience and Human Freedom." *RelS* 15 (1979) 303-16.

[*De ecclesia*] "Dogmatic Constitution on the Church." In *The Documents of Vatican II*. Ed. Walter M. Abbott. London: Chapman; New York: Herder & Herder, 1966. Pp. 9-106. ET of "Constitutio dogmatica de ecclesia." *AAS* 57 (1965) 1-71.

Deissler, Alfons. *Die Grundbotschaft des Alten Testaments*. Freiburg: Herder, 1972.

Dentan, Robert C. *Preface to Old Testament Theology*. New Haven: Yale University; London: Oxford University, 1950; rev. ed., New York: Seabury, 1963.

————. "*The Land: Place as Gift, Promise and Challenge in Biblical Faith*, by Walter Brueggemann." *JBL* 97 (1968) 577-78.

Diem, Hermann. *Dogmatics.* Philadelphia: Westminster; Edinburgh: Oliver & Boyd, 1959. ET of *Theologie als kirchliche Wissenschaft.* Vol. 2: *Dogmatik: Ihr Weg zwischen Historismus und Existentialismus.* Munich: Kaiser, 1955.

Diepold, Peter. *Israels Land.* BWANT 95. Stuttgart: Kohlhammer, 1972.

Dietrich, Walter. *Israel und Kanaan: Vom Ringen zweier Gezellschaftssysteme.* SBS 94. Stuttgart: Katholisches Bibelwerk, 1979.

_____. "Gott als König: Zur Frage nach den theologischen und politischen Legitimät religiöser Begriffsbildung." *ZTK* 77 (1980) 251-68.

Dilthey, Wilhelm. "Beiträge zum Studium der Individualität." In *Die Geistige Welt: Einleitung in die Philosophie des Lebens.* Vol. 1 (*Gesammelte Schriften,* vol. 5). Leipzig: Teubner, 1924. Pp. 241-316.

Dinkler, Erich. "Bibelautorität und Bibelkritik." *ZTK* 47 (1950) 70-93.

Douglas, Mary. *Implicit Meanings: Essays in Anthropology.* London: Routledge, 1975.

_____. *Purity and Danger: An Analysis of Concepts of Pollution and Taboo.* London: Routledge; New York: Praeger, 1966.

Driver, Samuel R. *The Book of Genesis.* Westminster Commentaries. London: Methuen; New York: Gorham, 1904.

_____. *A Critical and Exegetical Commentary on Deuteronomy.* ICC. Edinburgh: T. & T. Clark; New York: Scribner's, 1895.

Dubarle, A. M. "Où en est l'étude de la littérature sapientielle?" *ETL* 44 (1968) 407-19. Repr. in *De Mari à Qumrân. L'Ancien Testament: Son milieu, ses écrits, ses relectures juives. Hommages à Mgr. J. Coppens.* Ed. H. Cazelles et al. Donum Natalicum Iosepho Coppens. Vol. 1. BETL 24. Gembloux: Duculot; Paris: Lethielleux, 1969. Pp. 246-58.

Dumas, André. *Political Theology and the Life of the Church.* London: SCM; Philadelphia: Westminster, 1978. ET of *Théologies politiques et vie de l'Église.* Lyon: Les Editions du Chalet, 1977.

Dunn, James D. G. *Christology in the Making: A New Testament Inquiry into the Origins of the Doctine of the Incarnation.* London: SCM; Philadelphia: Westminster, 1980.

_____. *Unity and Diversity in the New Testament: An Inquiry into the Character of Earliest Christianity.* London: SCM; Philadelphia: Westminster, 1977.

_____. "The Authority of Scripture according to Scripture." *Churchman* 96 (1982) 104-22, 201-25.

Dupont, Jacques. *See* Schnackenburg, Rudolph, and Jacques Dupont.

Ebeling, Gerhard. *Luther: An Introduction to His Thought.* Philadelphia: Fortress; London: Collins, 1970. ET of *Luther: Einführung in sein Denken.* Tübingen: Mohr, 1964.

_____. *The Study of Theology.* Philadelphia: Fortress, 1978; London: Collins, 1979. ET of *Studium der Theologie: Eine enzyklopädische Orientierung.* Tübingen: Mohr, 1975.

_____. "Dogmatik und Exegese." *ZTK* 77 (1980) 269-86.

_____. "Reflections on the Doctrine of the Law." In *Word and Faith.* London: SCM; Philadelphia: Fortress, 1963. Pp. 247-81. ET of "Erwägungen zur Lehre vom Gesetz." *ZTK* 55 (1958) 270-306. Repr. in *Wort und Glaube*. Tübingen: Mohr, 1960. 1:255-93.

————. "The Meaning of Biblical Theology." *JTS* 6 (1955) 210-25. Repr. in *On the Authority of the Bible: Some Recent Studies*. By Leonard Hodgson et al. London: SPCK, 1960. Pp. 49- 67. Repr. in *Word and Faith*. London: SCM; Philadelphia: Fortress, 1963. Pp. 79-97. ET of "Was heisst 'Biblische Theologie'?" In *Wort und Glaube*. Tübingen: Mohr, 1960. 1:69-81.

Eckert, Willehad P., et al., eds. *Jüdisches Volk— gelobtes Land*. Munich: Kaiser, 1970.

Edwards, Richard A. *A Theology of Q: Eschatology, Prophecy and Wisdom*. Philadelphia: Fortess, 1976.

Eichrodt, Walther. *Theology of the Old Testament*. 2 vols. OTL. London: SCM; Philadelphia: Westminster, 1961 and 1967. ET of *Theologie des Alten Testaments*. 3 vols. Leipzig: Hinrichs, 1933, 1935, 1939; rev. ed. (2 vols.) Stuttgart: Klotz, 1957-61.

————. "*A Guide to the Understanding of the Bible* . . . , by Harry Emerson Fosdick." *JBL* 65 (1946) 205-17.

————. "Covenant and Law: Thoughts on Recent Discussion." *Int* 20 (1966) 302-21.

————. "Darf man heute vom einem Gottesbund mit Israel reden?" *TZ* 30 (1974) 193-206.

————. "Hat die alttestamentliche Theologie noch selbständige Bedeutung innerhalb der alttestamentlichen Wissenschaft?" *ZAW* 47 (1929) 83-91.

Eissfeldt, Otto. *The Old Testament: An Introduction*. Oxford: Blackwell; New York: Harper & Row, 1965. ET of *Einleitung in das Alte Testament*. Tübingen: Mohr, 1934; 3rd ed., 1964.

————. "El and Jahweh." *JSS* 1 (1956) 25-37. ET of "El und Jahweh." In *Kleine Schriften*. Tübingen: Mohr, 1966. 3:386-97.

————. "Israelitisch-jüdische Religionsgeschichte und alttestamentliche Theologie." *ZAW* 44 (1926) 1-12. Repr. in *Kleine Schriften*. Tübingen: Mohr, 1962. 1:105-14.

————. "Geschichtliches and Übergeschichtliches im Alten Testament: Volk und 'Kirche' im Alten Testament." *TSK* 109 (1947) 9-23.

Eliade, Mircea. "Methodological Remarks on the Study of Religious Symbolism." In *The History of Religions: Essays in Methodology*. Ed. Mircea Eliade and Joseph M. Kitagawa. Chicago: University of Chicago, 1959; repr., 1973. Pp. 86-107.

Eliot, T. S. *The Complete Poems and Plays*. London: Faber; New York: Harcourt, Brace, 1969.

Ellis, Peter F. *The Yahwist: The Bible's First Theologian*. Notre Dame, IN: Fides, 1968; London: Chapman, 1969.

Ellul, Jacques. *The Politics of God and the Politics of Man*. Grand Rapids: Eerdmans, 1972. ET of *Politique de Dieu, politiques de l'homme*. Paris: Éditions Universitaires, 1966.

Elon, Amos, and Sana Hassan. *Between Enemies: An Arab-Israeli Dialogue*. London: Deutsch; New York: Random House, 1974.

Epstein, Isidore. *Judaism: A Historical Presentation*. Harmondsworth: Penguin, 1959.

Epstein, Louis M. *Marriage Laws in the Bible and the Talmud*. Harvard Semitic Series 12. Cambridge: Harvard University, 1942.

Eslinger, Lyle. "The Case of an Immodest Lady Wrestler in Deuteronomy xxv 11-12." *VT* 31 (1981) 269-81.

Evans, Christopher F. *Explorations in Theology* 2. London: SCM, 1977.

Evans-Prichard, E. E. "Nuer Rules of Exogamy and Incest." In *Social Structure*. Ed. Meyer Fortes. Oxford: Oxford University, 1949. Pp. 85-101. Repr. as "Where the Women Are, the Cattle Are Not." In *Rules and Meanings: The Anthropology of Everyday Life—Selected Readings*. Ed. Mary Douglas. Harmondsworth: Penguin, 1973. Pp. 38-44.

Farrer, Austin. *The Glass of Vision*. Bampton Lectures. London: Dacre, 1948.

_____. *A Study in St. Mark*. London: Dacre; New York: Macmillan, 1951.

_____. *St. Matthew and St. Mark*. London: Dacre, 1954.

Fensham, F. Charles. "Widow, Orphan, and the Poor in Ancient Near Eastern Legal and Wisdom Literature." *JNES* 21 (1962) 129-39. Repr. in *Studies in Ancient Israelite Wisdom*. Ed. James L. Crenshaw. New York: Ktav, 1976. Pp. 161-71.

Fiorenza, Elisabeth Schussler. "Wisdom Mythology and the Christological Hymns of the New Testament." In *Aspects of Wisdom in Judaism and Early Christianity*. Ed. Robert L. Wilken. Notre Dame, IN: University of Notre Dame, 1975. Pp. 17-41.

Fishbane, Michael. "*In Man We Trust: The Neglected Side of Biblical Faith*, by Walter Brueggemann." *JBL* 93 (1974) 457-59.

Fisher, Eugene J. "Cultic Prostitution in the Ancient Near East? A Reassessment." *BTB* 6 (1976) 225-36.

Flanagan, James W. "Chiefs in Israel." *JSOT* 20 (1981) 47-73.

_____. "The Relocation of the Davidic Capital." *JAAR* 47 (1979) 223-44.

Flesseman-van Leer, Ellen. "Dear Christopher, . . ." In *What about the New Testament? Essays in Honour of Christopher Evans*. Ed. Morna Hooker and Colin Hickling. London: SCM, 1975. Pp. 234-42.

Flew, R. Newton. *Jesus and His Church: A Study of the Idea of the Ecclesia in the New Testament*. London: Epworth, 1938.

Fohrer, Georg. *History of Israelite Religion*. Nashville: Abingdon, 1972; London: SPCK, 1973. ET of *Geschichte des israelitischen Religion*. Berlin: de Gruyter, 1968.

_____. *Introduction to the Old Testament. See* Sellin, Ernst, and Georg Fohrer.

_____. *Theologische Grundstrukturen des Alten Testaments*. Berlin: de Gruyter, 1972.

_____. "Action of God and Decision of Man in the Old Testament." In *Biblical Essays: Proceedings of the Ninth Meeting of "Die Ou-Testamentiese Werkgemeenskap in Suid-Afrika."* Potchefstroom: Pro Rege-Pers, 1967. Pp. 31-39.

_____. "Altes Testament—'Amphiktyonie' und 'Bund'?" *TLZ* 91 (1966) 801-16, 893-904. Repr. in *Studien zur alttestamentlichen Theologie und Geschichte (1949-1966)*. BZAW 115. Berlin: de Gruyter, 1969. Pp. 84-119.

_____. "Prophetie und Geschichte." *TLZ* 89 (1964) 481-500. Repr. in *Studien zur alttestamentlichen Prophetie (1949-1965)*. BZAW 99. Berlin: Töpelmann, 1967. Pp. 265-93.

Ford, J. Massyngberde. "Jewish Law and Animal Symbolism." *JSJ* 10 (1979) 203-12.

Ford, Lewis S. *The Lure of God: A Biblical Background for Process Theism.* Philadelphia: Fortress, 1978.

_____. "Biblical Recital and Process Philosophy." *Int* 26 (1972) 198-209. Repr. in *The Lure of God: A Biblical Background for Process Theism.* Philadelphia: Fortress, 1978. Pp. 15-28.

Fosdick, Harry Emerson. *A Guide to Understanding the Bible.* London: SCM; New York: Harper & Row, 1938.

_____. *The Modern Use of the Bible.* New York: Macmillan; London: SCM, 1924.

Frankfort, Henri. *Kingship and the Gods: A Study of Ancient Near Eastern Religion as the Integration of Society and Nature.* Chicago: University of Chicago, 1948; repr., 1978.

Freedman, David Noel. "*The Old Testament and Christian Faith: A Theological Discussion*, edited by Bernhard W. Anderson." *TToday* 21 (1964-65) 225-28.

Fuchs, Ernst. *Marburger Hermeneutik.* Tübingen: Mohr, 1968.

_____. "Alte und neue Hermeneutik." In *Hören und Handeln: Festschrift für Ernst Wolf zum 60. Geburtstag.* Munich: Kaiser, 1962. Pp. 106-32. Repr. in *Gesammelte Aufsätze.* Vol. 3: *Glaube und Erfahrung: Zum Christologischen Problem im Neuen Testament.* Tübingen: Mohr, 1965. Pp. 193-230.

Galling, Kurt. "Das Gemeindegesetz in Deuteronomium 23." In *Festschrift für Alfred Bertholet zum 80. Geburtstag.* Ed. W. Baumgartner et al. Tübingen: Mohr, 1950. Pp. 176-91.

_____. "Das Königsgesetz im Deuteronomium." *TLZ* 76 (1951) 133-38.

Gebser, Hans/Jean. *Ursprung und Gegenwart.* 2 vols. Stuttgart: Deutsche, 1949-53.

Gehman, Henry S. "Natural Law and the Old Testament." In *Biblical Studies in Memory of H. C. Allemann.* Ed. Jacob M. Myers et al. Locust Valley, NY: Augustin, 1960. Pp. 109-22.

Gemser, Berend. "The Importance of the Motive Clause in Old Testament Law." In *Congress Volume: Copenhagen 1953* (in memoriam Aage Bentzen). VTSup 1. Leiden: Brill, 1953. Pp. 50-66. Repr. in *Adhuc Loquitur: Collected Essays.* Leiden: Brill, 1968. Pp. 96-115.

_____. "The Spiritual Structure of Biblical Aphoristic Wisdom: A Review of Recent Standpoints and Theories." In *Adhuc Loquitur: Collected Essays.* Leiden: Brill, 1953. Pp. 138-49. Repr. in *Studies in Ancient Israelite Wisdom.* Ed. James L. Crenshaw. New York: Ktav, 1976. Pp. 208-19.

Gerlemann, Gillis. *Esther.* BKAT 21. Neukirchen: Neukirchener, 1973.

Gerstenberger, Erhard. *Wesen and Herkunft des "apodiktischen Rechts."* WMANT 20. Neukirchen: Neukirchener, 1965.

_____. "Covenant and Commandment." *JBL* 84 (1965) 38-51.

Gerstenberger, Erhard, and Wolfgang Schrage. *Suffering.* Nashville: Abingdon; London: SPCK, 1980. ET of *Leiden.* Stuttgart: Kohlhammer, 1977.

Gese, Hartmut. *Essays on Biblical Theology.* Minneapolis: Augsburg, 1981. ET of *Zur biblischen Theologie: Alttestamentliche Vorträge.* BEvT 78. Munich: Kaiser, 1977.

_____. "Erwägungen zur Einheit der biblischen Theologie." *ZTK* 67 (1970) 417-36. Repr. in *Vom Sinai zum Zion: Alttestamentliche Beiträge zur biblischen Theologie.* BEvT 64. Munich: Kaiser, 1974. Pp. 11-30.

_____. "Die Krisis der Weisheit bei Koheleth." In *Les sagesses du Proche Orient ancien: Colloque de Strasbourg 17-19 mai 1962.* Centre d'Études Supérieures Specialisé de l'Histoire des Religions de Strasbourg. Paris: Presses Universitaires, 1963. Pp. 139-51. Repr. in *Vom Sinai zum Zion: Alttestamentliche Beiträge zur biblischen Theologie.* BEvT 64. Munich: Kaiser, 1974. Pp. 168-79.

_____. "Das Problem von Amos 9,7." In *Textgemäss: Aufsätze und Beiträge zur Hermeneutik des Alten Testaments—Festschrift für Ernst Würthwein zum 70. Geburtstag.* Ed. A. H. J. Gunneweg and Otto Kaiser. Göttingen: Vandenhoeck & Ruprecht, 1979. Pp. 33-38.

_____. "Tradition and Biblical Theology." In *Tradition and Theology in the Old Testament.* Ed. Douglas A. Knight. Philadelphia: Fortress; London: SPCK, 1977. Pp. 301-26.

_____. "Wisdom, Son of Man, and the Origins of Christology: The Consistent Development of Biblical Theology." *Horizons in Biblical Theology* 3 (1981) 23-57. ET of "Die Weisheit, der Menschensohn und die Ursprünge der Christologie als konsequente Entfaltung der biblischen Theologie." *SEA* 44 (1979) 77-114.

Geus, C. H. J. de. *The Tribes of Israel: An Investigation into Some of the Presuppositions of Martin Noth's Amphictyony Hypothesis.* Studia Semitica Neerlandica 18. Assen: van Gorcum, 1976.

Geyer, Hans Georg. "Zur Frage der Notwendigkeit des Alten Testamentes." *EvT* 25 (1965) 207-37.

Gibson, John C. L. "The Last Enemy." *SJT* 32 (1979) 151-69.

Gilkey, Langdon B. "Cosmology, Ontology, and the Travail of Biblical Language." *JR* 41 (1961) 194-205.

Gilmer, Harry W. *The If-You Form in Israelite Law.* SBLDS 15. Missoula, MT: Scholars, 1975.

Ginsberg, H. L. "The Oldest Interpretation of the Suffering Servant." *VT* 3 (1953) 400-404.

Goldingay, John. *Approaches to Old Testament Interpretation.* Leicester/Downers Grove, IL: InterVarsity, 1981.

_____. "The Arrangement of Isaiah xli-xlv." *VT* 29 (1979) 289-99.

_____. "The Chronicler as a Theologian." *BTB* 5 (1975) 99-126.

_____. "Diversity and Unity in Old Testament Theology." *VT* 34 (1984) 153-68.

_____. "History, Culture, Mission and the People of God in the Old Testament." *Evangelical Fellowship for Missionary Studies Bulletin* 5 (1975) 1-30.

_____. "The Man of War and the Suffering Servant: The Old Testament and the Theology of Liberation." *TynBul* 27 (1976) 79-113.

_____. "The 'Salvation History' Perspective and the 'Wisdom' Perspective within the Context of Biblical Theology." *EvQ* 51 (1979) 194-207.

Gordis, Robert. *The Song of Songs and Lamentations: A Study, Modern Translation and Commentary*. Rev. ed. New York: Ktav, 1974.

_____. "Religion, Wisdom and History in the Book of Esther—A New Solution to an Ancient Crux." *JBL* 100 (1981) 359-88.

Gottwald, Norman K. *The Tribes of Yahweh: A Sociology of the Religion of Liberated Israel 1250-1050 B.C.E.* Maryknoll, NY: Orbis, 1979; London: SCM, 1980.

_____. " 'Holy War' in Deuteronomy: Analysis and Critique." *RevExp* 61 (1964) 296-310.

_____. "Theologische Grundstrukturen des Alten Testaments, by Georg Fohrer." *JBL* 93 (1974) 594-96.

_____. "Walther Eichrodt's Theology of the Old Testament." *ExpT* 74 (1962-63) 209-12.

_____. "W. Eichrodt, *Theology of the Old Testament*." In *Contemporary Old Testament Theologians*. Ed. Robert B. Laurin. Valley Forge, PA: Judson; London: Marshall, 1970. Pp. 23-62.

Grässer, Erich. "Offene Fragen im Umkreis einer Biblischen Theologie." *ZTK* 77 (1980) 200-221.

Gray, John. *Joshua, Judges and Ruth*. NCBC. Camden, NJ: Nelson, 1967; repr., London: Marshall, Morgan & Scott, 1977; rev. ed., London: Marshall, Morgan & Scott; Grand Rapids: Eerdmans, 1986.

_____. *I & II Kings: A Commentary*. OTL. London: SCM; Philadelphia: Westminster, 1963; rev. ed., 1970.

_____. *The Legacy of Canaan: The Ras Shamra Texts and Their Relevance to the Old Testament*. VTSup 5. Leiden: Brill, 1957; rev. ed., 1965.

Grech, Prosper. "The Old Testament as a Christological Source in the Apostolic Age." *BTB* 5 (1975) 127-45.

_____. "The 'Testimonia' and Modern Hermeneutics." *NTS* 19 (1972-73) 318-24.

Greenberg, Moshe. "The Biblical Conception of Asylum." *JBL* 78 (1959) 125-32.

_____. "Some Postulates of Biblical Criminal Law." In *Yehezkel Kaufmann Jubilee Volume*. Ed. Menaham Haran. Jerusalem: Magnes, 1960. Pp. 5-28.

Griffin, David. "Is Revelation Coherent?" *TToday* 28 (1971-72) 278-94.

Grillmeier, Aloys. "The People of God." In *Commentary on the Documents of Vatican II*. London: Burns & Oates; New York: Herder, 1967. Pp. 153-85. ET of "Constitutio Dogmatica De Ecclesia: Kommentar." (On chaps. 1-2.) In *LTK: Das zweite vatikanische Konzil. Konstitutionen, Dekrete und Erklärungen.*

Kommentare: Teil I. Ed. Herbert Vorgrimler. Freiburg: Herder, 1966. Pp. 159-209.

Grollenberg, Lucas. *Palestine Comes First*. London: SCM, 1980. ET of *Vor een Israel zonder grenzen*. Bilthoven: Ambo, 1970; rev. ed., Uitgeverij In der Toren, 1977.

Gunneweg, Antonius H. J. *Understanding the Old Testament*. OTL. London: SCM; Philadelphia: Westminster, 1978. ET of *Vom Verstehen des Alten Testaments: Eine Hermeneutik*. ATD Ergänzungsreihe 5. Göttingen: Vandenhoeck & Ruprecht, 1977.

_____. "Herrschaft Gottes und Herrschaft des Menschen: Eine alttestamentliche Aporie von aktueller Bedeutung." *KD* 27 (1981) 164-79.

_____. " 'Theologie' des Alten Testaments oder 'Biblische Theologie'?" In *Textgemäss: Aufsätze und Beiträge zur Hermeneutik des Alten Testaments. Festschrift für Ernst Würthwein zum 70. Geburtstag*. Ed. A. H. J. Gunneweg and Otto Kaiser. Göttingen: Vandenhoeck & Ruprecht, 1979. Pp. 39-46.

Guthrie, Harvey Henry. *Wisdom and Canon: Meanings of the Law and the Prophets*. Evanston: Seabury-Western Theological Seminary, 1966.

Gutiérrez, Gustavo. *A Theology of Liberation: History, Politics and Salvation*. Maryknoll, NY: Orbis, 1973; London: SCM, 1974. ET of *Teología de la liberación: Perspectivas*. Lima: CEP, 1971.

Halbe, Jorn. " 'Altorientalisches Weltordnungsdenken' und alttestamentliche Theologie: Zur Kritik eines Ideologems am Beispiel des israelitischen Rechts." *ZTK* 76 (1979) 381-418.

Hall, Roger Alan. "Post-exilic Theological Streams and the Book of Daniel." Ph.D. diss., Yale University, 1974.

Hamerton-Kelly, Robert. *God the Father: Theology and Patriarchy in the Teaching of Jesus*. Overtures to Biblical Theology 4. Philadelphia: Fortress, 1979.

Hanson, Paul D. *The Dawn of Apocalyptic*. Philadelphia: Fortress, 1975.

_____. *The Diversity of Scripture: A Theological Interpretation*. Overtures to Biblical Theology 11. Philadelphia: Fortress, 1982.

_____. *Dynamic of Transcendence*. Philadelphia: Fortress, 1978.

_____. "Jewish Apocalyptic against Its Near Eastern Environment." *RB* 78 (1971) 31-58.

_____. "Masculine Metaphors for God and Sex-Discrimination in the Old Testament." *The Ecumenical Review* 27 (1975) 316-24. Repr. in *The Diversity of Scripture: A Theological Interpretation*. Overtures to Biblical Theology 11. Philadelphia: Fortress, 1982. Pp. 136-47.

_____. "Old Testament Apocalyptic Reexamined." *Int* 25 (1971) 454-79. Repr. in *Visionaries and Their Apocalypses*. Ed. P. D. Hanson. Philadelphia: Fortress; London: SPCK, 1983. Pp. 37-60.

_____. "The Theological Significance of Contradiction within the Book of the Covenant." In *Canon and Authority: Essays in Old Testament Religion and Theology*. Ed. George W. Coats and Burke O. Long. Philadelphia: Fortress, 1977. Pp. 110-31.

Harrelson, Walter. *From Fertility Cult to Worship*. Garden City, NY: Doubleday, 1969.

_____. "Life, Faith, and the Emergence of Tradition." In *Tradition and Theology in the Old Testament*. Ed. Douglas A. Knight. Philadelphia: Fortress; London: SPCK, 1977. Pp. 11-30.

Hart, Ray L. *Unfinished Man and the Imagination: Toward an Ontology and a Rhetoric of Revelation*. New York: Herder, 1968.

Harvey, Julien. "The New Diachronic Biblical Theology of the Old Testament (1960-1970)." *BTB* 1 (1971) 5-29.

Hasel, Gerhard F. *Old Testament Theology: Basic Issues in the Current Debate*. Grand Rapids: Eerdmans, 1972; 2nd ed., 1975; 3rd ed., 1982.

_____. *The Remnant: The History and Theology of the Remnant Idea from Genesis to Isaiah*. Berrien Springs, MI: Andrews University, 1972.

_____. "The Problem of the Center in the OT Theology Debate." *ZAW* 86 (1974) 65-82.

Hay, L. S. "What Really Happened at the Sea of Reeds?" *JBL* 83 (1964) 397-403.

Hebblethwaite, B. L. "Some Reflections on Predestination, Providence and Divine Foreknowledge." *RelS* 15 (1979) 433-48.

Hedenquist, Göte, ed. *The Church and the Jewish People*. London: Edinburgh House, 1954.

Heiler, Friedrich. "The History of Religions as a Preparation for the Co-operation of Religions." In *The History of Religions: Essays in Methodology*. Ed. Mircea Eliade and Joseph M. Kitagawa. Chicago: University of Chicago, 1959; repr., 1973. Pp. 132-60.

Hempel, Johannes. *Das Ethos des Alten Testaments*. BZAW 67. Berlin: Töpelmann, 1938; rev. ed., 1964.

_____. "Vom irrenden Glauben." *ZST* 7 (1930) 631-60. Repr. in *Apoxysmata: Vorarbeiten zu einer Religionsgeschichte und Theologie des Alten Testaments. Festgabe zum 30. Juli 1961*. BZAW 81. Berlin: de Gruyter, 1961. Pp. 174-97.

_____. "Die Wurzeln des Missionswillens im Glauben des AT." *ZAW* 66 (1954) 244-72.

Hendry, George S. *Theology of Nature*. Philadelphia: Westminster, 1980.

_____. "The Eclipse of Creation." *TToday* 28 (1971-72) 406-25.

Herder, Johann Gottfried von. *The Spirit of Hebrew Poetry*. Burlington: Edward Smith, 1833; repr., Naperville, IL: Allenson, 1971. ET of *Vom Geist der hebräischen Poesie*. Leipzig: Barth, 1787; rev. ed., 1822.

Herion, Gary A. "The Role of Historical Narrative in Biblical Thought: The Tendencies Underlying Old Testament Historiography." *JSOT* 21 (1981) 25-57.

Hermisson, Hans-Jürgen. "Observations on the Creation Theology in Wisdom." In *Israelite Wisdom: Theological and Literary Essays in Honor of Samuel Terrien*. Ed. John G. Gammie et al. Missoula, MT: Scholars, 1978. Pp. 43-57. Repr. (abridged) in *Creation in the Old Testament*. Ed. B. W. Anderson. Issues in Religion and Theology 6. Philadelphia: Fortress; London: SPCK, 1984. Pp. 118-34.

_____. "Weisheit und Geschichte." In *Probleme biblischer Theologie:*

Gerhard von Rad zum 70. Geburtstag. Ed. Hans Walter Wolff. Munich: Kaiser, 1971. Pp. 136-54.

_____. "Zeitbezug des prophetischen Wortes." *KD* 27 (1981) 96-110.

Herrmann, Siegfried. *A History of Israel in Old Testament Times.* London: SCM; Philadelphia: Fortress, 1975. ET of *Geschichte Israels in alttestamentlicher Zeit.* Munich: Kaiser, 1973.

_____. "Die Konstructive Restauration: Das Deuteronomium als Mitte biblischer Theologie." In *Probleme biblischer Theologie: Gerhard von Rad zum 70. Geburtstag.* Ed. Hans Walter Wolff. Munich: Kaiser, 1971. Pp. 155-70.

Hertzberg, H. W. *Der Prediger.* KAT 17/4. Gütersloh: Mohn, 1963.

_____. *Werdende Kirche im Alten Testament.* Theologische Existenz heute 20. Munich: Kaiser, 1950.

Hesse, Franz. *Abschied von der Heilsgeschichte.* Theologische Studien 108. Zürich: EVZ, 1971.

_____. "The Evaluation and Authority of Old Testament Texts." In *Essays on Old Testament Hermeneutics.* Ed. Claus Westermann. Richmond: Knox, 1963. = *Essays on Old Testament Interpretation.* London: SCM, 1963. Pp. 285-313. ET of "Zur Frage der Wertung und der Galtung alttestamentlicher Texte." In *Festschift Friedrich Baumgärtel zum 70. Geburtstag.* Ed. Johannes Herrman and Leonhard Rost. Erlanger Forschungen: Reihe A, Band 10. Erlangen: Universitätsbund, 1959. Pp. 74-96. Repr. in *Probleme alttestamentlicher Hermeneutik: Aufsätze zum Verstehen des Alten Testaments.* Ed. Claus Westermann. TBü 11. Munich: Kaiser, 1960. Pp. 266-94.

Hirsch, Emanuel. *Geschichte der neuern evangelischen Theologie* 4. Gütersloh: Bertelsmann, 1952.

Hobbes, Thomas. *Leviathan; or, The Matter, Forme and Power of a Commonwealth Ecclesiastical and Civil.* 1651. Ed. Michael Oakeshott. Oxford: Blackwell, 1946. New York: Macmillan, 1947.

Hobhouse, Leonard T. *Morals in Evolution: A Study of Comparative Ethics.* London: Chapman & Hall; New York: Henry Holt, 1906; rev. ed., 1915.

Horst, Friedrich. "Recht und Religion im Bereich des Alten Testaments." *EvT* 16 (1956) 49-75. Repr. in *Gottes Recht: Gesammelte Studien zum Recht im Alten Testament.* TBü 12. Munich: Kaiser, 1961. Pp. 260-91.

Hubbard, David A. "The Wisdom Movement and Israel's Covenant Faith." *TynBul* 17 (1966) 3-34.

Hübner, Hans. "Das Gesetz als elementares Thema einer Biblischen Theologie?" *KD* 22 (1976) 250-76.

Humbert, Paul. "Le substantif to'eba et le verbe t'b dans l'Ancien Testament." *ZAW* 72 (1960) 217-37.

Jacob, Edmond. *Grundfragen alttestamentlicher Theologie.* Stuttgart: Kohlhammer, 1970.

_____. *Theology of the Old Testament.* London: Hodder; New York: Harper & Row, 1958. ET of *Théologie de l'Ancien Testament.* Neuchâtel: Delachaux, 1955; rev. ed., 1968.

_____. "Principe canonique et formation de l'Ancien Testament." In *Congress Volume: Edinburgh 1974.* VTSup 28. Leiden, Brill, 1975. Pp. 101-22.

Jacobsen, Thorkild. *The Treasures of Darkness: A History of Mesopotamian Religion*. New Haven: Yale University, 1976.

Janssen, Enno. *Juda in der Exilseit: Ein Beitrag zur Frage der Entstehung des Judentums*. FRLANT 69. Göttingen: Vandenhoeck & Ruprecht, 1956.

Janzen, J. Gerald. "Eschatological Symbol and Existence in Habakkuk." *CBQ* 44 (1982) 394-414.

_____. "Modes of Power and the Divine Relativity." *Encounter* (Indianapolis) 36 (1975) 379-406.

_____. "The Old Testament in 'Process' Perspective." In *Magnalia Dei: The Mighty Acts of God: Essays on the Bible and Archeology in Memory of G. Ernest Wright*. Ed. Frank Moore Cross et al. Garden City, NY: Doubleday, 1976. Pp. 480-509.

Jepsen, Alfred. "Kanon und Text des Alten Testaments." *TLZ* 74 (1949) 65-74.

Jeremias, Joachim. *Jesus' Promise to the Nations*. SBT 1/24. London: SCM; Chicago: Regnery, 1958. ET of *Jesu Verheissung für die Völker*. Stuttgart: Kohlhammer, 1956.

Jeremias, Jörg. "משפט im ersten Gottesknechtslied (Jes. xlii 1-4)." *VT* 22 (1972) 31-42.

Johnson, Aubrey R. *The One and the Many in the Israelite Conception of God*. Cardiff: University of Wales, 1942; rev. ed., 1961.

Johnson, Luke Timothy. *Sharing Possessions: Mandate and Symbol of Faith*. Overtures to Biblical Theology 9. Philadelphia: Fortress, 1981.

Johnson, Marshall D. *The Purpose of the Biblical Genealogies, with special reference to the Setting of the Genealogies of Jesus*. SNTSMS 8. Cambridge: Cambridge University, 1969.

Johnstone, William. "The Authority of the Old Testament." *SJT* 22 (1969) 197-209.

Jones, Douglas R. *Haggai, Zechariah and Malachi*. Torch Bible Commentaries. London: SCM, 1962.

Jones, Gwilym H. " 'Holy war' or 'Yahweh war'?" *VT* 25 (1975) 642-58.

Käsemann, Ernst, ed. *Das Neue Testament als Kanon: Dokumentation und kritische Analyse zur gegenwärtigen Diskussion*. Göttingen: Vandenhoeck & Ruprecht, 1970.

_____. "The Canon of the New Testament and the Unity of the Church." In *Essays on New Testament Themes*. SBT 1/41. London: SCM; Naperville, IL: Allenson, 1964. Pp. 95-107. ET of "Begrundet der neutestamentliche Kanon die Einheit der Kirche?" *EvT* 11 (1951-52) 13-21. Repr. in *Exegetische Versuche und Besinnungen*. Göttingen: Vandenhoeck & Ruprecht, 1959. 1:214-23.

_____. "Unity and Diversity in New Testament Ecclesiology." *NovT* 6 (1963) 290-97. Repr. in *New Testament Questions of Today*. London: SCM; Philadelphia: Fortress, 1969. Pp. 252-59. ET of "Einheit und Vielfalt in der neutestamentlichen Lehre von der Kirche." *Ökumenische Rundschau* 13 (1964) 58-63. Repr. in *Zeichen der Zeit* 18 (1964) 81-85. Repr. in *Exegetische Versuche und Besinnungen*. Göttingen: Vandenhoeck & Ruprecht, 1964. 2:262-67.

_____. "New Testament Questions of Today." In *New Testament Questions of Today*. London: SCM; Philadelphia: Fortress, 1969. Pp. 1-22. ET of "Neutestamentliche Fragen von heute." *ZTK* 54 (1957) 1-21. Repr. in *Exegetische Versuche und Besinnungen*. Göttingen: Vandenhoeck & Ruprecht, 1964. 2:11-31.

_____. "Paul and Early Catholicism." *JTC* 3 (1967) 14-27. Repr. in *New Testament Questions of Today*. London: SCM; Philadelphia: Fortress, 1969. Pp. 236-51. ET of "Paulus und der Frühkatholizismus." *ZTK* 60 (1963) 75-89. Repr. in *Exegetische Versuche und Besinnungen*. Göttingen: Vandenhoeck & Ruprecht, 1964. 2:239-52.

_____. "The Problem of a New Testament Theology." *NTS* 19 (1972-73) 235-45.

Kant, Immanuel. *Religion within the Limits of Reason Alone*. La Salle, IN: Open Court, 1934; repr., New York: Harper & Row, 1960. ET of *Die Religion innerhalb der Grenzen der blossen Vernunft*. 1793, 1794. Repr. in *Gesammelte Schriften* 6:1-202. Berlin: Reimer, 1914.

Kapelrud, Arvid S. "Tradition and Worship: The Role of the Cult in Tradition Formation and Transmission." In *Tradition and Theology in the Old Testament*. Ed. Douglas A. Knight. Philadelphia: Fortress; London: SPCK, 1977. Pp. 101-24.

Katz, Peter. "The Old Testament Canon in Palestine and Alexandria." *ZNW* 47 (1956) 191-217. Repr. in *The Canon and Masorah of the Hebrew Bible*. Ed. Sid Z. Leiman. New York: Ktav, 1974. Pp. 72-98.

Kaufman, Gordon D. *An Essay on Theological Method*. Missoula, MT: Scholars, 1975; rev. ed., 1979.

_____. "On the Meaning of 'Acts of God.' " *HTR* 61 (1968) 175-201. Repr. in *God the Problem*. Cambridge: Harvard University, 1972. Pp. 119-47.

_____. "What Shall We Do with the Bible?" *Int* 25 (1971) 95-112.

Kaufmann, Yehezkel. *The Religion of Israel from Its Beginnings to the Babylonian Exile*. Chicago: University of Chicago, 1960; London: Allen & Unwin, 1961. Abridged ET of תולדות האמונה הישראלית. Vols. 1-7. Tel Aviv: Bialik Institute/ Dvir, 1937-48.

Keel, Othmar. *Das Böcklein in der Milch seiner Mutter und Verwandtes im Lichte eines altorientalischen Bildmotivs*. Freiburg: Universitätsverlag; Göttingen: Vandenhoeck & Ruprecht, 1980.

Kegler, Jürgen. Summary of *Politisches Geschehen und theologisches Verstehen: Zum Geschichtsverständnis in der frühen israelitischen Königzeit*. (Stuttgart: Calwer, 1977), in *TLZ* 102 (1979) 315-18.

Kellermann, Ulrich. *Nehemiah: Quellen, Überlieferung und Geschichte*. BZAW 102. Berlin: Töpelmann, 1967.

Kermode, Frank. *The Genesis of Secrecy: On the Interpretation of Narrative*. Cambridge: Harvard University, 1979.

Kirk, J. Andrew. *Liberation Theology: An Evangelical View from the Third World*. London: Marshall; Atlanta: Knox, 1979.

Kitamori, Kazoh. *Theology of the Pain of God*. Richmond: Knox, 1965; London: SCM, 1966. ET of *Kami No Itami No Shingaku*. Tokyo: Shinka Shuppansha, 1946; 5th ed., 1958.

Klein, Ralph W. *Israel in Exile: A Theological Interpretation.* Overtures to Biblical Theology 6. Philadelphia: Fortress, 1979.

Knierim, Rolf. "Cosmos and History in Israel's Theology." *Horizons in Biblical Theology* 3 (1981) 59-123.

Knight, Douglas A., ed. *Tradition and Theology in the Old Testament.* Philadelphia: Fortress; London: SPCK, 1977.

Knight, George A. F. *A Biblical Approach to the Doctrine of the Trinity.* SJT Occasional Papers 1. Edinburgh: Oliver & Boyd, 1953.

————. *A Christian Theology of the Old Testament.* Richmond: Knox; London: SCM, 1959; rev. ed., London: SCM, 1964.

————. *Law and Grace: Must a Christian Keep the Law of Moses?* London: SCM, 1962.

Koch, Klaus. "Ezra and the Origins of Judaism." *JSS* 19 (1974) 173-97.

————. "Gibt es ein Vergeltungsdogma im Alten Testament?" *ZTK* 52 (1955) 1-42. Repr. in *Um das Prinzip der Vergeltung in Religion und Recht des Alten Testaments.* Ed. Klaus Koch. Darmstadt: Wissenschaftliche Buchgesellschaft, 1972. Pp. 130-80.

————. "Der Tod des Religionsstifters: Erwägungen über das Verhältnis Israels zur Geschichte der altorientalischen Religionen." *KD* 8 (1962) 100-123.

————. "Wort und Einheit des Schöpfergottes in Memphis und Jerusalem: Zur Einzigartigkeit Israels." *ZTK* 62 (1965) 251-93.

Köhler, Ludwig. *Old Testament Theology.* London: Lutterworth; New York: Harper & Row, 1957. ET of *Theologie des Alten Testaments.* Tübingen: Mohr, 1936.

Koester, Helmut. "*Gnomai diaphoroi:* The Origin and Nature of Diversification in the History of Early Christianity." *HTR* 58 (1965) 279-318. Repr. in *Trajectories through Early Christianity.* By James M. Robinson and Helmut Koester. Philadelphia: Fortress, 1971. Pp. 114-57.

————. "The Theological Aspects of Primitive Christian Heresy." In *The Future of our Religious Past: Essays in Honour of Rudolf Bultmann.* London: SCM; Philadelphia: Fortress, 1971. Pp. 65-83. ET of "Häretiker im Urchristentum als theologiches Problem." In *Zeit und Geschichte: Dankesgabe an Rudolf Bultmann zum 80. Geburtstag.* Ed. Erich Dinkler. Tübingen: Mohr, 1964. Pp. 61-76.

Koester, Helmut, and James M. Robinson. *Trajectories through Early Christianity.* Philadelphia: Fortress, 1971.

Kohlberg, Lawrence. "From Is to Ought: How to Commit the Naturalistic Fallacy and Get Away with It in the Study of Moral Development." In *Cognitive Development and Epistemology.* Ed. Theodore Mischel. New York: Academic, 1971. Pp. 151-235.

Kornfeld, Walter. "L'adultère dans l'Orient antique." *RB* 57 (1950) 92-109.

Kraus, Hans-Joachim. *Die biblische Theologie: Ihre Geschichte und Problematik.* Neukirchen: Neukirchener, 1970.

————. *The People of God in the Old Testament.* London: Lutterworth; New York: Association, 1958. ET of *Das Volk Gottes im Alten Testament.* Zürich: Zwingli, 1958.

————. *Psalmen.* 2 vols. BKAT 15/1-2. Neukirchen: Neukirchener, 1961.

————. *Theologie der Psalmen.* BKAT 15/3. Neukirchen: Neukirchener, 1979.

————. "Freude an Gottes Gesetz: Ein Beitrag zur Auslegung der Psalmen 1; 19B und 119." *EvT* 10 (1950-51) 337-51.

————. "Das heilige Volk: Zur alttestamentlichen Bezeichnung ʿam qādoš." In *Freude am Evangelium: Alfred de Quervain zum 70. Geburtstag am 28. Sept. 1966.* Ed. Johann Jakob Stamm and Ernst Wolf. Munich: Kaiser, 1966. Pp. 50-61. Repr. in *Biblisch-theologische Aufsätze.* Neukirchen: Neukirchener, 1972. Pp. 37-49.

————. "Schöpfung und Weltvollendung." *EvT* 24 (1964) 462-85. Repr. in *Biblisch-theologische Aufsätze.* Neukirchen: Neukirchener, 1972. Pp. 151-78.

Kümmel, Werner Georg. *The New Testament: The History of the Investigation of Its Problems.* Nashville: Abingdon; London: SCM, 1972. ET of *Das Neue Testament: Geschichte der Erforschung seiner Probleme.* Orbis Academicus 3/3. Freiburg: Alber, 1958.

Küng, Hans. *On Being a Christian.* London: Collins; Garden City, NY: Doubleday, 1976. ET of *Christ sein.* Munich: Piper, 1974.

————. *The Church.* London: Burns & Oates; New York: Sheed & Ward, 1967. ET of *Die Kirche.* Freiburg: Herder, 1967.

————. *Structures of the Church.* New York: Nelson, 1964; London: Burns & Oates, 1965. ET of *Strukturen der Kirche.* Freiburg: Herder, 1962.

————. "'Early Catholicism' in the NT as a problem in controversial theology." In *The Living Church: Reflections on the Second Vatican Council.* London: Sheed & Ward, 1963. Pp. 233-93. ET of "Der Frühkatholizismus im Neuen Testament als kontroverstheologisches Problem." *TQ* 142 (1962) 385-424. Repr. in *Kirche im Konzil.* Freiburg: Herder, 1963; 2nd ed., 1964.

Kutsch, Ernst. *Verheissung und Gesetz: Untersuchungen zum sogenannten 'Bund' im Alten Testament.* BZAW 131. Berlin: de Gruyter, 1973.

Lambert, William G. "Destiny and Divine Intervention in Babylon and Israel." *OTS* 17 (1972) 65-72.

————. "History and the Gods: A Review Article." *Or* 39 (1970) 170-77.

Landau, Rudolf. "'... der hoch in der Höhe thront—der tief in die Tiefe sieht': Einige Aspekte zur Bedeutung des Psalters für die Praxis der Kirche." In *Werden und Wirken des Alten Testaments: Festschrift für Claus Westermann zum 70. Geburtstag.* Ed. Rainer Albertz et al. Göttingen: Vandenhoeck & Ruprecht; Neukirchen: Neukirchener, 1980. Pp. 334-54.

Landes, George M. "Creation and Liberation." *USQR* 33 (1977-78) 79-89. Repr. (abridged) in *Creation in the Old Testament.* Ed. B. W. Anderson. Issues in Religion and Theology 6. Philadelphia: Fortress; London: SPCK, 1984. Pp. 135-51.

Landy, Francis. "The Song of Songs and the Garden of Eden." *JBL* 98 (1979) 513-28.

Lash, Nicholas. "Continuity and Discontinuity in the Christian Understanding of God." *ITQ* 44 (1977) 291-302. Repr. in *Doing Theology on Dover Beach.* London: Darton, Longman & Todd; Ramsey, NJ: Paulist, 1979. Pp. 28-44.

Lauha, Aarre. *Kohelet.* BKAT 19. Neukirchen: Neukirchener, 1978.

Laurin, Robert B. "Tradition and Canon." In *Tradition and Theology in the Old Testament.* Ed. Douglas A. Knight. Philadelphia: Fortress; London: SPCK, 1977. Pp. 261-74.

Lebram, J. C. H. "Aspekte des alttestamentlichen Kanonbildung." *VT* 18 (1968) 173-89.

Leenhardt, Franz J. *Two Biblical Faiths: Protestant and Catholic.* Philadelphia: Westminster; London: Lutterworth, 1964. ET of *La parole et le buisson de feu: Les deux sources de la spiritualité chrétienne et l'unité de l'Église.* Neuchâtel: Delachaux, 1962.

Lenski, Gerhard. *See* Buss, Martin J., and Gerhard Lenski.

Leonard, Jeanne-Marie. "Invitation à la prudence dans l'emploi de l'expression 'Peuple de Dieu.' " *Communio Viatorum* 19 (1976) 35-60.

Levenson, Jon D. "The Davidic Covenant and Its Modern Interpreters." *CBQ* 41 (1979) 205-19.

―――. "The Theologies of Commandment in Biblical Israel." *HTR* 73 (1980) 17-33.

Lévêque, J. "Le contrepoint théologique apporté par la reflexion sapientielle." In *Questions disputées d'Ancien Testament: Méthode et Théologie.* Ed. C. Brekelmans. BETL 33. Gembloux: Duculot; Louvain: Louvain University, 1974. Pp. 183-202.

Levine, Baruch A. *In the Presence of the Lord: A Study of Cult and Some Cultic Terms in Ancient Israel.* SJLA 5. Leiden: Brill, 1974.

Lewis, C. S. "The Funeral of a Great Myth." In *Christian Reflections.* London: Bles; Grand Rapids: Eerdmans, 1967. Pp. 82-93.

L'Hour, Jean. "Les interdits to'eba dans le Deutéronome." *RB* 71 (1964) 481-503.

―――. "The People of the Covenant Encounters the Nations: Israel and Canaan." In *Evangelization, Dialogue, and Development: Selected Papers of the International Theological Conference, Nagpur (India) 1971.* Ed. Mariasusai Dhavamony. Documenta Missionalia 5. Rome: Gregorian University, 1972. Pp. 77-86.

―――. "Une législation criminelle dans le Deutéronome." *Bib* 44 (1963) 1-28.

Lind, Millard C. *Yahweh Is a Warrior: The Theology of Warfare in Ancient Israel.* Scottdale, PA: Herald, 1980.

―――. "The Concept of Political Power in Ancient Israel." *ASTI* 7 (1970) 4-24.

―――. "Paradigm of Holy War in the Old Testament." *BR* 16 (1971) 16-31.

Lindeskog, Gösta. "The Theology of Creation in the Old and New Testaments." In *The Root of the Vine: Essays in Biblical Theology.* By Anton Fridrichsen et al. London: Dacre; New York: Philosophical Library, 1953. Pp. 1-22.

Link, Christian. *Die Welt als Gleichnis: Studien zum Problem der natürlichen Theologie.* BEvT 73. Munich: Kaiser, 1976.

Loader, J. A. "Esther as a Novel with Different Levels of Meaning." *ZAW* 90 (1978) 417-21.

Loewe, Raphael. "The Targums and Rabbinic Literature: An Introduction to Jewish Interpretations of Scripture, by John Bowker." JTS 21 (1970) 459-64.

Lönning, Inge. "Kanon im Kanon": Zum dogmatischen Grundlagenproblem des neutestamentlichen Kanons. Oslo: Universitets Forlaget; Munich: Kaiser, 1972.

Lohfink, Norbert. The Christian Meaning of the Old Testament. Milwaukee: Bruce, 1968; London: Burns and Oates, 1969. ET of Das Siegeslied am Schilfmeer: Christliche Auseinandersetzungen mit dem Alten Testament. Frankfurt: Knecht, 1965.

——. "Beobachtungen zur Geschichte des Ausdrucks יהוה עם." In Probleme biblischer Theologie: Gerhard von Rad zum 70. Geburtstag. Ed. Hans Walter Wolff. Munich: Kaiser, 1971. Pp. 275-305.

——. "Darstellungskunst und Theologie in Dtn 1,6–3,29." Bib 41 (1960) 105-34.

Lonergan, Bernard J. F. Method in Theology. London: Darton, Longman & Todd; New York: Herder & Herder, 1972.

——. "The Ongoing Genesis of Methods." SR 6 (1976-77) 341-55.

Long, Burke O. "The Social World of Ancient Israel." Int 36 (1982) 243-55.

Lumen Gentium. See [De Ecclesia.]

Lust, J. "A Gentle Breeze or a Roaring Thunderous Sound?" VT 25 (1975) 110-15.

Luther, Martin. "How Christians Should Regard Moses." In Luther's Works. Vol. 35. Ed. E. Theodore Bachman. Philadelphia: Fortress, 1960. Pp. 155-74. ET of "Eyn Unterrichtung wie sich die Christen yn Mosen sollen schicken." 1525. Repr. in WA 16:363-93. Weimar: Hermann Bohlaus Nachfolger, 1899.

——. "Prefaces." In Luther's Works. Vol. 35. Ed. E. Theodore Bachman. Philadelphia: Fortress, 1960. Pp. 233-411. ET of "Vorreden" to Old and New Testaments and to Individual Books. 1522-46. Repr. in WA, Deutsche Bibel 6-12. Weimar: Hermann Bohlaus Nachfolger, 1888-1960.

Lys, Daniel. The Meaning of the Old Testament: An Essay on Hermeneutics. Nashville: Abingdon, 1967. Expanded ET of "A la recherche d'une méthode pour l'exégèse de l'Ancien Testament." ETR 30/3 (1955) 1-73; and "L'appropriation de l'Ancien Testament." ETR 41/1 (1966) 1-12.

——. "Le cantique des cantiques: Pour une sexualité non ambiguë." Lumière et Vie 144 (1979) 35-53.

McCarter, P. Kyle. I Samuel: A New Translation with Introduction, Notes and Commentary. AB 8. Garden City, NY: Doubleday, 1980.

McCarthy, Dennis J. "Berît and Covenant in the Deuteronomistic History." In Studies in the Religion of Ancient Israel. VTSup 23. Leiden: Brill, 1973. Pp. 65-85.

——. "Berît in Old Testament History and Theology." Bib 53 (1972) 110-21.

Macholz, Christian. "Psalm 29 und 1. Könige 19: Jahwes und Baals Theophanie." In Werden und Werken des Alten Testaments: Festschrift für Claus Westermann zum 70. Geburtstag. Ed. Rainer Albertz et al. Göttingen: Vandenhoeck & Ruprecht; Neukirchen: Neukirchener, 1980. Pp. 325-33.

Macholz, Georg Christian. "Das Verständnis des Gottesvolkes im Alten Testament." *Jüdisches Volk—gelobtes Land.* Ed. Willehad P. Eckert et al. Munich: Kaiser, 1970. Pp. 169-87.

Mack, Burton L. *Logos und Sophia: Untersuchungen zur Weisheitstheologie im hellenistischen Judentum.* SUNT 10. Göttingen: Vandenhoeck & Ruprecht, 1973.

_____. "Wisdom Myth and Myth-ology: An Essay in Understanding a Theological Tradition." *Int* 24 (1970) 46-60.

McKane, William. *Prophets and Wise Men.* SBT 1/44. London: SCM; Naperville, IL: Allenson, 1965.

_____. *Proverbs: A New Approach.* OTL. London: SCM; Philadelphia: Westminster, 1970.

_____. "Functions of Language and Objectives of Discourse according to Proverbs, 10–30." In *La sagesse de l'Ancien Testament.* BETL 51. Ed. Maurice Gilbert. Gembloux: Duculot, Louvain: Louvain University, 1979. Pp. 166-85.

McKay, John W. "Man's Love for God in Deuteronomy and the Father/Teacher—Son/Pupil Relationship." *VT* 22 (1972) 426-35.

McKeating, Henry. "The Development of the Law on Homicide in Ancient Israel." *VT* 25 (1975) 46-68.

_____. "Sanctions against Adultery in Ancient Israelite Society, with Some Reflections on Methodology in the Study of Old Testament Ethics." *JSOT* 11 (1979) 57-72.

McKenzie, John L. *A Theology of the Old Testament.* New York: Macmillan; London: Chapman, 1974.

_____. "The Four Samuels." *BR* 7 (1962) 3-18.

_____. "Reflections on Wisdom." *JBL* 86 (1967) 1-9.

Macquarrie, John. *The Faith of the People of God: A Lay Theology.* London: SCM; New York: Scribner's, 1972.

Malamat, Abraham. "The Ban in Mari and in the Bible." In *Biblical Essays: Proceedings of the Ninth Meeting of "Die Ou-Testamentiese Werkgemenskap in Suid-Afrika."* Potchefstroom: Pro Rege-Pers, 1967. Pp. 40-49.

Malfroy, Jean. "Sagesse et loi dans le Deutéronome." *VT* 15 (1965) 49-65.

Mantel, Hugo (Haim Dov). "The Dichotomy of Judaism during the Second Temple." *HUCA* 44 (1973) 55-87.

Marks, John H. "God's Holy People." *TToday* 29 (1972-73) 22-33.

Martens, Elmer A. *Plot and Purpose in the Old Testament.* Leicester: IVP, 1981. = *God's Design.* Grand Rapids: Baker, 1982.

Martin, Brice L. "Some Reflections on the Unity of the New Testament." *SR* 8 (1979) 143-52.

Martin-Achard, Robert. *Actualité d'Abraham.* Neuchâtel: Delachaux, 1969.

_____. *From Death to Life: A Study of the Development of the Doctrine of the Resurrection in the Old Testament.* Edinburgh: Oliver & Boyd, 1960. ET of *De la mort à la résurrection d'après l'Ancien Testament.* Neuchâtel: Delachaux, 1956.

———. *A Light to the Nations: A Study of the Old Testament Concept of Israel's Mission to the World.* Edinburgh: Oliver & Boyd, 1962. ET of *Israël et les nations: La perspective missionnaire de l'Ancien Testament.* Neuchâtel: Delachaux, 1959.

———. "La signification théologique de l'élection d'Israël." *TZ* 16 (1960) 333-41.

Marxsen, Willi. *The New Testament as the Church's Book.* Philadelphia: Fortress, 1972. ET of *Das Neue Testament als Buch der Kirche.* Gütersloh: Mohn, 1966.

Mayes, Andrew D. H. *Deuteronomy.* NCBC. London: Oliphants; Grand Rapids: Eerdmans, 1979.

———. *Israel in the Period of the Judges.* SBT 2/29. London: SCM; Naperville, IL: Allenson, 1974.

———. "Israel in the Pre-Monarchy Period." *VT* 23 (1973) 151-70.

———. "*The Tribes of Yahweh . . .* , by Norman K. Gottwald." *JTS* 32 (1981) 472-83.

Mays, James L. "Historical and Canonical: Recent Discussion about the Old Testament and Christian Faith." In *Magnalia Dei: The Mighty Acts of God: Essays on the Bible and Archaeology in Memory of G. Ernest Wright.* Ed. Frank Moore Cross et al. Garden City, NY: Doubleday, 1976. Pp. 510-28.

Mays, James L. and Patrick D. Miller [?]. "Introduction." *Int* 29 (1975) 115-17.

Meeks, M. Douglas. "God's Suffering Power and Liberation." *JRT* 33 (1977) 44-54.

Melly, George. *Revolt into Style.* London: Allen Lane, 1970; Garden City, NY: Doubleday, 1971; Harmondsworth: Penguin, 1972.

Mendelsohn, Isaac. *Slavery in the Ancient Near East: A Comparative Study of Slavery in Babylonia, Assyria, Syria, and Palestine from the Middle of the Third Millennium to the End of the First Millennium.* New York: Oxford University, 1949.

———. "On the Preferential Status of the Eldest Son." *BASOR* 156 (1959) 38-40.

———. "Samuel's Denunciation of Kingship in the Light of the Akkadian Documents from Ugarit." *BASOR* 143 (1956) 17-22.

Mendenhall, George E. *The Tenth Generation: The Origins of the Biblical Tradition.* Baltimore: Johns Hopkins University, 1973.

———. "Ancient Oriental and Biblical Law." *BA* 17 (1954) 26-46. Repr. in *BAR* 3:3-24. Garden City, NY: Doubleday, 1970.

———. "Covenant Forms in Israelite Tradition." *BA* 17 (1954) 50-76. Repr. in *BAR* 3:25-53. Garden City, NY: Doubleday, 1970.

———. "The Hebrew Conquest of Palestine." *BA* 25 (1962) 66-87. Repr. in *BAR* 3:100-120. Garden City, NY: Doubleday, 1970.

———. "The Monarchy." *Int* 29 (1975) 155-70.

———. "Samuel's Broken Rib." In *No Famine in the Land: Studies in Honor of John L. McKenzie.* Ed. James W. Flanagan and Anita Weisbrod Robinson. Missoula, MT: Scholars, 1975. Pp. 117-26.

————. "The Shady Side of Wisdom: The Date and Purpose of Genesis 3." In *A Light unto my Path: Old Testament Studies in Honor of Jacob M. Myers*. Ed. Howard N. Bream et al. Philadelphia: Temple University, 1974. Pp. 319-34.

————. "Social Organization in Early Israel." In *Magnalia Dei: The Mighty Acts of God: Essays on the Bible and Archaeology in Memory of G. Ernest Wright*. Ed. Frank Moore Cross et al. Garden City, NY: Doubleday, 1976. Pp. 132-51.

Merleau-Ponty, Maurice. *Signs*. Evanston, IL: Northwestern University, 1964. ET of *Signes*. Paris: Gallimard, 1960.

Meyers, Carol. "Norman K. Gottwald, *The Tribes of Yahweh*." *CBQ* 43 (1981) 104-9.

Michaelis, Johann David. *Moral*. 3 vols. Göttingen: Vandenhoeck & Ruprecht, 1792-1802.

Milgrom, Jacob. "The Alleged 'Demythologization and Secularization' in Deuteronomy: A Review Article." *IEJ* 23 (1973) 156-61.

————. "Religious Conversion and the Revolt Model for the Formation of Israel." *JBL* 101 (1982) 169-76.

Miller, Charles H. "Esther's Levels of Meaning." *ZAW* 92 (1980) 145-48.

Miller, John W. "Prophetic Conflict in Second Isaiah: The Servant Songs in the Light of Their Context." In *Wort—Gebot— Glaube: Beiträge zur Theologie des Alten Testaments: Walther Eichrodt zum 80. Geburtstag*. Ed. Hans Joachim Stoebe et al. ATANT 59. Zürich: Zwingli, 1971. Pp. 77-85.

Miller, Patrick D. *The Divine Warrior in Early Israel*. HSS 5. Cambridge: Harvard University, 1973.

————. "*Biblical Theology in Crisis*, by Brevard S. Childs." *JBL* 90 (1971) 209-10.

————. "The Gift of God: The Deuteronomic Theology of the Land." *Int* 23 (1969) 451-65.

Miranda, José Porfirio. *Being and the Messiah: The Message of St. John*. Maryknoll, NY: Orbis, 1977. ET of *El ser y el mesías*. Salamanca: Sígueme, 1973.

Miskotte, Kornelis H. *When the Gods Are Silent*. London: Collins; New York: Harper & Row, 1967. ET with revisions and additions of *Als de goden zwijgen*. Amsterdam: Uitgeversmaatschappij, 1956.

Moltmann, Jürgen. *The Theology of Hope: The Ground and the Implications of a Christian Eschatology*. New York: Harper & Row, 1967. ET of *Theologie der Hoffnung: Untersuchungen zur Begründung und zu den Konsequenzen einer christlichen Eschatologie*. Munich: Kaiser, 1964.

Moran, William L. "The Ancient Near Eastern Background of the Love of God in Deuteronomy." *CBQ* 25 (1963) 77-87.

————. "The End of the Unholy War and the Anti-Exodus." *Bib* 44 (1963) 333-42.

Morgan, G. Campbell. *The Answers of Jesus to Job*. London: Marshall, 1934; New York: Revell, 1935.

Morgan, Robert. *The Nature of New Testament Theology: The Contribution of William Wrede and Adolf Schlatter.* SBT 2/25. London: SCM; Naperville, IL: Allenson, 1973.

Mowinckel, Sigmund. *The Old Testament as Word of God.* Nashville: Abingdon, 1959; Oxford: Blackwell, 1960. ET of *Det Gamle Testament som Guds Ord.* Oslo: Gyldendal, 1938.

_____. *The Psalms in Israel's Worship.* 2 vols. Oxford: Blackwell, 1962; Nashville: Abingdon, 1963. ET of *Offersang og sangoffer: Salmediktning i Bibelen.* Oslo: Aschehoug, 1951.

Müller, Hans Michael. *Das Alte Testament: Christlich/Jüdisch/Weltlich— Ein Beitrag zur ökumenischen Frage.* Leipzig: Hinrichs, 1937.

Müller, Hans-Peter. "Neige der althebräischen 'Weisheit': Zum Denken Qohäläts." *ZAW* 90 (1978) 238-64.

Müller-Vollmer, Kurt. *Towards a Phenomenological Theory of Literature: A Study of Wilhelm Dilthey's Poetik.* The Hague: Mouton, 1963.

Murphy, Roland E. "Assumptions and Problems in Old Testament Wisdom Research." *CBQ* 29 (1967) 407-18.

_____. "The Interpretation of Old Testament Wisdom Literature." *Int* 23 (1969) 289-301.

_____. "The Kerygma of the Book of Proverbs." *Int* 20 (1966) 3-14.

_____. "Wisdom and Yahwism." In *No Famine in the Land: Studies in Honor of John L. McKenzie.* Ed. James W. Flanagan and Anita Weisbrod Robinson. Missoula, MT: Scholars, 1976. Pp. 117-26.

_____. "Wisdom: Theses and hypotheses." In *Israelite Wisdom: Theological and Literary Essays in Honor of Samuel Terrien.* Ed. John G. Gammie et al. Missoula, MT: Scholars, 1978. Pp. 35-42.

Myers, Jacob M. "Walter Brueggemann, *In Man We Trust.*" *CBQ* 35 (1973) 367-68.

Nel, Philip. "Authority in the Wisdom Admonitions." *ZAW* 93 (1981) 418-26.

Neufeld, Edward. *Ancient Hebrew Marriage Laws with Special Reference to General Semitic Laws and Customs.* London: Longmans, 1944.

_____. "The Emergence of a Royal-Urban Society in Ancient Israel." *HUCA* 31 (1960) 31-53.

Neusner, Jacob. "Ritual without Myth: The Use of Legal Materials for the Study of Religions." *Religion* 5 (1975) 91-100.

Neusner, Jacob, ed. *Understanding Jewish Theology: Classical Issues and Modern Perspectives.* New York: Ktav, 1973.

Nicholson, Ernest W. *Deuteronomy and Tradition.* Oxford: Blackwell; Philadelphia: Fortress, 1967.

_____. *Preaching to the Exiles: A Study of the Prose Tradition in the Book of Jeremiah.* Oxford: Blackwell; New York: Schocken, 1970.

Niebuhr, H. Richard. *The Meaning of Revelation.* New York: Macmillan, 1941; repr. New York: Macmillan; London: Collier-Macmillan, 1960.

Nielsen, Eduard. " 'Weil Jahwe unser Gott ein Jahwe ist' (Dtn 6,4f)." In *Beiträge zur alttestamentlichen Theologie: Festschrift für Walther Zimmerli zum 70. Geburtstag.* Ed. Herbert Donner et al. Göttingen: Vandenhoeck & Ruprecht, 1977. Pp. 288-301.

Nixon, Robin E. *The Exodus in the New Testament*. London: Tyndale, 1963.

Noonan, John T. "The Muzzled Ox." *JQR* 70 (1979-80) 172-75.

Noth, Martin. "The Laws in the Pentateuch: Their Assumptions and Meaning." In *The Laws in the Pentateuch and Other Studies*. Edinburgh: Oliver & Boyd; Philadelphia: Fortress, 1966. Pp. 1-107. ET of *Die Gesetze im Pentateuch: Ihre Voraussetzungen und ihr Sinn*. Halle: Niemeyer, 1940. Repr. in *Gesammelte Studien zum Alten Testament*. TBü 6. Munich: Kaiser, 1957. Pp. 9-141.

Ogden, Schubert. "The temporality of God." In *Zeit und Geschichte: Dankesgabe an Rudolf Bultmann zum 80. Geburtstag*. Ed. Erich Dinkler. Tübingen: Mohr, 1964. Pp. 381-98. Repr. in *The Reality of God and Other Essays*. New York: Harper, 1966; London: SCM, 1967. Pp. 144-63.

_____. "What Sense Does It Make to Say, 'God Acts in History'?" *JR* 43 (1963) 1-19. Repr. in *The Reality of God and Other Essays*. New York: Harper, 1966; London: SCM, 1967. Pp. 164-87.

Orlinsky, Harry M. "Nationalism-Universalism and Internationalism in Ancient Israel." In *Translating and Understanding the Old Testament: Essays in Honor of Herbert Gordon May*. Ed. Harry Thomas Frank and William L. Reed. Nashville: Abingdon, 1970. Pp. 206-36.

Otto, Eckart. "Erwägungen zu den Prolegomena einer Theologie des Alten Testaments." *Kairos* 19 (1977) 53-72.

_____. "Hat Max Webers Religionssoziologie des antiken Judentums Bedeutung für eine Theologie des Alten Testaments?" *ZAW* 94 (1982) 187-203.

Pannenberg, Wolfhart. *Jesus—God and Man*. Philadelphia: Westminster; London: SCM, 1968. ET of *Grundzüge der Christologie*. Gütersloh: Mohn, 1964.

_____. "Glaube und Wirklichkeit im Denken Gerhard von Rads." In *Gerhard von Rad: Seine Bedeutung für die Theologie*. By Hans Walter Wolff, Rolf Rendtorff, and Wolfhart Pannenberg. Munich: Kaiser, 1973. Pp. 37-54, 57-58.

_____. "Redemptive Event and History." In *Basic Questions in Theology*. London: SCM; Philadelphia: Westminster, 1970. 1:15-80. ET of "Heilsgeschehen und Geschichte." *KD* 5 (1959) 218-37, 259-88. Repr. in *Grundfragen systematischer Theologie: Gesammelte Aufsätze*. Göttingen: Vandenhoeck & Ruprecht, 1967. Pp. 22-78.

Pannenberg, Wolfhart, ed. *Revelation as History*. New York: Macmillan; London: Collier-Macmillan, 1968; London: Sheed & Ward, 1969. ET of *Offenbarung als Geschichte*. KD Beiheft 1. Göttingen: Vandenhoeck & Ruprecht, 1961; 2nd ed., 1965.

Patrick, Dale. *The Rendering of God in the Old Testament*. Overtures to Biblical Theology 10. Philadelphia: Fortress, 1981.

Peacocke, Arthur R. *Creation and the World of Science: The Bampton Lectures, 1978*. Oxford: Oxford University, 1979.

Pearson, Birger A. "Hellenistic-Jewish Wisdom Speculation and Paul." In *Aspects of Wisdom in Judaism and Early Christianity*. Ed. Robert L. Wilken. Notre Dame, IN: University of Notre Dame, 1975. Pp. 43-66.

Pedersen, Johannes. *Israel: Its Life and Culture*. 4 vols. repr. in 2. London: Oxford University, 1926-40. ET of *Israel*. 2 vols. Copenhagen: Pios Boghandel, 1926; and Copenhagen: Branner, 1940.

Perlitt, Lothar. *Bundestheologie im Alten Testament*. WMANT 36. Neukirchen: Neukirchener, 1969.

_____. "Die Vorborgenheit Gottes." In *Probleme biblischer Theologie: Gerhard von Rad zum 70. Geburtstag*. Ed. Hans Walter Wolff. Munich: Kaiser, 1971. Pp. 367-82.

Perrin, Norman. *Jesus and the Language of the Kingdom: Symbol and Metaphor in New Testament Interpretation*. Philadelphia: Fortress; London: SCM, 1976.

Peterson, David L. *Late Israelite Prophecy: Studies in Deutero-Prophetic Literature and in Chronicles*. SBLMS 23. Missoula, MT: Scholars, 1977.

Phillips, Anthony. *Ancient Israel's Criminal Law: A New Approach to the Decalogue*. Oxford: Blackwell; New York: Schocken, 1970.

_____. "Another Look at Adultery." *JSOT* 20 (1981) 3-25.

_____. "Nebalah—A Term for Serious Disorderly and Unruly Conduct." *VT* 25 (1975) 237-42.

Plöger, Josef G. *Literarkritische, formgeschichtliche und stilkritische Untersuchungen zum Deuteronomium*. BBB 26. Bonn: Hanstein, 1967.

Plöger, Otto. *Theocracy and Eschatology*. Richmond: Knox, 1968. ET of *Theokratie und Eschatologie*. WMANT 2. Neukirchen: Neukirchener, 1959.

Pope, Marvin H. *Song of Songs: A New Translation with Introduction and Commentary*. AB 7c. Garden City, NY: Doubleday, 1977.

Porteous, Norman W. *Living the Mystery: Collected Essays*. Oxford: Blackwell, 1967.

_____. "The Present State of Old Testament Theology." *ExpT* 75 (1963-64) 70-74.

Porter, J. Roy. *The Extended Family in the Old Testament*. Occasional Papers in Social and Economic Administration 6. London: Edutext, 1967.

_____. "Johs Pedersen: Israel." *ExpT* 90 (1978-79) 36-40.

Preuss, Horst Dietrich. "Alttestamentliche Weisheit in christlicher Theologie?" In *Questions disputées d'Ancien Testament: Méthode et Théologie*. Ed. C. Brekelmans. BETL 33. Gembloux: Duculot; Louvain: Louvain University, 1974. Pp. 165-81.

_____. "Erwägungen zum theologischen Ort alttestamentlicher Weisheitsliteratur." *EvT* 30 (1970) 393-417.

_____. "Das Gottesbild der alteren weisheit Israels." In *Studies in the Religion of Ancient Israel*. VTSup 23. Leiden: Brill, 1972. Pp. 117-45.

Priest, John F. "Humanism, Skepticism, and Pessimism in Israel." *JAAR* 36 (1968) 311-26.

_____. "Where Is Wisdom to Be Placed?" *JBR* 31 (1963) 275-82.

Pritchard, James B., ed. *Ancient Near Eastern Texts Relating to the Old Testament*. Princeton: Princeton University; London: Oxford University, 1950; 3rd ed., 1969.

Procksch, Otto. *Theologie des Alten Testaments*. Gütersloh: Bertelsmann, 1950.

Prussner, Frederick C. "The Covenant of David and the Problem of Unity in Old Testament Theology." In *Transitions in Biblical Scholarship*. Ed. J.C. Rylaarsdam. Chicago: Chicago University, 1968. Pp. 17-41.

Rad, Gerhard von. *The Message of the Prophets*. London: SCM; New York: Harper & Row, 1968. ET of *Die Botschaft der Propheten*. Munich: Siebenstern, 1967.

————. *Studies in Deuteronomy*. SBT 1/9. London: SCM; Chicago: Regnery, 1953. ET of *Deuteronomium-Studien*. FRLANT 58. Göttingen: Vandenhoeck & Ruprecht, 1947. Repr. in *Gesammelte Studien zum Alten Testament*. TBü 48. Munich: Kaiser, 1973. 2:109-53.

————. *Genesis: A Commentary*. OTL. London: SCM; Philadelphia: Westminster, 1961; 2nd ed., 1963; 3rd ed., 1972. ET of *Das erste Buch Mose: Genesis*. ATD. Göttingen: Vandenhoeck & Ruprecht, 1953; 9th ed., 1972.

————. *Deuteronomy: A Commentary*. OTL. London: SCM; Philadelphia: Westminster, 1966. ET of *Das fünfte Buch Mose: Deuteronomium*. ATD. Göttingen: Vandenhoeck & Ruprecht, 1964..

————. *Gesammelte Studien zum Alten Testament*. 2 vols. 3rd ed. TBü 8, 48. Munich: Kaiser, 1965, 1973.

————. *Das Gottesvolk im Deuteronomium*. BWANT 47. Stuttgart: Kohlhammer, 1929. Repr. in *Gesammelte Studien zum Alten Testament*. TBü 48. Munich: Kaiser, 1973. 2:9-108.

————. *Der Heilige Krieg im alten Israel*. ATANT 20. Zürich: Zwingli, 1951.

————. *Old Testament Theology*. Vol. 1: *The Theology of Israel's Historical Traditions*. Edinburgh: Oliver & Boyd; New York: Harper, 1962. Vol. 2: *The Theology of Israel's Prophetic Traditions*. Edinburgh: Oliver & Boyd; New York: Harper, 1965. 2 vols. repr., London: SCM, 1975. ET of *Theologie des Alten Testaments*. Vol. 1: *Die Theologie der geschichtlichen Überlieferungen Israels*. Munich: Kaiser, 1957. Vol. 2: *Die Theologie der prophetischen Überlieferungen Israels*. Munich: Kaiser, 1960.

————. "Offene Fragen im Umkreis einer Theologie des Alten Testaments." TLZ 88 (1963) 401-16. Repr. in *Gesammelte Studien zum Alten Testament*. TBü 48. Munich: Kaiser, 1973. 2:289-312. (ET in *Old Testament Theology*. Edinburgh: Oliver & Boyd; New York: Harper, 1965. 2:410-29.)

————. *Wisdom in Israel*. London: SCM; Nashville: Abingdon, 1972. ET of *Weisheit in Israel*. Neukirchen: Neukirchener, 1970.

————. "Some Aspects of the Old Testament World-View." In *The Problem of the Hexateuch and Other Essays*. Edinburgh: Oliver & Boyd; New York: McGraw-Hill, 1966. Pp. 144-65. ET of "Aspekte alttestamentlichen Weltverständnisses." *EvT* 24 (1964) 57-73. Repr. in *Gesammelte Studien zum Alten Testament*. 3rd ed. TBü 8. Munich: Kaiser, 1965. 1:311-31.

————. "Christliche Weisheit?" *EvT* 31 (1971) 150-54. Repr. in *Gesammelte Studien zum Alten Testament*. TBü 48. Munich: Kaiser, 1973. 2:267-71.

————. "There Remains Still a Rest for the People of God: An Investigation of a Biblical Conception." In *The Problem of the Hexateuch and Other Essays*. Edinburgh: Oliver & Boyd; New York: McGraw-Hill, 1966. Pp. 94-102. ET of "Es ist noch eine Ruhe vorhanden dem Volke Gottes: Eine biblische Begriffsuntersuchung." *Zwischen den Zeiten* 11 (1933) 104-11. Repr. in

Gesammelte Studien zum Alten Testament. 3rd ed. TBü 8. Munich: Kaiser, 1965. 1:101-8.

_____. " 'Righteousness' and 'Life' in the Cultic Language of the Psalms." In *The Problem of the Hexateuch and Other Essays.* Edinburgh: Oliver & Boyd; New York: McGraw-Hill, 1966. Pp. 243-66. ET of " 'Gerechtigkeit' und 'Leben' in der Kultsprache der Psalmen." In *Festschrift für Alfred Bertholet zum 80. Geburtstag.* Ed. Walter Baumgartner et al. Tübingen: Mohr, 1950. Pp. 418-37. Repr. in *Gesammelte Studien zum Alten Testament.* 3rd ed. TBü 8. Munich: Kaiser, 1965. 1:225-47.

_____. "Ancient Word and Living Word: The Preaching of Deuteronomy and Our Preaching." *Int* 15 (1961) 3-13. ET of "Die Predigt des Deuteronomiums and unsere Predigt." In *Gesammelte Studien zum Alten Testament.* TBü 48. Munich: Kaiser, 1973. 2:154-64.

_____. "The Theological Problem of the Old Testament Doctrine of Creation." In *The Problem of the Hexateuch and Other Essays.* Edinburgh: Oliver & Boyd; New York: McGraw-Hill, 1966. Pp. 131-43. Repr. in *Creation in the Old Testament.* Ed. B. W. Anderson. Issues in Religion and Theology 6. Philadelphia: Fortress; London: SPCK, 1984. Pp. 53-64. ET of "Das theologisches Problem des alttestamentlichen Schöpfungsglaubens." In *Werden and Wesen des Alten Testaments.* Ed. Johannes Hempel. BZAW 66. Berlin: Töpelmann, 1936. Pp. 138-47. Repr. in *Gesammelte Studien zum Alten Testament.* 3rd ed. TBü 8. Munich: Kaiser, 1965. 1:136-47.

_____. "Typological Interpretation of the Old Testament." *Int* 15 (1961) 174-92. Repr. in *Essays on Old Testament Hermeneutics.* Ed. Claus Westermann. Richmond: Knox, 1963. = *Essays on Old Testament Interpretation.* London: SCM, 1963. Pp. 17-39. ET of "Typologische Auslegung des Alten Testaments." *EvT* 12 (1952-53) 17-33. Repr. in *Vergegenwärtigung: Aufsätze zur Auslegung des Alten Testaments.* Ed. Hans Urner. Berlin: Evangelische, 1955. Pp. 47-65. Repr. (abbreviated) in *Probleme alttestamentlicher Hermeneutik: Aufsätze zum Verstehen des Alten Testaments.* Ed. Claus Westermann. TBü 11. Munich: Kaiser, 1960. Pp. 11-17. Repr. in *Gesammelte Studien zum Alten Testament.* TBü 48. Munich: Kaiser, 1973. 2:272-88.

_____. "The Promised Land and Yahweh's Land in the Hexateuch." In *The Problem of the Hexateuch and Other Essays.* Edinburgh: Oliver & Boyd; New York: McGraw-Hill, 1966. Pp. 79-93. ET of "Verheissenes Land und Jahwes Land im Hexateuch." *ZDPV* 66 (1943) 191-204. Repr. in *Gesammelte Studien zum Alten Testament.* 3rd ed. TBü 8. Munich: Kaiser, 1965. 1:87-100.

_____. "Verheissung: Zum gleichnamigen Buch Fr Baumgärtels." *EvT* 13 (1953) 406-13.

Rahner, Karl. *The Shape of the Church to Come.* London: SPCK; New York: Seabury, 1974. ET of *Strukturwandel der Kirche als Aufgabe und Chance.* Freiburg: Herder, 1972.

_____. "The Old Testament and Christian Dogmatic Theology." In *Theological Investigations.* Vol. 16: *Experience of the Spirit: Source of Theology.* London: Darton, Longman & Todd; New York: Seabury, 1979. Pp. 177-90. ET of "Altes Testament und christliche Dogmatik." In *Schriften zur Theologie Band XII: Theologie aus Erfahrung des Geistes.* Einsiedeln: Benziger, 1975. Pp. 224-40.

_____. "A Theological Interpretation of the Position of Christians in the

Modern World." In *Mission and Grace: Essays in Pastoral Theology*. London: Sheed & Ward, 1963. 1:3-55. ET of "Theologische Deutung der Position des Christen in der modernen Welt." In *Sendung und Gnade: Beiträge zur Pastoraltheologie*. Innsbruck: Tyrolia, 1961. Pp. 13-47.

――――. "Theology in the New Testament." In *Theological Investigations*. Vol. 5: *More Recent Writings*. London: Darton, Longman & Todd; Baltimore: Helicon, 1966. Pp. 23-41. ET of "Theologie im Neuen Testament." In *Schriften zur Theologie Band V: Neuere Schriften*. Einsiedeln: Benziger, 1962. Pp. 33-53.

Rast, Walter E. *Joshua, Judges, Samuel, Kings*. Proclamation Commentaries. Philadelphia: Fortress, 1978.

Reich, Charles A. *The Greening of America*. New York: Random, 1970; London: Allen Lane, 1971; Harmondsworth: Penguin, 1972.

Reid, Gavin. *The Elaborate Funeral*. London: Hodder, 1972.

Renckens, Henry. *The Religion of Israel*. New York: Sheed & Ward, 1966; London: Sheed & Ward, 1967. ET of *De godsdienst van Israël*. Roermond: Romen, 1962.

Rendtorff, Rolf. "Geschichtliches und weisheitliches Denken im Alten Testament." In *Beiträge zur alttestamentlichen Theologie: Festschrift für Walther Zimmerli zum 70. Geburtstag*. Ed. Herbert Donner et al. Göttingen: Vandenhoeck & Ruprecht, 1977. Pp. 344-53.

――――. "Das Land Israel im Wandel der alttestamentlichen Geschichte." *Jüdisches Volk—gelobtes Land*. Ed. Willehad P. Eckert et al. Munich: Kaiser, 1970. Pp. 153-68.

――――. "Weisheit und Geschichte im Alten Testament: Zu einer offenen Frage im Werk Gerhard von Rads." *EvK* 9 (1976) 216-18.

Rengstorf, Karl Heinrich. "The Jewish Problem and the Church's Understanding of Its Own Mission." In *The Church and the Jewish People*. Ed. Göte Hedenquist. London: Edinburgh House, 1954. Pp. 27-46.

Reventlow, Henning Graf. "Basic Problems in Old Testament Theology." *JSOT* 11 (1979) 2-22.

――――. "Die Eigenart des Jahweglaubens als geschichtliches und theologisches Problem." *KD* 20 (1974) 199-217.

――――. "Grundfragen der alttestamentlichen Theologie im Lichte der neueren deutschen Forschung." *TZ* 17 (1961) 81-98.

――――. " 'Internationalismus' im den Patriarchenüberlieferungen." In *Beiträge zur alttestamentlichen Theologie: Festschrift für Walther Zimmerli zum 70. Geburtstag*. Ed. Herbert Donner et al. Göttingen: Vandenhoeck & Ruprecht, 1977. Pp. 354-70.

Ricoeur, Paul. *Freud and Philosophy: An Essay on Interpretation*. New Haven: Yale University, 1970. ET of *De l'interprétation: Essai sur Freud*. Paris: Seuil, 1965.

――――. *The Rule of Metaphor: Multi-disciplinary Studies of the Creation of Meaning in Language*. Toronto: University of Toronto, 1977; London: Routledge, 1978. ET of *La métaphore vive*. Paris: Seuil, 1975.

――――. *The Symbolism of Evil*. New York: Harper & Row, 1967; Boston: Beacon, 1969. ET of *La symbolique du mal. Philosophie de la volunté*, Vol. 2/2. Paris: Aubier-Montaigne, 1960.

————. "Biblical Hermeneutics." In *Paul Ricoeur on Biblical Hermeneutics*. Ed. John Dominic Crossan. Semeia 4. Missoula, MT: SBL/Scholars, 1975. Pp. 29-148.

————. "The Hermeneutics of Symbols and Philosophical Reflection." *International Philosophical Quarterly* 2/2 (1962) 191-218. Repr. in *The Conflict of Interpretations: Essays in Hermeneutics*. Evanston: Northwestern University, 1974. Pp. 287-314. ET of *Le conflit des interpretations*. Paris: Seuil, 1969.

————. "The Narrative Function." In *The Poetics of Faith: Essays Offered to Amos Niven Wilder*. Part 2: *Imagination, Rhetoric, and the Disclosures of Faith*. Ed. William A. Beardslee. Semeia 13. Missoula, MT: SBL/Scholars, 1978. Pp. 177-202.

Ringgren, Helmer. *Sacrifice in the Bible*. London: Lutterworth, 1962; New York: Association, 1963.

————. "Monotheism." In *IDBSup*. Ed. Keith Crim et al. Nashville: Abingdon, 1976. Pp. 602-4.

Roberts, J. J. M. "The Davidic Origin of the Zion Tradition." *JBL* 92 (1973) 329-44.

Robinson, H. Wheeler. *Inspiration and Revelation in the Old Testament*. Oxford: Clarendon; New York: Oxford University, 1946.

Robinson, James M. "A Critical Inquiry into the Scriptural Bases of Confessional Hermeneutics." *JES* 3 (1966) 36-56. Repr. in *Encounter* (Indianapolis) 28 (1967) 17-34.

————. "The Dismantling and Reassembling of the Categories of New Testament Scholarship." *Int* 25 (1971) 63-77. Repr. in *Trajectories through Early Christianity*. By James M. Robinson and Helmut Koester. Philadelphia: Fortress, 1971. Pp. 1-19.

————. "The Historicality of Biblical Language." In *The Old Testament and Christian Faith: A Theological Discussion*. Ed. Bernhard W. Anderson. New York: Harper & Row, 1963; repr. New York: Herder & Herder, 1969. = *The Old Testament and Christian Faith: Essays by Rudolf Bultmann and Others*. Ed. Bernhard W. Anderson. London: SCM, 1964. Pp. 124-58.

————. "Jesus as Sophos and Sophia: Wisdom Tradition and the Gospels." In *Aspects of Wisdom in Judaism and Early Christianity*. Ed. Robert L. Wilken. Notre Dame, IN: University of Notre Dame, 1975. Pp. 1-16.

————. "Kerygma and History in the New Testament." In *The Bible in Modern Scholarship: Papers Read at the 100th Meeting of the Society of Biblical Literature, December 28-30, 1964*. Ed. James Philip Hyatt. Nashville: Abingdon, 1965; London: Carey Kingsgate, 1966. Pp. 114-50. Repr. in *Trajectories through Early Christianity*. By James M. Robinson and Helmut Koester. Philadelphia: Fortress, 1971.

Robinson, James M., and John B. Cobb, eds. *The Later Heidegger and Theology*. New Frontiers in Theology 1. New York: Harper & Row, 1963.

Robinson, James M., and Helmut Koester. *Trajectories through Early Christianity*. Philadelphia: Fortress, 1971.

Robinson, John A. T. *The Human Face of God*. London: SCM; Philadelphia: Westminster, 1973.

Rodd, Cyril S. "Max Weber and Ancient Judaism." *SJT* 32 (1979) 457-69.

Römer, W. H. P. "Randbemerkungen zur Travestie von Deut. 22,5." In *Travels in the World of the Old Testament: Studies Presented to Professor M. A. Beek*.

Ed. M. S. H. G. Heerma van Voss et al. Assen: Van Gorcum, 1974. Pp. 217-22.

Rogers, Jack B., and Donald K. McKim. *The Authority and Interpretation of the Bible: An Historical Approach.* San Francisco: Harper & Row, 1979.

Rogerson, John W. "The Old Testament View of Nature: Some Preliminary Questions." In *Instruction and Interpretation: Studies in Hebrew Language, Palestinian Archaeology and Biblical Exegesis—Papers Read at the Joint British-Dutch Old Testament Conference held at Louvain, 1976.* Ed. A. S. van der Woude. OTS 20. Leiden: Brill, 1977. Pp. 67-84.

Roifer, Alexander. "The Breaking of the Heifer's Neck." *Tarbiz* 31 (1961-62) i. [Summary of עגלה ערופה, pp. 119-43.]

Rost, Leonhard. "Die Bezeichnungen für Land und Volk im Alten Testament." In *Festschrift Otto Procksch zum 60. Geburtstag.* Leipzig: Deichert, 1934. Pp. 125-48. Repr. in *Das kleine Credo und andere Studien zum Alten Testament.* Heidelberg: Quelle & Meyer, 1965. Pp. 76-101.

―――. "Erwägungen zu Hosea 14,13f." In *Festschrift für Alfred Bertholet zum 80. Geburtstag.* Ed. Walter Baumgartner et al. Tübingen: Mohr, 1950. Pp. 451-60. Repr. in *Das kleine Credo und andere Studien zum Alten Testament.* Heidelberg: Quelle & Meyer, 1965. Pp. 53-63.

―――. "Sinaibund und Davidsbund." *TLZ* 72 (1947) 129-34.

Roszak, Theodore. *The Making of a Counter Culture: Reflections on the Technocratic Society and its Youthful Opposition.* New York: Doubleday, 1969; London: Faber, 1970.

Rowley, Harold Henry. *The Re-discovery of the Old Testament.* London: Clarke; Philadelphia: Westminster, 1946.

―――. *Worship in Ancient Israel: Its Forms and Meaning.* London: SPCK; Philadelphia: Fortress, 1967.

Rücker, Heribert. "Das 'heilige Volk' als Moralprinzip im Deuteronomium." In *Dienst der Vermittlung: Festschrift zum 25- jährigen Bestehen des philosophisch-theologischen Studiums im Priesterseminar Erfurt.* Ed. W. Ernst et al. Leipzig: St Benno, 1977. Pp. 39-47.

Rudolph, Wilhelm. "Präparierte Jungfrauen? (Zu Hosea 1)." *ZAW* 75 (1963) 65-73.

Ruether, Rosemary Radford. "Feminism and Patriarchal Religion: Principle of Ideological Critique of the Bible." *JSOT* 22 (1982) 54-66.

Ruler, Arnold A. van. *The Christian Church and the Old Testament.* Grand Rapids: Eerdmans, 1971. ET of *Die christliche Kirche und das Alte Testament.* BEvT 23. Munich: Kaiser, 1955.

Runia, Klaas. *Karl Barth's Doctrine of Holy Scripture.* Grand Rapids: Eerdmans, 1962.

Russell, Letty M. "Feminist Critique: Opportunity for Cooperation." *JSOT* 22 (1982) 67-71.

Rylaarsdam, J. Coert. *Revelation in Jewish Wisdom Literature.* Chicago: University of Chicago, 1946; repr. 1974.

―――. "Jewish-Christian Relationship: The Two Covenants and the Dilemmas of Christology." *JES* 9 (1972) 249-70.

Saggs, H. W. F. *The Encounter with the Divine in Mesopotamia and Israel.* London: Athlone; Atlantic Highlands, NJ: Humanities, 1978.

_____. "Assyrian Warfare in the Sargonid Period." *Iraq* 25 (1963) 145-54.

Sahlin, Harold. "The New Exodus of Salvation according to St. Paul." In *The Root of the Vine: Essays in Biblical Theology*. By Anton Fridrichsen et al. London: Dacre; New York: Philosophical Library, 1953. Pp. 81-95.

Sakenfeld, Katharine D. "The Problem of Divine Forgiveness in Numbers 14." *CBQ* 37 (1975) 317-30.

Sanders, E. P. *Paul and Palestinian Judaism: A Comparison of Patterns of Religion*. Philadelphia: Fortress; London: SCM, 1977.

Sanders, James A. *Torah and Canon*. Philadelphia: Fortress, 1972.

_____. "Adaptable for Life: The Nature and Function of Canon." In *Magnalia Dei: The Mighty Acts of God: Essays on the Bible and Archaeology in Memory of G. Ernest Wright*. Ed. Frank Moore Cross et al. Garden City, NY: Doubleday, 1976. Pp. 531-60.

_____. "Habakkuk in Qumran, Paul, and the Old Testament." *JR* 39 (1959) 232-44.

_____. "Hermeneutics in True and False Prophecy." In *Canon and Authority: Essays in Old Testament Religion and Theology*. Ed. George W. Coats and Burke O. Long. Philadelphia: Fortress, 1977. Pp. 21-41.

Sandys-Wunsch, John. "Spinoza—The First Biblical Theologian." *ZAW* 93 (1981) 327-41.

Sarna, Nahum M. *Understanding Genesis*. New York: Jewish Theological Seminary, 1966; repr., New York: Schocken, 1970.

Schelkle, Karl Hermann. *Die Petrusbriefe: Der Judasbrief*. HTKNT 13/2. Freiburg: Herder, 1961.

Schlier, Heinrich. "Biblical and Dogmatic Theology." In *The Relevance of the New Testament*. London: Burns & Oates; New York: Herder & Herder, 1968. Pp. 26-38. ET of "Biblische und Dogmatische Theologie." In *Diskussion über die Bibel*. Ed. Ludwig Klein. Mainz: Matthias-Grünewald, 1963. Pp. 85-98. Repr. in *Besinnung auf das Neue Testament: Exegetische Aufsätze und Vorträge*. Freiburg: Herder, 1964. 2:25-34.

_____. "The Meaning and Function of a Theology of the New Testament." In *The Relevance of the New Testament*. London: Burns & Oates; New York: Herder & Herder, 1968. Pp. 1-25. ET of "Über Sinn und Aufgabe einer Theologie des Neuen Testaments." *BZ* 1 (1957) 6-23. Repr. in *Besinnung auf das Neue Testament: Exegetische Aufsätze und Vorträge*. Freiburg: Herder, 1964. 2:7-24.

Schmid, Hans Heinrich. *Gerechtigkeit als Weltordnung: Hintergrund und Geschichte des alttestamentlichen Gerechtigkeitsbegriffes*. Tübingen: Mohr, 1968.

_____. *Wesen und Geschichte der Weisheit: Eine Untersuchung zur altorientalischen und israelitischen Weisheitsliteratur*. BZAW 101. Berlin: Töpelmann, 1966.

_____. "Schöpfung, Gerechtigkeit und Heil: 'Schöpfungstheologie' als Gesamthorizont biblischer Theologie." *ZTK* 70 (1973) 1-19. Repr. in *Altorientalische Welt in der alttestamentlichen Theologie: Sechs Aufsätze*. Zürich: TVZ, 1974. Pp. 9-30. Abridged ET: "Creation, Righteousness, and Salvation: 'Creation Theology' as the Broad Horizon of Biblical Theology." In

Creation in the Old Testament. Ed. B. W. Anderson. Issues in Religion and Theology 6. Philadelphia: Fortress; London: SPCK, 1982. Pp. 102-17.

_____. "Das alttestamentliche Verständnis von Geschichte in seinem Verhältnis zum gemeinorientalischen Denken." WD 13 (1975) 9-21.

Schmidt, Werner H. Das erste Gebot: Seine Bedeutung für das Alte Testament. Theologische Existenz heute 165. Munich: Kaiser, 1969.

_____. Zukunftsgewissheit und Gegenwartskritik. Grundzüge prophetscher Verkündigung. BibS(N) 64. Neukirchen: Neukirchener, 1973.

_____. "Kritik am Königtum." In Probleme biblischer Theologie: Gerhard von Rad zum 70. Geburtstag. Ed. Hans Walter Wolff. Munich: Kaiser, 1971. Pp. 440-61.

Schmitt, Hans-Christoph. " 'Priesterliches' und 'prophetisches' Geschichtverständnis in der Meerwundererzählung Ex 13,17-14,31: Beobachtungen zur Endredaktion des Pentateuch." In Textgemäss: Aufsätze zur Hermeneutik des Alten Testaments—Festschrift für Ernst Würthwein zum 70. Geburtstag. Ed. A. H. J. Gunneweg and Otto Kaiser. Göttingen: Vandenhoeck & Ruprecht, 1979. Pp. 139-55.

Schnackenburg, Rudolf, and Jacques Dupont. "The Church as the People of God." Concilium (London) 1/1 (1965) 56-61.

Schoeps, Hans Joachim. "Faith and the Jewish Law today." In The Church and the Jewish People. Ed. Göte Hedenquist. London: Edinburgh House, 1954. Pp. 63-76.

Schofield, John N. "Otto Procksch, Theology of the Old Testament." In Contemporary Old Testament Theologians. Ed. Robert B. Laurin. Valley Forge, PA: Judson; London: Marshall, 1970. Pp. 91-120.

Schrage, Wolfgang. See Gerstenberger, Erhard, and Wolfgang Schrage.

Schweizer, Alexander. Die christliche Glaubenslehre nach protestantischen Grundsätzen. 2 vols. Leipzig: Hirzel, 1863-72.

Schweizer, Eduard. Church Order in the New Testament. SBT 1/32. London: SCM; Naperville, IL: Allenson, 1961. ET of Gemeinde und Gemeindeordnung im Neuen Testament. ATANT 35. Zürich: Zwingli, 1959.

Scott, Ernest F. The Varieties of New Testament Religion. New York: Scribner's, 1943.

Scott, R. B. Y. "Priesthood, Prophecy, Wisdom, and the Knowledge of God." JBL 80 (1961) 1-15.

Seebass, Horst. "Der Beitrag des Alten Testaments zum Entwurf einer biblischen Theologie." WD 8 (1965) 20-49.

Seeligmann, I. L. "Menschliches Heldentum und göttliche Hilfe." TZ 19 (1963) 385-411.

Segal, J. B. "The Jewish Attitude towards Women." JJS 30 (1979) 121-37.

Segundo, Juan Luis. Liberation of Theology. Maryknoll, NY: Orbis, 1976; Dublin: Gill and Macmillan, 1977. ET of Liberación de la teología. Buenos Aires: Lohlé, 1975.

_____. A Theology for Artisans of a New Humanity. Vol. 5: Evolution and Guilt. Maryknoll, NY: Orbis, 1974. ET of Teología abierta para el laico adulto. Vol. 5: Evolución y culpa. Buenos Aires: Lohlé, 1972.

Seitz, Gottfried. *Redaktionsgeschichtliche Studien zum Deuteronomium.* BWANT 93. Stuttgart: Kohlhammer, 1971.

Sellin, Ernst. *Alttestamentliche Theologie auf religionsgeschichtlicher Grundlage.* 2 vols. Leipzig: Quelle & Meyer, 1933.

————. *Introduction to the Old Testament.* New York: Doran, 1923. ET of *Einleitung in das Alte Testament.* Leipzig: Quelle & Meyer, 1910.

[Sellin, Ernst and] Georg Fohrer. *Introduction to the Old Testament.* Nashville: Abingdon, 1968; London: SPCK, 1970. ET of Sellin and Fohrer, *Einleitung in das Alte Testament.* 10th ed. Heidelberg: Quelle & Meyer, 1965.

Semler, Johann Salomo. *Abhandlung von freier Untersuchung des Canon.* 4 vols. Halle: Hemmerde, 1771-75. Rev. ed. of 1:1-128 by Heinz Scheible, Gütersloh: Mohn, 1967.

Shepherd, John J. "Man's Morals and Israel's Religion." *ExpT* 92 (1980-81) 171-74.

Sheppard, Gerald T. *Wisdom as a Hermeneutical Construct: A Study in the Sapientalizing of the Old Testament.* BZAW 151. Berlin: de Gruyter, 1980.

Simpson, D. C., ed. *The Psalmists: Essays on Their Religious Experience and Teaching, Their Social Background, and Their Place in the Development of Hebrew Psalmody.* London: Oxford University, 1926.

Simundson, Daniel J. *Faith under Fire: Biblical Interpretations of Suffering.* Minneapolis: Augsburg, 1980.

Sloyan, Gerald S. "Who Are the People of God?" In *Standing before God: Studies on Prayer in Scriptures and in Tradition with Essays in Honor of John M. Oesterreicher.* Ed. Asher Finkel and Lawrence Frizzell. New York: Ktav, 1981. Pp. 103-14.

Smart, James D. *The Interpretation of Scripture.* Philadelphia: Westminster; London: SCM, 1961.

Smend, Rudolf. *Yahweh War and Tribal Confederation: Reflections upon Israel's Earliest History.* Nashville: Abingdon, 1970. ET of *Jahwekrieg und Stammebund: Erwägungen zur ältesten Geschichte Israels.* FRLANT 84. Göttingen: Vandenhoeck & Ruprecht, 1963.

————. *Die Mitte des Alten Testaments.* Theologische Studien 101. Zürich: EVZ, 1970.

————. "Das Nein des Amos." *EvT* 23 (1963) 404-23.

————. "Zur Frage des altisraelitischen Amphiktyonie." *EvT* 31 (1971) 623-30.

Smith, Morton. *Palestinian Parties and Politics That Shaped the Old Testament.* New York: Columbia University, 1971.

————. "The Common Theology of the Ancient Near East." *JBL* 71 (1952) 135-47.

————. "On the Difference between the Culture of Israel and the Major Cultures of the Ancient Near East." *JANESCU* 5 (1973) 389-95.

Soler, Jean. "The Dietary Prohibitions of the Hebrews." *The New York Review of Books,* 14 June 1979, pp. 24-30. ET of "Sémiotique de la nourriture dans la Bible." *Annales: Economies, Sociétés, Civilisations* 28 (1973) 943-55.

Sontag, Frederick. "Is God Really in History?" *RelS* 15 (1979) 379-90.

Speiser, E. A. *Genesis: Introduction, Translation and Notes.* AB 1. Garden City, NY: Doubleday, 1964.

——. " 'People' and 'Nation' of Israel." *JBL* 79 (1960) 157-63. Repr. in *Oriental and Biblical Studies: Collected Writings.* Philadelphia: University of Pennsylvania, 1967. Pp. 160-70.

Spinoza, Benedict de. *The Correspondence of Spinoza.* Ed. A. Wolf. New York: Dial, 1927; London: George Allen, 1928. ET of *Epistolae.* 1661-76. Repr. in *Spinoza Opera.* Ed. Carl Gebhardt. Heidelberg: Carl Winters Universitätsbuchhandlung, 1925. 4:1-342.

——. *A Theologico-political Treatise.* In *The Chief Works of Benedict de Spinoza.* Ed. R. H. M. Elwes. London: Bell, 1883. 1:1-278. ET of *Tractatus theologico-politicus.* 1670. Repr. in *Spinoza Opera.* Ed. Carl Gebhardt. Heidelberg: Carl Winters Universitätsbuchhandlung, 1925. 3:1-267.

Spriggs, David G. *Two Old Testament Theologies: A Comparative Evaluation of the Contributions of Eichrodt and von Rad to Our Understanding of the Nature of Old Testament Theology.* SBT 2/30. London: SCM; Naperville, IL: Allenson, 1974.

Stamm, Johann Jakob. *The Ten Commandments in Recent Research,* by Johann Jakob Stamm, with Maurice Edward Andrew. SBT 2/2. London: SCM; Naperville, IL: Allenson, 1967. ET of *Der Dekalog im Lichte der neueren Forschung.* Berne: Evangelisch-reformierten Landeskirche, 1958; Berne: Haupt, 1962.

Steck, Odil Hannes. *Israel und das gewaltsame Geschick der Propheten: Untersuchungen zur Überlieferung des deuteronomistischen Geschichtsbildes im Alten Testament, Spätjudentum und Urchristentum.* WMANT 23. Neukirchen: Neukirchener, 1967.

——. *World and Environment.* Nashville: Abingdon; London: SCM, 1980. ET of *Welt und Umwelt.* Stuttgart: Kohlhammer, 1978.

——. "Das Problem theologischer Strömungen in nachexilischer Zeit." *EvT* 28 (1968) 445-58. Repr. in *Wahrnehmungen Gottes im Alten Testament.* TBü 70. Munich: Kaiser, 1982. Pp. 291-317.

——. "Theological Streams of Tradition." In *Tradition and Theology in the Old Testament.* Ed. Douglas A. Knight. Philadelphia: Fortress; London: SPCK, 1977. Pp. 183-214.

Stendahl, Krister. "Biblical Theology, Contemporary." In *IDB.* Ed. George Arthur Buttrick et al. Nashville: Abingdon, 1962. 1:418-32.

——. "Method in the Study of Biblical Theology." In *The Bible in Modern Scholarship: Papers Read at the 100th Meeting of the Society of Biblical Literature, December 28-30, 1964.* Ed. James Philip Hyatt. Nashville: Abingdon; 1965; London: Carey Kingsgate, 1966. Pp. 196-209.

Stendebach, Franz Josef. "Das Schweinopfer im Alten Orient." *BZ* 18 (1974) 263-71.

——. "Überlegungen zum Ethos des Alten Testaments." *Kairos* 18 (1976) 273-81.

Stoebe, Hans-Joachim. "Überlegungen zur Theologie des Alten Testaments." In *Gottes Wort und Gottes Land: Hans Wilhelm Hertzberg zum 70. Geburtstag*. Ed. Henning Graf Reventlow. Göttingen: Vandenhoeck & Ruprecht, 1965. Pp. 200-220.

Strathmann, Hermann. "Die Krisis des Kanons der Kirche: Joh. Gerhards und Joh. Sal. Semlers Erbe." *TBl* 20 (1941) 295-310. Repr. in *Das Neue Testament als Kanon: Dokumentation und kritische Analyse zur gegenwärtigen Diskussion*. Ed. Ernst Käsemann. Göttingen: Vandenhoeck & Ruprecht, 1970. Pp. 41-61.

Stuhlmacher, Peter. *Historical Criticism and Theological Interpretation of Scripture: Towards a Hermeneutics of Consent*. Philadelphia: Fortress, 1977; London: SPCK, 1979. ET of "Historische Kritik und theologische Schriftauslegung." In *Schriftauslegung auf dem Wege zur biblischen Theologie*. Göttingen: Vandenhoeck & Ruprecht, 1975. Pp. 59-127.

————. "Das Gesetz als Thema biblischer Theologie." *ZTK* 75 (1978) 251-80. Repr. in *Versohnung, Gesetz und Gerechtigkeit: Aufsätze zur biblischen Theologie*. Göttingen: Vandenhoeck & Ruprecht, 1981. Pp. 136-65.

————. " '. . . in verosteten Angeln.' " *ZTK* 77 (1980) 222-38.

Suggs, M. Jack. *Wisdom, Christology, and Law in Matthew's Gospel*. Cambridge: Harvard University Press; London: Oxford University, 1970.

Swanson, Guy E. *The Birth of the Gods: The Origin of Primitive Beliefs*. Ann Arbor: University of Michigan, 1960.

Terrien, Samuel. *The Elusive Presence: Toward a New Biblical Theology*. San Francisco: Harper & Row, 1978.

————. "The Play of Wisdom: Turning Point in Biblical Theology." *Horizons in Biblical Theology* 3 (1981) 125-53.

Tertullian, Quintus Septimius Florens. *Against Marcion*. In *ANF* 3. Ed. Alexander Roberts and James Donaldson. Edinburgh: T. & T. Clark, 1870; repr. Grand Rapids: Eerdmans, 1957. Pp. 269-475. ET of *Adversus Marcionem*. 208. Repr. in *PL* 1:239-54. Paris: Migne, 1844.

Thomas, David Winton. "*Kelebh* 'dog': Its Origin and Some Usages of It in the Old Testament." *VT* 10 (1960) 410-27.

Thompson, Leonard L. "The Jordan Crossing: Ṣidqot Yahweh and World Building." *JBL* 100 (1981) 343-58.

Thompson, R. J. *Moses and the Law in a Century of Criticism since Graf*. VTSup 19. Leiden: Brill, 1970.

Tillich, Paul. *The Shaking of the Foundations*. New York: Scribner's, 1948; London: SCM, 1949; repr. Harmondsworth: Penguin, 1962.

————. *Systematic Theology*. 3 vols. Chicago: University of Chicago, 1951-63. London: Nisbet, 1953-64.

Towner, Wayne Sibley. "The Renewed Authority of Old Testament Wisdom for Contemporary Faith." In *Canon and Authority: Essays in Old Testament Religion and Theology*. Ed. George W. Coats and Burke O. Long. Philadelphia: Fortress, 1977. Pp. 132-47.

Trible, Phyllis. *God and the Rhetoric of Sexuality*. Overtures to Biblical Theology 2. Philadelphia: Fortress, 1978.

Tromp, Nicolas J. *Primitive Conceptions of Death and the Nether World in the Old Testament.* BibOr 21. Rome: Pontifical Biblical Institute, 1969.

———. "Wisdom and the Canticle: Ct., 8,6c-7b: Text, Character, Message and Import." In *La sagesse de l'Ancien Testament.* Ed. Maurice Gilbert. BETL 51. Gembloux: Duculot; Louvain: Louvain University, 1979. Pp. 88-95.

Tunyogi, Andrew C. *The Rebellions of Israel.* Richmond: Knox, 1969.

Tupper, E. Frank. *The Theology of Wolfhart Pannenberg.* Philadelphia: Westminster, 1973; London: SCM, 1974.

Turner, Harold W. *From Temple to Meeting House: The Phenomenology and Theology of Places of Worship.* The Hague: Mouton, 1979.

Turner, Victor. *Dramas, Fields, and Metaphors: Symbolic Actions in Human Society.* Ithaca: Cornell University, 1974.

Vance, Eugene. "*Pas de trois:* Narrative, Hermeneutics, and Structure in Medieval Poetics." In *Interpretation of Narrative.* Ed. Mario J. Valdés and Owen J. Miller. Toronto: University of Toronto, 1978. Pp. 118-34.

Vaux, Roland de. *The Early History of Israel.* 2 vols. repr. in 1. Philadelphia: Westminster, 1978. Repr. of *The Early History of Israel to the Exodus and Covenant of Sinai* and *The Early History of Israel to the Period of the Judges.* 2 vols. London: Darton, Longman & Todd, 1978. ET of *Histoire ancienne d'Israël.* 2 vols. Paris: Gabalda, 1971-73.

———. "The 'Remnant of Israel' according to the Prophets." In *The Bible and the Ancient Near East.* Garden City, NY: Doubleday, 1971; London: Darton, Longman & Todd, 1972. Pp. 15-30. ET of "Le 'rest d'Israël' d'apres les prophètes." *RB* 42 (1933) 526-39. Repr. in *Bible et Orient.* Paris: Cerf, 1967. Pp. 25-40.

———. "The Sacrifice of Pigs in Palestine and in the Ancient East." In *The Bible and the Ancient Near East.* Garden City, NY: Doubleday, 1971; London: Darton, Longman & Todd, 1972. Pp. 252-69. ET of "Les sacrifices de porcs en Palestine et dans l'ancien Orient." In *Von Ugarit nach Qumran: Beiträge zur alttestamentlichen und altorientalischen Forschung Otto Eissfeldt zum 1 September, 1957.* Ed. Johannes Hempel et al. BZAW 77. Berlin: Töpelmann, 1958. Pp. 250-65. Repr. in *Bible et Orient.* Paris: Cerf, 1967. Pp. 499-516.

Vawter, Bruce. *Biblical Inspiration.* Philadelphia: Westminster; London: Hutchinson, 1972.

———. "A Tale of Two Cities: The Old Testament and the Issue of Personal Freedom." *JES* 15 (1978) 261-73.

Vermes, Geza. "Bible and Midrash: Early Old Testament Exegesis." In *The Cambridge History of the Bible.* Vol. 1: *From the Beginnings to Jerome.* Ed. Peter R. Ackroyd and Christopher F. Evans. Cambridge: Cambridge University, 1970. Pp. 199-231. Repr. in *Post-Biblical Jewish Studies.* SJLA 8. Leiden: Brill, 1975. Pp. 59-91.

Vincent, John J. *The Para Church: An Affirmation of New Testament Theologies.* SE 55 in *Study Encounter* 10/1 (1974).

Vischer, Wilhelm. *The Witness of the Old Testament to Christ.* Vol. 1: *The Pentateuch.* London: Lutterworth, 1949. ET of *Das Christuszeugnis des Alten Testaments.* Vol. 1: *Das Gesetz.* Munich: Kaiser, 1934.

Voegelin, Eric. *Order and History.* Vol. 1: *Israel and Revelation.* Baton Rouge: Louisiana State University, 1956.

―――――. "Equivalences of Experience and Symbolisation in History." In *Eternità e storia: I valori permanenti nel divenire storico―A cura dell' Istituto accademico di Roma*. Florence: Vallechi, 1970. Pp. 215-34.

Vogels, Walter. *God's Eternal Covenant: A Biblical Study*. Ottawa: University of Ottawa, 1979.

Vriezen, Theodorus C. *The Religion of Israel*. London: Lutterworth; Philadelphia: Westminster, 1967. ET of *De godsdienst van Israel*. Arnhem: de Haan, 1963.

―――――. *An Outline of Old Testament Theology*. Oxford: Blackwell; Newton, MA: Branford, 1958; 2nd ed., 1970. ET of *Hoofdlijnen der theologie van het Oude Testament*. Wageningen: Veenman, 1949; 2nd ed., 1954; 3rd ed., 1966.

Waal, Victor de. *What Is the Church?* London: SCM, 1969.

Wagner, Siegfried. " 'Biblische Theologien' und 'Biblische Theologie.' " *TLZ* 103 (1978) 785-98.

Waldow, Hans Eberhard von. "Israel and Her Land: Some Theological Considerations." In *A Light unto My Path: Old Testament Studies in Honor of Jacob M. Myers*. Ed. Howard N. Bream et al. Philadelphia: Temple University, 1974. Pp. 493-508.

Wallis, Gerhard. "Torah und Nomos." *TLZ* 105 (1980) 321-32.

Watson, Philip S. "The Nature and Function of Biblical Theology." *ExpT* 73 (1961-62) 195-200.

Watts, John D. W. *Basic Patterns in Old Testament Religion*. New York: Vantage, 1971.

―――――. "The People of God." *ExpT* 67 (1955-56) 232-37.

Weber, Hans-Ruedi. *The Promise of the Land*. SE 16 in *Study Encounter* 7/4 (1971).

Weber, Max. *Ancient Judaism*. New York: Free Press; London: Collier-Macmillan, 1952. ET of *Gesammelte Aufsätze zur Religionssoziologie*. Vol. 3: *Das antike Judentum*. Tübingen: Mohr, 1921.

Weber, Otto. *Foundations of Dogmatics*. 2 vols. Grand Rapids: Eerdmans; Exeter: Paternoster, 1982-83. ET of *Grundlagen der Dogmatik*. 2 vols. Neukirchen: Neukirchener, 1955; 5th ed., 1973.

Weinfeld, Moshe. *Deuteronomy and the Deuteronomic School*. Oxford: Clarendon; New York: Oxford University, 1972.

―――――. "Berît―Covenant vs. Obligation." *Bib* 56 (1975) 120-28.

―――――. "On 'Demythologization and Secularization in Deuteronomy.' " *IEJ* 23 (1973) 230-33.

Weippert, Manfred. *The Settlement of the Israelite Tribes in Palestine: A Critical Survey of Recent Scholarly Debate*. SBT 2/21. London: SCM; Naperville, IL: Allenson, 1971. ET of *Die Landnahme der israelitischen Stämme in der neueren wissenschaftlichen Diskussion*. FRLANT 92. Göttingen: Vandenhoeck & Ruprecht, 1967.

―――――. " 'Heiliger Krieg' in Israel und Assyrien: Kritische Anmerkungen zu Gerhard von Rads Konzept des 'Heiligen Krieges im alten Israel.' " *ZAW* 84 (1972) 460-93.

Weiser, Artur. *Die Profetie des Amos*. BZAW 53. Giessen: Töpelmann, 1929.

———. *Samuel: Seine geschichtliche Aufgabe und religiöse Bedeutung—Traditionsgeschichtliche Untersuchungen zu 1. Samuel 7-12.* FRLANT 81. Göttingen: Vandenhoeck & Ruprecht, 1962.

———. "Samuel und die Vorgeschichte des israelitischen Königtums: 1 Samuel 8." *ZTK* 57 (1960) 141-61. Repr. in *Samuel: Seine geschichtliche Aufgabe und religiöse Bedeutung—Traditionsgeschichtliche Untersuchungen zu 1. Samuel 7-12.* FRLANT 81. Göttingen: Vandenhoeck & Ruprecht, 1962. Pp. 25-45.

Welch, Adam C. *The Work of the Chronicler: Its Purpose and Its Date.* Schweich Lectures 1938. London: Oxford University, 1939.

Wellhausen, Julius. *Prolegomena to the History of Ancient Israel.* Edinburgh: Black, 1885; repr. Gloucester, MA: Peter Smith, 1973. ET of *Geschichte Israels.* Vol. 1. Berlin: Reimer, 1878. Repr. in *Prolegomena zur Geschichte Israels: Zweite Ausgabe der Geschichte Israels.* Vol. 1. Berlin: Reimer, 1883.

Wenham, Gordon J. "The Restoration of Marriage Reconsidered." *JJS* 30 (1979) 36-40.

———. "The Theology of Unclean Food." *EvQ* 53 (1981) 6-15.

Westerholm, Stephen. *Jesus and Scribal Authority.* ConBNT 10. Lund: Gleerup, 1978.

Westermann, Claus. *The Old Testament and Jesus Christ.* Minneapolis: Augsburg, 1970. ET of *Das Alte Testament und Jesus Christus.* Stuttgart: Calwer, 1968.

———. *Beginning and End in the Bible.* FBBS 31. Philadelphia: Fortress, 1972. ET of *Anfang und Ende in der Bibel.* Stuttgart: Calwer, 1969.

———. *Isaiah 40–66: A Commentary.* OTL. London: SCM; Philadelphia: Westminster, 1969. ET of *Das Buch Jesaja: Kap. 40–66 übersetzt und erklärt.* ATD 19. Göttingen: Vandenhoeck & Ruprecht, 1966.

———. *Genesis 1–11: A Commentary.* Minneapolis: Augsburg, 1984. ET of *Genesis.* Vol. 1: *Genesis 1–11.* BKAT 1/1. Neukirchen: Neukirchener, 1974.

———. *Creation.* Philadelphia: Fortress; London: SPCK, 1974. ET of *Schöpfung.* Stuttgart: Kreuz, 1971.

———. *Blessing in the Bible and in the Life of the Church.* Overtures to Biblical Theology 3. Philadelphia: Fortress, 1978. ET of *Der Segen in der Bible und im Handeln der Kirche.* Munich: Kaiser, 1968.

———. *What Does the Old Testament Say about God?* London: SPCK; Atlanta: Knox, 1979.

———. "Creation and History in the Old Testament." In *The Gospel and Human Destiny.* Ed. Vilmos Vajta. Minneapolis: Augsburg, 1971. Pp. 11-38. ET of "Gottes Handeln in Schöpfung und Geschichte im Alten Testament." In *Das Evangelium und die Bestimmung des Menschen.* Ed. Vilmos Vajta. Göttingen: Vandenhoeck & Ruprecht, 1972. Pp. 11-37.

———. "The Way of Promise through the Old Testament." In *The Old Testament and Christian Faith: A Theological Discussion.* Ed. Bernhard W. Anderson. New York: Harper & Row, 1963. Repr., New York: Herder & Herder, 1969. = *The Old Testament and Christian Faith: Essays by Rudolf Bultmann and Others.* Ed. Bernhard W. Anderson. London: SCM, 1964. Pp. 200-224. ET of "Der Weg der Verheissung durch das Alte Testament." In *Forschung am Alten Testament: Gesammelte Studien.* Munich: Kaiser, 1974. 2:230-49.

———. "The Interpretation of the Old Testament" and "Remarks on the Theses of Bultmann and Baumgärtel." In *Essays on Old Testament Hermeneutics.* Ed. Claus Westermann. Richmond: Knox, 1963. = *Essays on Old Testament Interpretation.* London: SCM, 1963. Pp. 40-49, 123-33. ET of "Zur Auslegung des Alten Testaments." In *Vergegenwärtigung: Aufsätze zur Auslegung des Alten Testaments.* Ed. Hans Urner. Berlin: Evangelische, 1955. Pp. 88-116. Repr. (abbreviated) in "Zur Auslegung des Alten Testaments" and "Bemerkungen zu den Thesen Bultmanns und Baumgärtels." In *Probleme alttestamentlicher Hermeneutik: Aufsätze zum Verstehen des Alten Testaments.* Ed. Claus Westermann. TBü 2. Munich: Kaiser, 1960. Pp. 18-27, 102-13.

Wette, Wilhelm M. L. de. *Das Wesen des christlichen Glaubens vom Standpunkte des Glaubens.* Basle: Schweighauser, 1846.

Whedbee, J. William. *Isaiah and Wisdom.* Nashville: Abingdon, 1971.

Wheelwright, Philip. *Metaphor and Reality.* Bloomington, IN: Indiana University, 1962.

Whybray, R. Norman. *Isaiah 40–66.* NCBC. London: Oliphants; Grand Rapids: Eerdmans, 1975.

———. *Thanksgiving for a Liberated Prophet: An Interpretation of Isaiah Chapter 53.* JSOTSup 4. Sheffield: JSOT, 1978.

———. *Two Jewish Theologies: Job and Ecclesiastes.* Hull: Hull University, 1980.

———. "Conservatisme et radicalisme dans Qohelet." In *Sagesse et religion: Colloque de Strasbourg (Octobre 1976).* Ed. Edmond Jacob. Paris: Presses Universitaires, 1979. Pp. 65-81.

———. "Yahweh-Sayings and Their Contexts in Proverbs, 10,1–22,16." In *La sagesse de l'Ancien Testament.* Ed. Maurice Gilbert. BETL 51. Gembloux: Duculot; Louvain: Louvain University, 1979. Pp. 153-65.

Wicker, Brian. *The Story-Shaped World: Fiction and Metaphysics—Some Variations on a Theme.* London: Athlone; Notre Dame, IN: University of Notre Dame, 1975.

Wildberger, Hans. *Jahwes Eigentumsvolk: Eine Studie zur Traditionsgeschichte und Theologie des Erwählungsgedankens.* ATANT 37. Zürich: Zwingli, 1960.

———. *Jesaja.* Vol. 1: *Jesaja 1–12.* BKAT 10/1. Neukirchen: Neukirchener, 1972.

———. "Auf dem Wege zu einer biblischen Theologie." *EvT* 19 (1959) 70-90.

———. "Israel und sein Land." *EvT* 16 (1956) 404-22.

———. "Jesajas Verständnis der Geschichte." In *Congress Volume: Bonn 1962.* VTSup 9. Leiden: Brill, 1963. Pp. 83-117. Repr. in *Jahwe und sein Volk: Gesammelte Aufsätze zum Alten Testament.* TBü 66. Munich: Kaiser, 1979. Pp. 75-109.

Wilder, Amos N. *The New Voice: Religion, Literature, Hermeneutics.* New York: Herder & Herder, 1969.

Wilken, Robert L., ed. *Aspects of Wisdom in Judaism and Early Christianity.* Notre Dame, IN: University of Notre Dame, 1975.

Williams, Colin W. *The Church.* New Directions in Theology Today 4. Philadelphia: Westminster, 1978; London: Lutterworth, 1969.

Williams, James G. "What Does It Profit a Man? The Wisdom of Koheleth." *Judaism* 20 (1971) 179-93. Repr. in *Studies in Ancient Israelite Wisdom.* Ed. James L. Crenshaw. New York: Ktav, 1976. Pp. 375-89.

Williamson, Hugh G. M. *Israel in the Books of Chronicles.* Cambridge: Cambridge University, 1977.

Willis, John T. "Micah 2:6-8 and the 'People of God' in Micah." *BZ* 14 (1970) 72-87.

Wirth, Wolfgang. "Die Bedeutung der biblischen Landverheissung für die Christen." In *Jüdisches Volk—gelobtes Land.* Ed. Willehad P. Eckert et al. Munich. Kaiser, 1970. Pp. 312-21.

Wittgenstein, Ludwig. *Philosophical Investigations—Philosophische Untersuchungen.* Oxford: Blackwell; New York: Macmillan, 1953.

Wolff, Hans Walter. *Anthropology of the Old Testament.* London: SCM; Philadelphia: Fortress, 1974. ET of *Anthropologie des Alten Testaments.* Munich: Kaiser, 1973.

_____. *The Old Testament: A Guide to Its Writings.* Philadelphia: Fortress, 1973; London: SPCK, 1974. ET of *Bibel—Das Alte Testament: Eine Einfuhrung in seine Schriften und in die Methoden ihrer Erforschung.* Stuttgart: Kreuz, 1970.

_____. *A Commentary on the Book of the Prophet Hosea.* Hermeneia. Philadelphia: Fortress, 1974. ET of *Dodekapropheton.* Vol. 1: *Hosea.* BKAT 14/1. Neukirchen: Neukirchener, 1961; rev. ed., 1965.

_____. "Masters and Slaves: On Overcoming Class-Struggle in the Old Testament." *Int* 27 (1973) 259-72. ET of "Herren und Knechte: Anstösse zur Überwindung der Klassengegensätze im Alten Testament." *TTZ* 81 (1972) 129-39.

_____. "The Kerygma of the Yahwist." *Int* 20 (1966) 131-58. Repr. in *The Vitality of Old Testament Traditions.* By Walter Brueggemann and Hans Walter Wolff. Atlanta: Knox, 1975. Pp. 41-66, 132-38. ET of "Das Kerygma des Jahwisten." *EvT* 24 (1964) 73-97. Repr. in *Gesammelte Studien zum Alten Testament.* TBü 22. Munich: Kaiser, 1964. Pp. 345-73.

_____. "Psalm 1." *EvT* 9 (1949-50) 385-94.

_____. "The Hermeneutics of the Old Testament." *Int* 15 (1961) 439-72. Repr. in *Essays on Old Testament Hermeneutics.* Ed. Claus Westermann. Richmond: Knox, 1963. = *Essays on Old Testament Interpretation.* London: SCM, 1963. Pp. 160-99. ET of "Zur Hermeneutik des Alten Testaments." *EvT* 16 (1956) 337-70. Repr. in *Probleme alttestamentlicher Hermeneutik: Aufsätze zum Verstehen des Alten Testaments.* Ed. Claus Westermann. TBü 2. Munich: Kaiser, 1960. Pp. 140-80. Repr. in *Gesammelte Studien zum Alten Testament.* TBü 22. Munich: Kaiser, 1964. Pp. 251-88.

_____. "The Elohistic Fragments of the Pentateuch." *Int* 26 (1972) 158-73. Repr. in *The Vitality of Old Testament Traditions.* By Walter Brueggemann and Hans Walter Wolff. Atlanta: Knox, 1975. Pp. 67-82, 138-40. ET of "Zur

Thematik der elohistischen Fragmente im Pentateuch." *EvT* 29 (1969) 59-72.

Wolff, Hans Walter, and Walter Brueggemann. *The Vitality of Old Testament Traditions.* Atlanta: Knox, 1975.

Wood, Charles M. *The Formation of Christian Understanding: An Essay in Theological Hermeneutics.* Philadelphia: Westminster, 1981.

World Council of Churches Commission on Faith and Order. *Study on the Authority of the Bible: Reports from Regional Groups.* FO/71:5 (R). Geneva: WCC, 1971.

_____. *Study on Biblical Hermeneutics and its Significance for the Ecumenical Movement: Reports from Regional Groups.* FO/67:20 (R). Geneva: WCC, 1967.

Wright, G. Ernest. *God Who Acts: Biblical Theology as Recital.* SBT 1/8. London: SCM; Chicago: Regnery, 1952.

_____. *The Old Testament against Its Environment.* SBT 1/2. London: SCM; Chicago: Regnery, 1950.

_____. *The Old Testament and Theology.* New York: Harper & Row, 1969.

Würthwein, Ernst. "Egyptian Wisdom and the Old Testament." In *Studies in Ancient Israelite Wisdom.* Ed. James L. Crenshaw. New York: Ktav, 1976. Pp. 113-33. ET of *Die Weisheit Ägyptens und das Alte Testament.* Marburg: Elwert, 1960. Repr. in *Wort und Existenz: Studien zum Alten Testament.* Göttingen: Vandenhoeck & Ruprecht, 1970. Pp. 197-216.

Yaron, Reuven. *Gifts in Contemplation of Death in Jewish and Roman Law.* Oxford: Clarendon, 1960.

_____. "Divorce in Old Testament times." *Revue Internationale des Droits de l'Antiquité* 3/4 (1957) 117-28.

_____. "The Restoration of Marriage." *JJS* 17 (1966) 1-11.

Yoder, John H. *Karl Barth and the Problem of War.* Nashville: Abingdon, 1970.

_____. "Exodus and Exile: The Two Faces of Liberation." In *Missionalia.* Pretoria: South African Missiological Society, 1974. 2:29-41.

Young, Norman. *Creator, Creation and Faith.* London: Collins; Philadelphia: Westminster, 1976.

Zevit, Ziony. "The *'egla* Ritual of Deuteronomy 21:1-9." *JBL* 95 (1976) 377-90.

Zimmerli, Walther. *Old Testament Theology in Outline.* Atlanta: Knox; Edinburgh: T. & T. Clark, 1978. ET of *Grundriss der alttestamentlichen Theologie.* Stuttgart: Kohlhammer, 1972.

_____. *The Law and the Prophets: A Study of the Meaning of the Old Testament.* Oxford: Blackwell, 1965; New York: Harper & Row, 1967. ET of *Das Gesetz und die Propheten: Zum Verständnis des Alten Testaments.* Göttingen: Vandenhoeck & Ruprecht, 1963.

_____. *Man and His Hope in the Old Testament.* SBT 2/20. London: SCM; Naperville, IL: Allenson, 1971. ET of *Der Mensch und seine Hoffnung im Alten Testament.* Göttingen: Vandenhoeck & Ruprecht, 1968.

_____. *The Old Testament and the World.* London: SPCK; Atlanta: Knox, 1976. ET of *Die Weltlichkeit des Alten Testaments.* Göttingen: Vandenhoeck & Ruprecht, 1971.

_____. "Alttestamentliche Traditionsgeschichte und Theologie." In *Probleme biblischer Theologie: Gerhard von Rad zum 70. Geburtstag.* Ed. Hans Walter Wolff. Munich: Kaiser, 1971. Pp. 632-47. Repr. in *Studien zur alttestamentliche Theologie und Prophetie: Gesammelte Aufsätze.* TBü 51. Munich: Kaiser, 1974. 2:9-26.

_____. "Die Bedeutung der grossen Schriftprophetie für das alttestamentliche Reden von Gott." In *Studies in the Religion of Ancient Israel.* VTSup 23. Leiden: Brill, 1972. Pp. 48-64. Repr. in *Studien zur alttestamentliche Theologie und Prophetie: Gesammelte Aufsätze.* TBü 51. Munich: Kaiser, 1974. 2:55-72.

_____. "Erwägungen zur Gestalt einer alttestamentlichen Theologie." *TLZ* 98 (1973) 81-98. Repr. in *Studien zur alttestamentlichen Theologie und Prophetie: Gesammelte Aufsätze.* TBü 51. Munich: Kaiser, 1974. 2:27-54.

_____. "Das Gesetz im Alten Testament." *TLZ* 85 (1960) 481-98. Repr. in *Gottes Offenbarung: Gesammelte Aufsätze zum Alten Testament.* TBü 19. Munich: Kaiser, 1963. Pp. 249-76.

_____. "The Place and Limit of the Wisdom in the Framework of the Old Testament Theology." *SJT* 17 (1964) 146-58. Repr. in *Studies in Ancient Israelite Wisdom.* Ed. James L. Crenshaw. New York: Ktav, 1976. Pp. 314-25. ET of "Ort und Grenze der Weisheit im Rahmen der alttestamentlichen Theologie." In *Les sagesses du Proche-Orient ancien: Colloque de Strasbourg 17-19 mai 1962.* Centre d'Études supérieures specialisé d'Histoire des Religions de Strasbourg. Paris: Presses Universitaires, 1963. Pp. 121-37. Repr. in *Gottes Offenbarung: Gesammelte Aufsätze zum Alten Testament.* TBü 19. Munich: Kaiser, 1963. Pp. 300-315.

_____. "Prophetic Proclamation and Reinterpretation." In *Tradition and Theology in the Old Testament.* Ed. Douglas A. Knight. Philadelphia: Fortress; London: SPCK, 1977. Pp. 69-100.

_____. "Wahrheit und Geschichte in der alttestamentlichen Schriftprophetie." In *Congress Volume: Göttingen 1977.* VTSup 29. Leiden: Brill, 1978. Pp. 1-15.

_____. "Zum Problem der 'Mitte des Alten Testaments.' " *EvT* 35 (1975) 97-118.

_____. "Zur Struktur der alttestamentlichen Weisheit." *ZAW* 51 (1933) 177-204. 56-61.

Index of Subjects

Abraham 10–11, 13, 15, 19, 32, 34, 60–64, 186, 213–14, 227, 229, 234
accommodation 116
activity: divine and human, 16–17, 41, 48–55, 57
acts of God. *See* history
Adam 217–18
afterlife. *See* death
Ahaz 54
Amalek 51, 144, 160
Amarna letters 63
Ammon 144
amphictyony 45, 69
angels 102, 197
anger 31
anthropology 124
antinomianism 7
Antiochus 57
apiru 63
apocalyptic 31, 49, 52, 54, 78–79, 87, 91, 94, 124, 152
apocrypha 210
apostasy 11–12, 138
ark 161, 182
Assyria 18, 23, 163, 192
asylum 150
Avvim 144

Baal(s) 21, 24, 63, 68, 219
Babylon 8, 50–51
Bar Kochba 81
Barak 51
Baruch 73
blessing 62, 64, 140–41, 146, 204–6, 210, 213–15, 224, 229–31, 233, 236–37
blood 157–58, 160
brotherhood 136–37, 156

Cain 224
Canaan 13, 37, 68–69, 134, 143, 145, 148–50, 153–54, 163–64, 203; Canaanisation, 70–71
canon 27, 30, 46, 100, 113; canon within the canon, 97, 122–27, 129–30; canonical criticism, 209
Caphtorim 144
cause-effect thinking 207, 220
centralization 150–51
church 74, 82–83, 85, 87, 89, 91–92, 95–96, 166, 212. *See also* people of God
class system 71
communion 112, 180
condescension 116, 154–66
Constantine 83
contradiction 15–25
conversion 79
covenant (בְּרִית) 3, 7, 11–12, 20, 44–48, 60, 63, 66–67, 69, 74, 79, 107, 113, 123, 137, 141, 147, 155, 171, 174–76, 178–80, 193, 200, 205–6, 218, 227, 231
creation 8–10, 15, 31, 36, 45, 65–66, 70, 103, 106, 128, 132, 146, 165–66, 191, 196, 198, 209, 213–16, 218, 225–26; and salvation, 200–239; continuous, 217; self-, 238
cross-section approach 167–72
cult 104–6, 125, 161–62, 191, 199, 231
cultures 42, 90, 157–61
curse 157
Cyrus 8, 31, 51, 75, 190

Darwin 203

Index of Authors

Index of Scripture